James Earl Russell

German Higher Schools

The History, Organization and Methods of Secondary Education in Germany

James Earl Russell

German Higher Schools
The History, Organization and Methods of Secondary Education in Germany

ISBN/EAN: 9783337158798

Printed in Europe, USA, Canada, Australia, Japan

Cover: Foto ©Andreas Hilbeck / pixelio.de

More available books at **www.hansebooks.com**

GERMAN HIGHER SCHOOLS

THE

HISTORY, ORGANIZATION AND METHODS

OF

SECONDARY EDUCATION IN GERMANY

BY

JAMES E. RUSSELL, Ph.D.

DEAN OF TEACHERS COLLEGE, COLUMBIA UNIVERSITY, NEW YORK

NEW YORK
LONGMANS, GREEN, AND CO.
LONDON AND BOMBAY
1899

PREFACE

No apology is necessary, I assume, in presenting to the reading public a book on the secondary schools of Germany. For many years American educators have drawn professional inspiration from German sources, and more recently it has become apparent that German ideas are taking root in British soil. The history, organization and methods of the German elementary schools are generally well understood. We have grown familiar with the German universities and have profited not a little from the relationship. But very little has been written in English on the secondary education which is the foundation of the German university training and the basis of all professional service in the Fatherland. Yet it is precisely in this sphere that German education can be studied to best advantage, and from it we have most to learn.

The Regents of the University of the State of New York, at Convocation in July, 1893, appointed me their European Commissioner, and shortly afterwards I was made Special Agent of the Bureau of Education of the United States for the study and investigation of German schools. These keys unlocked all doors. During the two years which I spent in Germany I visited more than forty towns and cities in order personally to acquaint myself with school affairs. By force of circumstances my attention was directed chiefly to the schools of central and northern Germany. It happens, therefore, that this study is concerned principally with the schools of Prussia. But as Prussia is the larger part of the Empire both in area and population, and by far the most important state politically in the Confederation, it is doing no great injustice to consider German schools from the Prussian standpoint.

A foreign institution, however simple it appears to the casual observer, presents a wonderful complexity to the student. And the longer he studies the more complex it grows. After a six months' residence abroad I was more confident of my ability to interpret the German school system than I am now, at the end of almost five years' continuous study and investigation. No one of my readers, I am sure, can be more dissatisfied than I am myself with this attempt to portray German ideals and German methods. The subject is too important to be lightly treated and too extensive to be understood on short acquaintance. I trust, however, that my work may lighten the labours of other students in this field and prove to be of some practical worth to educators.

Sermonizing on the basis of foreign customs is always of doubtful expediency. It is, indeed, questionable whether there is anything peculiar to the German theory and practice of teaching which is directly applicable to British or American conditions. Each nation must educate itself in its own way and for its own ends. The chief value of foreign examples consists in a rational understanding of the foreign way of adapting means to ends in the realization of great ideals. In this work, therefore, I have studiously resisted the temptation to point out the moral of every tale. The intelligent reader is capable of drawing his own conclusions; he who reads merely to imitate needs no encouragement.

It has been my aim to make each chapter as complete in itself as possible, even at the risk of some repetition of important facts. References have been cited in foot-notes wherever it has seemed necessary to refer to original documents or authorities of consequence. At the end of each chapter I have appended a short bibliographical list, through which students may easily acquaint themselves with the literature of the various topics. In the space at my disposal it would manifestly be impossible to cite all that has been written. Complete bibliographies will generally be found in the Hand-books and Encyclopedias mentioned in the lists of "general references." The chapters dealing with methods of instruction, the progress of school reform and the merits and defects of the German system, are obviously little dependent on books, except as they may serve to present other points of view.

The study as a whole, while demanding some familiarity with books, is much more indebted to the personal factor. Without the acquaintance and assistance of many German educationists it would have remained impossible for me to interpret the mass of material that has come to my hands. I cannot speak too highly of the many favours which were so freely extended to a very inquisitive and persistent stranger. The men whom I most wanted to consult were men fully occupied in places of great responsibility, but I could always count on a generous allotment of their time. To some of these friends I am indebted not only for personal interviews, but also for searching criticisms of parts of my manuscript. It is not their fault if I have gone astray; any errors of fact or judgment herein contained are my own.

I desire especially to acknowledge my obligations to *Oberschulrat* Dr. Waetzoldt, of Magdeburg; Professor Urtel, inspector of schools in Weimar; Drs. Muff and Quiehl, school directors in Cassel; Drs. Reinhardt and Walter, school directors in Frankfort-am-Main; Dr. G. Richter, gymnasial rector in Jena; Dr. Wernekke, director of the *Realgymnasium* in Weimar; Dr. Fries, director of the *Franckesche Stiftungen* in Halle, Drs. Richter and Wychgram, directors of secondary schools in Leipsic; Dr. Hausknecht, school director in

Berlin; and Professor Rein of the University of Jena, Professor Volkelt of Leipsic, Professor Paulsen of Berlin and Professor Schiller of Giessen. My thanks are due also to Mr. Edgar Kesner and Mr. W. M. Shafer, former students of mine in the University of Colorado, for clerical assistance, and to my colleague, Mr. Walter H. Nichols, who has kindly prepared the index to this volume.

J. E. R.

NEW YORK, December, 1898.

CONTENTS

CHAPTER I.
BEGINNINGS OF GERMAN SCHOOLS, ... PAGE 1

CHAPTER II.
THE RISE OF PROTESTANT SCHOOLS, ... 17

CHAPTER III.
THE PERIOD OF TRANSITION, ... 46

CHAPTER IV.
THE RECONSTRUCTION OF THE HIGHER SCHOOLS, . . 76

CHAPTER V.
THE PRUSSIAN SCHOOL SYSTEM, ... 108

CHAPTER VI.
THE HIGHER SCHOOLS OF PRUSSIA, ... 121

CHAPTER VII.
FOUNDATION AND MAINTENANCE OF HIGHER SCHOOLS, 138

CHAPTER VIII.
RULES, REGULATIONS AND CUSTOMS, ... 156

CHAPTER IX.
EXAMINATIONS AND PRIVILEGES, . . . 175

CHAPTER X.
STUDENT LIFE IN THE HIGHER SCHOOLS, ... 194

CHAPTER XI.
INSTRUCTION IN RELIGION, ... 213

CHAPTER XII.
INSTRUCTION IN GERMAN, ... 227

CHAPTER XIII.
INSTRUCTION IN GREEK AND LATIN, ... 245

CHAPTER XIV.
INSTRUCTION IN THE MODERN LANGUAGES, . . 266

CHAPTER XV.
INSTRUCTION IN HISTORY AND GEOGRAPHY, . 291

CHAPTER XVI.
INSTRUCTION IN MATHEMATICS, . . . 312

CHAPTER XVII.

PAGE

INSTRUCTION IN THE NATURAL SCIENCES, . . 329

CHAPTER XVIII.

THE PROFESSIONAL TRAINING OF TEACHERS, . 352

CHAPTER XIX.

APPOINTMENT, PROMOTION AND EMOLUMENTS OF TEACHERS, ... 370

CHAPTER XX.

TENDENCIES OF SCHOOL REFORM, ... 388

CHAPTER XXI.

MERITS AND DEFECTS OF GERMAN SECONDARY EDUCATION, ... 406

APPENDIX A.

THE PRIVILEGED HIGHER SCHOOLS OF GERMANY IN 1897, 425

APPENDIX B.

ATTENDANCE IN HIGHER SCHOOLS OF PRUSSIA, . 426

APPENDIX C.

SYSTEM OF PRIVILEGES, . . 427

APPENDIX D.

SALARY SCHEDULES, . . . 429

APPENDIX E.

Pensions of Teachers in the Higher Schools of Germany, ... 438

APPENDIX F.

Extracts from the General Pension Laws of Prussia, 439

APPENDIX G.

Leading Educational Journals of Germany, 442

Index, ... 445

GERMAN HIGHER SCHOOLS

CHAPTER I

BEGINNINGS OF GERMAN SCHOOLS
718–1490

THE schools of Germany have ever been a means to the realization of the highest spiritual ideals of the German people. They were called into existence to support the tenets of the Christian faith, and upon the union of Church and State they were taken over bodily into the service of the broader national life. Hence the clew to the systematic development of the German school system, at least until the present century, must be sought in the religious ideals of the successive periods as tempered by the prevailing social, economic and political influences.

<small>Educational Ideals.</small>

As long as the only classes in society were the nobility and the peasantry a practical training in the arts of gaining a livelihood, of making war and of diplomacy sufficed. Custom, modified only by new exigencies, afforded all the discipline needed for their mode of life. But a new era dawned with the introduction of Christianity in the eighth century. Columban and Boniface began their missionary work from the west and sought to convert the pagan Germans.[1] Monasteries and churches

<small>Influence of the Church.</small>

---

[1] See the interesting and naïve *Life of St. Columban*, by the Monk Jonas (University of Pennsylvania, *Translations and Reprints from the Original Sources of European History*, Vol. II., No. 7). Columban "feared lest, ensnared by the lusts of the world, he should in vain have spent so much

were founded everywhere in order to make sure of the conversion of the whole country. About these institutions arose a third important class, the clergy. The source of inspiration for this class lay outside the semi-barbarous customs of the people among whom they lived. The nobles and peasants alike were ignorant of letters, and this made easy the introduction of the Latin language to which the ecclesiastics, as priests and missionaries of the Roman Church, were naturally partial. The progress of Christianity was conditioned very largely by the acceptance of the Latin language. For purposes of international communication, too, the ability to use the Latin tongue was indispensable. Here, then, were conditions demanding an innovation in existent educational methods; schools were founded to satisfy these demands.

The Church alone recognized the need of schools, and throughout the Middle Ages all instruction proceeded from the clergy. The imparting of a new religion and a new culture was the chief motive that actuated the German missionaries. Monasteries and schools grew up together. The earliest schools were under the direction of monastic orders or bishops of the Church. Their aim was preparation for the priesthood.

---

labour on grammar, rhetoric, geometry and the Holy Scriptures. . . . Having collected a band of brethren, St. Columban asked the prayers of all that he might be assisted in his coming journey and that he might have their pious aid. So he started out in the twentieth (or thirtieth) year of his life, and under the guidance of Christ went to the seashore with twelve companions. Here they waited to see if the mercy of the Almighty would allow their purpose to succeed, and learned that the spirit of the all-merciful Judge was with them. So they embarked, and began the dangerous journey across the channel, and sailed quickly with a smooth sea and favourable wind to the coast of Brittany. Here they rested for awhile to recover their strength and discussed their plans anxiously, until finally they decided to enter the land of Gaul. They wanted zealously and shrewdly to inquire into the disposition of the inhabitants, in order to remain longer if they found they could sow the seeds of salvation; or, in case they found the hearts of the people in darkness, go on to the nearest nations."

Of the early orders the Benedictines were most devoted to the cause of education. From the famous monastery of Monte Casino, for the administration of which St. Benedict prescribed his more famous rules in 529,[1] there proceeded a ray of light down through all the dark ages. **The Benedictines.** The Benedictine monks, though secluded from the world, found eventually within claustral walls a little world of their own.[2] The duties of every hour were carefully enjoined, and to a strict religious life under vows of poverty, chastity and obedience were added the demands of manual labour and the duty of instructing the young. The example of Cassiodorus, the prime minister of Theodoric the Great, who retired about 540 to a monastery, and there devoted his life to literary pursuits, had a wholesome influence on the ecclesiastics of his day. The rapid growth of religious orders and the accumulation of property required no little administrative ability. This led eventually to many monks becoming learned men; in every monastery some scholars were a necessity. And with the development of the idea that the Church was the Kingdom of God on Earth, the Benedictines became the tools of the Bishops of Rome in conquering the world.

It is a significant fact that the great apostle to the Germans, the Anglo-Saxon Winfried, better known as St. Boniface, introduced the monastic rules of St. Benedict throughout Germany. The labours of the Irish missionaries early in the seventh century had been restricted to southern Germany and Switzerland. But they founded there monastic schools, notably Reichenau and St. Gall, which became the models of all northern Europe. Boniface, a century later, received a commission from the Pope (718), to Christianize and Roman-

---

[1] Henderson, *Select Historical Documents of the Middle Ages*, London, 1892, gives an English translation of "The Rule of St. Benedict." See pp. 274–314.

[2] Putnam, *Books and Their Makers During the Middle Ages*, New York, 1896, Vol. I., pp. 106–145, gives an account of the literary activities of the Benedictines.

ize all Germany. The results of his labours were truly marvellous; in five years he had succeeded in planting the standard of Rome in all parts of Thuringia and Hesse, and as strongholds of the faith cloisters grew up under his fostering care. In 732 he was made archbishop, the head of an ecclesiastical system including many bishoprics and important clerical institutions. At the time of his death in 755 the Roman Catholic conquest of Germany was nearly complete; the Bishop of Rome was supreme.[1] And with Roman Catholicism came the elements of Latin learning and the culture of the Church.

Boniface seems to have been not less interested in Romanizing Germany than in giving the youth of Germany a Christian education. The German abbeys were every one of them mission schools. The enthusiasm of the great apostle inspired his disciples, men and women alike, to heroic efforts. The monasteries of Fitzlar, Büraburg, Heidesheim, Eichstätt, Erfurt and Fulda, and the nunneries of Bischofsheim, Kitzingen and Ochsenfurt, were centres of educational influence, training-schools for native missionaries.

Monastic Schools.

The aim of these schools was naturally enough to promote the work of the Church. Boys of five to seven years of age were dedicated to the holy office and reared within convent walls. The church language and singing stood first in a curriculum theoretically composed of the Trivium—grammar, rhetoric and dialectic; and of the Quadrivium—arithmetic, geometry, astronomy and music. Upon these seven liberal arts, as on seven impregnable pillars, the superstructure, theology, was built.[2]

Under the influence of Charles the Great and Alcuin, educational ideals ceased to be exclusively ecclesiastical. The purpose of the schools became something more than that of preparation for the priesthood. A dawning national self-

---

[1] The Councilium Germanicum recognized the Roman Pontiff as head of the Church in 748.

[2] *Cf.* Schiller, *Geschichte der Pädagogik: Die Klosterschulen*, Leipzig, 1894, p. 35 f.

consciousness led to a dream of Empire, but an Empire in harmony with the Church. Those who aspired to the rule of the Roman Empire must needs be somewhat acquainted with Roman learning. Hence the rise of the "Palace School" at the court of Charles the Great, the pioneer school for the nobles of the realm.[1]

Charles the Great.

The task of Alcuin was nothing less than the introduction and diffusion of learning among the Franks, a task of no little difficulty when we consider the deplorable condition of education consequent on the barbaric rule of the Merovingian kings. The church schools were no longer the seats of learning; some of them had fallen a prey to selfish royal favourites; others had abandoned themselves to the lusts of the flesh. For the upbuilding of that "more excellent Athens," which Alcuin hoped to establish in Frankland, it was necessary that the monastic and cathedral schools be reformed and enthused with new life.[2] More than that, the common people would have to be rescued from barbarism and raised by Christian education to an appreciation of Christian citizenship. The famous proclamation of Charles, issued in 787 to the abbots of the different monasteries, sometimes called the first general charter of education for the Middle Ages, shows clearly the intent of Alcuin in regard to the schools. The copy addressed to Bangulf, abbot of Fulda, runs as follows:

Alcuin.

"Be it known to your devotion, pleasing to God, that in conjunction with our faithful we have judged it to be of utility that, in the bishoprics and monasteries committed by Christ's favour to our charge, care should be taken that there shall be not only a regular manner of life and one conformable to holy religion,

First general Charter of Education.

---

[1] Cramer, *Geschichte der Erziehung und des Unterrichts in den Niederlanden während des Mittelalters*, Stralsund, 1843, gives an interesting account of educational progress under Charles the Great.

[2] See G. B. Adams' *Civilization During the Middle Ages*, p. 163 ff.; Bryce's *Holy Roman Empire*, ch. v.; and Oman's *The Dark Ages*, p. 379 ff.

but also the study of letters, each to teach and learn them according to his ability and the divine assistance. For even as due observance of the rule of the house tends to good morals, so zeal on the part of the teacher and the taught imparts order and grace to sentences; and those who seek to please God by living aright should also not neglect to please him by right speaking. It is written 'by thine own words shalt thou be justified or condemned;' and although right doing be preferable to right speaking, yet must the knowledge of what is right precede right action. Every one, therefore, should strive to understand what it is that he would fain accomplish; and this right understanding will be the sooner gained according as the utterances of the tongue are free from error. And if false speaking is to be shunned by all men, especially should it be shunned by those who have elected to be the servants of the truth. During past years we have often received letters from different monasteries informing us that at their sacred services the brethren offered up prayers in our behalf; and we have observed that the thoughts contained in these letters, though in themselves most just, were expressed in uncouth language, and while pious devotion dictated the sentiments, the unlettered tongue was unable to express them aright. Hence there has arisen in our minds the fear lest, if the skill to write rightly were thus lacking, so too would the power of rightly comprehending the Sacred Scriptures be far less than was fitting, and we all know that, though verbal errors be dangerous, errors of the understanding are yet more so. We exhort you, therefore, not only not to neglect the study of letters, but to apply yourself thereto with perseverance and with that humility which is well pleasing to God; so that you may be able to penetrate with greater ease and certainty the mysteries of the Holy Scriptures. For as these contain images, tropes and similar figures, it is impossible to doubt that the reader will arrive far more readily at the spiritual sense according as he is the better instructed in learning. Let there, therefore, be chosen for this work men who are able and willing to learn, and also desirous of instructing others; and let them apply themselves to the work with a zeal equalling the earnestness with which we recommend it to them.

"It is our wish that you may be what it behooves the soldiers of the Church to be,—religious in heart, learned in discourse, pure in act, eloquent in speech; so that all who approach your house in order to invoke the Divine Master or to behold the excellence of the religious life, may be edified in beholding you and instructed in hearing you discourse or chant, and may return home rendering thanks to God most High.

"Fail not, as thou regardest our favour, to send a copy of this letter to all thy suffragans and to all the monasteries; and let no monk go beyond his monastery to administer justice or to enter the assemblies and the voting-places. Adieu."[1]

The ideal ecclesiastic should be "religious in heart, learned in discourse, pure in act, eloquent in speech," a man both "able and willing to learn, and also desirous of instructing others." As a faithful soldier of the Church it is incumbent on him to see to it that, for the sake of a right comprehension of the mysteries of the Holy Scriptures, the study of letters be not neglected. Again Charles writes:

"As it is our desire to improve the condition of the Church, we make it our task to restore, with most watchful zeal, the study of letters, a task almost forgotten through the neglect of our ancestors. We therefore enjoin on our subjects, so far as they may be able, to study the liberal arts, and we set them the example."[2]

The immediate effect of these injunctions was a quickened activity in the old church schools and the foundation of new ones. Generally speaking the sole function of the monastic and cathedral schools had been hitherto the training of churchmen; the doors were now opened to laymen—but cau-

---

[1] I. Migne, *Patrologia Latina*, xcviii., 895. Mullinger, *Schools of Charles the Great*, 97-99.

[2] Pertz, *Leges*, I., 44. Quoted by West, *Alcuin*, New York, 1892, p. 54.

tiously.[1] Boys who were dedicated to the monastic life, *oblati*, were trained in the *interior* school; the *exterior* school,

<small>Progress under Charles the Great.</small> outside the convent walls, was reserved for the secular clergy and laymen.[2] The cathedral schools were in many respects similar to the exterior schools of the monasteries. But under Charles the Great a separation was commonly made between the ecclesiastical and the lay students. The prevailing ignorance, superstition and immorality of the lower priesthood, which Charles sought to correct, was due in part to lack of education and in part to the custom of taking candidates from the lowest social class, very often from among the serfs. The remedy for this evil was instruction in letters and a life under monastic rule. Hence as the custom arose of collecting all the clergy of a diocese about the bishop's

<small>Cathedral Schools.</small> church, a special school was needed for the canons. Herein the cathedral schools found their chief work, but as a rule both the monastic and the cathedral schools were also open to those who had no intention of leading a strictly religious life. The discipline of the *interni* was naturally more rigorous than that of the *externi*, and, too, the novices were taught more of the Scriptures, more of church music and ritual. But the course of study for beginners was practically the same for all. Pupils were admitted when about seven years of age. Their first task was to commit the Latin Psalter to memory. Along with this went reading, writing and a little arithmetic. The enforced use of the Latin language at all times, in school and out, eventually gave them a second mother-tongue. To make their pupils adepts in the *use* of this tongue was, next to a knowledge of Holy Writ, the chief aim of the mediæval schools. As a means to this end Roman authors, especially

---

[1] Basilius, bishop of Cæsarea in Cappadocia (370-379), is said to have been the first to divide the cloistral schools into *schola claustri s. interior* and *schola canonica s. exterior*.

[2] See *Encyc. Britan.*, Vol. I., under "Abbey" for the arrangement at St. Gall.

the poets, were carefully studied—not for what they said so much as for their way of saying it. This was the work of grammar and rhetoric; dialectics seem not to have been much in evidence except in the greatest schools. Of the *Realien* the only subject of moment was music—church music at that. Just enough arithmetic was taught for the computation of the church calendar. It will be seen, therefore, that Latin formed the main part of the curriculum—its prominence being due to the fact that Latin was the language of the Bible, of the Church and the learned world. Greek was almost unknown in Germany; yet not wholly lost, as a pupil of Swiss Reichenau (815-825) tells us in his autobiography that besides Vergil, Lucan, Statius, Cicero, Quintilian, Sallust, Livy and other so-called sacred and scientific authors he mastered several books of Homer's Iliad.[1]

The elevation of the clergy was undoubtedly hampered by the practice of drawing recruits largely from the servile class. Charles insisted that candidates for the priesthood should be taken from the sons of freemen. The Church was the light of the world; its representatives should be men capable and worthy of their high office. And as the custodians of learning they should give to others even as had been given to them. Not only in the monastic and cathedral schools were teachers needed, but every parish priest should be a teacher to those about him. A capitulary of 802 enjoined that "everyone should send his son to study letters, and that the child should remain at school with all diligence until he should become well instructed in learning."[2]

Condition of the Clergy.

The most notable conception of Charles and Alcuin was that of a state school system, a system that provided instruction for all classes of society—nobles, clergy and peasantry. From the "Palace School" at court proceeded that influence

---

[1] Kellner, *Sketches and Pictures of Educational History*, Essen, 1862, Vol. I., p. 132. *Cf.* also Ekkehart, *Lib. Benedict.*, p. 345.

[2] Pertz, *Leges*, I., 107. Cited by West in *Alcuin*, p. 54.

which infused new life into the schools of the monasteries and bishoprics, and these in turn were responsible for the teachers and the teaching of the parish schools. It should not be forgotten, however, that the entire system was in the hands of the Church. Alcuin himself was a monk educated in a monastic school, and died the abbot of the monastery in Tours (804).

The enthusiasm of Charles and Alcuin penetrated the schools of Germany and served to uphold for a time the hands of her teachers. Fulda attained great renown early in the tenth century, under the leadership of Rabanus Maurus, a disciple of Alcuin. A century later the cloistral school of Hersfeld enjoyed a high reputation. Among the leading cathedral schools of the eleventh century may be mentioned those of Cologne, Mainz, Worms, Speyer, Hildesheim and Magdeburg.

In the general collapse of the tenth century most of the gains of the eighth were lost. The period of chaos following the reign of Charles the Great was a sorry time for German schools. There could be little thought of education when men's minds were most concerned with the preservation of their lives; but finally, after terrible sacrifice, order was restored and another period of progress was entered upon. The life of the period, however, was vastly different from that of the eighth century. New educational ideas gave rise to new pedagogical methods.

Feudalism had gained a firm foothold in Germany. Class distinctions were more closely drawn than ever before. The separation of the nobility, secular and ecclesiastical, from the peasantry was now sharply marked. Wealth, which meant power, was a chief desideratum; its possession exalted a man, the want of it brought him low. The spirit of chivalry was intensified by the crusades, and at every court noble bards, guiltless of the rudiments of letters, sang the praises of woman and wine. Success in battle, the chase, or the tournament, in making love or writing verses—any or all were worth striving for and it

Feudalism.

mattered little in which domain the prize was won. For the realization of such ideals some systematic training of the young was necessary. For this purpose the seven liberal arts of the church school were supplanted by the seven *Frömmigkeiten* of feudalism,—riding, swimming, archery, fencing, hunting, whist-playing and rhyming. The arts of reading and writing were quite unnecessary; in fact it was considered somewhat effeminate to dally long with books. But a speaking knowledge of French was useful and was sometimes taught at court by private tutors. In the training of the young noble, therefore, schools were entirely superfluous.

Feudalism was essentially antagonistic to the schools; scholasticism gave them new life. The efforts of the schoolmen to reconcile the revealed dogmas of the Church with natural reason, "to render the dogma acceptable to reason," supplied new motives for study. *Influence of Scholasticism.* The alliance between theology and philosophy developed an imperative demand for close syllogistic reasoning. The scholar must be a skilful dialectician. The study of grammar and rhetoric led to the comprehension of the mysteries of the Holy Scriptures; this, with the faith to believe the patristic dogmas of the Church, was all the old education sought to attain. Scholasticism marks the dawn of a scientific era. The rise of the University of Paris marks the corresponding advance in the history of education.

During the period of political disorder that preceded the establishment of feudalism the Germans were compelled to seek safety within walled inclosures. These grew in time into cities and formed the chief centres of trade and commerce when travel again became safe *Rise of Cities.*

---

[1] "In Wahrheit ist das Mittelalter gar nicht weltflüchtig und lebenssatt, sondern voll Freude und Verlangens. Kampf und Eroberung, mit den Waffen und im Handel, ist sein Tagewerk, Jagd und Kampfspiel seine Erholung, macht und Reichtum sein Ziel. Der Inhalt seiner Lieder ist Liebeslust und Liebesleid."—Paulsen, *Gesch. d. Gel Unterrichts*, Leipzig, 1885, p. 6. *Cf.* also Wilson, *The State*, Boston, 1892, ch. vii., on the feudal system.

and profitable. The guilds of the Middle Ages, secret organizations of people engaged in the same occupation and with like interests, greatly facilitated commercial activity. After the reign of the Hohenstaufen, say about 1254, the leading cities of Germany gained complete political independence. Back of these political changes were social changes of equal importance. The expansion of trade and the increase of wealth in the cities placed the balance of power in the hands of the *Bürger*, a new social class midway between the earlier extremes. Tradesmen, master workmen and skilled mechanics were as thoroughly differentiated from the peasant class below as from the nobles above. Nor were their needs identical with the needs of the clergy. New ideals of life and new standards of living obviously demanded a new mode of education. But learning was the property of the Church. Only by an alliance with the Church could the benefits of learning be secured. Cathedral schools, monastic schools and specially endowed church schools there were in considerable numbers, but they all were ill-adapted to the practical needs of practical men. The next step was the establishment in every city of schools designed to extend the benefits of learning to the middle classes.[1] Notwithstanding these schools were under city patronage, supported from public funds and designed to give a practical education, they were still connected with the Church and under clerical supervision and direction. So completely had the idea permeated all grades of society that the Church was the sole dispenser of spiritual gifts, that a secular school system seems scarcely to have been considered. Even the founding of city schools required the assent of episcopal authority—a favour sometimes granted only after a long struggle with the bishops and final appeal to the Pope. And despite the secular aim of the city schools, their organization, subject-matter and methods of instruction did

---

[1] Specht, *Geschichte des Unterrichtswesens in Deutschland von den ältesten Zeiten bis zur Mitte des dreizehnten Jahrhunderts*, Stuttgart, 1885, p. 241 ff.

not materially differ from the older church schools. They were "Latin schools," as the others were, but their ultimate aim was the making of citizens and business men instead of priests of the Roman Church.

The obvious result of this system of semi-public schools was wide-spread knowledge of letters among the burghers. In the fourteenth and fifteenth centuries, when the cities reached their zenith, it is said that the citizens were better educated than the contemporary nobles.[1] Although the city schools were theoretically of the same type as the church schools it is probable that the practical ends for which they were striving had the effect of making them quite independent. Certainly less emphasis was placed on Latin and singing. The vernacular was growing into a vigorous tongue, and its use was essential to the commercial life of the tradesmen. Hence the schools were inclined to give more attention to the common branches.

City Schools.

Contemporaneous with the period of greatest activity in feudal circles and with the rise of a middle class in society the attention of learned Germany was directed to the new movement in higher education inaugurated with the founding of the University of Paris.[2] This movement was a part of ecclesiastical policy. The Pope was its final authority, and the masters of the university and most of the students were in holy orders. Nevertheless instruction in the subtleties of Aristotelian philosophy and the mysteries of ancient science exercised a profound influence upon the higher thought of Germany. Following at a respectful distance, Germany, a century later than France, England, Italy and Spain, became the patron of the three scholastic sciences of Theology, Jurisprudence and Medicine.

The University Movement.

---

[1] The records of the city of Frankfort show that from about 1417 onwards the members of the guilds coming from all parts of Germany signed their names to the registers "by the hundreds." *Cf.* Kriek, *Deutsches Bürgerthum im Mittelalter; das Schulwesen*, Frankfort, 1870.

[2] *Cf.* Rashdall, *Universities of Europe in the Middle Ages*, Oxford, 1895, Vol. I., 25-74, 271 ff.

The first German University was founded by Emperor Charles IV., at Prague in 1348 with the purpose, as its charter reads, that his "faithful subjects who continually hungered for the fruits of science might find satisfaction at home and no longer be compelled to girdle the earth in the search for knowledge, to hunt out strange peoples and to beg in foreign lands." Six others[1] were established in rapid succession, and in the following century, under the influence of humanism, nine more [2] were added to the list.

As first planned, the universities were ecclesiastical establishments, defenders of the faith, foundations of the Church for the higher education of the clergy. But in the support so freely given by civil rulers and city corporations there was evidence of secular co-operation. Gradually the faculties of Law and Medicine adjusted themselves to the professional needs of the times. It should be remarked, however, that in the theological atmosphere of the Middle Ages the Church cast its shadow over every science. Canon law was regarded as the main part of jurisprudence, and the art of healing a gift of God. The study of the liberal arts was but a preparation for higher work, itself presupposing the training of the Latin schools. Yet from the Bachelors and Masters of Arts of the universities who did not advance to the higher faculties a new class of learned men was being formed with ideals somewhat at variance with the established traditions of the Church. Many of these becoming teachers in the lower schools prepared the way for a learned class outside the ecclesiastical fold.[3]

University Ideals.

---

[1] Vienna, 1365—reorganized, 1384; Heidelberg, 1385; Cologne, 1388; Erfurt, 1392; Leipsic, 1409; Rostock, 1419.

[2] Griefswald, 1456; Frieburg, 1457; Basel, 1460; Ingolstadt, 1472; Trier, 1473; Mainz, 1477; Tübingen, 1477; Wittenberg, 1502; Frankfort-on-the-Oder, 1506.

[3] *Cf.* Rashdall, *Universities of Europe in the Middle Ages*, II., 211, 232-282, 593 ff.; Paulsen, *German Universities*, New York, 1895, pp. 16-88; Laurie, *Rise and Constitution of Universities*, ch. x.; and Denifle, *Die Entstehung der Universitäten des Mittelalters bis 1400*, Berlin, 1885.

The fourteenth and fifteenth centuries mark the completion of a process toward the liberation of the commons, the working classes. Under feudalism, slavery became territorial and was transformed into serfdom. *Common Schools.* Towns and cities, under the impulse of trade and commerce, enfranchised the commons. Later, for selfish reasons, and because of the church teachings, agricultural serfs were freed. This large class in society came to possess personality and importance; freedom gave it rights and ideals. The needs and the ideals, the conditions and stage of political development under which this class became a factor in society, led to the establishment of schools for the common people.[1]

The Latin language, which had long been the polite tongue as well as the medium of official intercourse, began here and there to give way to the vernacular. The common people could live without a knowledge of Latin. City officials could not longer disregard the language of the commons. The legal documents and accounts of the fourteenth century were mainly in German—a form intelligible at least within a limited area. Indeed, the charters establishing these schools were written in the vernacular. A desire for learning spread among the commons, because the ability to read and write was a means to advancement. Wandering monks and teachers went about giving instruction, thereby helping on the movement for the founding of schools.

But just as the city Latin schools were the old church schools secularized, so the common schools were in reality Latin schools without Latin. And even here ecclesiastical influence was not wanting. City magistrates might establish the schools, provide for their support, and nominate teachers, but the Church confirmed the appointments and supervised all school-work. And in return for this concession—for any recognition of secular education was deemed a concession by

---

[1] For good short accounts of the period see G. B. Adams' *Civilization During the Middle Ages*, pp. 279-310; Thatcher and Schwill's *Europe in the Middle Age*, pp. 434 ff. and 563 ff.

the Church—the tuition fees of the pupils often went into the coffers of the Church.

At the end of the mediæval period, therefore, we find a well-defined school system, embracing the common schools of the people at one extreme and the universities at the other. The significant fact is that it is the product of a gradual development brought into existence by the growth of different social classes, with their respective ideals of life, and dominated throughout by the Roman Catholic Church.

Summary.

GENERAL REFERENCES :—*Geschichte des deutschen Schulwesens* in Rein's *Encyklopädisches Handbuch der Pädagogik*, II., 693-747; K. A. Schmid, *Geschichte der Erziehung*, Stuttgart, 1892, II., 94-548; Schmidt, *Geschichte der Pädagogik*, II., 125-379; Stein, *Das Bildungswesen des Mittelalters*, Stuttgart, 1883; Willmann, *Didaktik als Bildungslehre*, II., 233-292; Kriek, *Deutsches Bürgerthum im Mittelalter*, Frankfort, 1871; Tetzner, *Geschichte der deutschen Bildung und Jugenderziehung von der Urzeit bis zur Errichtung von Stadtschulen*, Gütersloh, 1897; Rashdall, *Universities of Europe in the Middle Ages*, Oxford, 1895; Drane, *Christian Schools and Scholars*; Geffcken, *Church and State*; Hinschius, *Staat und Kirche—Handbuch des öffentlichen Rechts*.

CHAPTER II

THE RISE OF PROTESTANT SCHOOLS
1490–1618

THE characteristic theme of the Middle Ages was the restoration and glorification of the kingdom of God on earth. Only so much knowledge of God and Man and Nature was tolerated as the Church thought safe to promulgate. The authority of the Church was supreme, not only in religious matters but in intellectual, social and political as well. The mediæval world, however, was not wholly enshrouded in intellectual night; there was considerable store of classical learning. But learning having sought refuge in the monasteries, became the handmaid of theology. The civilization of the Middle Ages was feudal and clerical. Both feudalism and the Church conspired to set at nought the natural rights of man.

The fifteenth century saw the first-fruits of a new ideal. The key-note of the new movement was the glorification of man, his greatness and his fame; the worship of the individual, his genius, his power, his immeasurable natural freedom. "The revival of classic learning broke through the barriers set by the Church; antiquity was discovered anew; the feeling of kinship with the spirit of its art and philosophy permeated and renovated the western world, and in the admiration and imitation of these works of classic paganism, men felt their relationship, not merely with Christians, but with the whole human race. Their mode of thought became humanistic at the same time with their studies; art and philosophy fol-

The Ideals of the Renaissance.

lowed in the same direction."[1] Interest in the humanities led to a revival of interest in the classic view of Nature. Thus science gained a place in the thought of the age, and to the conquest of the historical treasures of Greece and Rome were quickly added the discovery of a new world in geography and a new solar system in astronomy. The study of the ancient tongues exhibited clearly the striking contrast between the pure Latin of Cicero and the barbarous dialect of the Church. What had passed for Latin, that to which the schools of Christendom were bending all their efforts, could no longer be venerated as a fountain of truth pure and undefiled. And the deeper investigation went, the more apparent it became that the historical teachings of the Church were hopelessly mixed with error, and that nothing but an appeal to original sources could set free the truth.

The whole movement of the Renaissance tended toward an awakened interest in humanity, a dissatisfaction with the formalism of the schoolmen and a consequent attempt to restore the ancient culture of Greece and Rome.[2] In Italy, once the home of Roman culture, Petrarch (1304–1374), and Boccaccio (1313–1375) lighted the torch of classical learning; the Medici took it from their hands and fanned it into a blaze that illuminated all western Europe. Italy became directly the scene of intense activity. Store-houses of books were ransacked for manuscripts; the contributions of Greece were joyously welcomed upon the fall of Constantinople (1453); artists gathered fresh inspiration from Grecian masterpieces; philosophers busied themselves with new views of life and new theories of the State. It meant a new civilization, or rather the transformation and regeneration of the old civilization.

New Interest in Humanity.

"It is impossible to exaggerate the benefit conferred upon

---

[1] Fischer, *Descartes*, p. 81.

[2] See Symonds' *Renaissance in Italy* and Burckhardt's *Civilization of the Renaissance in Italy* for an exhaustive treatment of the subject. G. B. Adams, *Civilization During the Middle Ages*, gives a convenient summary in the chapter on " The Renaissance."

Europe by the Italians at this epoch. The culture of the classics had to be reappropriated before the movement of the modern mind could begin; before the nations could start upon a new career of progress, the chasm between the old and new world had to be bridged over. *The Renaissance in Italy.* This task of reappropriation the Italians undertook alone, and achieved at the sacrifice of their literary independence and their political freedom. The history of Renaissance literature in Italy is the history of a national genius deviating from the course of self-development into the channels of scholarship and antiquarian research. The language created by Dante as a thing of power, polished by Petrarch as a thing of beauty, trained by Boccaccio as the instrument of melodious prose, was abandoned even by the Tuscans in the fifteenth century for revived Latin and newly discovered Greek. Patient acquisition took the place of proud inventiveness; laborious imitation of classical authors suppressed originality of style. The force of mind which in the fourteenth century had produced a *Divine Comedy* and a *Decameron*, in the fifteenth was expended upon the interpretation of codices, the settlement of texts, the translation of Greek books into Latin, the study of antiquities, the composition of commentaries, encyclopædias, dictionaries, ephemerides. While we regret this change from creative to acquisitive literature, we must bear in mind that those scholars who ought to have been poets accomplished nothing less than the civilization, or, to use their own phrase, the humanization of the modern world. At the critical moment when the Eastern Empire was being shattered by the Turks, and when the other European nations were as yet unfit for culture, Italy saved the arts and sciences of Greece and Rome and interpreted the spirit of the classics. Devoting herself to what appears the slavish work of compilation and collection, she transmitted an inestimable treasure to the human race; and though for a time the beautiful Italian tongue was superseded by a jargon of dead languages, yet the literature of the Renaissance yielded in the end the poetry of

Ariosto, the political philosophy of Machiavelli, the histories of Guicciardini and Varchi. Meanwhile the whole of Europe had received the staple of its intellectual education."[1]

Late in the fifteenth century the movement passed beyond the Alps. Enthusiastic scholars rivalled the Italians in their zeal for the resuscitation and purification of Latin. The University of Paris was the storm centre. The Brethren of the Common Life early admitted the new learning to a place in their schools. The institution founded by Groote (1340–1384) in Deventer, had as its leaders in the fifteenth century such enlightened humanists as Agricola (1443–1485), Hegius (1433–1498) and Murmellius (1479–1517). And here Erasmus (1466–1536) received his first impulse to humanistic studies. In south Germany Reuchlin (1455–1522) and Wimpheling (1450–1528) stand out as the clearest figures in the first dawn of the new day. Under such teachers as these Germany received its first lesson in Ciceronian Latin, in Greek and in Hebrew. Erasmus said of Agricola that he was "*Græcorum græcissimus, Latinorum latinissimus*," and in a letter to Cardinal Raphael he wrote thus in defence of Reuchlin: "It is to him really that Germany owes such knowledge as it has of Greek and Hebrew. He is a learned, accomplished man, respected by the Emperor, honoured among his own people, and blameless in life and character."[2] Of his own work he said in 1521, it has been "to restore a buried literature, and recall divines from their hair-splittings to a knowledge of the New Testament."[3]

Humanism in Germany.

The Renaissance in Italy early showed two main tendencies, the one toward the revival of antiquity, the other toward a better comprehension of modern life. The one mode of thought found its chiefest satisfaction in the enjoyment of the restored literatures, the other in reforming art, philosophy, society and the state. The

Two main Tendencies.

---

[1] Symonds, *Renaissance in Italy—The Revival of Learning*, ch. ii.
[2] Ep. clxviii. Cited by Froude, *Erasmus*, ch. ix.
[3] Ep. dlxiii. *Ib.*, ch. xiv.

humanists of Germany exhibited unmistakably the former tendency; they were almost to a man teachers of the classical languages. Yet they were more than linguists. They shared in the scientific spirit of the age; yet the truth for which they sought lay buried in manuscripts. Their task it was to unearth the truth and publish it abroad. Distance from classic soil and the invention of printing[1] conspired to make the German humanists bookish from the start.

An irresistible craving for truth for its own sake everywhere characterized the leading spirits of the Renaissance.[2] In their zeal to get at the facts it was inevitable that they should find opposition once they touched the dogmas of theology. Notwithstanding that the movement in its inception was favoured by the higher clergy and throughout its course the foremost humanists, the most profound scholars, remained loyal sons of the Church; its influence was distinctly opposed to the dictatorial authority of the Church. Not only did increasing familiarity with pagan learning tend to array the humanists against the Church, but the spirit of independence, the taste for freedom of thought, yes, even the study of the Scriptures and the patristic writings, militated strongly against clerical tyranny. The Church submerged the individual; humanism exalted him. The theologians and the scholars could not long live peaceably together.

Erasmus and Reuchlin soon found themselves confronted by a threatening storm. "Theology," Erasmus wrote to Colet, "is the mother of the sciences. But nowadays the good and the wise keep clear of it, and leave the field to the dull and the sordid, who think themselves omniscient."[3] Again, in the *Encomium Moriæ*, he launches out vigorously against the scholastic divines: "They live in the third heaven, adoring their own persons and disdaining the poor crawlers

Evils of Monasticism.

---
[1] *Cf.* Putnam, *Books and Their Makers in the Middle Ages*, pp. 348-402.
[2] *Cf.* Francke, *Social Forces in German Literature*, New York, 1896, p. 141.
[3] Froude, *Erasmus*, ch. iii.

upon earth. They are surrounded with a body-guard of definitions, conclusions, corollaries, propositions explicit and propositions implicit. They will tell you how the world was created. They will show you the crack where Sin crept in and corrupted mankind. . . . They lift their theologic brows. They talk of their doctors solemn, doctors subtle and most subtle, doctors seraphic, doctors cherubic, doctors holy, doctors irrefragable. They practise all the tricks of the platform, and use them badly, and yet they are admired —wonderfully admired—by women who are on bad terms with their husbands."[1] Against such lampooning as this no wonder the theologians were prompted to call Erasmus a "heretic," and "bring thunderbolts out of their arsenals" to train on him.

Nor were the clerical party the only opponents of humanism in Germany. Scholasticism, firmly intrenched in the universities, had its partisans and valiant defenders. How fiercely the battle raged can be seen in the *Epistolæ Obscurorum Virorum*, anonymous publications which appeared during the second decade of the sixteenth century. They attacked the clerical party with keen satirical denunciation, and held up to ridicule the ablest university professors of the country. Thus the seed of dissension was sown which was destined to grow into revolution.

The Beginnings of Dissension.

If the Renaissance inspired a deeper respect for the humanities and pointed out the way to independent research and inductive reasoning, the Reformation finished the work in exalting the intrinsic worth of the individual. Guizot says the Reformation was "a vast effort made by the human mind to achieve its freedom; it was a new-born desire to think and judge, freely and independently, of facts and opinions which till then Europe received, or was considered bound to receive, from the hands of authority. It was a

---

[1] Froude, *Erasmus*, ch. viii. *Cf.* also *Erasmus's Familiar Colloquies* translated by Bailey, Glasgow, 1877, pp. 184 ff.

great endeavour to emancipate human reason, and to call things by their right names; it was an insurrection of the human mind against the absolute power of spiritual order."[1] Luther in emphasizing the personal responsibility of the individual immeasurably increased the dignity of man and established a principle of supreme importance in the national life. Nothing short of revolution could result from it—revolution not only in religious and political matters, but revolution within the schools and universities.[2]

Without the Reformation the revival of learning would have remained comparatively uninfluential in Germany. The Renaissance was throughout an aristocratic movement. In Germany especially, to use Paulsen's phrase, it was "an imitation of an imitation;" it took its cue from the south.[3] It failed to reach the people. Still a few were filled with its spirit; the real leaders, Reuchlin and Erasmus, Hegius and Wimpheling, Mosellanus and Melanchthon were profound scholars and earnest teachers. To their influence was due the founding of chairs of eloquence and of the Greek language everywhere in Germany even before the Reformation; to them may be traced a movement for purer Latin and certain rational reforms in the organization of the schools. But it is under the combined influences of both Renaissance and Reformation that we find the great changes in the educational system of Germany that mark the rise of the Protestant Schools. And it is of especial significance that in Germany alone of the leading European countries the Reformers—they who alone reached the masses and strongly influenced the national life —were for the most part eminent humanists.[4] Melanchthon and Erasmus were not only participants in the revolt against Romish oppression, but they were indefatigable exponents of

The Renaissance an Aristocratic Movement.

---

[1] Guizot, *History of Civilization*, New York, 1877, p. 255. *Cf.* Hazlitt's translation, London, 1851, Vol. I., p. 220.

[2] *Cf.* G. B. Adams' *Civilization During the Middle Ages*, pp. 416-442.

[3] *Cf.* Paulsen, *Geschichte des Gelehrten Unterrichts*, p. 34 ff.

[4] Arnold, *Higher Schools and Universities in Germany*, pp. 1-6.

the new classical learning.[1] In the union of humanistic ideals with the Christian faith born anew in the Reformation we find the thread that will guide us through the confused period of reorganization of the German school system.

Among the early humanists of northern Europe Erasmus easily held first place. His word was law in the learned world, so profound was his scholarship and so striking his genius. To him, probably more than to any of his contemporaries, was due what of life and spirit was infused into the early humanism of Germany. While accepting Quintilian's theory of education of the orator he never lost sight of Quintilian's dictum that the good orator must first be a good man. It is not enough, he reiterated, to compass heaven and earth in the search for elegancies of expression—even for those of Cicero. Cicero uses words as the signs of ideas, and both words and ideas are invariably suited to his special purpose. Bare imitation, therefore, must always be a senseless task. Hence, true eloquence must be born of a good purpose, directed to definite ends and give expression to lofty thought. It is the purpose of education to make a happy, contented, broad-minded, God-fearing man. Such a man must needs be a scholar and a gentleman, a philosopher filled with the ancient wisdom and trained in the school of experience. His life transcends the petty limitations of nationality; he is the true citizen of the world of letters.

Erasmus and His Educational Ideals.

The schools of Germany were not much affected by the ideals of humanism until toward the end of the fifteenth century.[2] In fact, it was not till the beginning of the sixteenth that many changes were introduced. The earliest teachers were wandering scholars, irrepressible, uncouth and boastful of their abilities. The possession of the new learning was riches enough;

Spread of Humanism.

---

[1] *Cf.* Taylor, *Studies in German Literature*, pp. 135-166.
[2] Kaemmel, *Geschichte des devtschen Schulwesens im Übergange vom Mittelalter zur Neuzeit*, Leipsic, 1882.

they affected to despise a settled position and worldly goods; even books were unnecessary to the man who carried the ancient world in his head. Between the years 1460 and 1490 Heidelberg, Erfurt and Leipsic were intermittently honoured by such masters of "Poetry." In 1494 Erfurt established a professorship of *Poesie und Eloquenz*. Greek, the classical literature and the New Testament gradually attained a place. Wittenberg, the first German University founded except by papal bull, was throughout humanistic from the beginning (1502). Luther began his lectures there in 1508; ten years later Melanchthon was called to the chair of Greek, and the same year instruction was first offered in Hebrew. Leipsic received her first professor of Greek in 1515, an Englishman who, after two years of residence, gave way to the learned Mosellanus. But even now the cause of humanism was won. The new scholars were the leaders in all the universities of the land. In 1519 both Erfurt and Leipsic, the strongest universities of central Germany, following the lead of Wittenberg, were reorganized in the humanistic sense. It was then that Erasmus could say that "the University of Leipsic, in which the old studies have long flourished, is now so enriched by the introduction of languages and sciences that she stands second to none." The same year also marks the beginning of the end of German humanism through Luther and the Reformation.

Contemporaneous with the progress of humanism in the universities, similar changes were under way in the schools. All over Germany, particularly in the wealthier cities, there was a growing demand for better instruction in Latin. Nuremberg was typical of all. Its city schools were slightly modified as early as 1485. In 1496 a "poet" was engaged to teach literature, chiefly Latin poetry. A few years later the demand for training in eloquence, the ability to read, write and speak Ciceronian Latin, compelled the rectors of the city schools to extend their Latin course "in the new *grammatica* and *poesie* or *arte oratoria*." The climax was reached in 1521, when a

Humanism Enters the Schools.

humanistic scholar was installed in the *Sebaldus-Schule* "to give instruction in Latin, Greek and Hebrew."[1]

Humanism reached its height in the first twenty years of the sixteenth century. Scarcely a university or school of importance but had been won over to the new learning. Greek was everywhere recognized as the natural supplement of Latin, and wherever the practical utility of linguistic study outweighed its æsthetic value Hebrew was added to the list. The fact that so much attention was given to the reading of the Scriptures in the original texts was of no little significance in view of Luther's appeal from the Church to the Bible.[2] He hatched a game-cock, as the monks declared, from the egg laid by the humanists.

Humanism Reaches its Height: 1520.

The Reformation was the natural sequence of the Renaissance. Men had been accustomed to go to the sources, to think for themselves and to find satisfaction in pagan culture. What more natural than that they should reason together about theology and the practices of the clergy, that they should come to doubt the authority for papal absolutism and the efficacy of papal indulgences. With Luther conviction passed quickly into action. And his action was of incalculably greater consequence for Germany than all that the humanists had done.[3] The humanists stood apart from the people; they represented a foreign civilization; they knew no nationality. Luther sprang from the common people; he was sympathetic, patriotic, and brave; he spoke the German language and he reached the German heart. At his bidding the traditions of centuries were broken, old associations ruthlessly cast aside and the bonds of authority set at naught. Thus the freedom that the

German Reformers also Humanists.

---

[1] The records of the Nuremberg schools are given by Paulsen, *Gel. Unt.*, pp. 105–108.

[2] Reuchlin's Hebrew Grammar, the first of its kind in Germany, appeared in 1506, and in 1516 the first edition of the New Testament in Greek was published by Erasmus.

[3] *Cf.* Francke, *Social Forces in German Literature*, p. 150 ff.

Renaissance assured to the learned was offered by the Reformation to all mankind.

Luther's whole life was dominated by a single idea, the salvation of human souls. With a singleness of purpose, that had been fanatical if not sublime, he fought "Beelzebub, Satan, the devil, the great dragon, the old serpent, and the god of this world" on every field. And for this warfare he conceived it every man's duty to prepare himself. The great purpose of life is to do the will of God and to escape the consequences of sin. "The will of God is everything which he requires us to believe, do and suffer, in order that His name may be hallowed and His kingdom come." "The consequences of sin are the wrath and displeasure of God, temporal death and eternal condemnation." Redemption is found in Christ alone. "Conversion is the work of the Holy Spirit, by which, through faith in Christ, we turn from darkness to light, and from the power of Satan to God." "Faith in Jesus Christ is personal trust in Him alone for salvation;" and salvation means to be with Christ, "to live under Him and in His kingdom, and to serve Him in everlasting righteousness, innocence and blessedness."[1]

<small>Luther's Aim.</small>

Luther took his stand squarely on the doctrine of justification by faith; his sole authority was the Bible, "the word of God." "God makes Himself known to us partly through His works, mainly through His word." Repentance and personal faith in Christ, for which a knowledge of the Scriptures is an almost indispensable prerequisite, is the corner-stone of Lutheranism. The "works" which the Roman Church had enjoined were useless except they came from a regenerated heart.

In putting aside the observances, customs and traditions of the Roman Church, Luther abolished that "law" which had been the "school-master" of mediæval Europe. By fasting, penances and prayer, by ritualistic worship in public and in private, by conversation, confession and preaching, by cate-

---

[1] Extracts from Luther's *Catechism*.

chising and formal discipline, the Roman clergy had fashioned the mediæval Christians according to the ideals of the Papacy. This was the true educational system of the Middle Ages, and in it the church schools played only a subordinate part; the masses of the people were trained in the school of life, a school permeated with ecclesiastical ideas and calculated to produce a simple, obedient laity.

<small>A Change of School-Masters.</small>

With the Reformation the authority of the Church was superseded by the authority of the Bible. All central Germany was let out of one school and invited to enrol itself under another teacher. Luther saw clearly the absolute necessity of making the new education as effective as the old had been, and accordingly he resolved to supplant the formal teachings of Rome with a rational training of head and heart. But an undertaking of such vast dimensions, freighted with such tremendous consequences, demanded the combined support of Family, State and Church. To secure harmony of action among these "three hierarchies established by God," and to see that the right means were used in the right way— this was the life-work of Luther once the Reformation of Germany was an assured fact. For this purpose he translated the Bible, wrote his two catechisms, composed popular hymns, and unweariedly laboured to uplift the peasantry and strengthen the government. The great pedagogical service of Luther, the most remarkable fact in a remarkable life, was his keen appreciation of Germany's need of an education broader than that of the schools if the shock of the protestant revolution were to be successfully withstood.

The duty thus imposed upon parents, Luther declares, is a divine requirement. "Married people should know that they can perform no better and no more useful work for God, Christianity, the world, themselves and their children, than by bringing up their children well. Pilgrimages to Rome and to Jerusalem, building churches, providing for masses, or whatever else the work may be called, is nothing in comparison with the right train-

<small>Duties of Parents.</small>

ing of children, for that is the straight road to heaven; and it cannot be more easily attained in any other way. It is the peculiar work of parents, and when they do not attend to it, there is a perversion of nature, as when fire does not burn or water moisten. On the other hand, hell cannot be more easily deserved, and no more hurtful work can be done, than by neglecting children, letting them swear, learn shameful words and songs, and do as they please." [1]

Again: "But this again is a sad evil that all live on as though God gave us children for our pleasure or amusement, and servants that we should employ them like a cow or ass, only for work, or as though all we had to do with our subjects were only to gratify our wantonness, without any concern on our part as to what they learn or how they live; and no one is willing to see that this is the command of the Supreme Majesty, who will most strictly call us to an account and punish us for it, nor that there is so great need to be so intensely anxious about the young. . . . Let every-one know, therefore, that above all things it is his duty (or otherwise he will lose the divine favour,) to bring up his children in the fear and knowledge of God; and if they have talents, to have them instructed and trained in a liberal education, that men may be able to have their aid in government and in whatever is necessary." [2]

Family government he considers the basis of all other government. Obedience to parents, therefore, is the child's chief duty. "For what is a city but a collection of houses? How then can a city be well governed, when there is no government in the separate houses, and neither child nor servant is obedient? Likewise, what is a province but a collection of cities, towns, and villages? When, therefore, the families are badly controlled, how can the province be well governed? Verily there can be nothing but tyranny, witchcraft, murders, *Family Government the Basis of all Government.*

---

[1] Cited by Painter, *Luther on Education*, pp. 117-118.
[2] Same, p. 116.

thefts, disobedience. A principality is made up of districts; a kingdom, of principalities; an empire, of kingdoms; these are all composed of families. Where the father and mother rule badly, and let the children have their own way, there neither city, town, village, district, principality, kingdom nor empire, can be well and peacefully governed."[1]

For the guidance of parents in the proper instruction of their children he prepared his catechisms. They consist of a critical exegesis of the ten commandments, the Creed and the Lord's Prayer, which "are the most necessary parts, which every Christian should first learn to repeat word for word, and which our children should be accustomed to recite daily when they arise in the morning, when they sit down to their meals, and when they retire at night; and until they repeat them they should be given neither food nor drink. The same duty is also incumbent upon every head of a household, with respect to his man-servants and his maid-servants, if they do not know these things and are unwilling to learn them. For a person who is so heathenish as to be unwilling to learn these things is not to be tolerated; for in these three parts everything contained in the Scriptures is comprehended in short and simple terms."[2]

That there was sufficient cause for alarm at the condition of education in the early years of the Reformation is clearly apparent from the tenor of Luther's "Letter to the Mayors and Aldermen of all the Cities of Germany in behalf of Christian Schools" (1524) and of the "Sermon on the Duty of Sending Children to School" (1530).[3] Herein we see reflected a state of affairs due partly to the open rupture with the past and partly to

Luther's Letter and Sermon.

---

[1] Luther's comments on the Fourth Commandment.
[2] From the introduction to the Catechism.
[3] English translations of these, the most famous of Luther's pedagogical writings, may be found in Painter's *Luther on Education*, Philadelphia, 1889. See also Köstlin's *Life of Luther*, New York, 1883, and Luther's *Pädagogische Schriften*, edited by Schumann, Vienna and Leipsic, 1884.

the popular interpretation of the doctrine of justification by faith rather than by works. "First of all," Luther writes, "we see how schools are deteriorating throughout Germany. The universities are becoming weak, the monasteries are declining. . . . For through the word of God the unchristian and sensual character of these institutions is becoming known. And because selfish parents see that they can no longer place their children upon the bounty of monasteries and cathedrals, they refuse to educate them. 'Why should we educate our children,' they say, 'if they are not to become priests, monks and nuns, and thus earn a support?'"

It is the work of the devil that the people are so neglectful of the higher education of their children. Therefore he appeals to the city magistrates and to the civil rulers to take the matter in hand. "If we must annually expend large sums on muskets, roads, bridges, dams, and the like, in order that the city may have temporal peace and comfort, why should we not apply as much to our poor, neglected youth, in order that we may have a skilful school-master or two?"

But Luther has little regard for the general run of schools, even those of the humanists. "I should prefer, it is true, that our youth be ignorant and dumb rather than that the universities and convents should remain as the only sources of instruction open to them. For it is my earnest intention, prayer and desire that these schools of Satan either be destroyed or changed into Christian schools. But since God has so richly favoured us, and given us a great number of persons who are competent thoroughly to instruct and train our young people, it is truly needful that we should not disregard His grace and let Him knock in vain. . . . Therefore it will be the duty of the mayors and councils to exercise the greatest care over the young. For since the happiness, honor, and life of the city are committed to their hands, they would be recreant before God and the world, if they did not, day and night, with all their power, seek its welfare and improvement. Now the welfare of the city does not consist alone in great treasures, firm walls, beautiful

Need of Schools.

houses, and munitions of war; indeed, where all these are found, and reckless fools come into power, the city sustains the greater injury. But the highest welfare, safety and power of a city consists in able, learned, wise, upright, cultivated citizens, who can secure, preserve and utilize every treasure and advantage. . . . Even if there were no soul (as I have already said), and men did not need schools and the languages for the sake of Christianity and the Scriptures, still, for the establishment of the best schools everywhere, both for boys and girls, this consideration is of itself sufficient, namely, that society; for the maintenance of civil order and the proper regulation of the household, needs accomplished and well-trained men and women."

It should be remembered, however, that in Luther's opinion the chief end of education is distinctly religious. "Able, learned, wise, upright, cultivated citizens" must also be earnest, active Christians. In the union of the Church and State the latter must be theoretically subordinate. The schools which Luther most wanted were Christian schools, in which the ancient languages should hold first rank. "The languages are the scabbard in which the Word of God is sheathed. They are the casket in which this jewel is enshrined; the cask in which this wine is kept; the chamber in which this food is stored. . . . If through neglect we lose the languages (which may God forbid), we will not only lose the Gospel, but it will finally come to pass that we will lose also the ability to speak and write either Latin or German." The degeneracy of the Church is due to the ignorance of the languages in the dark ages, and the only remedy is the knowledge of them. "Since, then, it behooves Christians at all times to use the Bible as their only book and to be thoroughly acquainted with it, especially is it a disgrace and a sin at the present day not to learn the languages, when God provides every facility, incites us to study, and wishes to have His word known."

Chief End of Education.

The schools should also give instruction in history, mathematics and handiwork. "My idea is that boys should spend an hour or two a day in school, and the rest of the time work at home, learn some trade and do whatever is desired, so that study and work may go on together, while the children are young and can attend to both. . . . In like manner, a girl has time to go to school an hour a day, and yet attend to her work at home; for she sleeps, dances, and plays away more than that. . . . But the brightest pupils, who give promise of becoming accomplished teachers, preachers, and workers, should be kept longer at school, or set apart wholly for study. . . . We must have persons qualified to dispense the Word of God and the Sacraments, and to be pastors of the people. But where will we obtain them, if schools are not established on a more Christian basis, since those hitherto maintained, even if they do not go down, can produce nothing but depraved and dangerous corruptors of youth?"

Luther's Curriculum.

"Finally, this must be taken into consideration by all who earnestly desire to see such schools established and the languages preserved in the German states: that no cost nor pains should be spared to procure good libraries in suitable buildings, especially in the large cities, which are able to afford it. For if a knowledge of the Gospel and of every kind of learning is to be preserved, it must be embodied in books, as the prophets and apostles did, as I have already shown. . . . But my advice is, not to collect all sorts of books indiscriminately, thinking of getting only a vast number together. I would have discrimination used, because it is not necessary to collect the commentaries of all the jurists, the productions of all the theologians, the discussions of all the philosophers, and the sermons of all the monks. Such trash I would reject altogether, and provide my library only with useful books; and in making the selection, I would advise with learned men. In the first place, a library should contain the Holy Scriptures in Latin, Greek, Hebrew, German, and other languages. Then the best and most ancient commentators in Greek, Hebrew, and Latin. Secondly, such books as are useful in acquiring the

Value of Books.

languages, as the poets and orators, without considering whether they are heathen or Christian, Greek or Latin. For it is from such works that grammar must be learned. Thirdly, books treating of all the arts and sciences. Lastly, books on jurisprudence and medicine, though here discrimination is necessary. A prominent place should be given to chronicles and histories, in whatever languages they may be obtained; for they are wonderfully useful in understanding and regulating the course of the world, and in disclosing the marvellous works of God."

It was characteristic of the great reformer that whatever he did he never left anyone in doubt as to his real intentions. His words went straight to the mark. So in discussing educational affairs there was no uncertainty as to his attitude. He wanted systematic family instruction; he stated clearly the purpose of it and supplied the means, even to question and answer, in his catechisms. He wanted schools for the people that likely boys might be discovered for the service of the Church and State. He wanted schools for the higher training of those who might become preachers and civil rulers. Above all things he wanted Christian schools in which everything taught should redound to the glory of God and the salvation of immortal souls. He approved of the study of the ancient languages, but not for humanistic reasons; the immediate end of language study, as he conceived it, was not the cultivation of literary style, nor yet the recovery of pagan learning, but rather the interpretation and understanding of the Word of God. Luther's position was diametrically opposed to the ideals of the humanists; nevertheless the course of events yoked together Luther, the reformer, and Melanchthon, the humanist, in the great work of reorganizing the German school system. The union was unique, but the situation demanded the co-operation of the two movements which they pre-eminently represented.

Luther the Reformer—Melanchthon the Humanist.

An adequate presentation of Melanchthon's pedagogical views and of the part he played in the history of German schools would transcend the limits of the present study. Suffice it to say that as a nephew and disciple of the famous Reuchlin he was a humanist of the humanists. His inaugural address on taking his chair in Wittenberg, *de corrigendis adolescentiæ studiis*, marked out the path which he followed the rest of his life. The only remedy for the ignorance of the Middle Ages, he assumed, was to go back to the sources of classical learning and start afresh. Greek he ranked on a par with Latin because of its content. For style Cicero stands pre-eminent; for training in conversational Latin, Terence. The immediate aim of all linguistic study is *dilucide et perspicue dicere;* the literature, fortified by theology, ethics, mathematics and the natural sciences, leads to *prudentia et humanitas*. As a teacher, organizer and maker of text-books, Melanchthon excelled all his contemporaries. His lectures at Wittenberg included almost the entire round of the linguistic and philosophical studies—dialectics and physics, ethics and history, mathematics and astronomy, Greek grammar, Cicero, Sallust, Tacitus, Quintilian, Vergil, Terence, Ovid, Horace, Homer, Hesiod, Demosthenes, Æschines, Lycurgus, Sophocles, Euripides, Aristophanes, Pindar, Theognis, Thucydides, Aristotle and the Greek New Testament. The text-books which he wrote on most of these subjects were in common use for more than a century after his death. But perhaps in no way did Melanchthon better deserve the title, *Preceptor Germaniæ*, than in his attention to the training of teachers for the higher schools. The best teachers of the Reformation age were Melanchthon's pupils. Through them the schools which he organized became famous, and his influence extended throughout all Germany.[1]

Melanchthon's Pedagogical Views.

In the general crash of the Reformation it is significant that monarchical Germany retained the episcopal form of

---

[1] For an account of Melanchthon's services to education in Germany, see Paulsen, *Gel. Unt.*, pp. 73–77, 135–139, 147–160; Rein's *Ency. Hdbk. d. Päd.*; and Kehrbach's *Monumenta Germaniæ Pædagogica*, Vol. VII.—*Philipp Melanchthon als Præceptor Germaniæ* by Hartfelder.

church government—in effect if not in name. Even before 1530 there was a marked tendency toward a territorial church, the head of which should be the ruler of the state. Saxony and Hesse led the way; others followed in rapid succession, until in 1540 practically every protestant state of Germany had its own church—a condition of affairs tolerable to Luther only on the ground that the state is a divine institution designed to enable its citizens the better to do the will of God.

The reorganization of the universities, especially of the theological faculties, was an imperative necessity in view of the fact that preachers were wanted, not priests —men learned in the Scriptures and the Lutheran doctrines, rather than men skilled in the use and manipulation of symbols. The University of Marburg was founded for this purpose in 1529. Wittenberg was reformed in the early 30's, and within a decade thereafter Tübingen, Leipsic, Basel, Frankfort-on-the-Oder, and Greifswald followed. With the founding of the universities of Königsberg (1544), Jena (1558) and Helmstädt (1559), and the reorganization of Heidelberg (1558) and Rostock (1563), the triumph of the Reformation was complete. Candidates for the ministry were thereafter enabled to get not only a Christian education, but provision was made in all the universities for supporting meritorious students by scholarships, bursaries and stipends of various sorts.

Founding of Protestant Universities.

Closely associated with the reorganization of the universities, and, like it, directly traceable to the movement for a state church, was the secularization of the school system. In this, too, as in the case of the universities, Melanchthon played a leading part. It is said that not a course of study was adopted, nor a school founded, in all protestant Germany during the first twenty years of the Reformation without his having something to do with it. The influence of Luther was not wanting, of course, but Melanchthon was the better educationalist and the better organizer.

Secularization of the School System.

THE RISE OF PROTESTANT SCHOOLS 37

The first protestant school, according to Paulsen,[1] was established in Magdeburg (1524) by the union of the old parochial schools under one management. In 1525 the Counts of Mansfield called upon the reformers to organize a school in Eisleben, the birthplace of Luther. *The First Protestant School.* Melanchthon's plan for this school is the oldest protestant school programme now extant. It provides for three classes. The first *classis* is the elementary school, in which reading and writing are the main subjects. The second *classis* is devoted chiefly to grammar, *i.e.*, the linguistic study of Terence and Vergil. The third *classis* deals with rhetoric and dialectic; Erasmus' *de duplici copia* serves as a text-book, and besides Livy, Sallust, Vergil, Horace and Cicero are studied. Favoured pupils may also make some beginning of Greek and Hebrew. Mathematics is considered desirable, but the exigencies of the schedule rule it out. Music gets one hour a day, and on Sunday there is instruction in religion.

Erasmus himself could not have devised a more humanistic course of study than the reformers placed before the little school at Eisleben. The ability to read, write and speak good Latin is the one chief end. If Melanchthon had no thought of making Latin orators, he certainly desired for these pupils a Ciceronian style. It is interesting to note here and in subsequent developments how barren were Luther's ideas wherever Melanchthon's influence extended.

The first step toward a state school system was taken by the Electorate of Saxony. The *Kursächsische Schulordnung* of 1528 was the first official response to Luther's appeal for the co-operation of municipalities in the founding of protestant schools.[2] It provided not only for schools, but for a uniform system of schools throughout the Electorate. This plan was also

---

[1] *Geschichte des Gelehrten Unterrichts*, p. 182

[2] *Cf.* Schiller, *Geschichte der Pädagogik*, p. 99. The best authority on the period is Burkhardt, *Geschichte der sächsischen Kirchen- und Schulvisitationen von 1524–45*, Leipzig, 1879.

Melanchthon's, but that it received Luther's approval as the best possible arrangement under existing conditions is equally certain. In general outline it was similar to the plan prescribed for Eisleben, but with some modifications, chiefly making for greater simplicity, which were probably the result of experience in the former instances. It contemplated the founding of Latin schools in all the towns and villages of Saxony. And they were to be Latin schools in fact as well as in name; no Greek, no Hebrew, not even a modicum of the mother-tongue, might find a place. Their chief function was to begin the preparation of boys for the university; the final preparation of such "lads of pairts" as they discovered were provided for as the emergencies arose.

The Saxony Latin schools had three classes or grades, each with rather indefinite time allotment. The lowest class was taught reading and writing from Melanchthon's Latin primer; the Creed, the Lord's Prayer, the Commandments, and a few classical selections were committed to memory. The second class studied grammar, syntax and prosody. Latin reading, Terence and Plautus, and conversational practice were given considerable attention. Music and religious instruction occupied a more conspicuous position. The third class, having been thoroughly drilled in Latin Grammar, read Vergil, Ovid and Cicero. They practised Latin declamations, made verses, and wrote letters and essays weekly. One day a week was devoted to religious instruction.

<small>Saxon Latin Schools.</small>

The need of higher schools was soon felt. In the early 40's three such schools were established by the state government and richly endowed with the possessions of secularized monasteries. The *Fürstenschulen*, also called *Landesschulen*, of Pforta, Meissen and Grimma were the first schools erected in Germany, not for the benefit of the municipalities, but in the interests of state and church. To these schools young nobles preparing for political careers and poor boys looking to the ministry as a profession were admitted on equal footing. The entire sup-

<small>The Fürstenschulen.</small>

port of likely boys was assured, a fact that had much to do with changing the attitude of parents, as remarked by Luther, toward the higher education of their sons.

The conduct of these schools seems to have been much influenced by their monastic environment. The pupils lived in cells, ate and worked together, and wore a common habit. The masters, at least in some schools founded a little later on the same plan, were pledged to celibacy. The discipline was always severe, the rod being much in evidence; little freedom was granted outside of the convent walls; vacations were short and far between. In fact, these schools came as near being monastic schools as was possible under protestant rule.

The *Landesschulen* of Saxony stood theoretically midway between the Latin schools of the cities and the universities, but for many years the line of demarcation at either extreme was not sharply drawn. Each school strove to do the utmost in its power. The Latin schools in some instances became strong enough to extend their course beyond the three grades and offered elementary instruction in Greek, Hebrew and mathematics. Schools such as these, wherein at least two ancient languages were taught, have been known since about the middle of the sixteenth century as *Gymnasien*. The *Fürstenschulen*, on the other hand, overlapped in many respects the university course. Admitting boys from the Latin schools at eleven to fifteen years of age, the curriculum of the higher schools included the three *artes dicendi*—grammar, rhetoric and dialectic; and the three ancient languages—Latin, Greek and Hebrew. The acquisition of a pure and facile style was the aim of all instruction; the means of its realization, chiefly the imitation of the classical authors. Wherever possible a beginning was made of professional study; not infrequently did the higher schools offer instruction in medicine, jurisprudence and theology.

Course of Study.

Notwithstanding the *Kursächsische Schulordnung* was designed to encourage the founding of schools and to secure uniformity in aim and method, the Latin schools of Saxony did not meet the high expectations of their founders. Supported by the municipal governments they were largely influenced by local considerations. As a system of public schools the most that can be said is that it was a confederacy of interests held together by the substantial inducements offered in the *Fürstenschulen* and the universities.

Würtemberg was the first German state to organize a complete system of public schools. In 1559 Melanchthon's plan, <small>School System of Würtemburg, 1559.</small> as tried in Saxony, but further modified and extended, was introduced in the Duchy. For the first time in Germany schools were provided for all the people and in a series that permitted of orderly progression from the elementary grades to the universities. And here was the real beginning of the common schools of Germany; not a radical and independent beginning, to be sure, but the development of what already existed under the influence of new religious, intellectual and economic conditions.

The *Württembergische Schulordnung*[1] provided that in every village there should be an elementary school where both <small>Elementary School.</small> boys and girls should be taught reading, writing, the art of reckoning, religion and singing. These schools were entirely in accord with Luther's idea that boys and girls should be taught for an hour or two each day the three R's and the catechism. The only thing lacking was some means of compelling attendance.

Each considerable town and city was to have also a *Particularschule*, a Latin school, with five or six classes according <small>Latin School.</small> to local needs. Here instruction should be given six hours a day in reading, writing and speaking Latin. A little mathematics was included and in the last year the elements of Greek were taught. The curriculum was altogether humanistic, but with the addition of religion according to Luther's catechism. These schools were intended chiefly for the education of burghers, and as a

---

[1] *Cf.* Schiller, *Geschichte der Pädagogik*, p. 102 ff.

matter of fact comparatively few students ever passed from these schools to the next higher grade. Nevertheless the way was open to graduates of the Latin schools to pass directly into the University of Tübingen and the *Pädagogium* of Stuttgart. These colleges—they could hardly be called universities—were higher schools attended principally by students in preparation for the civil service. For intending theologians thirteen cloistral schools were established, on the plan of the *Fürstenschulen* of Saxony, to which graduates of the Latin schools were admitted on competitive examination.

<small>Cloistral Schools for Clergy.</small>

The school system of Würtemberg was in advance of the times. It was too comprehensive for effectual realization, but the experience of the Duchy taught Germany how to provide instruction for all classes of society, how to make transition easy from one school to another, and especially how to combine central control with a fair share of local self-government. The rector of the college in Stuttgart had charge of the *Land-Examen* which regulated the admission of Latin-school pupils into the higher schools, while the immediate supervision of the schools rested with the mayors of the different towns and committees composed of ministers and citizens. All needy theological students received stipends in the cloistral schools, and a few young nobles of special promise were awarded scholarships at the university which in certain cases might be retained even during three or four years of study abroad.

<small>Würtemberg's Plan a Type for Others.</small>

. The example of Würtemberg was everywhere followed in protestant Germany. Even Saxony in 1580 made use of all the improvements that Würtemberg had devised and reformed her plan of 1528 to accord therewith. This date, 1580, indicates the high-water mark of the protestant schools as the products of the Renaissance and the Reformation; after that, a period of transition, which is the subject of the following chapter.

<small>Saxon Reforms of 1580.</small>

It is obvious that so many and such far-reaching reforms could never have been carried through without the loyal support of many capable teachers and educationists. Melanchthon's students have already been mentioned as his trusty lieutenants. But of all the school-masters of the time John Sturm (1507–1589) of Strassburg was the most celebrated.[1] He combined in himself all the important tendencies of the age. He was a humanist, and no humanist was ever more deeply impressed than he with the almightiness of the classical languages; he was a protestant of the Calvinistic type, but in full sympathy with the Lutheran position; he was a practical man of affairs, an experienced diplomat, at one time or another in the service of most of the leading European courts; he was an able teacher and organizer, if we can judge anything from his work in Strassburg.

It matters little in this connection whether Sturm was merely the product of his age or whether he was in reality a creative genius. At any rate he had the ability to combine all the good points in school management, as they were then conceived, and direct them systematically toward the commonly accepted ends of education, *sapiens atque eloquens pietas*. Concerning the results attained it is enough to know that the Strassburg *Gymnasium*, of which Sturm was rector for forty-three years after its foundation in 1538, became the most famous school in Europe. The dominant ideas of the sixteenth century were concentrated in this school, and for two hundred years it remained the typical school of the "good old times" when schools were "what they ought to be."

Sturm's Position.

Sturm provided for a ten years' course of study (only nine years' at first, later ten). His pupils entered at six years of age and immediately began the Latin grammar. Seven years they laboured to acquire a correct and fluent use of the Latin tongue (*Latinitas pura*); three years more were devoted to the acquisition of a

His Course of Study.

---

[1] The best accounts of Sturm's work will be found in Schmidt's *La vie et les travaux de Jean Sturm*, Strassburg, 1855, and in Laas' *Die Pädagogik des Joh. Sturm*, Berlin, 1872.

fine style (*Latinitas ornata*). Thus for ten years "Latin was exclusively taught, read, spoken, written, every day four hours long." Sturm never seems to have doubted his ability to turn German boys back sixteen centuries; his aim was to produce Ciceronian orators. Environment had nothing to do with the case; all that was necessary was to Latinize it. And so in getting a vocabulary his boys were first taught the Latin names of every-day things and the commonest expressions of use in conversation. They were compelled to imagine themselves Roman youths in an imaginary Roman atmosphere. Naturally enough under such conditions imitation was a virtue and a good memory the greatest of intellectual endowments. In fact, the reproduction of whole orations of Cicero and of whole books of Vergil, was a favourite exercise because of its value in strengthening the memory and in forming taste.

How far the protestant schools toward the end of the century were now removed from the ideals of Erasmus and Melanchthon can be clearly seen in the case of Strassburg. We hear nothing more of "content" or "substance;" everything is "form," "style," "eloquence." To be sure, Sturm included Greek in his curriculum—six years of it—but both Greek and Latin were looked upon either as ends in themselves, so far as the school was concerned, or else as means to higher professional study of a nature demanding a knowledge of language and skill in its use. Sturm's curriculum contained no history, no mathematics, no natural sciences, and it is said that for thirty years no time was found to teach even the elements of arithmetic as scheduled for the two highest classes.

Scholastic Humanism.

But as a schoolmaster Sturm was a success. His curriculum accorded strictly with the educational ideals of his time, although we cannot fail to observe that the Reformation in emphasizing the value of the classical languages for biblical interpretation had strenghtened the worst element in the humanistic movement, the formal, "bookish" element. He introduced unity into the whole school-plan whereby the end that was desired might the more certainly be attained; he

made a clear-cut, logical arrangement of the materials which
he used; he proposed methods of teaching whereby the materials of instruction were rendered of incalculably greater
educational value. His entire scheme was a model of concentration, both in subject-matter and methods of presentation. In this respect Sturm's work remains unsurpassed.

A glance at the pedagogical progress of the sixteenth century discloses marvellous changes in educational thought.
First, the humanistic movement completely
shattered within twenty years the scholastic
traditions of centuries. The mediæval Latin of the Church
was replaced by the pure Latin of classical antiquity; Greek
was awarded a prominent place and Hebrew came in for a
share of attention. Accurate translations of the classical
writers, philosophers and scientists took the place of the fac-
titious interpretations of the Middle Ages. Man's sympathies were broadened, his understanding of life enormously
extended, and his mental attitude completely changed—all
the result of careful investigation and the habit of appealing
to the original sources for information. Next came the Reformation, the logical consequence of the Renaissance, and
with it a new view of life and new duties corresponding to
the responsibilities now for the first time laid on individual
consciences. The authority of the Church gave way to the
authority of the Bible. To do God's will one must first know
God's word, not as distorted by ignorant commentators, but
as it is given in the original tongues. Scholarship must not
perish from the earth if true religion is to remain. Schools
are indispensable. But the chief end of the schools is by no
means absorption in pagan learning; the ability to use the
classical languages is worth far more than the acquaintance
with classical antiquity. Protestant schools were rapidly established to meet the requirements of Lutheranism; but they
were humanistic schools in fact, protestant only in theory.
More than that they rapidly became state schools more or
less closely fitted into a comprehensive system, supported in
part by state funds and supervised by state authority. Both

within and without the protestant schools corresponded to the *Zeitgeist;* but conditions obtained in the political and religious worlds, as well as in the pedagogical sphere, that rendered impossible any settled educational system. A period of transition was at hand.

GENERAL REFERENCES :—Voigt, *Wiederbelebung des classischen Alterthums;* Fisher, *History of the Reformation;* Häusser, *Period of the Reformation;* Bryce, *Holy Roman Empire;* Bluntschli, *Theory of the State;* Ranke, *History of the Reformation in Germany;* Freytag, *Bilder aus der deutschen Vergangenheit* and *Neue Bilder aus dem Leben des deutschen Volkes;* K A. Schmid, *Geschichte der Erziehung;* Schmidt, *Geschichte der Pädagogik;* Rein, *Encyklopädisches Handbuch der Pädagogik;* Ziegler, *Geschichte der Pädagogik,* in Baumeister's *Handbuch der Erziehungs- und Unterrichtslehre für höhere Schulen.*

CHAPTER III

THE PERIOD OF TRANSITION
1618-1805

THE first decades of the sixteenth century saw the rise of protestant schools in Germany under the combined influences of the humanists and the reformers. The early humanists had sought out the ancient classics for their spirit and content; with an exalted idea of man they found in the old civilization a higher realization of individual freedom than was offered in the mediæval world. Lutheranism checked the growth of the humanistic movement. It converted intellectual and humanitarian interests into civil and religious interests. It turned man's attention from the life of the past to life in the present as a preparation for the life that is to come. A knowledge of God's word as found in the Greek and Hebrew Scriptures was of paramount importance both in shaping human action in this world and for the adequate appreciation of the glories of the next. Hence an acquaintance with the ancient languages was indispensable, but the pagan literatures of Greece and Rome, much more other records of these corrupt civilizations, were of little value, even if not positively harmful.

Tendencies of Protestantism.

The protestant schools of Germany, in their zeal for the education of the clergy and the uplifting of the masses, had one pre-eminent ... the promotion of a better and purer religious life ... the people and the salvation of human souls. How well fitted ... cceeded in alienating all classes from the Roman Church ... establishing them in the protestant faith, is best evidenced in the adoption of schools as the most effective weapons of the Counter Reformation. Sturm could have received no greater compliment than was paid him by the Society of Jesus in incorporating so many of his methods into the new catholic schools. The Jesuits, in employing schools to check the growth of heresy and to win back to the Church apostate Germany, merely borrowed the devil's artillery to fight the devil with. And they used it to good effect.

"In the year 1551 they [the Jesuits] had no settled position in Germany; in 1566, their institutions held possession of Bavaria and the Tyrol, Franconia and Swabia, a large part of the Rhenish provinces and Austria. They had penetrated, also, into Hungary, Bohemia, and Moravia. The effect of their exertions soon became perceptible. So early as the year 1561 the papal nuncio declares that 'they are winning many souls, and doing great service to the holy see.' This was the first effectual counteraction of protestant labours, the first enduring impression made against them in Germany." [1]

The Counter Reformation.

It is safe to say that the world has never seen a more powerful religious order than this Society of the Jesuits. Ranke finds the secret of its strength in its extreme military character. "For in the order of Jesuits, obedience takes the place of every motive or affection that usually awakens men to activity—obedience, absolute and unconditional, without one thought or question as to its object or consequences. No man shall aspire to any rank above that he holds. The secular coadjutor may not even learn to read or write without permission, if it happen that he do not possess these attainments. With the most unlimited abjuration of all right of judgment, in total and blind subjection to the will of his superiors, must he resign himself to be led, like a thing without life, as the staff, for example, that the superior holds in his hand, to be turned to any purpose

Society of Jesus.

---

[1] Ranke, *History of the Popes*, I., 415, Bohn's Library.

seeming good to him. The society is to him as the representative of the divine providence."[1]

The success of the Jesuits can scarcely be credited to their learning or their piety, says Ranke, but rather to the exactness and nicety of their methods. "With them all was nicely calculated, every movement and action had its definite end and aim. Such a combination of learning sufficing to its purpose with unwearying zeal, of studies and persuasion, of pomp and asceticism, of widely extended influence and unity in the governing principle and intention, has never been exhibited in the world before or since. At once diligent and visionary, worldly wise, yet full of enthusiasm; well-bred men and attractive companions; disregarding their personal interests, but labouring for the advancement of each other—we cannot wonder that they were successful."[2]

Success of the Jesuits.

The three great lines of the order's activity, according to the plans of its founder, Ignatius Loyola, were preaching, confession—"for by this they were to hold the immediate guidance and government of consciences"—and the education of youth. And of these the last was the most important. "To gain the rising generation was among the purposes most earnestly pursued. They laid aside all secondary matters, devoting themselves wholly to such labours as were essential, of immediate result, and calculated for the extension of their influence."

The means which the Jesuits found most serviceable in the training of their own novices they soon carried into the education of others. The schools of the semi-protestant regions in which the society first began its work were pretty thoroughly tinctured with humanistic ideas—a mode of education that by the middle of the sixteenth century was by no means acceptable to Rome. Gradually the Jesuits found their way into all the schools and universities of the outlying provinces of Germany, and at the

Jesuit Schools.

---

[1] Ranke, *History of the Popes*, I., 168.   [2] *Ibid.*, p. 417.

end of the century the protestant states were surrounded, except for the Baltic coast, by Jesuits firmly intrenched in the educational institutions of the people and at the courts of their rulers.[1]

Perhaps the real secret of the popularity of the Jesuit schools with the majority of the people was the fact that wherever one of their colleges was founded "no private person needed further to incur expense for the education of his children." Their instruction was altogether gratuitous; the asking or receiving any remuneration whatsoever was strictly prohibited. And with children to instruct the Jesuits knew far better how to attain their ends than did the protestant school-masters of their time. We are told that " It was found that young people gained more with them in six months, than with other teachers in two years; even protestants removed their children from distant schools, to place them under the care of the Jesuits."

An extended discussion of the ideals of the Jesuits and of their methods of work is foreign to the purpose of this essay. Nevertheless it is impossible to ignore the influence of their teachings on the subsequent development of the German school system. *Influence of Jesuits on School System.* First, because the schools of catholic Germany have remained almost as the Jesuits left them, even well into the present century; and second, because the protestant schools, forced to recognize the superior skill of their adversaries, were gradually reformed the better to act on the defensive.

Catholic and protestant schools alike at the beginning of

---

[1] Zirngiebl, *Studien über das Gesellschaft Jesu mit besonderer Berücksichtigung der pädagogischen Wirksamkeit dieses Ordens in Deutschland*, Leipzig, 1870. Probably the most valuable work on this subject from the educational stand-point that has been published in German. Hughes, *Loyola, and the Educational System of the Jesuits*, New York, 1892, is perhaps the most instructive book for English readers. The *Ratio studiorum et Institutiones scholasticæ Societatis Jesu* (by Pachtler) will be found in Vols. II., V., IX. and XVI. of Kehrbach's *Monumenta Germaniæ Pædagogica*.

the seventeenth century gave little heed to the substance of the ancient civilization; both alike were earnestly devoted to the study of the Latin language—the Jesuits, because it was the universal speech of their order; the protestants, because it was the first step toward a knowledge of Holy Writ. The Jesuits, too, made much of disputation and declamation in Latin as a means of formal discipline; the protestants found themselves increasingly engaged in theological discussion among themselves, an exercise no less destructive of peace than the encroachments of a rejuvenated Catholicism. The tendency was everywhere to neglect the study of Greek and Hebrew. So long as eloquence was the immediate aim of all instruction the imitation of Latin orators held a prominent place. At the turn of the century, however, teachers were inclined to content themselves with the Latin of philosophical and theological compendiums. In fact, the petty jealousies among the protestants themselves and the aggressiveness of the Jesuits were giving rise to a new scholasticism. Scholars found themselves engulfed in a maelstrom of theological disputation; all their energies were bent on building up or tearing down some dogma of the new faith.[1]

Tendency toward Scholasticism.

It has already been noted that the natural tendency of the protestant schools was toward a formal study of the ancient languages, regardless of their cultural content. We now see how this formalism tended to develop into a rehabilitated scholasticism. Accompanying the revival of the old hairsplittings in the learned world, the shade of the mediæval dialectic appeared in the schools.

The result of the movement was on the one hand to exclude the masses of the people from all participation in the learning of the time, and on the other hand to alienate the sympathies of the nobility. The vague speculations of the scholars concerning philosophy and theology had no

---

[1] *Cf.* Wakeman, *Europe, 1598-1715*, London, 1894, pp. 39-52, on the Counter Reformation in Germany.

attractions for the upper classes, and for the lower classes it was all an unknown region. And just as in the Middle Ages the rise of scholasticism was accompanied by the growth of feudalism, so in the seventeenth century alongside of the new scholastic movement we find the nobility following ideals of its own.

From about the middle of the sixteenth century the courts of western Germany had been more or less closely in touch with court life in France. German nobles affected the French language and aped French customs. They professed a liking for French literature.[1] They sent their children to French schools or employed French tutors at home. Dissatisfaction with the education at home and admiration for everything foreign soon worked a complete change in the ideals of the German nobility. The highest ambition of the young noble was to become a "perfect cavalier." To know the latest Parisian fads, fashions and customs; to know how to dance, fence and ride like a born Frenchman; to be accomplished in speech and manner,—all this was of more importance than a knowledge of Latin or the art of disputation. French political ideas readily found a place in many German states, and the "perfect cavalier" gradually came to need special preparation for civil and military service. The new ideal carried with it the desire for an acquaintance with mathematics and physics and their practical applications. The new political sciences, political history, jurisprudence, geography and statistics, heraldry and genealogy, were all a part of the educational life of the *galant homme*. To be sure, the formal disciplines—religion, ethics, rhetoric and dialectics, were not altogether abandoned; nor was Latin wholly supplanted by French and the other modern languages. But the fact is these old-fashioned studies were relegated to

---

[1] *Cf.* Taylor's *Studies in German Literature*, New York, 1891, pp. 167-199; Francke, *Social Forces in German Literature*, p. 172 ff.; Scherer, *Geschichte der deutschen Litteratur*, 7th ed., Berlin, 1894, p. 367 ff.

places in the rear rank; all that pertained to fine manners, practical conduct, and civil and military functions, came to the front.

To satisfy the demands of this borrowed ideal of life, there arose schools designed to afford the means of cultivating and refining the German youth. This new school, thoroughly characteristic of the period in which it arose, was the *Ritterakademie*. It succeeded the reign of private tutors, and, established only in capital cities, it always remained a part of court life. A *Collegium illustre* was established in Tübingen in 1589 for noble youths. In 1599 the *Collegium Mauritianum* was founded in Cassel, and in 1618 it was converted into a *Ritterakademie*—the first of its kind.[1] These schools were the direct outgrowth of French influence, and manned mostly by French teachers they sought to extend the French ideals of life. In their way they were effective, but a still more effective way was at hand. It was war.

Schools for Nobles.

The Thirty Years' War (1618–1648) was the culmination of the political and ecclesiastical complications of the sixteenth century. The great schism struck a blow not only at the Church of Rome but also at the Holy Roman Empire. The subsequent rise of national churches coextensive with the territorial areas of the several protestant states, and the designation of civil rulers as Lords of the Church or Defenders of the Faith, gave to petty princes a taste of power that they had not previously enjoyed. It weakened their allegiance to the Roman Emperor at the same time that it rejected the supremacy of the Pope of Rome. But protestantism was unable at once to shake off the habits of centuries; a church that stood primarily for freedom of conscience and individual reason soon became almost as intolerant as the body from which it had separated. This intolerance, quickened by the aggressiveness of the Jesuits and supported by political jealousies, at length

The Thirty Years' War.

---

[1] Paulsen, *Geschichte des Gelehrten Unterrichts*, p. 339.

plunged Germany into a cruel and horrible war. The hatred of a century's religious strife burst forth with uncontrollable fury in Bohemia and kindled a conflagration that lasted thirty years long. It was the gift of Jesuit intrigue and protestant intolerance to Europe.

The conduct of the war on the one side was in the hands of men trained by the Jesuits to act on the belief that the end justifies the means, and on the other side it devolved largely upon leaders actuated by French ideals and inspired by Richelieu's judicious grants of money from the French treasury. *Protestantism vs. Catholicism.* No wonder that at the end of the struggle the common people on both sides were well-nigh exterminated! So cruel and relentless had been the war that a population of thirty millions was reduced to less than ten millions; the country was laid waste, cities razed to the ground, homes made desolate; want and poverty and starvation stared the German peasantry in the face; too weak to stand alone and too poor to command assistance the common man became the prey of a conscienceless aristocracy. The destruction of trade and commerce by a war that had lasted a generation meant the decline of the free cities and the ruin of the burghers. The Peace of Westphalia (1648) made an end of war, but in making the princes absolute in their own petty dominions it also gave Germany over to feudalism, a "feudalism from which all the feelings that once ennobled it had departed." Germany instead of being an empire was a jumble of two or three hundred principalities, "each with its own laws, its own court (in which the ceremonious pomp of Versailles was faintly reproduced), its little army, its separate coinage, its tolls and custom-houses on the frontier, its crowd of meddlesome and pedantic officials, presided over by a prime minister who was generally the unworthy favourite of his prince and the pensioner of some foreign court."[1]

---

[1] *Cf.* Bryce, *Holy Roman Empire*, chap. xix. On the life of the German peasant, see Freytag's *Pictures of German Life*, second series, translated by Mrs. Malcolm, London, 1863, I., 9-77.

The school that withstood the ravages of the Thirty Years'
War, that had pupils and could pay teachers, was, indeed, a
strong one. The great majority of educational
institutions, universities and secondary schools
included, went to the wall, or were so weakened
as to be scarcely recognizable.[1] And when the war was over
the dearth of funds and pupils left many of the survivors in
a precarious condition. But worse yet, there was little demand on the part of those still interested in education for the
education of the typical German school, whether protestant
or catholic. Now, even more than in the period before the
war, the nobility turned away from poor, devastated, wretched
Germany to the splendor of a foreign culture. The brilliancy
of the Court of Louis XIV. dazzled all eyes and seemed the
one thing desirable in a gloomy age. The French language
became the polite speech; French literature was eagerly
sought after, and it carried with it an interest in Italian,
Spanish and English; French customs and manners were a
considerable part of the *galant homme*.

Destruction of the Schools.

For the realization of these ideals a new scheme of education was bound to develop. Schools for nobles (the common
people had no share in the prevailing fad for
things French) were an imperative necessity.[2]
Hence the revival of the *Ritterakademien*.
During the last half of the seventeenth century and the first
quarter of the eighteenth, the really influential schools of

Revival of Schools for Nobles.

---

[1] For a picture of the condition of the schools, see Reuss, *M. Samuel Gloner ein Strassburger Lehrerbild aus den Zeiten des dreisigjährigen Krieges*, Strassburg, 1888.

[2] One of the earliest announcements of the course of study in the French *Gymnasium* of Berlin, founded about 1690, runs as follows: "Die Frantzösische und Italiänische Sprache, durch deren Gebrauch und durch die Grammatische Regeln zu erlernen, wie auch die Teutsche Sprache für die Frömbden.—Das Tantzen.—Das Fechten.— Die Exercitien mit der Pique, mit der Mousquet und mit der Fahne.—Die Vocal- und Instru-mental-Music.—Die Geographie.—Die Fortification.—Die Bau-Kunst.—Die Mahlerey.—Die Perspective.—Die Zeichenkunst, nach den Principien, wie sie insgemein unterwiesen werden muss.—N.B. Der Autor erbietet

Germany were these schools in which the masses of the people had no interest—schools utterly devoid of sincere religion and honest patriotism. The common schools of the people were well-nigh extinct. The *Gymnasien* and Latin schools went begging for scholars, except as they could offer free places and substantial benefits to applicants. The entire school system of protestant Germany, schools for nobles excepted, was manipulated in the interests of a church that had been tried as by fire, and if its temper were not just perfect it was doubtless the result of over-heating.

The schools and universities of Germany—yes, of all Europe as well—between 1625 and 1725 were not the workshops of the leaders of thought. It is significant that the philosophers—Bacon (1561–1626), Hobbes (1588–1679), Descartes (1596–1650), Locke (1632–1704), Spinoza (1632–1677) and Leibnitz (1646–1716); and the scientists—Harvey (1578–1657), Boyle (1627–1691), Huygens (1629–1693) and Newton (1642–1727)—almost without exception were rarely, or never at all, in touch with university life; they were men of the world, interested in the practical workings of Man and Nature and the State, and largely dependent their lives long on the bounty of lords and princes whose satellites they chose to be.

Decadence of the Universities.

Leibnitz, better than anyone else, represents the tendency of the age in Germany. A bitter opponent of the formalism

---

sich, die Zeichen-Kunst auff eine gantz sonderbahre Art zu informiren, so vermittelst eines Instruments geschieht, welches er erfunden hat.—Er verpflichtet sich, den Gebrauch dieses Instruments in kurtzer Zeit denjenigen, so niemahls Zeichen gelernet, zu zeigen, also das sie allerhand Sachen, als Landschafften, Städte, Dörffer, Schlösser, in Summa alles, was sich dem Gesichte unbeweglich prasentiren wird, eben so wol als die besten Mahler sollen abzeichen können.—Die Arithmetic.—Die Frantzösische, Italiänische und Teutsche Schreib-Kunst.—Die Höfflichkeit und andere Sachen mehr, welche theils nöhtig, theils curios seyn, und die als dann, wann man einen guten Fortgang in den oberwehnten sehen wird, benennet werden sollen." (From the history of the *Französisches Gymnasium*, Berlin, in the *Festschrift*, 1890.)

of the schools, almost as much a Frenchman as a German, a go-between in religion, he sought by attaching himself to influential courts, rather than from a professor's chair, to accomplish his mission. He was much interested in education; he wrote pedagogical treatises, outlined school curricula, and introduced school reforms. But in it all he worked from the outside; he was at home only in the *Ritterakademien* and for them he did good service. He valued Latin highly, but lamented that so much time was wasted in its acquisition. There are so many other things to learn, he declared, some of them valuable in themselves, others because custom makes them so; but in every instance that which makes a thing worth knowing is its utility, its worth in practical life. It matters not whether the study be etiquette or statute law, philology or history, politics or natural science, its place in the curriculum must be determined by the needs of the pupils in relation to the demands of public life. Logic, mathematics, physics and geography are indispensable; the ability to speak well and to appear well in good society are second in importance only to the ability to reason well.[1] The poetry and eloquence of the Latin schools, their barren philosophy and endless theological controversies, deserve no part in the education of a gentleman. So far did French influence carry the leading thinker of the century away from all that was truly German.

Closely connected with the introduction of French views of life into German society was the movement toward a rationalistic philosophy and scientific method. As for method the early humanists had demonstrated the value of inductive research; they had appealed from scholastic authority to the original sources. But in proving the utter futility of speculative inquiry as a means of reaching truth, they had recourse to the wisdom of the ancients, and by it they were held entranced.

---

[1] *Cf.* Paulsen, *Geschichte des Gelehrten Unterrichts*, p. 336.

The perfection that they beheld seemed to them absolutely complete; the whole duty of fallen man, it was argued, was to regain paradise and hold fast to it. Hence the devotion to the literary master-pieces of Greece and Rome, for they contained the words of the perfect life. Hence the ceaseless round of imitation in the schools, the attempt to blot out the Middle Ages and to live the life of the past in the present.

French scepticism and English common-sense could not countenance idolatry even at Minerva's shrine. Bacon, grasping the full significance of the inductive method, boldly turned from the past to the present and future. Descartes ably demonstrated that there is something even in modern man worthy of respect. Progress, not stagnation, was their motto. The invention of the compass and the telescope had already supplied the means of getting at a new heaven and a new earth. The Belgian Vesale (1553) and the Englishman Harvey (1628) afforded a new view of man. Columbus and Kepler and Galileo prepared the way for the scientific advance of the seventeenth century.

Bacon's aphorism that "we must lead men to the particulars themselves, and their series and order; while men on their side must force themselves for awhile to lay their notions by and begin to familiarize themselves with facts," was echoed by Descartes when he told the queen of Sweden, pointing to a skeleton, "Here are my books." This was the spirit that directed the advance of the positive sciences; it based reasoning solely on the observation of facts; no authority save the authority of reason was accepted.

The scientific movement in Germany aroused by the discoveries of Kepler, began to make itself felt in the early years of the seventeenth century. Jungius, a professor in Rostock, founded in 1619 a Natural Science Association whose purpose was "to free from sophistry all the arts and sciences that are dependent on reason and experience, to lead them back to

The First Natural Science Association.

demonstrative certainty, and to expand them by correct experimentation and fortunate discoveries."[1] It was the natural reaction against the extreme formalism into which the Latin schools of the country, protestant and catholic alike, were falling.

The ideals of the scientists soon found a reception in the schools of the nobles—at least in so far as such ideals were capable of practical realization. On the other hand the classical schools have never since been entirely free from the influences that the scientific movement then first brought to bear on them. In the *Ritterakademien* it meant the admission of mathematics and physics and other *Realien* into the curriculum; in the classical schools it suggested reforms in method and a revival of the true religious spirit.

<small>Influence on the Schools.</small>

The first man to offer himself as mediator between the humanists and the advocates of the positive sciences was Comenius (1592–1671). He was himself a humanist in his respect for Latin, a realist in his admiration for Bacon and the empirical philosophy, a religionist in that he believed the supreme aim of education —and life as well—is "eternal happiness in and with God." Hence he, even more than his forerunner Ratke, emphasized the need of reform in language teaching; and as for Latin, while indispensable, it must be learned quickly in order that time may be had for the serious business of life. What a man most needs to know, next to a knowledge of God and of his own nature, is the natural environment in which he lives. It is possible, so argued Comenius, to get considerable information about things while learning words; in fact, words are valuable only when learned in connection with things, as the signs of things or ideas. In thus economizing time and energy life is prolonged and man the better fitted for eternity. In order to teach school-masters their business Comenius wrote his famous series of text-books

<small>Comenius.</small>

---

[1] Paulsen, *Geschichte des Gelehrten Unterrichts*, p. 306.

that perpetuated his ideas when the man himself was forgotten.[1]

Comenius served the cause of the ultra-realists in thus exposing the defects in the prevailing methods of teaching Latin and the utter uselessness of learning mere words. Even Sturm had taught the classic authors chiefly for the purpose of illustrating grammatical and rhetorical rules. *His Services to Secondary Education.* Both Ratke and Comenius looked upon the Latin language like the vernacular, as a living, organic whole. And as such they considered it only one of many spheres of empirical knowledge.

The intensely religious character of Comenius gained him many sympathizers among those protestants who remained true to the original spirit of the Reformation. The formalism of the Lutheran Church, its subserviency to Aristotelianism and the scholastic philosophy, was not a pleasing prospect to believers in practical piety. They believed that religion was an affair of the heart as well as of the head, that true religion involved not only a knowledge of God's word but also a disposition to cherish and obey divine commands. The reaction against protestant formalism slowly ripened into the movement known as Pietism, of which Spener and Francke were the most distinguished representatives. The gospel of love and benevolence as preached by these men contrasted strangely with the theological dissensions of the times. It is to their credit that they upheld the worth of the inner life in an age given over to externalism.

Pietism had nothing in common with the scientific movement, except its uncompromising opposition to the scholasticism of school and church. Rationalism —worldly, aristocratic and cultured—was the obverse of pietism. It was the logical outcome of scientific *Rationalism.*

---

[1] The standard work on Comenius in English is Laurie's *Comenius: His Life and Educational Works*. Quick's *Essays on Educational Reformers* gives a good account of his work. See also the *Educational Review*, New York, Vol. III.

inquiry and the appeal to facts within the reach of observation and reason. Pushing in from the west, it found supporters at the courts and among the nobility; before the end of the seventeenth century it had become the dominant mode of thought among the ruling classes of Germany. It inspired the entire eighteenth century with a joyous consciousness of its own power; it spoke with pride of what had been accomplished, and looked forward with enthusiastic hope to the future. Its culmination in the Enlightenment was the full fruition of the hope of the early humanists; it was the extreme limit of individualism.

Both pietism and rationalism were unfavourable to humanistic studies. Pietism looked upon them as dangerous; rationalism, as unnecessary. Both movements turned away from the past. The pietists would live a holy life in the present, a life of praise and prayer and supplication, for the sake of an eternal reward in heaven; the rationalists, unwilling to believe that the bounds of knowledge were fixed by the ancients, and unable to find any basis in reason for implicit faith in the glories of a life to come, devoted themselves wholly to the joys of the present. Under the influence of French court life the latter part of the seventeenth century saw the introduction into Germany of a profligacy and libertinism utterly foreign to its own civilization. But sensual indulgence, excused on philosophic grounds, played an important part in weakening the grasp of the nobility on the middle classes. The rise of the democratic spirit toward the end of the eighteenth century was made possible if not actually promoted by the hideous corruption in high places. Rationalism was essentially liberal and liberalizing; and if occasionally it plunged weaklings into dissipation, it gave strong-minded men the impulse to free themselves from the thraldom of tradition and authority. Moreover, in the intellectual sphere, it did not immediately set up a standard of its own to which reason must conform; it left each man free to follow his own bent; it offered a fair field and no favour. Science cut loose from the Greeks; phil-

Pietism.

osophy and political economy and jurisprudence assumed a modern aspect; even the dry bones of the church, both evangelical and catholic, began to feel the stir of life under the combined attacks of atheism and pietism.

The foundation of the University of Halle (1694) ushered in the new era in German life. In Halle, Thomasius and Francke, both of whom had been expelled from the orthodox University of Leipsic because of their too liberal ideas, joined hands in opposing the old spiritual order. *The University of Halle and Lehrfreiheit.* Thomasius was a type of the perfect cavalier; Francke was the leading pietist of the day. Francke's influence dominated the theological faculty; Thomasius was supreme in the rest of the University. That one and the same institution could harbour two such men and assure them freedom of action was the most significant fact in the whole matter. It was the beginning of *Lehrfreiheit* in Germany, and for that reason Halle is counted the first really modern university. It stood for freedom of teaching modern subjects in a modern tongue and according to modern methods.

The atmosphere of Halle was conducive to the growth of a modern philosophy. Christian Wolff, professor from 1707 to 1723 and again from 1740 to 1754, was the first who succeeded in making "philosophy speak German." *Wolff's Philosophy.* His system was the first to supersede Aristotelianism, and it was so well received that it dominated the German schools till the advent of Kantianism. "Nothing without sufficient cause" was its ruling principle. "It aimed no longer to be *ancilla theologiæ*, but without prejudice sought after truth, and mathematics and the natural sciences in their modern form composed its foundation. And in equal degree it disclaimed all transcendental authority for morals and for law, basing them exclusively upon the nature of man and of society."[1]

It was no mere accident that the period of Enlightenment

---

[1] Paulsen, *German Universities*, New York, 1895, p. 60.

in Germany was coincident with the reign of Frederick the Great. On ascending the throne he announced that his mission was "to further the country's well-being, and to make everyone of our [his] subjects happy." The character of the whole forty-six years of his reign was clearly indicated in the principal acts of the first week,[1] viz., the abolition of legal torture in criminal trials, an order looking to more equitable administration of the laws, a (partial) guarantee of the freedom of speech and of the press, the enunciation of the principle of religious toleration, and the encouragement of independent, scientific research. "All religions must be tolerated," he declared, "for in this country every man must get to heaven in his own way." In giving orders for the immediate recall of Wolff, who had been banished by Frederick's father at the instigation of the pietists, the King said, "A man that seeks truth, and loves it, must be reckoned precious in any human society." In his efforts to resuscitate the Berlin Academy he urged M. de Maupertuis to leave Paris and "come and insert into this wild crab-tree the graft of the sciences, that it may bear fruit."

Frederick the Great.

This period, under the leadership of so enlightened a prince, embodied and united all the forces that were making for a new spiritual and social life. The national spirit was stirred; forms of misgovernment were abolished and economical administration introduced. The resources of the country were developed, industries of all kinds encouraged, the territory extended by fortunate conquests and the army increased to formidable proportions. In a word, the electorate of Brandenburg was now become the kingdom of Prussia, a kingdom not only in name, but a recognized power in European politics.

His Reforms.

It has been said that in the Enlightenment "an effort was made to raise man, so far as he is a rational individual, into a position of supremacy over everything."[2] Two dominant

---

[1] *Cf.* Carlyle, *Frederick the Great*, X., 231-261.
[2] Erdmann, *History of Philosophy*, I., 283.

motives determined all action in this direction : (1) the perfection of the individual, and (2) the mastery over environment. These two ideas also entered into the educational ideals of the time, and directed the development of the school system. The one was essentially humanistic as pertaining to the perfection of the human subject; the other was essentially realistic as pertaining to the control of things in the objective world. The Courtly-French ideal, at least as formulated by Leibnitz, embodied both notions, and for this reason it is often considered the typical educational ideal of this transition period. But it is equally certain that in the great undercurrent of German thought the two ideas were but loosely joined. They held together at first for prudential considerations in the face of united opposition from State and Church, but they quickly differentiated when each could maintain itself alone. Humanistic ideas had never been entirely expelled from the schools and universities, but throughout the seventeenth century they were inactive and uninfluential. It was not till toward the middle of the eighteenth century that they again became dynamic and exercised a power in the educational world. *The Two Motives of the Enlightenment.*

We have already noted the growth of the sciences and the spread of the scientific spirit in Germany. In accord with this spirit Ratke and Comenius emphasized the study of things ; natural science, physics, mathematics, history, and the mother-tongue, all deserve a place in the curriculum on a par with the classical languages. In fact, Latin and Greek, like the rest, are valuable only for practical purposes. Weigel (1625-1699), a professor in the University of Jena, and Reyher, rector of the *Gymnasium* in Gotha and author of the famous Saxe-Gotha *Schulordnung* of 1642, worked assiduously for the reform of the Latin schools in the realistic sense. Francke (1663-1727) was no sooner settled in Halle than he began the foundation of that remarkable group of schools and charitable institutions which still bears his name. All Francke's schools, especially *I. The Mastery of Environment.*

those for the common people, were strongly pietistic. The study of the Bible and the catechism, the learning of hymns and prayers, and participation in religious exercises, were the all-important part of the curriculum; nevertheless three hours a day were devoted in the lower schools to secular subjects, and in the higher schools the course was determined by the requirements for admission to the university. But however much Francke was hampered in the development of his higher schools by the traditional demands of the universities, he managed to find a place for geography, history, mathematics and French, and by a judicious use of "recreation hours" he succeeded in introducing his pupils to nature study and manual training.

Francke had the rare ability to see clearly what needed doing and then to do it regardless of obstacles or consequences.

Francke and Realistic Education. The magnitude of his work in Halle is simply marvellous, and yet what he actually accomplished is insignificant in comparison with what he inspired others to do.[1] He showed how practical Christianity could be incorporated in the work of the common schools; his plan was immediately adopted by Frederick William I. and made well-nigh universal in Prussia. He showed how the *Realien* could be profitably employed in a Latin school, and even made a constituent part of a university preparatory course; as a result of his methods, and especially of his suggestion that schools should be founded for the exclusive purpose of fitting the youth of the citizen class for practical life, there has since grown up in Germany a class of *Real*-schools. Herein Francke acted in conformity with the rationalistic spirit of his times. Whatever may have been his opinion of the *Ritterakademie* as an institution for the practical training of the nobility, he certainly believed in the wisdom of a practical training for the learned professions, for the business occupations of the citizen class, and for the needs of the people generally. The *Real*-school, therefore, is the

---

[1] Frick, *Die Franckeschen Stiftungen*, 1892.

direct response to the educational ideal that lays special emphasis on the mastery of environment. It is the outgrowth of one phase of the rationalistic mode of thought.

Francke's efforts in Halle were seconded by Semler, one of Weigel's students, who was the first to establish a school in which the *Realien* took first place.[1] His idea was to give manual training to pupils from both the common and the Latin schools. Semler's plan was altogether impracticable, but his dream was destined to be realized by Hecker, a clergyman who had served an apprenticeship as teacher in Francke's orphan school. In 1747 he established in Berlin an "*oekonomisch-mathematische Realschule*" for the higher training of those pupils who had no intention of entering the learned professions. Instruction was offered in religion and ethics, the German, French and Latin languages, writing, arithmetic, drawing, history, geography, and the elements of geometry, mechanics and architecture. An important feature of the founder's plan was a series of optional courses designed to give pupils an insight into the practical workings of the various trades and occupations of burgher life.

The Real-Schools.

The success of Hecker's undertaking was assured almost from the start. With the hearty approval of Frederick the Great there was little difficulty in putting the institution on a permanent basis and in winning popular support. The school was soon overrun with pupils, and additional facilities were demanded. Moreover, the plan found numerous imitators outside of Berlin. Within a few years all the flourishing commercial centres of Germany were supplied with *Real*-schools occupying a position in the school system midway between the common schools and the classical *Gymnasien*.

The pedagogical character of the *Real*-school was established by Basedow and his followers. Originally the plan was to provide for the middle classes what would be called

---

[1] Heubaum, *Christoph Semlers Realschule und seine Beziehung zu A. H. Francke* in *Neue Jahrbücher für Philologie und Pädagogik*, 1893.

nowadays manual training schools in which the scientific principles underlying the various trades and business vocations should have a prominent place. These schools were to be one step removed from the trade schools for the lower classes. But under the influence of the Philanthropinists the *Real*-school was transformed into a modern humanistic school and placed in competition with the humanistic *Gymnasium*. The wisdom of such a step may be questioned from the fact that for half a century the *Real*-school was held in check. The only advantage gained was the demonstration that almost any kind of instruction was preferable to the antiquated Latin school with its scholastic methods and dreary round of Latin imitation.

Their Pedagogical Character.

The utilitarian conceptions of the rationalistic view of life found complete expression in the conventional training of the *Ritterakademie* and in the *Real*-school.[1] They represent the reaction in the pedagogical sphere against the empty, sterile dogmatism of the preceding age. As champions of the new learning and modern culture they were the fittest representatives of an "enlightened" educational ideal, and their triumph would doubtless have been complete had not another force gained the ascendancy at the very hour of victory. This new force was likewise a part of the rationalistic movement, but instead of

Reaction Against the Formalism of the Latin Schools.

---

[1] The building up of great national governments during this period necessitated large military operations. These required large forces of men and great funds of wealth. The feudal system no longer supplied the one, nor could royal domains, however vast, supply the other. National governments and armies necessitated taxation in order to secure the funds of precious metals. Industrial and commercial activities alone could bear this burden. In order to foster industry and commerce, the welfare of the masses must be secured and their capacities developed. Hence, the *Realschule*. The attitude of mind which revealed itself on the economic side as mercantilism, on the educational side revealed itself as a realistic tendency. Cf. Ingram, *History of Political Economy*, New York, 1894, pp 36-54. Cossa, *Introduction to the Study of Political Economy*, London, 1893, pp. 193-210.

making for practical utility in commonplace life it tended toward the perfection of man as a free, rational individual. In other words, the growth of the democratic spirit came in to check the development of institutions calculated to perpetuate the existing social order and to intensify prevailing class distinctions.

Notwithstanding the efforts made by the early humanists to exalt the individual by striking off the fetters of obsolete tradition, a hundred years of religious fanaticism left him even more than before the sport of despotic power. The anarchy of the Thirty Years' War was followed by an absolutism that was as inquisitorial as it was petty. The spirit of the people, crushed by a generation of disaster, was still further oppressed by the exactions of relentless task-masters. Literature and art and religion were enslaved to aristocratic vanity. What of hope there was for freedom hardly dared express itself for a full hundred years. Yet it would be misleading if this state of affairs were interpreted as furnishing no evidences of progress.

In politics the little electorate of Brandenburg stepped into a unique position; transformed into the kingdom of Prussia under Frederick I. (1688–1713), it became ambitious to be counted among the independent states of Europe. It was an absolute monarchy, to be sure, but then as now the rule of the Hohenzollerns subordinated all pretensions of the aristocracy and privileged classes to the higher interests of the commonweal. *Rise of Prussia.*

From the time of the Great Elector to Frederick the Great there was certain if slow progress in the alleviation of the burdens of the peasantry; the citizen class gradually regained an enviable position as the growth of the cities and political stability made trade and commerce more safe and profitable; and at the same time the scions of nobility were gathered into the army or left to exterminate themselves by their own debauchery. The century following the peace of Westphalia was the seed-time of political and social reforms. The idea that the welfare of a nation is best subserved when its citizens are contented and happy has as its counterpart the idea that the welfare of the whole presupposes the well-being of all its parts. In teaching the masses of the people to respect themselves as rational beings, as free moral agents, the seeds of democracy were sown from which a harvest was reaped at a later day.

The growth of an independent spirit is also clearly discernible in the literature of the period. During the seventeenth century, despite the example of the reformers, the use of the German language was an evidence of boorishness. The scholars spoke Latin; the nobles, French. Nevertheless just at this time Ratke and Comenius threw all their influence on the side of the mother-tongue; a society was formed in 1617, with the Prince of Anhalt at its head, for the purpose of promoting "good and pure German speech;" Thomasius dared to use the German language in his class-room in Leipsic even at the risk of exile; and a little later Wolff shocked the learned world by treating philosophy in the vernacular. And while the *belles-lettres* of this period "were the most depraved and abject mockery that has ever usurped the name of literature,"[1] there was nevertheless a deep undercurrent of native independence. In the religious lyrics of Fleming and Gerhardt a strong and manly sentiment was aroused that despised the vice and frivolity of the princely courts, and "from more than one solitary country parsonage there shone forth a light which in due time was to mingle with the dawning of a better day." Keen satirists reawakened an interest in the homely German life by exposing the follies of French imitators, and in the mass of rubbish called literature there might occasionally be found a genuine expression of the emotions of a heart pulsating with hope. Poor as it may have been, the best there was in literature came from the common people. In the spread of individualism class distinctions were being levelled down. English public opinion, English philosophy and English lit-

Growth of an Independent Spirit.

---

[1] Francke, *Social Forces in German Literature*, New York, 1896, p. 187.

erature, which were carried through France into Germany about the middle of the eighteenth century, re-enforced the democratic movement and inspired the middle classes to heroic effort. Then there arose from the ranks of the people master workmen in prose and verse, who put the ideas of the people in enduring form. Klopstock, Gellert, Lessing, Herder, Kant, Fichte, Goethe and Schiller—all rising from the ranks —overthrew French classicism and built on its ruins the stately edifice of classic German literature.

The "Storm and Stress" agitation, which marked the concentration of forces that had been gathering for a century or more, disclosed to Germany a new aristocracy, a nobility of worth instead of a nobility of birth. If bloodshed was averted it was because the old order recognized in the new its legitimate suzerain. Hereditary rights and privileges counted for naught as compared with individual character. "The ideal of human perfection which inspired the movement was not man as a social being, dependent upon and determined by the force of surrounding conditions, but man as such, man lifted above the barriers of his political, social, moral environment, man in the full autonomy of his own free, spiritual nature."[1] In this passionate devotion to the human subject the objective world was ignored, nay, even argued out of existence except as it exists as a show-world for the creative self. Humanity in its largest sense was the characteristic theme of the age. Nothing that concerns man, nothing that enters into his life at all, nothing that gives him deeper experience, truer insight, nobler emotions, purer character, can be unworthy of study and investigation. Says Herder, the greatest preacher of the gospel of humanity: "Whatever belongs to the nature of our race, every possible means of its improvement and progress, this is the object which a humane man has in mind, this is the centre of his work. Since our race must work out its own destiny, none of its members has

II. The Perfection of the Human Type.

---

[1] Francke, *Social Forces in German Literature*, p. 317.

a right to be idle in this work. Everyone must take part in the weal and woe of the whole, everyone must willingly sacrifice his share of reason, his mite of activity, to the genius of the race. No one, however, can contribute to the welfare of mankind who does not make himself what he can and ought to be made. Everyone, therefore, must cultivate the seed of humanity, most of all on the bed where he himself is planted. We all carry in us an ideal of what we ought to be and are not. The dross which we ought to cast away, the perfection which we ought to attain, we all know. And since we can become what we ought to be only through ourselves and others from whom we receive or whom we affect, our own humanity necessarily becomes at one with the humanity of others." [1]

Herder and Kant, Goethe and Schiller, stand at the parting of the ways. They represent the best that individualism has to offer without its serious defects; they are products of a rationalistic age without sharing overmuch in its sensual realism; but at the same time they look on life as an organic whole, a whole made up of parts all harmoniously working for the common good. While they glorify freedom, humanity, individuality, they find the perfection of the individual, and of humanity as well, in the perfection of the national type. In Kant's categorical imperative, "Act as if the maxim from which you act were to become through your will a universal law of nature," we see the moral injunction that converts eighteenth century particularism into nineteenth century nationalism.

What more natural than that there should be a "return to the Greeks" in quest of the perfect realization of the human idea! The versatility of the Greek type, the fearlessness and subtlety of Greek thought, the exquisite beauty of Greek art, the clear, exact, expressive character of the Greek language, fill the German

A New Humanism.

---

[1] Herder, *Briefe zur Beförderung der Humanität*, III. Cited by Francke.

mind with admiration. At every turn the modern explorer finds exemplified the union of beauty and truth, art and science; everywhere is exhibited the supremacy of mind over sense, of spirit over matter. Here human development attains complete perfection. From the fountain-head of Greek genius flows a clear and sparkling stream of boundless life and freedom—life in the fullest sense, joyous, unrestrained; freedom in all its branches, moral, intellectual, political, social. It is this conception of humanity that the German mind pictures as its highest ideal of life.

Klopstock called himself an "apprentice of the Greeks;" Winckelmann taught his countrymen to appreciate the beauty of Greek art; Lessing and Goethe and Schiller were filled with the Greek spirit, and through them it became the common possession of the nation. The result was a blending of the spiritual life of the present with classical life and thought—a modern Renaissance that indicated the rise of a New Humanism. *Return to the Greeks.*

The ideal of the new humanism was radically different from the humanistic ideal that had held undisputed sway in the learned world for upward of two centuries. It is no longer the mastery of the Latin language, the imitation of classic style, the acquisition of eloquence or skill in disputation; the aim now is to develop the all-round man by infusing into his being the vitalizing spirit of classical culture. The Greek language advances to first place, not for the language alone but for the literature, for the content rather than the form. Moreover, language and literature are only partial records of the past; art and philosophy and history speak with a thousand tongues. "History," Herder says, "opens to us beautiful bowers of friendship and discourse with the upright and thoughtful of all times. Here Plato stands before me: there I hear Socrates's kindly questionings, and share in his last fate. When Marcus Antoninus in his chamber communes with his heart, he also speaks to mine; and poor Epictetus gives commands more powerful than those of a king. The ill-starred Tullius, the unfortunate Boëthius speak to me, confiding to me the circumstances of their lives, the anguish and comfort of their souls. Thus history leads us, as it were, into the council of fate, teaches us the eternal laws of human nature, and assigns to us our own place in the great organism in which reason and goodness have to struggle, to be sure, with chaotic forces, but always, according to their very nature, must create order and go forward on the path of victory."[1] "The Germans," it was said, "should unite the virtues of the Greeks and Romans with their own. They should study the Greeks and Romans merely to become thereby the better Germans, and in every kind of virtue to surpass them."

It was inevitable that so complete a change in the spiritual ideals of a people should induce a corresponding change in their schools. The new Hanoverian University of Göttingen became the centre of the pedagogical reforms; a considerable part of its fame belongs to one man, J. M. Gesner, who at the opening of the University was called to the chair of classical languages from the rectorship of the *Thomasschule* in Leipsic. For twenty-seven years Gesner devoted all his marvellous ability as teacher and scholar to the cause of humanity. He was the first of the new humanists, a broad-minded man, interested in the modern literature and familiar with modern science and philosophy. Therefore, unlike the pedants of his day, he would have his students enjoy the classical literature in order that they might thereby acquire a correct standard of judgment and taste applicable to modern morals, nationality, language, thought and feeling. The teacher's duty, he conceived, is to direct attention to the thought-content, to note the interdependence of cause and effect, to make clear the conditions which determine the course of events. What does the author mean? How does he prove it? Is he right or wrong? What objections can be urged?—these are the questions that give life to language-study.

Leaders of the Movement.

---

[1] Herder, *Ideen*, XV., 5. Cited by Francke.

Gesner's work was ably carried on by his successor, Heyne, who did perhaps more than anyone else to popularize Greek poetry. In Saxony, the chief apostle of the new humanism was Ernesti, who followed Gesner as rector of the *Thomasschule*. Ernesti and Heyne were teachers of teachers; their students carried with them into the schools of central and north-western Germany the humanistic spirit. Saxony, Hanover, Hesse-Cassel and the country round about officially encouraged the new reforms. In Prussia the utilitarian theories of the realists offered considerable opposition to the realization of the humanistic ideal, but with the entrance of von Zedlitz into the ministry of Frederick the Great in 1771 a change was apparent. The cabinet order of 1779 gave von Zedlitz an opportunity to attempt reforms in some of the more important higher schools of the kingdom, but for lack of co-operation on the part of local school authorities his efforts were not altogether successful.[1] But in Gedike and Meierotto, respectively rectors of the *Friedrich-Werdersche Schule* and the *Joachimstalsches Gymnasium* in Berlin, he found able and willing collaborators. These men entered heartily into the new methods of teaching the classics, adopted a new curriculum and did not a little to fix the character of the humanistic *Gymnasium*. Gedike especially was an ardent believer in the doctrine of formal discipline in accordance with the Wolffian psychology. He recognized the value of thought-content in literature, but he was also persuaded that the study of the classical languages is a most excellent mental gymnastic. " You can become a successful business man," he declared, "an excellent judge and lawyer, a famous physician, even a beloved and useful preacher, without Greek; you will find in all these positions plenty of able men who learned it as youths only to forget it as men. But what is the inference?—that the time given to it was wasted? This

(Effects on the Schools.)

---

[1] Rethwisch, *Der Staatsminister Freiherr von Zedlitz und Preussens höheres Schulwesen im Zeitalter Friedrichs des Grossen*, Berlin, 1886.

would be the case if the study were pursued only as a means of information." The fact is it serves another purpose : the all-round training of the mental faculties. "So be assured that if you forget your Greek, yes, even your Latin too, you still have the advantage of having given your mind a training and discipline that will go with you into your future occupation."

It is clearly apparent that there is chance for serious conflict between the doctrine of formal discipline and the theory of classical culture. But it is interesting historically to know that both notions spring from the same ideal, the perfection of the individual or *Bildung zur Humanität*.

The pedagogical character of the humanistic *Gymnasium*, which at the end of the eighteenth century was universally recognized as the type of school corresponding to the new educational ideal, was largely the work of one man, Frederick August Wolf. He strove to set up a golden mean between the extremes so sharply accentuated by Gedike. His aim was to effect a harmonious union between culture and discipline, form and substance. I cannot state his view better than to quote the words of Professor Paulsen regarding the purpose of the *Gymnasium:* "Its object is the development of all the faculties in every possible direction. To this end, a study of the ancient languages is regarded as of the utmost importance ; for, by cultivating the Greek and Roman languages and literatures, we acquire skill in all mental operations. The grammar assists us greatly in formulating our ideas ; the classical poets awaken our sense of the æsthetic, and cultivate a taste for beauty and simplicity ; the study of the historical and philosophical writers broadens our horizon, fills us with noble sentiment and furnishes a historical basis for the proper conception of the present. The study of mathematics ranks next in importance, and also furnishes an excellent training to the faculties. The new era despises the utilitarian and encyclopedic attainments so highly valued by the previous epoch. True human culture, and not utility, is its aim. It is characteristic of ignoble souls to appreciate only what is absolutely utilitarian, and to overlook entirely the importance of a free, beautiful, and perfect culture of the inner life."[1]

The utilitarian tendencies of the Enlightenment were easily overcome after the death of Frederick the Great. A new ideal began to rule, an ideal born of rationalistic thought and nurtured by the democratic spirit of the times. The theory that all men are created equal was not to the German mind, as to the French and American, a self-evident truth, but the perfectibility of the individual through education was a part of the universal creed of the eighteenth century. From the German point of view the development of man as man, the attainment of the highest type of manhood, was possible only through humanistic training according to the standards of the Greeks. And as particularism grew into nationalism the humanistic ideal as interpreted by Stein, Fichte and Humboldt became the ideal of the nation. From the confusion of two hundred years there emerged one dominant form of higher education; it was neither ecclesiastical nor partisan, although both secular and religious. The inactivity of the protestant Latin schools, the secularization of the colleges of the Jesuits consequent upon the suppression of the order in 1773, and the decline of the *Ritterakademien* paved the way for the complete reconstruction of the higher schools of Germany on a national basis. This has been the work of the nineteenth century.

Summary.

GENERAL REFERENCES :—Ziegler, *Geschichte der Pädagogik*, in Baumeister's *Handbuch der Erziehungs- und Unterrichtslehre;* Schmid's, Schmidt's and Rein's Encyclopedias; Paulsen, *Geschichte des Gelehrten Unterrichts ;* Wiese, *Das höhere Schulwesen im Preussen*, Vol. I.; Whitman, *Imperial Germany*, Leipsic, 1890; Hegel, *Philosophy of History ;* Baring-Gould, *Germany, Present and Past ;* Wakeman, *Europe, 1598-1715 ;* Taylor, *Studies in German Literature ;* Japp, *German Life and Literature ;* Lowell, *Governments and Parties in Continental Europe.*

---

[1] Paulsen, *The Forum*, XXIII., 5 : 606-7.

CHAPTER IV

THE RECONSTRUCTION OF THE HIGHER SCHOOLS
1806-1892

THE chief characteristic of modern political history is the foundation of great national states. The rise of Prussia to a commanding position in continental politics and her subsequent leadership in the formation of the German Empire, are the central facts in the later history of Europe. The keynote to educational progress in Germany, therefore, must be sought in the ideas which have actuated Prussian leadership and led to Prussian success. That key-note is the concentration of political forces and the struggle for national unity.

At the opening of the century German patriotism was at a low ebb. There was no common bond of sympathy between the various states and no mutual ambitions. The national spirit was dormant. Prussia herself had fallen from the high estate of Frederick the Great. The successors of that able monarch were totally unfit to carry on his work. Where he strove to improve the conditions of the people and to abolish unjust class distinctions, they suffered themselves to be led by base intriguers and favoured courtiers. Under Frederick William II. "the people who had learnt already to associate energy and heroism with irreligion, were now taught to associate religion with vice, misgovernment and disgrace."[1] Even the well-meaning Frederick William III. continued on the downward path. Corruption in high places went hand in hand with the op-

(marginal note: Germany at the Beginning of the Century.)

---

[1] Seeley, *Life and Times of Stein.* Pt. II., chap. 2.

pression of the common people. Worse than that, the venality of the ruling class made Germany an easy prey to French aggression.

The defeat of the Prussian army at Jena and Auerstädt recalled the king and his councillors to their senses; Prussia lay prostrate and bleeding at the feet of Napoleon. The Treaty of Tilsit was the penalty for "sleeping upon the laurels of Frederick the Great." *Victory of Napoleon at Jena.*
By that treaty Prussia lost nearly half of her territory—all that between the Rhine and the Elbe, besides her share of Poland—and was so humiliated by the severe terms of Napoleon that one wonders any national spirit was left. "The state seemed to have fallen in pieces because it had no principle of cohesion, and was held together by an artificial bureaucracy. It had been created by the energy of its government and the efficiency of its soldiers, and now it appeared to come to an end because its government had ceased to be energetic and its soldiers to be efficient. The catastrophe could not but seem as irremediable as it was sudden and complete."[1]

The war which dragged along for seven years was a war for the liberation of Prussia from the Napoleonic yoke. That it was finally successful is due in the first instance to a remarkable transformation in the loyalty and patriotism of the people. The reforms of Stein, Hardenburg, Scharnhorst and Gneisenau, in political and military affairs, were ably seconded by Arndt, Fitche, von Humboldt, and a score of others who strove passionately to enthuse the nation with a higher and nobler spirit. *The War of Liberation.*

Baron von Stein began in 1807 the silent revolution by proposing the Emancipating Edict[2] which abolished class distinctions in the tenure of land and business occupation and struck the final blow at serfdom. He aimed to liberate the cities from the obnoxious and selfish *Civil Reforms.*

---

[1] Seeley, *Life and Times of Stein*, Pt. III., chap. 4.
[2] A translation of the Edict is given in *Translations and Reprints*, issued by the University of Pennsylvania, *The Napoleonic Age*, Vol. II., No 2, Philadelphia, 1895.

control of a bureaucracy and to strengthen the state by admitting the people to a share in its government. Naturally such radical proposals were displeasing to Napoleon and not altogether satisfactory to the royal favourites who were so largely responsible for the degradation of Prussia. Stein was soon forced to lay down his office and quit the country, but the seed he had planted came to fruition under Hardenburg, who extended the rights of citizenship and laid the foundations for legislation by representative assemblies.

The year 1807 saw also the beginnings of far-reaching reforms in the organization of the army. Napoleon had permitted the retention of only 42,000 men under arms, but by the foresight of Scharnhorst this little band became the nucleus of the grand army which under Blücher seven years afterward helped to make Napoleon's overthrow complete. The universal liability to military service and the constitution of a trained reserve force ready to take up arms at a moment's notice, innovations forced on Prussia by the exigencies of the situation, marked a new epoch in European military procedure. Instead of the old army, "Frederick's army grown twenty years older," there arose a new army which could be maintained only by adequate recognition of merits and fitness in all its parts. It was seen that "Nothing but attainments in education in peace, distinguished gallantry, activity and comprehension in war can establish the claim to the post as officer. Hitherto, through the restriction of these honours to a single class, all the talents and requirements of the rest of the nation were lost to the army, and this class found itself relieved of the necessity of acquiring military talents, being raised to the highest military posts by birth and long life."[1]

Military Reforms.

The reforms of Stein, Hardenburg, Scharnhorst and their co-workers were the official recognition of mighty changes in the social consciousness. The one thought was the overthrow of Napoleon and the restoration of national indepen-

---

[1] Seeley, *The Life and Times of Stein*, Pt. IV., chap. 4.

dence. In this great undertaking minor differences of men and states sank into insignificance; there was no place for petty bickerings and factional strife. The leaders knew that success could be attained only through united effort. Secret societies sprang up whose members were pledged to promote the interests of the state. Through books and pamphlets and public addresses patriotic men unceasingly sought to inflame the people. The stirring appeals of Arndt came at a time when "songs were sermons and sermons were songs." One of his pamphlets, *"The Rhine, Germany's River, but never Germany's Boundary,"* seems now like an inspired prophecy. He, in common with many others of his time, was filled with the idea of German unity—not merely the aggrandizement of Prussia, but the birth of a German Empire. In one of his great war-songs he asks the question,

Changes in the Social Consciousness.

> " What is the German's Fatherland?
> Is it Prussia, or the Swabian's land?
> Is it where the grape glows on the Rhine?
> Where sea-gulls skim the Baltic's brine? "

The answer finally is found:

> " Where'er resounds the German tongue,
> Where'er its hymns to God are sung!
> That is the land,
> Brave German, that thy Fatherland!"

The services of Arndt in the liberation of his country cannot be lightly regarded. He firmly believed in the imperial policy and remained steadfast in that faith, as may be seen from the fact that forty years afterward he was one of the deputation to offer the imperial crown to the King of Prussia, Frederick William IV. The influence of Arndt, however, was mostly with the common people. Stein, in one of his letters, designates the philosopher Fichte as performing remarkable services among the leaders in thought and action. He says: "Fichte's *Addresses to the Germans,* delivered during the French oc-

Services of Arndt and Fichte.

cupation of Berlin, and printed under the censorship of M. Bignon, the Intendant, had a great effect upon the feeling of the cultivated class." Seeley, in citing this comment of Stein, observes "that in the midst of such weighty matters he should remember to mention Fichte's addresses is a remarkable testimony to the effect produced by them on the public mind, and at the same time it leads us to conjecture that they must have strongly influenced his own."[1]

Certain it is that this philosopher, confident in his own moral freedom and conscious of a growing perfection in the race, moved his countrymen as they had not been moved since the days of the Reformation. He reminds them that "a nation that is capable, if it were only in its highest representation and leaders, of fixing its eyes firmly on the vision from the spiritual world, Independence, and being possessed with a love of it, like our earliest ancestors, will assuredly prevail over a nation that is only used as the tool of foreign aggressiveness and for the subjugation of independent nations, like the Roman armies; for the former have everything to lose and the latter only something to gain." Again he exhorts them: "On you it depends whether you will be the end and last of a race worthy of little respect . . . or whether you will be the beginning and germ of a new time, glorious beyond all your imaginations, and those from whom posterity will reckon the years of their welfare." By such words as these he urged his people to action. "That we can no longer resist openly has been already assumed and universally admitted. Having then lost the first object of life, what remains for us to do? Our constitutions will be made for us, our treaties and the use of our military forces will be prescribed to us, a code will be given us, even the right of judicial trial and decision, and the exercise of it will be at times taken away; for the present we shall be relieved of all these cares. Education alone has been overlooked; if we want an occupation let us take to this.

Fichte's Addresses to the German Nation.

---

[1] Seeley, *Life and Times of Stein*, Pt. IV., chap. 1.

... I hope to convince some Germans and bring them to see that nothing but education can rescue us from all the miseries that overwhelm us. I count especially upon our being made more disposed to observation and earnest reflection by our needs."[1]

The course of events in Prussia during the war, despite French domination, was wonderfully changed for the better. Not only in Prussia but in all Germany reforms were executed which did much to alleviate the hard condition of the peasantry and remove restrictions which had so hampered the commercial and industrial activities of the middle and upper classes. Such loyalty and devotion had been engendered that when independence was attained further effort toward political freedom was easily checked by those interested in perpetuating the sovereignty of local potentates. Notwithstanding it had been proclaimed in 1813 by the Prussian King that the object of his alliance with Russia was "to aid the German peoples in recovering freedom and independence, and to afford to them effective protection and defence in re-establishing a venerable Empire," the Act of Confederation, adopted a week before Waterloo, "made only the feeblest provisions for the concession of popular rights and the establishment of representative institutions in the several states."[2] For a time Austrian influence was supreme. The Carlsbad Conference of 1819 approved the repressive measures of Metternich which were aimed at the freedom of the press, university teaching, political discussion and free intercourse. Thus did the selfishness of rulers and the greed of royal sycophants triumph over the desires of the people for freedom, national unity and national greatness.

Results of the War.

The years from 1819 to 1848 marked a period of utter hopelessness for the liberal policy. That which had seemed so nearly attained in 1814 to all appearances was irretriev-

---

[1] Fichte, *Reden an die Deutsche Nation*; translation by Seeley.
[2] Bryce, *Holy Roman Empire*, p. 412.

6

ably lost. The strict censorship of the press and the lack of all constitutional methods of bringing pressure to bear on the government effectually checked the development of free institutions. Nevertheless the exigencies of trade and industry united all Germany, save Austria, in 1836 in a *Zollverein* which in its own way contributed to the Revolution of 1848. Then for a time the petty rulers of Germany were thoroughly frightened, and by liberal promises to their peoples they succeeded in averting the threatened storm, only to fall back into the old ways once the danger was passed. The fifteen years following 1850 seemed as devoid of hope as the thirty years and more that preceded. One advantage, however, had been gained: It was becoming increasingly clear that German sovereigns could be frightened into making liberal promises, and the notion was gaining ground that possibly they could be compelled to grant radical reforms. The rivalry between Prussia and Austria afforded a chance for even a comparatively weak party to exert considerable influence. The trend of events, especially the Schleswick-Holstein affair, showed unmistakably that Prussia was in the ascendancy, and with Prussia the weaker states were forced to unite. The union, foreshadowed in the North German Confederation, was finally accomplished on December 31, 1870, when in the palace of the French Emperors the King of Prussia accepted the imperial crown which his brother had rejected in 1849.

Repressive Measures.

The German Empire of to-day is not altogether the ideal toward which German liberalism has been striving for three-quarters of a century, but it conforms nearly enough to that ideal to secure the allegiance of the old-time reformers. It is in fact little more than a confederation of states, some of which, notably Bavaria, are practically as independent as ever. There is still a censorship of the press and much official interference with the freedom of speech and assembly; property qualifications and the privileges of birth still continue to beget socialistic discord. But notwithstanding these short-comings there is a

German Empire a Confederation of States.

universal feeling that the fortunes of the German people are indissolubly bound up with the future of Prussia. This state, with an area and a population greater than the other twenty-five together, and whose king is German Emperor by hereditary right, must continue to dominate the policy of the Empire. If complete unity has not been attained it is acknowledged that it can be secured in case of need. The lesson of German history teaches that progress comes in time of war, and Prussia stands armed cap-à-pie, ready to lead in the next conflict as she has in the past. One more desperate struggle and national unity may be perfected.[1]

The idea of national unity which has given colour to all the later political aspirations of the German people was powerfully re-enforced during the earlier decades of the century by the idealistic tendency in all departments of thought. That "enlightened" view of the world which saw the universe as a machine and God the master workman, that conception of mind as a store-house of ideas which gave no chance for individual initiative and personal responsibility, that notion of art and literature which subjected them to rule and reason—all characteristic of the eighteenth century—were transformed at the touch of the leading spirits of the new era. Kant showed that it is man's understanding, working on the things of sense, that gives laws to nature, and that human experience would be forever impossible without those forms of sense perception which "lie *a priori* in the mind, ready to be applied to all sensations as they arise."[2] In the realm of scientific discovery "it was seen that reason has insight only into that which it produces after a plan of its own, and that it must itself lead the way with principles of judgment based upon fixed laws, and force nature to answer its questions."[3] The outer world, ac-

German Idealism.

---

[1] See the chapter on *The New German Empire* in Bryce's *Holy Roman Empire*, London, 1894.
[2] Kant, *Critique of Pure Reason*, introduction to the *Transcendental Æsthetic*.
[3] Kant, Introduction to the *Critique of Pure Reason*.

cording to Kant, is a show-world, a world of phenomena; the real world, the realm of things as they are, is utterly unknowable. The world which we know, the world in which we live and move and have our being, is nothing apart from the apperceiving mind; the world which man delights to conquer and in which he must perform his part as in the sight of God is the world of human thought.

German idealism, born of Kant and nurtured by Fichte and the Romantic School, culminated in the philosophy of Hegel. As a finished product, Hegelianism exercised a profound influence on the educational history of Germany. "In fact," says Paulsen, "his philosophy may well be called the Prussian state-philosophy during the years from 1820 to 1840, and in a double sense; it was the philosophical system officially acknowledged by the state or at least by the Ministry of Education, and on the other hand Hegel was the enthusiastic apostle of the 'state-idea.'"[1] But potent as was Hegelianism, it was rather a static than a dynamic force. Its subtleties made it a convenient shelter for all manner of reactionary and repressive measures. It was never so indubitably progressive as the earlier representatives of the idealistic school. During the generation preceding 1805, men of genius were almost deified in the select circles of their adorers. Jena and Weimar sprang into eminence because moved by the presence of Goethe and Schiller, Herder and Fichte, and their satellites.

Influence of Hegelianism.

The world, as Fichte conceived it, is the world that the self makes, the world that it freely chooses to make, and because of its imperfections and limitations the self must needs work to overcome it. This is the whole duty of man: work to upbuild the moral order of the universe. The world is what we make it, good or bad, great or small, bond or free. Go forth and do something in a world that can be made better by your action. This is the spirit that cried out in

---

[1] Paulsen, *German Universities*, New York, 1895, p. 68.

the *Addresses to the German Nation* that it bethink itself of the duty resting upon it to create the truly civilized state and give back freedom to the world. Never did philosophy find a more eloquent advocate or touch more surely a nation's heart!

The philosophy of the Romantic school lacked the ethical basis of Fichte's idealism. In its practical aspects it bordered on the immoral by granting to the budding philosophers, literati, and professed geniuses a freedom of action which amounted in many cases to unbridled license. *The Philosophy of the Romantic School.* But it must be acknowledged that in this circle there was a buoyancy of spirit and an enthusiasm in action which inevitably made for progress. That *Weltanschauung* which leaves to man's caprice the determination of his own world does not conduce to social stability, but it may serve a good purpose in casting aside useless traditions. In breaking with the past the Romantic School saw fit to dispense with foreign culture, whether in classical or modern garb, except as it contributed to German needs. German literature, art and philosophy were advanced to first place. The *Nibelungenlied* was heralded as the German Iliad, and the half-forgotten singers of the sixteenth century, despised in their own day because they could use only the peasant speech, were now lauded because they wrote in German. In deference to this increasing respect for the individual man, especially if he be German, we find an increasing interest in the homelier element of life, a broader sympathy for all that is human. The folk-tales of the brothers Grimm and all the wealth of song and story which to-day seems so characteristically German must be credited to this romantic movement.

A survey of the spiritual forces current in German life at the turn of the century easily discovers the secret of the political and military strength of the German nation. From the ashes of the Thirty Years' War there had sprung a proud and ambitious people determined to redeem the Fatherland. *Civic Ideals of Education.* Deprived of their inheritance from the Renaissance of the fifteenth century by circumstances over which they had no control, but of which they were an integral part, they profited in the eighteenth from their birthright. In the meantime the stern lessons of history had taught them the value of co-operation and the dignity and worth of manhood. True, the lesson had been but imperfectly learned; nevertheless it was clearly apparent to the leaders in the reconstruction of Germany that nobility of birth supported by a foreign culture must eventually give way to a higher and more patriotic nobility rooted in a truly German civilization. The problem was how best to weld together the discordant elements in the state and to realize in the national life the highest ideals of individual and social excellence. Down to the Napoleonic era this had been regarded as peculiarly the prerogative of the church; the trend of events guided by the collectivistic idea imposed this task in self-defence upon the state. The reconstruction of the school system and its adaptation to this end followed as a matter of course.

In the reorganization of the schools to conform to the civic ideal of education two main tendencies are noticeable: First, the centralization of the school system, the conversion of a vast collection of schools of all grades into a single system capable of direction, supervision and management by a central authority acting for the state; second, the selection of materials of instruction, the formation of courses of study and the methods of teaching best calculated to subserve the needs of the different classes of society while promoting the interests of the state. The former deals with the external affairs of the schools; the latter is concerned solely with their internal arrangement and methods of work. The one has always enjoyed a close relationship with practical politics and differs in the various states according to the political peculiarities of each; the other, independent of state boundaries, is conditioned primarily by the social, industrial and spiritual needs of the people.

[Problems of School Reform.]

The development of central control of the schools in Prussia has been even more closely in touch with the political expansion of the monarchy than in most other German states. A direct and systematic inspection of the evangelical schools followed the Reformation in Brandenburg, and Joachim II. established in 1552 a consistory for church and school affairs. In 1573 the Elector, John George, prescribed regulations for the inspection and general conduct of schools. In the privy council of Joachim Frederick there appeared in 1604 a special board to which was delegated supervisory powers over the church consistory. But inasmuch as all school inspectors were clergymen there was no thought of making the schools independent of the church. During the Thirty Years' War all was lost that had been gained. The wanton destruction of property and the loss of population effectually checked all educational progress. In 1687 Elector Frederick William made an urgent plea for the re-establishment of the school system on the lines marked out by his predecessors. The founding of the Prussian kingdom in 1701 first gave an opportunity for effectual centralization. Under Frederick William II. regulations were enforced which secured considerable uniformity. Frederick the Great continued the development along the lines marked out by his father. In 1750 he placed all the provincial consistories, except that of Silesia, under the jurisdiction of the Berlin consistory, and by so doing school affairs were brought more than ever under one central control. A practical result was that from a large number of weak Latin schools with no definite course of study there were evolved a few really good *Gymnasien,* with uniform curricula. In 1771, Baron von Zedlitz became head of the Department of Lutheran Church and School Affairs. From that time on till his retirement from office in 1788 there was rapid progress. At his instance King Frederick William II. instituted in 1787 the *Oberschulcollegium,* a board charged with the reorganization of the school system and the oversight of all school affairs in the monarchy.[1]

Development of Central Control.

---

[1] The duty of the board, according to the royal rescript, was "*das gesammte Schulwesen in Unseren Landen auf das zweckmässigste einzu-*

Von Zedlitz was placed at the head of the board, and with him were associated the Berlin school-masters, J. H. Meierotto and Frederick Gedike, who were to be travelling inspectors of schools in the provinces. One of the most important regulations of the *Oberschulcollegium* was the edict (1788) instituting a system of leaving examinations in all the higher schools (*Abiturientenprüfungen*).[1] This regulation, however, like most of those that had gone before, was of little practical importance. Whatever was pleasing to the church or the clerical parties was sure to succeed; whatever was opposed to clerical interests was equally certain of failure. In fact it was the King's settled policy in all his enactments to bind the school more closely to the church, and for this purpose the *Oberschulcollegium* was filled up with representatives of the clerical parties. More than that, Gedike's dream of a centralized and uniform school system was officially dispelled by a refusal to extend the jurisdiction of the *Oberschulcollegium* even to all the higher schools of the monarchy. At the end of the century there was really no state school system; such system as obtained was directly under the control of the church and only indirectly responsible to the state.

The first step in the secularization of the schools was taken in 1794 by the promulgation of the *Allgemeine Landrecht*, the Prussian Magna Charta, itself the surest guarantee of the strength of the democratic spirit. The common law basis for educational institutions was stated in these unequivocal

---

richten, und nach den Umständen der Zeit und der Beschaffenheit der Schulen immer zu verbessern. Es muss darauf Acht haben, dass nach Verschiedenheit der Schulen in jeder der nothwendige und nützlichste Unterricht ertheilt werde; es muss mit Nachdruck darauf halten, dass überall zweckmässige Schulbücher gebraucht und eingeführt, und wo solche mangeln, durch tüchtige Männer eingeführt werden.—Wir legen dem O. S. C. die Befugniss bei, an alle Landesregierungen und Consistorien, auch an das ostpreuss, Staatsministerium Rescripte und Befehle zu erlassen." (Wiese, *Das höhere Schulwesen in Preussen*, I., p. 3.)

[1] The various regulations governing the examinations down to 1863 are given in Wiese, *Das höhere Schulwesen in Preussen*, I., pp. 478-524. Later details are given by Kübler.

terms: "Schools and universities are state institutions, charged with the instruction of youth in useful information and scientific knowledge. Such institutions may be founded only with the knowledge and consent of the state. All public schools and educational institutions are under the supervision of the state, and are at all times subject to its examination and inspection." These were brave words, but they had little actual significance until the people were fully roused to the necessities of national independence and national unity. *[Separation of Church and School.]*

The organization of the Prussian school system waited on the reorganization of the Prussian state. On October 5, 1807, Baron von Stein was placed at the head of the entire civil administration of the monarchy. One of his first acts was to abolish the *Oberschulcollegium* in order effectually to rid himself of clerical domination. In 1808 the bureau of public instruction was transferred to the Department of the Interior, in which it formed one of the six sections. The *Section für Cultus und den öffentlichen Unterricht* was presided over by William von Humboldt. "The Providential man appeared in Humboldt, as great a master of the science and art of education as Scharnhorst was master of the organization of war. Not only was he himself, as a scholar and an investigator, on a level with the very first of his age, not only had he lived with precisely those masters of literature, Schiller and Goethe, who were most deliberate in their self-culture, and have therefore left behind most instruction on the higher parts of education, but he had been especially intimate with F. A. Wolf. Formed by such teachers, and supported by a more intense belief in culture than almost any man of his time, Humboldt began his work in April, 1809."[1] His efforts were directed from the first to making the education of the Prussian youth commensurate with the responsibilities of Prussian citizenship. The schools must exist for the state *[The Work of Humboldt.]*

---

[1] Seeley, *Life and Times of Stein*, Pt. VI., chap. 3.

and must learn how to train up intelligent, God-fearing, patriotic citizens. For the most part his efforts were directed to the internal improvement of the schools, but it was seen that no radical change could be made without first putting the schools in such a position that unwilling pedagogues should be forced to obey governmental requests. So far as the higher schools were concerned there was little uniformity in the courses of study and no guarantee that their graduates were fitted for university work and the civil service, except the uncertain entrance tests applied by the universities themselves. Accordingly in 1812 the system of final examinations which had fallen into abeyance was revived and enforced. But the time was not ripe for its universal application. Failure to pass this examination, which was conducted by local school officers under the personal supervision of a state inspector, did not prevent a student's admission to the university nor to the civil service; the only penalty was ineligibility for the many valuable stipends controlled by the state. Not till the second decade of the century was the privilege of admission to the civil service withdrawn from those who failed to pass the final examinations of the *Gymnasien*. The decisive step was taken in 1834, when it was decreed that candidates for the learned professions must have as a prerequisite for admission to the state examinations a certificate of graduation from an approved higher school. Inasmuch as the leaving examinations of the higher schools are conducted by a board of school officers in the presence of a representative of the department of public instruction, whose approval is necessary in passing a candidate, it will be seen how completely the essential control of the schools had passed into the hands of the central board.

The plan of administration as proposed by Stein and elaborated by Humboldt and his successors continued in force down to the year 1817, when that section of the Interior Department which included the bureau of education was erected into an independent ministry, called the *Ministerium der geistlichen und Unter-*

The Triumph of Bureaucracy.

richtsangelegenheiten. The chief of the new Department was Baron Von Altenstein, who remained in office until his death in 1840—a regime which marks the triumph of bureaucracy, as may be inferred from the fact that for eight years, 1824–1832, the Director of the Police Bureau was officially in charge of the department of public instruction.[1]

---

[1] "In 1817, the students of several universities assembled at the Wartburg in order to celebrate the tercentenary of the Reformation. In the evening, a small number of them, the majority having already left, were carried away by enthusiastic zeal, and, in imitation of Luther, burnt a number of writings recently published against German freedom, together with other emblems of what was considered hateful in the institutions of some of the German states. These youthful excesses were viewed by the governments as symptoms of grave peril. At the same time, a large number of students united to form one great German *Burschenschaft* (association of students), whose aim was the cultivation of a love of country, a love of freedom, and the moral sense. Thereupon increased anxiety on the part of the governments, followed by vexatious police interference. Matters grew worse in consequence of the rash act of a fanatical student, named Sand. It became known that the Russian government was using all its powerful influence to have liberal ideas suppressed in Germany, and that the play-wright Kotzebue had secretly sent to Russia slanderous and libellous reports on German patriots. Sand travelled to Mannheim and thrust a dagger into Kotzebue's heart. The consequences were most disastrous to the cause of freedom in Germany. The distrust of the governments reached its height: it was held that this bloody deed must needs be the result of a wide-spread conspiracy: the authorities suspected demagogues everywhere. . . . Many young men were thrown into prison; gymnastic and other societies were arbitrarily suppressed; a rigid censorship of the press was established, and the freedom of the universities restrained; various professors, among them Arndt, whose songs had helped to fire the enthusiasm of the *Freiheits-kämpfer*—the soldiers of freedom—in the recent war, were deprived of their offices; the *Burschenschaft* was dissolved, and the wearing of their colours, the future colours of the German Empire, black, red, and gold, was forbidden. . . . The universities continued to uphold the national idea; the *Burschenschaft* soon secretly revived as a private association, and as early as 1820 there again existed at most German universities *Burschenschaften*, which, though their aims were not sharply defined, bore a political colouring and placed the demand for German unity in the foreground." (Krause, *The Growth of German Unity*, chap. 8.)

The external organization of the school-system was fully accomplished in 1825 when provincial school-boards (*Provinzial Schulcollegien*), responsible to the Ministry of Education, were instituted in the several provinces of the kingdom side by side with the church consistories. At this point the schools were finally separated from the church and state control was assured.

The great work, however, which Humboldt set himself to do was the vitalizing of the schools from within. It need not be related here in detail how that work was done in the field of elementary or of university education. "The movement in behalf of popular schools commenced by inviting C. A. Zeller, of Würtemberg, to Prussia. Zeller was a young theologian who had studied under Pestalozzi in Switzerland, and was thoroughly imbued with the method and spirit of his master. On his return he had convened the school-teachers of Würtemberg in barns, for want of better accommodations being allowed him, and inspired them with a zeal for Pestalozzi's methods, and for a better education of the whole people. On removing to Prussia he first took charge of the seminary at Koenigsberg, soon after founded the seminary at Karalene, and went about into different provinces meeting with teachers, holding conferences, visiting schools and inspiring school officers with the right spirit. The next step taken was to send a number of young men, mostly theologians, to Pestalozzi's institution at Iferten, to acquire his method, and on their return to place them in new or reorganized teachers' seminaries. To these new agents in school improvement were joined a large body of zealous teachers, and patriotic and enlightened citizens, who, in ways and methods of their own, laboured incessantly to confirm the Prussian state, by forming new organs for its internal life, and new means of protection from foreign foes. They proved themselves truly educators of the people. Although the government thus not only encouraged, but directly aided, in the introduction of the methods of Pestalozzi into the public schools of Prussia, still the school-boards in the

Reforms in Elementary Education.

different provinces sustained and encouraged those who approved and taught on different systems. . . . Music, which was one of Pestalozzi's great instruments of culture, was made the vehicle of patriotic songs, and through them the heart of all Germany was moved to bitter hatred of the conqueror who had desolated her fields and homes, and humbled the pride of her monarchy. All these efforts for the improvement of the elementary education, accompanied by expensive modifications in the establishments of secondary and superior education, were made when the treasury was impoverished, and taxes the most exorbitant in amount were levied on every province and commune of the kingdom."[1] From such beginnings has grown the most magnificent system of common schools in the world.

The influence of the reformers was felt quite as distinctly in university education. Seeley says that "it was on the highest department of education that Humboldt left his mark most visibly. He founded the University of Berlin; he gave to Europe a new seat of learning, which has ever since stood on an equality with the very greatest of those which Europe boasted before. We are not indeed to suppose that the idea of such a university sprang up for the first time at this moment, or in the brain of Humboldt. Among all the losses which befell Prussia by the Peace of Tilsit none was felt more bitterly than the loss of the University of Halle, where Wolf himself had made his fame. Immediately after the blow fell, two of the professors of Halle made their way to Memel and laid before the King a proposal to establish a High School at Berlin. This was on August 22, 1807. . . . A university is not founded in a day, and accordingly while Stein held office the design did not pass beyond the stage of discussion. . . . Humboldt sent in his report on May 12, 1809, and on August 16th followed the Order of Cabinet assigning to the new University, along with the Academies of Science and Art, an annual do-

Reforms in University Education.

---

[1] H. Barnard, *Am Journal of Education*, VIII., 405.

nation of 150,000 thalers, and the palace of Prince Henry as its residence. During the rest of his term of office Humboldt was occupied in negotiations with eminent men of science all over Germany, whose services he hoped to procure. He was certainly not unsuccessful. He secured Fichte for philosophy; Schleiermacher, De Wette, and Marheineke for theology; Savigny and Schmalz for jurisprudence; Friedländer, Kolrausch, Hufeland, and Reil for medicine; Wolf, Buttmann, Böckh, Heindorf, and Spalding for the study of antiquity; Niebuhr and Rühs for history; Tralles for mathematics (Gauss refused the invitation). The University was opened at Michaelmas of 1810, and as the first result of it the first volume of Niebuhr's *Roman History*, opening so vast a field of historical speculation, was published in 1811."[1]

The reforms which were inaugurated in the higher schools were characteristic of the age and reflect the personalities of the great leaders in educational thought. Humboldt and Wolf were ardent humanists; both were profound students and enthusiastic admirers of Greek culture. It was natural that their influence should be exerted in favour of the new humanism which had already won a place for itself in central and northern Germany under the leadership of the University of Göttingen. Wolf, himself, had been for years a missionary of the new cult in Halle; Herder had made it at home in the *Gymnasium* in Weimar. It might seem, therefore, to the casual observer that nothing could prevent the triumph of Greek ideals. But Humboldt was in office only about a year and Wolf's temperament was not such as to make him a popular leader of men. More than that the reforms of the higher schools were scarcely more than begun when the reactionary tendency in all lines of civic and mental activity began to set in. To be sure much had been accomplished before the true significance of the reforms were fully realized, and a machinery had been set in motion which had to be directed and could not be stopped.

[Sidenote: Reforms in Secondary Education.]

---

[1] Seeley, *Life and Times of Stein*, Pt. VI., chap. 3.

The direction, however, was not altogether in harmony with the views of those who had planned the educational reforms.

A survey of the educational field at the beginning of the century discloses two radically different types of classical schools. The Weimar *Gymnasium* was a leading representative of the new humanistic ideal ; Schulpforta was the best known institution of the old type. Both were strong and vigorous schools and well calculated for leadership in the educational world. Schulpforta made the doctrine of formal discipline the chief article in its creed ; the critical study of the ancient languages was the all-important means to this end. Its supporters were especially numerous in southern Germany and wherever clerical influence, particularly Jesuitical, was felt. The Weimar school was the creation of Herder, who set as his educational ideal the *Bildung zur Humanität*. In effect the opposition was strictly between the old humanism and the new.

<small>Main Problems.</small>

There can be little doubt that if Humboldt and Wolf had come into power ten years earlier the victory of the new ideas would have been more complete. As it was they were forced to reckon with the conservatism of school-masters and found it insuperable. Yet no one but possibly they themselves would count their labour lost. While they did not attain the heights of their ambition they made the higher schools of the kingdom a hundred-fold more efficient than they had ever been before. The ideals of Greek culture were so built into the very foundations of the school system that it has since been impossible to remove them.

Perhaps the wisest measure that Humboldt introduced was the one relating to the certification of teachers as set forth in the edict of 1810.[1] This measure provided for a searching examination of all candidates for teachers' positions and effectually checked what had been a common practice of permitting theological

<small>Certification of Teachers.</small>

---

[1] See Wiese, *Das höhere Schulwesen in Preussen*, I., pp. 545 ff.

students to eke out an existence while waiting for a suitable post in the church. The position of teacher was raised at once to something like professional dignity. And from that day to this the teaching profession has steadily grown in technical and social importance.

The introduction of leaving examinations in 1812 put a premium on uniformity in school work. It was also decreed at the same time that all classical schools, en-
<small>Final Examinations.</small> titled to fit students for the universities, whether known by the title of *Gymnasium, Lyceum, Pädagogium, Collegium, Lateinische Schule,* or what not, should henceforth be called *Gymnasien.*

For the guidance of these schools Humboldt commissioned Süvern, a pupil of Fichte and Wolf and later a member of Gedike's seminar, to prepare a general course
<small>General Course of Study.</small> of study. This was laid before Wolf for his criticism as early as 1811, but its publication was delayed till 1816. It did not meet Wolf's approval, but Paulsen suggests[1] that perhaps his opposition was due as much to the fact that he himself was not asked to prepare it as to the actual contents of the document. Be this as it may, it is certainly true that while Wolf may justly be called the father of the modern *Gymnasium,* the child was not exactly the image of the parent. Throughout the ten years' course the main subjects of instruction were Latin, Greek and mathematics. The time allotment in the upper classes was as follows: Latin, 8 hours a week; Greek, 7; German, 4; mathematics, 6; history and geography, 3; religion, 2; and science, 2. No provision whatsoever was made for instruction in the elements of philosophy, French, or subjects designed to afford "useful information." This was the opposite of eighteenth century utilitarianism. The aim of instruction in the higher schools was "the formal development of good understanding and righteous judgment."

The *Lehrplan* of 1816 was evidently a compromise. The

---

[1] Paulsen, *Geschichte des Gelehrten Unterrichts,* p. 576.

special importance attached to Greek was pleasing to the new humanists; the increased number of hours devoted to mathematics was a sop to the realists and those who upheld the value of formal mental discipline. As a result it was generally unsatisfactory and never universally adopted.[1] Teachers could not be found who knew enough of Greek or mathematics to meet the demands of the official program. How to secure able teachers and make their work most effective was the problem of the next twenty years.

Lehrplan of 1816 not a Success.

The first requirement was better scholarship. With better prepared students the universities were soon able to turn out more scholarly graduates. Not only was the general university instruction steadily improved during the early decades of the century, but special attention was everywhere given to the training of teachers. Philological seminars were established in all the universities before 1825[2] which ably carried on the work so well marked out by Gesner in Göttingen and Wolf in Halle. Pedagogical seminars were also established at this time which did much to develop the professional spirit.[3] In 1826, a year of trial teaching (*Probejahr*) was required of all candidates, and in 1831 new orders were issued for the conduct of teachers' examinations. All candidates for positions in the higher schools, whether holders of doctor's degrees from universities or not, were obliged to take examinations in the main subjects of the higher school course and in philosophy, pedagogy and theology. Distinguished excellence

Better Teachers Needed.

---

[1] See Wiese, *Höheres Schulwesen*, I., p. 21.

[2] Königsberg, 1810; Berlin, 1812; Greifswald, 1820; Breslau, 1812; Münster, 1825; Bonn, 1819.

[3] Herbart's seminar in Königsberg was officially recognized in 1810; Gedike's seminar in Berlin was formally taken over by the University in 1812; the seminar in Stettin, founded in 1804, was reorganized in 1816; Breslau began pedagogical work in 1813; and in 1817 it was stated that the purpose of the reorganized seminar in Halle was "the training of skilled teachers for the *Gymnasien*." (Wiese, *Höheres Schulwesen*, I., 539.)

was required in one of the three main groups—(a) Greek, Latin and German; (b) mathematics and the natural sciences; (c) history and geography—and a reasonable knowledge of the other two. According to the standing obtained in this examination candidates were licensed to teach (after a successful trial year) in the higher, middle or lower grades of the higher schools. Promotion was strictly dependent upon scholarly and professional attainments, the one as tested by examination, the other chiefly by skill in teaching.

In the development of school affairs the example of Prussia was closely followed by the Grand Duchy of Hesse and the other northern states, but central and southern Germany followed their own devices. In Saxony the leadership of the great cloister-schools, Schulpforta, Grimma and Meissen, was generally acknowledged, and this tended distinctly toward a one-sided classical training, and that mainly philological. In Bavaria, Frederick Thiersch introduced the Saxon plan and carried out reforms which were in most respects opposed to the new humanism. According to his program, which was published in 1829 and officially adopted in all main points in 1830, Latin was given 16 hours a week during the first two years, 12 hours a week during the next four years, and 10, 9, 8 and 6 hours a week respectively during the last four years of the course. Greek was taught throughout the last eight years with a total of 51 hours. Logic and philosophy, German and history, were to be taught incidentally in connection with the classics. For mathematics 3 or 4 hours a week were considered sufficient. Würtemberg followed much the same line of development. Baden was considerably more liberal and inclined to the Prussian plan, but, on the whole, southern Germany was loath to abandon the old mode of education. Undoubtedly the influence of the Jesuits did much to maintain the supremacy of Latin in the schools, but even in protestant districts no reform has successfully combated the popular faith in classical scholarship.

The period from 1820 to 1840 is one of consolidation and

organization; it is not a period of progress in German education, except from the stand-point of practical politics. During these years the school system of Prussia was converted into a mighty political force and made obedient to the will of the state. The regulations concerning the governmental administration of the schools, the preparation and certification of teachers, and the control of school instruction through the final examinations, have already been mentioned as the work of Altenstein's ministry under the guidance of Johannes Schulze, chief of the bureau of education.[1] One further consideration and the review of the period will be complete. *The Period 1820–1840.*

The first impulse of the reformers of the revolutionary period was to make Greek the centre of all gymnasial instruction. Even Herbart, who had little sympathy with the roseate views of the idealists, earnestly advocated the claims of the Greek language and literature for the purpose of educative instruction. The program of 1816 gave it a prominent place, but, as Wolf well knew, not all schools were prepared to teach Greek to the extent recommended, nor were all teachers of the subject new humanists. In consequence some provision had to be made for the acceptance of equivalents. Up to 1824 it was possible to graduate from the *Gymnasien* without Greek. Substitution was then made permissible only with the consent of the provincial school-boards, and in 1837 Greek became an obligatory study. *The Place of Greek.*

At first sight it looks as if the victory were slowly on the side of the reformers, but in fact it was their defeat. In the early 20's it became apparent that the first care of the administration was to restore the supremacy of Latin. The philological seminars of the universities were ordered to give more attention to Latin composition. Occasional courses in Latin were given *Latin Takes the Lead.*

---

[1] Varrentrapp, *Johannes Schulze und das höhere Unterrichtswesen in seiner Zeit*, 1889.

by the Faculties of Law and Medicine, thanks to a little
official inspiration from the ministry, and finally the requirements of the final examinations as announced in 1834 showed
precisely where the schools were expected to stand. The
certificate of graduation could be given only to him who
could write Latin without grammatical errors and in a style
tolerably free from Germanisms, and who could speak the
language readily enough to satisfy the examiners thereby of
his knowledge of the other subjects of the course. Latin
was not the only object of official test; but as the examination
in other studies, Greek included, was conducted through the
Latin, it is safe to say that no candidate would fail to put
the stress in the proper place. If Greek was made obligatory,
Latin was absolutely indispensable. The truth is it was
necessary officially to bolster up the study of Greek to keep it
from disappearing entirely under the bureaucratic zeal for
excellence in Latin.

Another innovation of this period which shows clearly
enough the trend of official thought was the introduction of
philosophical propædeutics. This consisted
Philosophy and Theology. principally of empirical psychology and logic
as a "preparation for the systematic study of
the true philosophy." But what of the true philosophy?
Some inconsiderate provincial boards raised the question and
were laughed at for their pains. The true philosophy, of
course, is the Hegelian, and he who would teach in the higher
schools must be prepared to believe in it as religiously as in
his theology. Philosophy not only found an entrance into
the schools but the universities were constrained to make it
a required subject for degrees and similar honours. Theology,
too, became a formal study for intending teachers, and the os-
tensible purpose of the eight years' reign of the Police Minister in the bureau of education was to promote the interests of a truly religious education among the people!

The gymnasial program of 1837 is the embodiment of all
that had gone before in the realm of internal school affairs.
It gives us the first all-round view of what the Prussian state

considered essential in the training of its future leaders in thought and action. It was the first program which was universally adopted in all Prussian *Gymnasien*, and its adoption marked the triumph of the Altenstein Ministry in its crusade against freedom and individual initiative in education. Uniformity was thereby attained and the school system effectually nationalized.[1]

The Program of 1837.

GYMNASIAL PROGRAM OF 1837.

SUBJECTS.	CLASSES.									
	VI.	V.	IV.	IIIb.	IIIa.	IIb.	IIa.	Ib.	Ia.	Total.
Latin	10	10	10	10	10	10	10	8	8	86
Greek			6	6	6	6	6	6	6	42
German	4	4	2	2	2	2	2	2	2	22
French				2	2	2	2	2	2	12
Religion	2	2	2	2	2	2	2	2	2	18
Mathematics	4	4	3	3	3	4	4	4	4	33
Physics						1	1	2	2	6
Philosophy								2	2	4
History and Geography	3	3	2	3	3	3	3	2	2	24
Natural History	2	2	2	2	2					10
Drawing	2	2	2							6
Writing	3	3	1							7
Singing	2	2	2	2	2					10
Hebrew (elective)						(2)	(2)	(2)	(2)	(8)
Total	32	32	32	32	32	30(2)	30(2)	30(2)	30(2)	

A new era in the history of Prussian education began in 1840 with the reign of Frederick William IV. The leaders of the preceding generation had been superseded by others who were of a different faith; Wolf, Goethe, Hegel, and Humboldt were all dead, and in their places stood men who were almost fanatically opposed to the philosophy and world-views which had characterized the first third of the century. Specialization was the watch-word of the new order. In philology, history, philosophy and theology scholars were coming to content themselves with a thorough knowledge of some particular

The Period 1840-70.

---

[1] The *Circular-Rescript von 24 October, 1837,* is given in full in Wiese-Kübler, *Verordnungen und Gesetze,* Pt. I., pp. 53-65.

branch of their subject rather than strive for a comprehensive view of the entire field ; much less, therefore, were they interested in a superficial knowledge of the world in general. Note the change in philology from Wolf's general science of antiquities : Bopp (1791-1867) developed comparative grammar on the basis of the Sanskrit ; Dietz (1794-1876) was the founder of Romance philology ; Ritschl (1806-1876) introduced his students to a study of the Latin inscriptions ; and Lepsius (1810-1884) sought his materials for Egyptology with a spade. In history, following the epoch-making work of Niebuhr (1776-1831) came Ranke (1795-1886), who led the way in investigation of the sources. Hegel (1770-1831) was succeeded by Schopenhauer (1788-1860) and Lotze (1817-1881), and a new field was opened up by Fechner (1801-1887) and Wundt (1832-) in psychology. Even the old theology found opponents in Baur and the Tübingen school, who introduced the higher criticism from the historical stand-point. Jurisprudence had its specialists and critics in von Savigny and Stahl. But the most significant change of all was the tendency in science. Müller (1801-1858) gave a new impulse to the study of pathological anatomy by the introduction of the microscope ; Schultze (1825-1874) systematized zoölogy ; Liebig (1803-1873) made a new chemistry, and Helmholtz (1821-1894) a new physics. In short, every object which attracted the attention of scholars was carefully investigated and set off into specialties.

The immediate effect upon the schools of the strictly scientific methods of research which were gradually introduced after 1830 was a tendency to discredit all that had before been attempted. But the work of the Altenstein Ministry could not easily be set aside ; nevertheless the Prussian Department of Education assiduously strove to bring unity into the classical schools by emphasizing still further the study of Latin.[1] The idea of

<small>The Tendency to Specialization.</small>

---

[1] Wiese gives an official summary of the years 1864-1869 in *Das höhere Schulwesen in Preussen*, II., pp. 1-32; 1869-1874, in III., pp. 1-60.

power and special knowledge thus manifested itself in the classical schools by a return to the method of the old humanists. The ability to read, write and speak Latin was the chief end of all instruction. A gymnasial program was issued in 1856 which incorporated many of the desired reforms. In the two lower classes the instruction in German was combined with the Latin, to which two hours weekly were added, and the time previously given to the natural sciences was almost entirely devoted to French and religion. The writing of Latin was an important exercise in all classes. Greek prose composition was included in the final examination, from which German literature, French, the natural sciences and philosophy were entirely omitted. Latin was the main part of the gymnasial course; everything was subsidiary to the classics.

There were forces operative in German life, however, which were destined in time to overcome the extreme leaning toward a classical training. The rise of modern science and the accompanying changes in the industrial world demanded a hearing. The development of rapid transit, the discovery of easy means of communication and the invention of labor-saving devices tended toward the growth of urban population. This in its turn produced unexpected effects upon the social conditions of the country. The political revolution of 1848 was outwardly a failure; but the industrial and social revolution which began to be felt in Germany in the 30's, and which grew steadily despite all hinderances during the succeeding forty years, finally found free scope in the re-established German Empire. So completely has the new order supplanted the old that within the last twenty-five years Germany has entered the markets of the world and become a dangerous rival for commercial supremacy. In this period Germany has been transformed from a mediæval agricultural nation into a highly developed industrial power.

Forces Opposed to Classical Training.

In the organization of the school system little thought was given to the practical needs of the people. The reformers were intent upon securing the ideal training for the ideal citizen. Enough was done, they apparently believed, when schools were provided on the one hand for the common people and on the other hand for those who were to be leaders in society. But *Real*-schools were in existence and they continued to exist. Many of the old city Latin schools were also tolerated, although they could not maintain the standards of the *Gymnasien*. Here then were two kinds of schools outside of the gymnasial system and sufficiently in disrepute to cater to the needs of the new industrial classes.

Growth of Real-Schools.

Up to 1855 the free growth of these schools was persistently and perversely checked by university scholars and state officials. But after the change in administration the *Real*-school soon received full recognition. By ministerial order of October 6, 1859,[1] two classes of *Realschulen* were instituted. Schools of the first-class (*Realschulen I. Ordnung*) were permitted to give a full nine years' course in Latin with a total of 44 week-hours. French was allotted 34 week-hours; German, 29 week-hours; geography and history, 30 week-hours; mathematics, 47 week-hours—as opposed to 17, 20, 25 and 32 week-hours respectively in the *Gymnasium*. As a still further offset for Greek 20 week-hours in English and over 30 week-hours in the sciences were added to the *Real*-school course.

Their Official Recognition.

The *Realschule II. Ordnung* was left largely dependent upon the goodwill of local communities. It might teach Latin, but it did not receive official recognition unless it conformed to the official standard. And herein was an especial cause of discontent. Latin was an indispensable prerequisite for admission to the civil service, and in most instances it was a condition of entrance to the higher industrial and technical schools. With rapidly increasing industrial demands a school was needed which should give a systematic and comprehensive training in modern languages, mathematics and the natural

---

[1] The text of the order is given in Wiese-Kübler, *Verordnungen und Gesetze*, Pt. I, pp. 70–84.

sciences. This result was fully attained in 1882,[1] when the Prussian government gave the *Realschule I. Ordnung* the title of *Realgymnasium* and elevated the burgher school to the rank of *Oberrealschule*. Graduates of these schools were also given certain privileges in the universities, schools of technology and the civil service.

The revision of the higher-school programs in 1882 apparently left little to be desired. In a way peculiarly German the problems of secondary education were worked out to a logical conclusion. But seeds of discontent had been sown. The *Real*-schools were popular—too popular for their own best interests—and they increased rapidly in number and in the attendance of pupils. Their adherents soon began to press for additional privileges and thus incur the enmity of the *Gymnasien*. The classical schools on the other hand had been strengthened on the side of modern languages and the natural sciences to the disadvantage of Latin—a reform most displeasing to the ultra-humanists. The outcome was the famous School Conference of December, 1890, in which the young Emperor took so prominent a part and which led to the revised programs of 1892.

The last act in the educational drama presents very clearly the underlying motive in all the reforms of the century. The tendency has been to nationalize the school system and to make it the principal support of the state. In Prussia the state government is monarchical; hence the upholding of the crown is the patriotic duty of the schools. Whatever may be thought of the political aspects of this principle, it certainly conforms to the ideas of modern German statesmen; it is the natural evolution of the nineteenth century. The Emperor stated the case admirably in his opening address to the Conference : "The main trouble lies in the fact that since 1870 the philologists have sat in their *Gymnasien* as *beati possidentes*, laying main stress upon the subject-matter, upon the learning and the knowing,

The Period 1870-92.

German Schools for German Youth.

---

[1] See Wiese-Kübler, *Verordnungen und Gesetze*, Pt. 1, pp. 110–161.

but not upon the formation of character and the needs of life. Less emphasis is being placed upon practice (*können*) than theory (*kennen*), a fact that can easily be verified by looking at the requirements for the examinations. Their underlying principle is that the pupil must, first of all, know as many things as possible. Whether this knowledge fits for life or not is immaterial. If anyone enters into a discussion with these gentlemen on this point and attempts to show them that a young man ought to be prepared, to some extent at least, for life and its manifold problems, they will tell him that such is not the function of the school, its principal aim being the discipline or gymnastic of the mind, and that if this gymnastic were properly conducted the young man would be capable of doing all that is necessary in life. I am of the opinion that we can no longer be guided by this doctrine.

"To return to schools in general and to the *Gymnasium* in particular—I will say that I am not ignorant of the fact that in many circles I am looked upon as a fanatical opponent of the *Gymnasium*, and that I have therefore often been played as a trump-card in favour of other schools. Gentlemen, this is a misapprehension. Whoever has been a pupil of a *Gymnasium* himself, and has looked behind the scenes, knows where the wrong lies. First of all, a national basis is wanting. The foundation of our *Gymnasium* must be German. It is our duty to educate men to become young Germans, and not young Greeks and Romans. We must relinquish the basis which has been the rule for centuries, the old monastic education of the Middle Ages, when Latin and a little Greek (*ein bisschen Griechisch*) were most important. These are no longer our standard; we must make German the basis, and German composition must be made the centre around which everything else revolves." [1]

This is the aim of secondary education in Germany. There may be a difference of opinion on how best to attain it, but

---

[1] *Educational Review*, I., pp. 202-203.

on the whole the Emperor speaks for the German people. The problem of the future is the preservation of the national culture and the satisfaction of the practical needs of an industrial people.

The purpose of this rapid sketch of the history of secondary education in Germany has been attained if it has demonstrated the proposition that the German school system is a living, progressive institution that has changed from age to age in response to the changing ideals of successive periods. At no time has it been a finished product which could be studied apart from the political, social, industrial and spiritual conditions of the people by whom it has been supported and for whom it still exists. It is the natural evolution of forces inherent in the German life; it is the result of a process of adaptation to German environment; it is an educational product peculiar to the Fatherland.

Conclusion.

GENERAL REFERENCES :—Wiese, *Das höhere Schulwesen in Preussen*, 3 vols., Berlin, 1864–1873; Wiese-Kübler, *Verordnungen und Gesetze für die höhere Schulen in Preussen*, 3d ed., 2 vols., Berlin, 1886–1888; Rönne, *Das Unterrichts-Wesen des Preussischen Staates*, 2 vols., Berlin, 1855; Paulsen, *Geschichte des Gelehrten Unterrichts*, Leipzig, 1885 (a new and enlarged edition of this excellent work has been recently issued); Ziegler, *Geschichte der Pädagogik mit besonderer Rücksicht auf das höhere Unterrichtswesen*, Vol. I., Pt. I., of Baumeister's *Handbuch der Erziehungs und Unterrichtslehre*, Munich, 1895; Rethwisch, *Deutschlands höheres Schulwesen im neunzehnten Jahrhundert*, Berlin, 1893; *Centralblatt für die gesammte Unterrichts- Verwaltung in Preussen*; and the Encyclopedias of Schmid and Rein.

CHAPTER V

THE PRUSSIAN SCHOOL SYSTEM

It will be apparent from the foregoing sketch of the history of education in Germany that no absolute uniformity in the school systems of the various states is to be expected. There are marked political and religious differences between the north and the south; even the racial characteristics of the people are not the same in all parts of the Empire. But the unquestioned supremacy of Prussia in imperial politics assures her also the first place in educational affairs. However much the smaller states may object to Prussian leadership it remains a fact that the German Empire is little more than Prussia enlarged. In considering the German school systems, therefore, I shall take the Prussian system as the standard and refer to the other states only as the differentiation makes it imperative.

The Prussian System a Type.

In Germany, as in the United States, educational affairs are directed by state officials in accordance with governmental policy, custom and laws. The school-laws of some of the states have been codified, but in general this has been found impossible in the larger states owing to the variety of interests and the strength of tradition. In Prussia, for example, many attempts have been made to secure the passage of some general measure which would at least simplify existing customs, but without success. Either the proposition has been too bureaucratic to suit the citizen party, too ecclesiastical to please the liberals, or too radical to secure the vote of the catholics.

No Imperial System of Education.

The foreigner who would familiarize himself with the Prussian school system finds here the first serious obstacle; volumes of ministerial rescripts and official instructions are placed at his disposal, but there is no knowing how much of it all is a dead letter. And even a German is not quite sure till he has the minister's word for it.

In Prussia, as in most of the German states, the control of the schools is exercised through governmental orders and instructions that proceed from the Department of Education. The government, however, is not absolute in its powers. Limits are set by the constitution of the Prussian state.

Frederick William I. first claimed the right of putting the schools under state control, and in 1794 Frederick William II. issued the *Allgemeine Landrecht*, the charter upon which are based all school ordinances and regulations. Its most important articles are as follows: *The Basis of School Laws.*

1. Schools and universities are state institutions charged with the instruction of youth in useful information and scientific knowledge.

2. Such institutions may be founded only with the knowledge and consent of the state.

3. All public schools and educational institutions are under the supervision of the state and are at all times subject to its examination and inspection.

4. No one shall be denied admission to the public schools on account of his religious belief.

5. Public-school children cannot be compelled to attend religious instruction at variance with their own creed.

6. Public schools designed to give instruction in the higher arts and sciences enjoy all the rights of corporate bodies.

7. These rights are vested in governmental boards in accordance with the existing school regulations of the district.

8. Boards appointed by the state are charged with the immediate direction and supervision of schools.

9. Where the appointment of teachers does not rest with

certain persons or corporations because of foundations or special privileges it belongs to the state.

10. Even where the immediate supervision of such schools or the appointment of teachers is left to certain private persons or corporations new teachers cannot be appointed, nor can any important change in organization or methods of instruction be made, without the knowledge and consent of the provincial school-boards.

11. Only persons of sufficient knowledge, good morals and sound judgment can be chosen for supervising officers.

12. Overseers must earnestly seek to dissuade young people from attempting intellectual work beyond their ability.

13. On the other hand they should encourage and support students of superior ability in the prosecution of their studies.

14. No native pupil shall be dismissed from a public school without a certificate signed by the teachers and school authorities showing the nature of his school work and his moral deportment.

15. Such a certificate shall be deemed an essential prerequisite for admission to the university.

16. The selection of the school which the child shall attend belongs primarily to the father, who is, however, to the extent of his ability, specially charged with the duty of securing for his child a religious training and a practical education.

17. Teachers of *Gymnasien* and other higher schools are considered officers of the state.

The *Allgemeine Landrecht* asserted, in vigorous and unequivocal terms, the authority of the state in all educational affairs. It was the first-fruits of the civic ideal; it meant the complete removal of the schools from clerical control and the restriction of private venture. The traditions of a thousand years were brushed aside with a stroke of the pen, but general acceptance of the spirit of the law was long delayed. It was the work of half a century to harmonize these principles with public opinion.

In 1850 it was decreed that "All religious organizations shall order and administer their own affairs independently [subject, of course, to the general laws of the state—a point made clear by special enactment in 1873], and shall remain in enjoyment of all their educational and charitable enterprises and foundations," and further that "Everyone is free to give instruction and to conduct educational institutions provided he first proves to the satisfaction of the proper state officials that he has the requisite moral, scientific and professional qualifications." So much is conceded to private venture, but at the same time it was affirmed that "Sufficient provision for the education of the young shall be made by means of public schools," and that "All educational institutions, public and private, shall be under the supervision of authorities appointed by the state." *Recent Modifications.*

The national ideal was still further realized by the school laws of 1872, which provided that all private schools should be subject to regular and systematic inspection by state officials, the same as public schools. In effect the present regulations permit any licensed teacher to conduct a school, but the government through its inspectors will see to it that every such school maintains at least the minimum standard of the corresponding grade of public schools. The private or sectarian school may surpass the public school, but it dare not fall behind. Thus in all essential respects it is a part of the public school system save that it draws no support from public funds.

The central authority in Prussia, charged with the administration of the school system in accordance with these principles, is the Minister for Religious, Educational and Medicinal Affairs (*Minister der geistlichen, Unterrichts- und Medicinal-Angelegenheiten*). *Administrative System.*
He is a cabinet officer and responsible only to the crown; yet any deviation from the principles above mentioned would surely occasion factional controversy, if not parliamentary inquiry. The rule of precedent is binding. More than one

minister has lost his place for attempting reforms too much at variance with established customs. As the court of last resort, the minister's chief function is to hear and determine appeals from the decisions of lower departmental officers. The rescripts and decrees of the Minister of Education thus become the basis of school administration in all parts of the kingdom.

The Minister of Education is dependent on the crown for his appointment and retention in office. He is usually a jurist by profession, a politician and diplomat by force of circumstances. He represents his department in the Prussian parliament, and introduces bills pertaining to its interests, for the enactment of which he is held, in a great measure, responsible; in fact the tenure of his office is often conditioned upon the passage of a bill on which the government has set its heart. His individual obligations are numerous. He has charge of the financial affairs of his own department; appoints, with the approval of the crown, counsellors and other officials; confers titles upon teachers, ratifies their appointments and makes promotions, except where this right has been granted to other authorities; and he is the court of final appeal in all matters connected with this branch of government.

1. Department of Education.

The Minister.

The duties of the department as a whole cover a broad field. It controls examination requirements and the privileges dependent upon them in all schools; determines the course of study; regulates tuition fees; fixes the salaries and has charge of the pensioning and retiring of teachers.

Properly speaking, Prussia has no Minister of Education. The ministry has three general departments, one each for educational, ecclesiastical and medicinal affairs. The Department of Education is presided over by an under secretary and two chief assistants (*Direktoren*), and on these officers, assisted by nineteen (in 1897) special counsellors (*Vortragende Räte*), devolves the general administration of the school system. And within the department

His Assistants.

itself there are two main subdivisions. One has charge of the common schools, normal schools, high schools for girls, and institutions for the education of defective children; the other division has the supervision of higher education, chiefly in the universities and secondary schools.

The immediate administration and supervision of secondary-school affairs is intrusted to provincial school-boards (*Provincial-Schulcollegien*), thirteen in number, one in each of the provinces of East Prussia, West Prussia, Brandenburg, Pomerania, Posen, Silesia, Saxony, Schleswig-Holstein, Hanover, Westphalia, Hesse-Nassau, the Rhine Province, and the Hohenzollern Territory. 2. Provincial School-boards.

The President of the province (*Ober-Präsident*) is chairman *ex officio* of the board. Since he is a jurist and usually unfamiliar with pedagogical affairs, his place is generally taken by the governor of the district in which the provincial capital is located. The board is composed of from three to five trained inspectors, who are selected by the minister from a long list of prominent principals of secondary schools. They receive their appointment from the crown and hold office till retired in regular order. The senior member, who is chief administrative officer, generally directs gymnasial affairs, a second member has oversight of the *Realschulen*, and a third of the *Volkschulen*. Organization.

According to the instructions of 1817 the duties of the provincial board are prescribed as follows:

1. The supervision of all pedagogical matters appertaining to educational institutions. Duties.

2. Revision of plans and ordinances of schools and educational institutions.

3. Examination of new regulations, and the revision of those already in force (including disciplinary laws, etc.); also giving advice for rectifying manifest abuses and supplying apparent needs.

4. Examination of the text-books in use, and, with the

consent of the ministry, the discontinuation of unsuitable ones and introduction of others.

5. The compilation of new text-books, which, however, cannot be printed without the consent of the minister.

6. Regulations for conducting the leaving examinations (*Maturitätsprüfung*) and revision of the reports of the same.

7. Inspection, revision, and direction of those higher schools which admit to the university.

8. Appointment, dismissal, suspension, and discipline of higher-school teachers (not directors).

The provincial school-boards are required to send to the Minister of Education once in three years a full report of their administration. They must make also an annual report of the higher schools, giving lists of graduates with their chosen occupations, the record of school attendance, the financial conditions of the various schools, etc. A semi-annual report concerning trial teachers, their location, proficiency and prospective movements, is also required. Copies of all important decisions must be immediately sent to departmental head-quarters. In short the provincial boards are expected to keep the minister fully informed of the state of school affairs throughout the provinces.

The provincial school-board, it will be seen, does not examine and certificate teachers. In order to avoid too great centralization and to place an effectual check on favouritism, that responsible duty is assigned to a special body of experts—the *Wissenschaftliche Prüfungs-Commission*; and, further, in order that this examination commission may be in closest touch with the latest scientific research and best scholarship of the times, its members are selected from the faculties of the state universities. Occasionally, however, it happens that a prominent director of a secondary school, or a provincial school inspector, is chosen to represent some subject of which he is a recognized master. The duty of this commission is to pass upon the scholarship of the candidates for teachers' positions in the secondary schools; other means, as will be seen later

3. Examination Commission.

on, are taken to test the applicants' practical ability to teach. The mere fact that leave to teach in the Prussian secondary schools depends upon the approval of two distinct authorities, one representing scholarly attainments, the other professional skill, places the Prussian teacher at once in the front rank of his profession.

The examination commission has some ten to twenty members, one or more members for each subject in which a candidate may be examined. These members are appointed by the Minister of Education for a term of one year. The seat of the commission is always a university town. East and West Prussia have but one commission, Königsberg; Silesia and Posen also unite in Breslau. *Organization.*

Prussian law requires that religion be taught in all schools; it provides, too, that each communion not only shall have the right to conduct schools of its own under the general laws of the state, but also shall be privileged to inspect the religious instruction in the public schools. The General Superintendent of the Evangelical Church in each province is specially charged with the duty of visiting each secondary school at least once in six years and reporting to the provincial school-board on the religious conditions of the schools visited, the character of the work done and changes that seem to be desirable.

A similar privilege is granted the Catholic Bishops, who are also expected to report upon their findings. It should be understood, however, that these clerical inspectors have no right to attend other classes than those in which their own religious faith is taught. Catholics, for example, may not visit classes even in religion taught by evangelical masters, much less classes in other subjects of the school course. As a matter of fact this office, though highly prized by the church for the sake of its privileges in case of emergency, is becoming more and more formal with each decade. To-day its chief function is to approve of suitable text-books for religious instruction *Supervision of Religious Affairs.*

and to advise with the provincial board on minor changes in the course of study.

4. Local School Boards.
Secondary schools under royal patronage are, as a rule, exclusively in charge of the provincial school-boards. But for some years there has been a tendency to diminish the number of these university preparatory schools with a view to the diminution of the "educated proletariat," as Bismarck called that large class in Germany who, though well-educated, are nevertheless unable to turn their knowledge to any practical account. This has touched local pride and in many cases has actually proved a stimulus to municipal ambition. The result has been the establishment within the last few years of many schools by cities and local organizations. This method of establishing schools gives rise to what are known as local school-boards which exercise more or less authority in their regulation—that is, when the school is wholly supported at municipal expense, the local board assumes control of all matters *externa* pertaining to the school; where the community merely assists in the maintenance of a public school the local officers then exercise joint rights of administration with the officers of the government. But in all internal regulations the state has exclusive power.

Organization.
The membership of local boards (*Schuldeputation*) varies. It usually consists of a standing committee of one to three members of the city council, called the *Magistrat*, including the mayor (a government appointee), a like number of elective councilmen, and the same number of citizens elected for a long term of years. In some cities, however, the *Magistrat* assumes full charge of local secondary-school affairs; sometimes, as in Berlin, Stettin, Magdeburg, Breslau and Dantzic, they choose an advisory member as inspector of schools, a city superintendent (*Stadtschulrat*) who is paid for his services.

Other schools are those under private patronage, whether founded by persons of wealth, by philanthropic associations, or by the church. To the patrons of such institutions certain rights and privileges are granted by royal charter. These are often seriously at variance with modern usage, but in a country so dependent on tradition as Germany custom prevails. The higher schools, being for the most part of more recent foundation, suffer less in this respect than do the elementary schools, where patrons, in some instances, have not only the right of nominating teachers and modifying the course of study, but even of setting the school hours before eight in the morning and after four in the afternoon, in order that the children may labour during the day in the interests of their landlords.

The powers of local school-boards, and of trustees of most schools under special endowment, are limited principally to the choice of the kind of school they will have, the nomination of teachers, and the supervision and direction of certain external affairs, such as the managing of school property, looking after the order and equipment of school premises and the necessary furnishings and repairs, the drawing up of the school estimate, the regulation of tuition fees, free scholarships, and other matters involving financial obligations, and representing the town at the annual examinations and school celebrations. *Powers of Local Boards.*

State schools are in no wise beholden to local authorities. They look directly to the provincial school-boards, to the minister, or to the crown. The city schools, too, when once in operation, are independent of local control or influence in all matters pertaining to their internal affairs. The local school-board may found a school, provide books and apparatus, adopt a schedule of salaries (which must be at least as good as the state schedule), and select a director and teachers (but only from the approved official list)—all with the knowledge and consent of the state authorities. But here its privileges end. The city may not inspect the school work, may not cut down appropriations, may not effect any change in the curriculum nor compel the introduction of a single textbook; in short the chief privileges of local boards of education in respect to established city schools are to nominate teachers and pay the bills. And these claims do not cease with the teacher's retirement from active work. The state pensions its superannuated teachers; the city cannot do less. Nor can a city alter its contract to the disadvantage of any teacher or employee. It must perform all its obligations to the letter; should it fail, the state will step in and raise the necessary funds by special assessment of city property.

Private schools exist to supply a temporary lack of educational facilities. The state will not consent to the establishment of such schools where the public schools suffice. They must comply with all the regulations of the state in regard to equipment and the conduct of the work. The course of study, the methods employed and the teachers must all be approved by the provincial school-board, to whom regular reports must be made. A provincial school inspector likewise conducts the leaving examinations in case special privileges are attached, as for example the right of one-year voluntary service in the army.

<small>Private Venture Schools.</small>

The chief responsibility in the administration of secondary-school affairs, it will be seen, rests with the members of the provincial school-board. The central authority, the *Ministerium*, formulates plans and inaugurates reforms, but even in such matters the provincial school inspectors usually have a voice. They are in daily communication with the actual work of the schools and test annually the attainments of the pupils. They know, therefore, at first hand the particular and most urgent needs of the schools, and are qualified to advise the ministry from facts of which they are personally cognizant. Furthermore, as will be explained in a later chapter, the provincial inspectors are indirectly responsible for the immediate conduct of the schools. With them rest the appointment of all teachers, the transfer of teachers from one school to another and the power to effect changes that will tend to make the schools individually more efficient. Americans are familiar with the possibilities for good inherent in the office of superintendent of city schools; the Prussian school inspectors are really "superintendents" with greatly increased powers. They are picked men, chosen especially with a view to the importance of their office and the peculiar qualifications demanded by it. The provincial school-boards are, in my opinion, the main-stay of the Prussian school system.

One often hears it said—indeed, it has been half-apologetically remarked to me by a high official in the Prussian Educational Department—that Prussia can never have a well-organized school system. Her territory is unusually diversified, ranging from the low sandy dunes of the north to the mountains of the south; the east is distinctively agricultural, the west industrial and commercial; some provinces are protestant, others mainly catholic. With such varied interests there is small chance of a school system strictly uniform in all its parts. Saxony and some of the other smaller states are pointed to with pride as being so homogeneous that one method of administration serves all sections. It is true that the schools of the smaller states are governed directly from the capital, the inspectors belong to the ministry and the entire administration is beautifully centralized. But, I think, the average American will agree with me that it is fortunate for the cause of education in Prussia that centralization cannot be carried to the extreme. The provincial school-boards, as mediators between the schools on the one hand and the ministry on the other, perform a function of inestimable value for the well-being of the Prussian state and for general educational progress in the Empire.

Merits of the Prussian System.

The higher schools of the smaller German states are controlled by a central board, usually a bureau of some state department, presided over by a minister of the crown. Much the same conditions obtain as in a Prussian province, and the central educational department is similar in function to the provincial board of Prussia. There is, however, this important distinction: the smaller the state the greater the power of the government for good or ill; the larger the state the more chance for local influence. The distinctive peculiarity of the Prussian system is its semi-

In Other States.

independent provincial boards, certain members of which are exclusively concerned with the management of secondary schools. They maintain the balance between extreme centralization and local option. The provincial inspector of schools is the very heart of the Prussian higher-school system.

GENERAL REFERENCES :—Wiese, *Das höhere Schulwesen in Preussen;* Wiese-Kübler, *Gesetze und Verordnungen ;* Baumeister's *Handbuch der Erziehungs- und Unterrichtslehre,* Vol. I., Pt. II.—*Die Einrichtung und Verwaltung des höheren Schulwesens in Preussen, u. s. w.;* Mushacke's *Schulkalendar—Statistisches Jahrbuch der höheren Schulen und heilpädagogischen Anstalten Deutschlands.*

CHAPTER VI.

THE HIGHER SCHOOLS OF PRUSSIA

GERMANY is nothing if not military. The school system is pervaded by the military spirit; many of the teachers are reserve officers, most of the pupils hope to be, and all know that army service awaits them at the end of the school days. The really impor- *The Military Spirit.* tant problem for the school-boy's consideration is whether he shall serve for two years as an ordinary conscript living in the barracks, a servant to some superior, or whether he shall serve but one year, living where he will and always standing in line of promotion. This latter privilege is a prize most alluring to the German youth; it can be won only by successfully completing a six-year course in an approved higher school (*Höhere Schule*).

There is perhaps no better criterion of what constitutes a higher school from the German point of view than the requirements for the one-year volunteer service in the army. This school differs from the ele- *Definition of Higher School.* mentary school in that it offers instruction beyond the necessities of life; it differs from the technical school in that its aim is a liberal education; and it prepares for the university and institutions of scientific research. An approved higher school must teach at least two foreign languages, geography, history, German literature, mathematics and natural science.

Technological and trade schools (*Gewerbe und Fachschulen*), agricultural schools (*Landwirtschaftschulen*), normal schools (*Schullehrer- und Lehrerinnen-Seminarien*) and mil-

itary schools (*Cadetten-Corps*) are, therefore, outside of the scope of the present work. The conditions imposed above give the following classification of the higher schools of Germany:
1. *Gymnasien* and *Progymnasien*.
2. *Realgymnasien* and *Realprogymnasien*.
3. *Oberrealschulen, Realschulen* and *Höhere Bürgerschulen*.
4. Special schools with approved curricula.

The aim of the *Gymnasium* is "to prepare its students through a broad humanistic training for the independent study of the arts and sciences." Paulsen says, "The ideal of the new education is a human being whose faculties enable him to form a clear and definite conception of the actual world; who, by virtue of his will, is able to recognize and follow his original bent; whose imagination and fine emotions are trained to the perception of the beautiful and the heroic. This is a man in the full sense of the word: this is true humanistic culture." At all times the *allgemeine wissenschaftliche Bildung* of the pupil is to be regarded as the chief function of the *Gymnasien*. Recently the term *Humanistische Gymnasien* has been employed to differentiate these schools from the *Realgymnasien*, which have given somewhat more attention to the practical side of education.

1. The Prussian Gymnasium.

Its Aim.

The Prussian *Gymnasium* has nine classes in three divisions of three classes each. The lower classes are *Sexta, Quinta* and *Quarta;* the middle classes, *Untertertia, Obertertia* and *Untersecunda;* and the upper classes, *Obersecunda, Unterprima* and *Oberprima.* One entire school year is given to each class. Admission to the *Gymnasium* requires that the pupil be at least nine years of age, and that he shall have had a three years' preparatory course in reading, writing, arithmetic and religion. This preparatory training may be obtained in the elementary schools, private and public, and in the special *Vorschulen* connected with many *Gymnasien*.

Classes.

The curriculum (*Lehrplan*) of the *Gymnasien*, as of all public schools, is outlined by the government, but considerable freedom is left to the school and to individual teachers both in the selection of material for instruction and in the methods of presentation. Two general divisions are made in the subjects of the course: (1) *Wissenschaftliche Fächer*, under which are classed religion, the German language and literature, Latin, Greek, French (English and Hebrew as electives), history and geography, mathematics, and natural sciences; (2) *Künste und Fertigkeiten*, including drawing, writing, singing and gymnastics. The course of study, as prescribed by ministerial rescript of January 6, 1892, for the Prussian *Gymnasien*, is as follows:

Curriculum.

LEHRPLAN OF THE PRUSSIAN GYMNASIEN.

Subjects.	VI.	V.	IV.	IIIb.	IIIa.	IIb.	IIa.	Ib.	Ia.	Total Week-Hours.
Religion	3	2	2	2	2	2	2	2	2	19
German and History Stories	3} 4 1}	2} 3 1}	3	2	2	3	3	3	3	26
Latin	8	8	7	7	7	6	6	6	6	62
Greek	..	..	..	6	6	6	6	6	6	36
French	..	..	4	3	3	3	2	2	2	19
English (Elective)	..	..	..	..	..	..	..	..	..	..
Hebrew (Elective)	..	..	..	..	..	..	..	..	..	..
History and Geography	2	2	2} 4 2}	2} 3 1}	2} 3 1}	2} 3 1}	3	3	3	26
Mathematics	4	4	4	3	3	4	4	4	4	34
Natural History	2	2	2	2	..	..	..	..	..	8
Physics, Elements of Chemistry and Mineralogy	..	..	..	..	2	2	2	2	2	10
Writing	2	2	..	..	..	..	..	..	..	4
Drawing	..	2	2	2	2	..	..	..	..	8
Singing	2	2	..	..	..	..	..	..	..	4
Gymnastics	3	3	3	3	3	3	3	3	3	27
Totals	30	30	31	33	33	33	31	31	31	283

The gymnasial curricula of the other German states are closely modelled after the Prussian type. The southern states, however, as is indicated in the following comparative table of week-hours, show a disposition to give relatively more time to the classics and less to mathematics and science.

In Other States.

Comparative Table of Gymnasial Curricula.

Subjects.	Prussia.	Bavaria.	Saxony.	Würtemberg.	Hamburg.	Weimar.
Religion	19	18	20	18	18	19
German	26	27	25	24	21	23
Latin	62	66	71–73	81	69	72
Greek	36	36	40–42	40	36	40
French	19	10	18	18	19	18
History and Geography	26	25	29	24	28	28
Mathematics	34	33	33	33	29	30
Physics	10					8
Natural History	8	5	15	14	16	10
Writing	4	4	3	4	4	4
Drawing	8	4	4	7	10	6
Totals (exclusive of Singing and Gymnastics)	252	228	258–62	263	250	256

The *Progymnasien* are *Gymnasien* lacking some of the higher classes. They are usually found in the smaller towns,

Progymnasium. where few pupils remain after completing the six years' course required for one year's voluntary service in the army. Those pupils who would naturally advance into the upper classes are sent to some neighboring town. Hence, as a rule, the *Progymnasien* have only the lower and middle classes, *i.e.*, a six years' course.

The *Gymnasien* are the classical preparatory schools for the universities. All roads to the learned professions and to

Position of the Gymnasium. the higher posts in the civil and military service lead out from these schools. Historically, they are the centre and strength of the German school system ; and while schools of a different nature have been established with a view to modern economic needs, popular prejudice is so strong that only graduates of the *Gymnasien* are regarded as cultured. The classics may be a fetich, but for the German mind they have a charm too powerful to be easily broken. "The classical literature is, and will continue to be, the source of all our culture. It must remain, therefore, not only an indispensable, but by far the most important study in our higher schools." This thought, expressed a century ago by Frederick Gedike, the first *Oberschulrat* of Prussia, has been the guiding principle of the *Gymnasien* to the present time.

In 1897 there were in Germany 439 *Gymnasien* and 92 *Progymnasien*, of which 277 *Gymnasien* and 53 *Progymnasien* were in Prussia. Bavaria stands next with 40 *Gymnasien*, and Saxony and Alsace-Lorraine each have 17; Würtemberg has 16 *Gymnasien* and 3 *Progymnasien;* Baden, 14 of the former and 2 of the latter. The other states of the empire have from 1 to 9 each. In 1895-96 the attendance at the Prussian *Gymnasien* was 76,078, and at the *Progymnasien*, 4,544, or about fifty-seven per cent. of the total number of pupils in the secondary schools.

Numbers and Attendance.

"The aim of the *Realgymnasien*, as of the humanistic *Gymnasien*, is to give the youth a liberal education founded, however, especially on instruction in the modern languages, mathematics and the natural sciences." The class divisions and the general requirements are the same as in the *Gymnasien*, but the curriculum is somewhat different. English takes the place of Greek, and more time is devoted to French and the natural sciences. The *Lehrplan* of these schools in Prussia is as follows:

2. The Prussian Realgymnasium.

LEHRPLAN OF THE PRUSSIAN REALGYMNASIEN.

Subjects.	VI.	V.	IV.	IIIb.	IIIa.	IIb.	IIa.	Ib.	Ia.	Total Week-Hours.
Religion	3	2	2	2	2	2	2	2	2	19
German and History Stories	3 \} 4 1 \}	2 \} 3 1 \}	3	3	3	3	3	3	3	28
Latin	8	8	7	4	4	3	3	3	3	43
French	..	..	5	5	5	4	4	4	4	31
English	..	..	..	..	3	3	3	3	3	18
History and Geography	\} 2	\} 2	2 \} 4 2 \}	2 \} 4 2 \}	2 \} 4 2 \}	2 \} 3 1 \}	3	3	3	28
Mathematics	4	4	4	5	5	5	5	5	5	42
Natural History	2	2	2	2	2	2	..	..	..	12
Physics	..	..	..	..	..	3	3	3	3	12
Chemistry and Mineralogy	..	..	..	..	..	..	2	2	2	6
Writing	2	2	..	..	..	..	..	..	..	4
Drawing	..	2	2	2	2	2	2	2	2	16
Singing	2	2	..	..	..	..	..	..	..	4
Gymnastics	3	3	3	3	3	3	3	3	3	27
Totals	30	30	32	33	33	33	33	33	33	290

In accordance with the recommendation of the King and of the Berlin Conference of December, 1890, the Prussian ministry has persistently sought to do away with the *Realgymnasien*. As a consequence, the attendance at these schools has decreased and some of them have adopted another curriculum. But even in Prussia, *Realgymnasien* still exist, and are likely to outlive the King who signed their death-warrant. Saxony has always stoutly defended the *Realgymnasien*, and, in fact, the southern states in general support them with greater liberality than does Prussia. This is evident in the following comparison of the number of week-hours allotted to the different subjects in the various states.

Policy of the Government.

COMPARATIVE TABLE OF REALGYMNASIAL CURRICULA.

Subjects.	Prussia.	Bavaria.	Saxony.	Würtemberg.	Hamburg.	Weimar.
Religion................	19	18	21	14	18	18
German	28	27	29	20	28	27
Latin.......	43	60	54	74½	53	54
French.................	31	20	34	27	24	32
English................	18	13	18	11	19	20
History and Geography..	28	26	30	22½	25	30
Mathematics	42	38	44	59	38	44
Natural History........	12	7	12	8½	18	12
Physics.................	12	6	12	8½	11	12
Chemistry and Mineralogy....................	6	5	6	2	8	6
Writing	4	4	3	5	4	4
Drawing................	16	23	18	25½	18	18
Totals (exclusive of Singing and Gymnastics) .	259	247	281	277½	264	277

The *Realgymnasium* arose to supply an actual want in the German school system. Yet from the beginning tradition has retarded its progress, and whatever gains have been made are the results of long and persistent struggle. Its curriculum is of especial interest to Americans, inasmuch as it more nearly corresponds to the course of study of the American high school. The likeness is even more striking when Greek is admitted as an elective, as is the case in some *Realgymnasien* of Alsace-Lorraine. The policy of retaining the *Realgym-*

Position of Realgymnasium.

nasium, and the pedagogical principles involved, will be discussed in a subsequent chapter. It is sufficient to say at this point that graduates of the *Realgymnasium* are admitted to university courses in mathematics, the natural sciences and modern languages, and to all technological schools. They are, however, denied admission to the professions of law, medicine and theology, and to certain coveted positions in the civil service. The slight put upon this school, especially by the Prussian government and the medical fraternity, serves to retard its progress and hamper its usefulness.

There are in Germany 128 *Realgymnasien* and 93 *Realprogymnasien*. Of the former there are 85 in Prussia, 10 in Saxony, 5 in Bavaria and 3 in Würtemberg; of the latter, Prussia claims 67 and Würtemberg 4. In each of the other states there are less than 10 of both kinds. In 1896 the Prussian *Realgymnasien* enrolled 24,534 pupils, the *Realprogymnasien* 6,465, making in all twenty-three per cent. of the total number of higher-school pupils in the kingdom.[1]

<small>Numbers and Attendance.</small>

Higher schools in which the classical languages are not taught are called *Realschulen*. Their normal number of classes is six; the *Oberrealschulen*, however, have three extra classes. The term *Höhere Bürgerschulen*, as applied to approved higher schools, is fast falling into disuse; it properly belongs to a high-grade elementary school. The *Realschulen* aim to fit their students for more effectual and intelligent participation in the actual business affairs of life; hence they place particular emphasis on the modern languages and the natural sciences. Graduates of the *Oberrealschulen* are admitted to university courses in mathematics and the natural sciences, and may eventually become teachers of these branches in the secondary schools. On the whole, their social standing is about on a par with the graduates of the *Realgymnasien;*

<small>3. Prussian Realschulen.</small>

---

[1] *Statistisches Jahrbuch der höheren Schulen*, 1897–1898.

both are commonly looked upon as inferior to the classical student. It is the special policy of the Prussian ministry to multiply the number of these schools at the expense of both the *Gymnasien* and the *Realgymnasien*. Their students are prepared to follow practical lines of activity, and to them the nation looks for leaders in industrial pursuits.

The curriculum of the Prussian *Oberrealschulen* is as follows:

LEHRPLAN OF THE PRUSSIAN OBERREALSCHULEN.

Subjects.	VI.	V.	IV.	IIIb.	IIIa.	IIb.	IIa.	Ib.	Ia.	Total Week-Hours.
Religion............	3	2	2	2	2	2	2	2	2	19
German and...... History Stories	4} 5 1}	3} 4 1}	4	3	3	3	4	4	4	34
French............	6	6	6	6	6	5	4	4	4	47
English...........	..	..	..	5	4	4	4	4	4	25
History and .... Geography	}2	2	2}4 2}	2}4 2}	2}4 2}	2}3 1}	3	3	3	28
Mathematics......	5	5	6	6	5	5	5	5	5	47
Natural History...	2	2	2	2	2	2	..	..	..	12
Physics...........	..	..	..	..	2	2	3	3	3	13
Chemistry and Mineralogy	..	..	..	..	..	2	3	3	3	11
Writing..	2	2	2	..	..	..	..	..	..	6
Free-Hand Drawing	..	2	2	2	2	2	2	2	2	16
Singing...........	2	2	..	..	..	..	..	..	..	4
Gymnastics........	3	3	3	3	3	3	3	3	3	27
Totals	30	30	31	33	33	33	33	33	33	289

Numbers.

Prussia had, in 1896, 26 *Oberrealschulen* and 60 *Realschulen;* Würtemberg had 6 *Oberrealschulen*, Baden had 3, Alsace-Lorraine had 3, and Oldenburg and Brandenburg each had 1; in the other states there were no schools of this kind. Bavaria had 46 *Realschulen;* Saxony, 23; Würtemberg, 9; Baden, 14; Hesse, 16; Alsace-Lorraine, 8; and all the remaining states, 22. This gives a total of 40 *Oberrealschulen* and 198 *Realschulen* in the empire.

The *Lehrplan* of the *Oberrealschulen* of Würtemberg for the last nine years of the course assigns to religion 19 weekhours; German, 28; French, 55; English, 18; history and geography, 28; mathematics, 83; natural history, 10; physics and chemistry, 10; writing, 6; and drawing, 25. The other states follow more closely the Prussian plan.

High schools attended by both sexes are unknown in Germany. Coeducation, so far as it exists at all, is restricted to the *Volksschulen*, where the pupils are under fourteen years of age. In fact, the secondary education of girls is largely a matter of convenience. In Prussia there are 568 higher schools for boys, and only 128 for girls. Of the boys' schools 272 are supported wholly or in part by the state; while only four girls' schools receive any state aid.[1] This means that girls' schools are almost exclusively under city patronage, or on special foundations, or exist for private gain; and, as a natural consequence, there is little uniformity in respect either to curriculum or methods. Moreover, uniformity has been unnecessary, since no special privileges have been attached to graduation from a girls' higher school. Women are not wanted in the university; hence there is no need of a gymnasial course of study. They are worthless as soldiers; hence no advantage in a specified curriculum that grants the privilege of one year of voluntary service in the army. Nevertheless, some needed reforms have been brought about within the past four or five years.[2]

4. Other Secondary Schools.

Girls' Schools.

An association of women teachers (*Allgemeiner Deutscher Lehrerinnen-Verein*) was formed in 1890 for the express purpose of advancing their professional standing. Their main object was to obtain the right to teach in the higher classes of the *Höhere Mädchenschulen*. It was argued that young women in the advanced grades of the secondary schools should not be taught exclusively by men; the sub-

---

[1] *Cf.* Wychgram, *Handbuch des höheren Mädchenschulwesens*, Leipsic, 1897, p. 55.

[2] See: Von der Decken, *Die gebildete Frau und die neue Zeit*, Göttingen; Ichenhäuser, *Die Ausnahmestellung Deutschlands in Sachen des Frauenstudiums*, Berlin; and files of *Die Frauenbewegung*, *Die Frau* and *Neue Bahnen*.

jects of religion, German and history at least, it was modestly suggested, could be satisfactorily presented by women. But this involved the problem of university training for women. Candidates for the position of teacher are required to pass a state examination; and in order to do this there must be adequate preparation. Women with the indiscriminate training of a girls' higher school could not aspire to the positions occupied by university men.

<small>Women as Teachers.</small>

The first step, therefore, toward a fixed curriculum for these schools was taken under the necessity of knowing with what sort of preparation women should undertake higher study.

A ministerial rescript, dated May 31, 1894, fixes a curriculum for the *Höhere Mädchenschulen*. It also provides for the appointment of women to any position in the upper grades, and requires that a woman be made associate principal in case a man is the head of the school, and that one of the three head teachers in any event be a woman. This is the first important concession made to women teachers by the Prussian government; and it fixes the minimum standard of the preparation expected of them.

<small>Present Status of Girls' Schools.</small>

Up to 1897 only thirty-nine girls' schools had been placed under the jurisdiction of the Prussian provincial school-boards, and thus given equal rank with the higher schools for boys. By far the larger part of girls' schools are thereby relegated to the rank of *Mittelschulen,* or high grade elementary schools; but for all schools in which two foreign languages are taught there are now the same ideals and a common standard. The activity and persistency manifested by the various organizations of women is turning public attention to the education of girls. There is promise of better things in the near future. The curriculum of the girls' higher schools in Prussia is as follows:

LEHRPLAN OF THE PRUSSIAN HÖHERE MÄDCHENSCHULEN.

Subjects.	Lower Division.			Middle Division.			Upper Division.			Total Week Hours.
	IX.	VIII.	VII.	VI.	V.	IV.	III.	II.	I.	
Religion............	3	3	3	3	3	3	2	2	2	24
German.............	10	9	8	5	5	5	4	4	4	54
French¹.............	..	..	..	5	5	5	4	4	4	27
English.............	..	..	..	..	..	..	4	4	4	12
Arithmetic........	3	3	3	3	3	3	2	2	2	24
History............	..	..	..	..	2	2	2	2	2	10
Geography.........	..	..	2	2	2	2	2	2	2	14
Natural Sciences....	..	..	..	2	2	2	2	2	2	12
Drawing............	..	..	..	..	}2	2	2	2	2	10 (8)
Writing............	..	3	2	2		..	..	..	..	7 (9)
Sewing, etc.........	..	..	2	2	2	2	2	2	2	14
Singing............	}2	}2	}2	2	2	2	2	2	2	12 (18)
Gymnastics.........				2	2	2	2	2	2	18 (12)
Totals.............	18	20	22	28	30	30	30	30	30	238

Pupils enter the *Mädchenschulen* at six years of age, there being no special *Vorschulen*, as for the boys' schools. The course of nine years, therefore, places the school in the same class as the *Progymnasien*, *Realprogymnasien* and *Realschulen*, which graduate their students normally at the age of sixteen years.

The reader may inquire whether German girls receive no school training after they are sixteen. According to the present Minister of Education, a twelve years' course of uninterrupted study would make such demands on the mental and physical powers of the girls that after graduation they would be unfitted for life's work. "It is further to be presumed that a girl who has gathered as much knowledge as is possible in a nine years' course under the favorable circumstances which now obtain in the *Höhere Mädchenschulen* will feel the need of specializing in particular branches, without being compelled to pursue studies for which she has no special liking or talents." Those who advocate the higher education of women pronounce such manifestoes as merely another way of saying

Attitude of the Government.

that men must continue to monopolize all positions in the learned professions.

The first attempt to give graduates of the *Höhere Mädchenschulen* a complete gymnasial training was made in Berlin, where a school was organized for the purpose in October, 1893. It has since been conducted by Fräulein Helene Lange, one of the foremost advocates of women's rights in Germany. The school aims to fit graduates of the *Höhere Mädchenschulen* in four years for the *Abiturienten-Examen,* which carries with it the privilege of university study. It remains to be seen, however, whether the Prussian universities will open their doors to women, even though they are as well qualified for entrance as young men. Some of them have already conceded the point, but many obstacles are yet to be overcome before it can be said that the German universities are coeducational institutions.

Girls' Gymnasien.

In 1893 a girls' *Gymnasium* was also opened at Carlsruhe, under the auspices of the *Frauenbildung-Reform-Verein.* Pupils entering this school must be at least twelve years of age; and after one year's preparation in a connecting class, they are expected to finish the regular classical course of the boys' school in five years. A similar school was established at Leipsic, in April, 1894, by the *Allgemeiner Deutscher Frauen-Verein,* under the principalship of Fräulein von Windscheid, the first woman to receive the degree of Ph.D. from the University of Heidelberg. The course is four years, and pupils must be fifteen years old at entrance. A similar school is under way in Munich.

In all these schools the curricula are planned to supplement the earlier training of the girls, that they may graduate on a level with the boys of the *Gymnasien.* They are recognised by the authorities to the extent of being allowed to exist, and it is probable that some means will be found to enable their graduates to continue their work at the universities. Heidelberg already admits women to the department of Science-Mathematics,

Women in the University.

and grants them the degree of Ph.D. if all the work has been done there. Göttingen allows women as "auditors," and has granted several Ph.D.'s to women. Freiburg admits women as guests in the departments of philosophy and medicine. Leipsic permits them to register and pay tuition fees, but professors have no legal right to receive them in the lecture-rooms. "We simply don't see them, if they happen to be there," a member of the faculty once naïvely remarked to me. All other German universities do not tolerate women at all, or hedge the privilege about to such an extent that very few can secure entrance.[1]

The public day schools of Germany are so peculiarly German, such perfect expressions of the national policy in education, that little is heard of that other class so prominent in England and America—the boarding-school. It exists, nevertheless, and is no less German than the former. There are private institutions, too, of all grades, though but few are recognised as "schools." The higher education of girls is mostly in private hands, or supported only in part by the community. In the city of Hamburg, for example, with 11 public and 7 private higher schools for boys, there are for girls 5 public and 65 private secondary schools. Of the Berlin higher schools, 38 are for boys and 32 for girls; all of the boys' schools are public, but only 9 of the girls' schools receive any state or city aid.[2]

Private Schools.

Church schools—evangelical, catholic and jewish—are plentiful and generally have boarding departments. Schools for backward pupils, and commercial and technical schools, are usually private or local. But of all the influences which tend to promote private schools for boys the strongest is the privilege of the one-year volun-

Church Schools.

---

[1] See *Die akademische Frau: Gutachten hervorragender Universitätsprofessoren, Frauenlehrer und Schriftsteller über die Befähigung der Frau zum wissenschaftlichen Studium und Berufe*, edited by Kirchhof, Berlin.

[2] Statistics of 1893.

teer service in the army; this may be secured only on the completion of a six years' course of study in a privileged higher school, or upon examination by a governmental board. It is possible for students dropped from the public schools, or for those who, from choice or necessity, would take a shorter course, to find instruction in private institutions whose sole aim is to fit for the state examination. As before stated, these are not "schools" from the German point of view, but *Fabriken* or *Pressen*—either term being suggestive enough of the methods employed.

The necessity for private venture in the education of girls naturally gives rise to many "finishing" schools, in which social rank plays a conspicuous *rôle*. The more pretentious the rank, the more likely is it to be a boarding-school. Many of these schools are under the honorary protection of the various German courts, and thereby enjoy decided popularity. Institutions for the education of backward pupils, as those for orphans and others of charitable aim, are naturally home schools. At the head of such institutions stands the renowned *Franckesche Stiftungen* in Halle, a group of schools of different grades for orphans of both sexes. But the question of home accommodations for higher school pupils, irrespective of sex, class or condition, is really more serious than in America. In Germany there are some 25,000 post-offices, each of which represents a centre of population. The pastor, physician and school-master, not to mention wealthy peasants and government officials, may aspire to give their sons the higher training. But in all Germany there are but 1,173 privileged higher schools, and the condition is made still clearer when one learns that the twenty-five largest cities have two hundred and eight of these schools. Or, to put it in another way, there are in Germany about 2,500 cities and towns of over 2,000 inhabitants, and these have less than forty per cent. of the total population. The number of boys that must leave home at nine or ten years of age to begin their university preparation is presumably greater than in the United States, where the 4,500 high schools have a total enrolment not appreciably larger than obtains in the German schools. But because of the uniform excellence of the public schools, and from motives of economy, the average country lad will make his home with a family residing near a public school which he enters as a day pupil.

The better grade boarding-schools are recruited mainly from two sources, the nobility and the commercial class. The gymnasial course leading to the university and to the highest posts in the army and civil service will naturally be sought by the former; the aim of the latter is to secure the privilege of but one year of army service and a practical preparation for business life.

Private venture schools are not suffered to exist in Germany unless they satisfy an actual public need, and have the ability to maintain the governmental standard. They must also conform to the prescribed curricula for secondary schools, if they would secure the privileges granted to schools of that grade. Girls' schools in general, and boys' schools, too, beyond the fixed requirements, may exercise considerable freedom in regulating their work along special lines. *Restrictions on Private Venture.*

The German school system is not designed to lead pupils step by step from the kindergarten to the university, to form a connected series of grades, each of which is the natural development of the preceding one. The elementary and secondary schools are quite independent of each other. It is true that certain *Mittelschulen*, technological and trade schools, receive pupils from the *Volkschulen*, but not one boy in ten thousand finds his way from the highest class of the elementary school into the *Gymnasium*. The parent is obliged to choose a school for his nine-year old son, and on this selection depends in a large measure the boy's future career. The necessity of practically determining the trend of a boy's education before his personality is adequately known, places a responsibility upon many parents which they cannot properly discharge. *Interrelations of Schools.*

Errors of judgment often result in the transference of pupils, after two or three years of training, from one kind of school to another better adapted to their abilities. The difficulties thereby encountered are obvious from a comparison of the various courses of study outlined in this chapter.

In Frankfort-on-the-Main a noteworthy attempt has been made, since Easter, 1892, to remedy these evils, and at the same time to infuse more life into the studies of the secondary schools by introducing shorter and more intensive courses. The plan, as designed by Dr. Karl Reinhardt, Director of the *Städtisches Gymnasium*, prescribes the same curriculum during the first three school-years for the *Gymnasium*, the *Realgymnasium* and the *Oberrealschule*. In this way transference is comparatively easy between all schools for three years ; and between the *Gymnasium* and the *Realgymnasium* it is possible as late as the beginning of the sixth school year. Inasmuch as the Frankfort plan has received the sanction of the Prussian Department of Education, and has been adopted in many places, it deserves mention here among the curricula of the approved higher schools.

The Frankfort Plan.

LEHRPLÄNE OF FRANKFORT GYMNASIUM AND REALGYMNASIUM.

Subjects.	VI.	V.	IV	IIIb.		IIIa.		IIb.		IIa.		Ib.		Ia.		Total Week-Hours.	
	Gym. & RG.			G.	RG.	G.	RG.	G.	RG.	G.	RG.	G.	RG.	G.	RG.	G.	RG.
Religion.......	3	2	2	2	2	2	2	2	2	2	2	2	2	2	2	19	19
German.......	5	4	4	3	3	3	3	3	3	3	3	3	3	3	3	31	31
Latin	..	..	..	10	8	10	8	8	6	8	6	8	6	8	6	52	40
Greek...	..	..	..	..	..	..	..	8	..	8	..	8	..	8	..	32	..
French........	..	6	6	2	4	2	4	2	3	2	3	2	3	2	3	30	38
English	..	..	..	..	..	..	..	..	6	..	4	..	4	..	4	..	18
History and Geography...	2	2	5	3	3	3	3	2	3	2	3	2	3	3	3	24	27
Mathematics .	5	5	5	4	4	4	4	3	4	4	5	4	5	3	5	37	42
Natural History	2	2	2	2	2	2	2	..	..	..	..	..	..	..	..	10	10
Physics	..	..	..	..	..	..	..	2	3	2	2	2	2	2	2	8	9
Chemistry	..	..	..	..	..	..	..	..	..	..	2	..	2	..	2	..	6
Writing...	2	2	..	..	..	..	..	..	..	..	..	..	..	..	..	4	4
Drawing.......	..	2	2	2	2	2	2	..	2	..	2	..	2	..	2	8	16
Totals	25	25	26	28	28	28	28	30	32	31	32	31	32	31	32	255	260

In the lower classes French is strongly emphasized, and is taught with special reference to the Latin that follows. Latin is introduced in the third year and studied only six years, and Greek is reduced to four years. As compared with the regular gymnasial program, the mother-tongue gets ten more week-hours; Latin, twenty-five hours less; Greek, eight hours less; mathematics, three hours more; French, nine hours more; history, four hours less; drawing, two hours more. The aim is to arrive at results as good as those attained by following the regular course, the difference being in the method of procedure. The final outcome of the scheme is awaited with intense interest both by its friends and foes. On its success or failure depends a possible solution of one of the most important pedagogical problems before the German educationists of the present time.

<small>Comparison with Regular Courses.</small>

GENERAL REFERENCES:—Wiese-Kübler, *Gesetze und Verordnungen; Lehrpläne und Lehraufgaben für die höheren Schulen,* Berlin, 1893; Schwartz, *Der Organismus der Gymnasien in seiner praktischen Gestaltung,* Berlin, 1876; *Statistisches Jahrbuch der höheren Schulen Deutschlands;* Kunze, *Kalendar für das höhere Schulwesen Preussens,* Breslau, 1894; Wychgram, *Handbuch des höheren Mädchenschulwesens,* Leipsic, 1897; Lange, *Entwicklung und Stand des höheren Mädchenschulwesens in Deutschland,* Berlin, 1893; Reinhardt, *Die Frankfurter Lehrpläne,* Frankfort, 1892; *Centralblatt,* and Encyclopedias of Schmid and Rein.

CHAPTER VII

FOUNDATION AND MAINTENANCE OF HIGHER SCHOOLS

THE *Gymnasium* was originally founded by the Church as a professional school for the training of the clergy. It was intended to teach especially what was considered necessary for a priest of the Church to know. The languages of the Bible and of the Church Fathers — Latin, Greek and Hebrew — were all-important, Latin above all others. Under the influence of the Renaissance and the Reformation these schools assumed a more general character, and yet in Germany their main purpose was unaltered. The Protestant Church, inspired with the worth of each immortal soul, demanded for its ministers a more liberal education than had been deemed necessary for the clergy of the Church of Rome. Schools prepared to afford this training—the highest in the land—in time were opened to any one who desired a preparation for the higher intellectual life. The sphere of their influence was extended, while their main purpose remained as before.

<small>Origin of the Gymnasium.</small>

Many of the early ecclesiastical foundations remain at the present day. The oldest of the existent classical schools of Germany was founded in Fulda in the eighth century. It is still catholic, although now supported by the Prussian government. The *Gymnasium* at Osnabrück, known as the Carolinum, was established under charter of Charles the Great, dated December 19, 804. Another interesting old school, founded by the Roman Church in the first quarter of the ninth century, is the *Gymnasium* of Hildesheim. It was taken over by the

<small>Old Schools still Existent.</small>

Jesuits in 1595, and is still supported by the Church. Of the other catholic *Gymnasien* of modern Prussia, one was founded in 1450, another in 1474, and seven between 1545 and 1580. The comparatively large number of classical schools still in existence which were established in the latter half of the sixteenth century is an interesting commentary on the work of the Jesuits. In addition to those already mentioned, no fewer than twenty-one of the present Prussian *Gymnasien* were originally on catholic foundations, but went over to the protestants at the time of the Reformation. One of these schools (Zeitz) had been established as early as 968—two in the twelfth century, five in the thirteenth, nine in the fourteenth, one in the fifteenth, and three in the sixteenth. For example, the city *Gymnasium* of Königsberg was founded in 1335 by the municipal authorities as a parochial school in connection with the Roman Catholic Church. Under the influence of the head-master who was in charge from 1518 to 1541, himself a convert to Luther's preaching, it became a protestant Latin school. The *Kneipfhöfisches Gymnasium* (Königsberg), founded probably as early as 1304 as a cathedral school, went over to the Lutherans at about the same time. The *Köllnisches Gymnasium* of Berlin, probably the oldest classical school of the province, has been protestant since 1540. The present site of the Berlin *Gymnasium zum grauen Kloster* belonged to the Franciscans from 1290 to 1539, when the monastery was closed. Elector Johann George afterward presented one-third of the cloister to the present *Gymnasium*, which opened for the first time in 1574. It is something to be thankful for that in those days "conscience money" went for educational purposes.

Schools on protestant foundations date, for the most part, from the sixteenth century. The steady progress of education and the extension of the school system under the guidance of Luther and Melanchthon are evident from the number of schools still existing in Prussia which sprang up in the sixteenth century. Three of the leading protestant *Gymnasien* of modern Prussia

Old Protestant Schools.

were established prior to 1530, five others between 1530 and 1540, twelve between 1540 and 1550, and twenty-four others before the close of the century. The majority of these schools were supported by the municipalities in which they were located. Occasionally one received special endowment from some wealthy citizen. Two in particular deserve special mention: one, Pforta, which owes its origin to the generosity of Duke Maurice of Saxony, who endowed it in 1543 with the Cistercian Abbey of St. Mary's, on the banks of the Saale, not far distant from Naumburg, the other, Rossleben, a cloistral school founded in 1554 by a nobleman of the province. I shall make mention later of some of the striking characteristics of these two old boarding-schools.

There are in Prussia at the present time two hundred and seventy-seven *Gymnasien*. Of this number it will be seen that seventy-seven, or nearly one-fourth, were established before 1600. In the seventeenth century only thirty-three of the now existent Prussian *Gymnasien* were established, and most of these were on catholic foundations. Some of the notable exceptions are the *Joachimsthalsches Gymnasium* of Berlin (1607), the *Francke'sche Stiftungen* in Halle (1695-1697) and the *Französisches Gymnasium* of Berlin (1689).

Foundation of Prussian Schools.

Mention should be made in this place of some of the renowned schools of the other German states. There is so much of the life of the German people, so many interesting facts connected with their history, stored up in these venerable institutions, that I find myself seriously tempted to stray from the narrow lines of this chapter. The *Fürstenschulen* of Meissen and Grimma in Saxony stand side by side with Pforta as monuments of the Elector Maurice. Then in Leipsic are the famous *Thomas-Schule* (1221), and the *Nicolai Gymnasium* which was founded by a bull of Boniface IX. in 1395. Hamburg boasts of the *Gelehrtenschule des Johanneums*, of which Johann Bugenhagen, Luther's apostle to the low Germans, was the first master. The protestant *Gymnasium* of Strassburg dates

In Other States.

from 1538, when Sturm began his work in that city. Tübingen, Stuttgart, Munich, Augsburg, Würzburg, Nüremberg, and many other cities of South Germany have schools that have come down from the sixteenth century.

The tendency in Prussia, as indeed in all the German states, has been for the government to absorb schools on special foundations, and by taking over their endowments to make them purely state schools. **Difficulties of Administration.** In some instances this has been done with a view to the equalization of school funds; but inasmuch as there is no comprehensive school law in Prussia many serious complications still continue. There are schools existing by special charter which have done a great work in the past, yet whose funds are now so depreciated that retrenchment must follow if state aid cannot be secured; there are schools established by municipalities to which the government makes annual grants; there are state schools supported in part by local rates; there are others which have several sources of income. This mixed state of affairs, which often renders it necessary to search back to records even five or six hundred years old in order to settle some detail of administration, is very unsatisfactory to the school and highly exasperating to the officials. An inspector once told me of a village school in his jurisdiction the teacher of which must look to eighteen different sources for his small income. He gets a fee for being church chorister; something more for conducting an evening continuation school; and even observances long obsolete, such as personally greeting all the families of the village on Christmas day, have each their particular cash value. Now when custom decrees that Christmas calls are no longer the mode, how is the poor school-master to get that portion of his salary which is dependent on this labour of love? Such problems are of vital interest—to the school-masters—and the government cannot pass them by. But it is no easy task to adjust these old legacies to modern requirements; often special acts of Parliament are necessary to overcome conditions imposed by charters centuries old. There are weak

Gymnasien, too, that would gladly become *Realschulen*, save that some clause in a charter centuries old requires that Latin be taught in that school for all eternity. Between giving up Latin and abandoning the foundation there can be no question. The dead hand rules. Herein are some of the disadvantages of tradition.

The lower schools are often hampered by the uncertain boundary between the rights of the clergy—also a survival of the times when the schools were wholly under the control of the church—and the duties of the state inspectors. Conflicts are by no means rare, especially in Roman Catholic communities; and the Minister is careful to avoid establishing any new precedent in these matters which might give rise to political complications.

In Elementary Schools.

The secondary schools are more fortunate. Difficulties increase with the number of patrons, but as a rule there is a precise understanding as to the rights of patronage. The enormous growth in the population of German cities since 1870 has rendered necessary the establishment of large numbers of secondary schools. Rivalry between competing cities, or the effort to build up a new suburb, is sure to create a demand for additional school facilities. For example, Berlin had in 1872 a population of 864,300; in 1893, 1,691,702. During these twenty years there was an annual average increase of more than 6,000 in the school population. This necessitated, besides many common schools, the establishment of nineteen higher schools, practically an average of one secondary school a year.[1]

In Secondary Schools.

A dozen instances of phenomenal growth of city population could be cited that would compare favourably with the most phenomenal of our western American towns.[2] I shall men-

---

[1] Report of *Schul-Deputation* of Berlin, April, 1894.
[2] See Shaw, *The Government of German Cities*, *Century Magazine*, Vol. xlviii.

tion only one. The census of Magdeburg in 1880 showed a population of 97,500; in 1890 it had increased to 202,234. The area within the city walls became altogether inadequate. As a means of relief the city purchased of the Prussian government the site of the old fortifications, paying almost enough, I have heard, to construct still stronger walls at a greater distance out. The city fathers immediately cut up the newly acquired tract into building lots, which were put on the market. But in order to induce a better class of residents and to enhance the value of the land, a *Gymnasium* was established in 1886 at city expense. At bottom this was a pure speculation, a land-boom of the most approved type, and but for the rapid increase in the population and wealth of the locality it would have become a serious drain upon the city treasury. The result is, however, that a flourishing town has sprung up and the city has made a fortune in the transaction.

As a rule cities are disposed to found *Gymnasien*, rather than *Real*-schools, because of the higher social standing of the former. The town with many *Realschulen*, or even many *Realgymnasien*, is popularly supposed to be an industrial centre; while *Gymnasien*, on the contrary, invariably bespeak a professional or wealthy class. Often the conflict between city and state waxes warm over the kind of school to be established. The state cannot compel the city to found one school rather than another; in fact, it cannot compel the foundation of any school at all. But if the city proposes a plan counter to the policy of the government, some exceptionally strong support, political, social or religious, will be necessary to avoid the Minister's veto. It is no simple matter for a town nowadays to secure an additional classical school. In the words of the Emperor, the times demand "young Germans, upright, God-fearing and patriotic citizens, instead of young Greeks and Romans."

Present Tendencies.

The relations sustained by the municipality to the state in educational affairs, and the general tendencies of the age, are perhaps best seen in the kingdom of Saxony. There are, all told, seventeen *Gymnasien* in the kingdom. Four of them—all founded prior to 1586, one dating back to the thirteenth century—are now under the joint patronage of city and state; six are state schools; two others, founded in 1300 and 1879 respectively, are exclusively city foundations; one has a special endowment (1638), and is under the administration of a lineal descendent of the original founder. Grimma (1550) and St. Afra in Meissen (1543) are *Kloster Schulen*, having been endowed by Maurice of Saxony with the possessions of secularized monasteries. The two oldest *Gymnasien* of Leipsic, the *Thomas-Schule* (1221) and the *Nicolai Gymnasium* (1395), are supported in part by special endowments, in part by the city. Of the ten *Realgymnasien*, all except two belong to the present century, while the specific character of each has been determined within the past fifty years. Seven of these schools are municipal, only three being royal. Moreover, there are twenty-three *Realschulen* in the kingdom, all of them under city control. The state, however, makes a special grant of 12,000 marks a year to some seventeen of these schools—those outside of Dresden, Leipsic and Chemnitz—and secures thereby the privilege of appointing the director and head-teachers. As to the relative interests of state and city in the founding of a new school, the history of Saxony since 1870 is very suggestive; of the twenty-seven secondary schools called into existence in the last twenty-five years, only four are under royal patronage.

Foundation of City Schools. When a city will establish a new school it enters into covenant with the state to house it properly, to provide suitable furnishings and equipment, and to support it in a becoming way from year to year. But first it devolves upon the municipality to show that the elementary education of the city is on a satisfactory basis, and that there is genuine need of a secondary school. The approval of the Minister of Education—and nothing can be done without his approval—is also conditioned on special reports made to him by government officials on such matters as, for example, the town's ability to support the proposed institution, and whether it might tend to weaken some other school already established. Approval once granted is further conditioned on the proper execution of essential details: the school site must be satisfactory; the plans and specifications of the building must be submitted to the supervising architect of the province and passed by him; the denominational character of the school, on which depends the selection of a faculty, must conform to the religious belief of the majority of the scholars; the proposed furnishings and equipment down to the drinking cups and blackboard erasers must be of proper quality and amount. Nothing goes unregulated to which a regulation can be at all applied.

Perhaps to English readers the most suggestive of all these requirements is the one pertaining to the school building and its equipment. In general the school-house must contain sufficient class-rooms, large, light and well-ventilated; an auditorium for religious exercises and public exhibitions; arrangements for library, museums and laboratories; teachers' assembly-room, and a study for the director. *Construction of School-Houses.*

The class-rooms, according to official regulations, may not exceed 9.5 metres long, by 5.7 metres to 7 metres wide, by 4.1 metres to 4.4 metres high. The teachers' platform (3.2 metres long, 1.3 metres wide, .2 metre to .3 metre high) is placed at one side of the room. *Class-Room Arrangements.* There shall be a suitable desk for the teacher with lock-drawers. At the side of the platform, usually on an easel, is the blackboard about 3 by 5 feet. The main aisle between the platform and front row of desks should be at least 1 metre wide; aisles next to the walls (and windows) at least .4 metre wide and the central aisle at least .5 metre wide. The central aisle is unnecessary except when more than six scholars would thereby have to sit together. This gives 3.9 to 4.3 cubic metres air space for the lower classes, and 4.3 to 4.8 for the middle classes. Twice the above areas are allowed for drawing, and the auditorium should provide for 6 square metres floor space for each pupil.

In 1879 the government had the space carefully measured which is allotted to each pupil's desk in the schools of Berlin and Cologne. The city schools of Berlin showed the most economical arrangement and their plan was thereupon recommended for general adoption. It is as follows:—

Ages and Classes of Scholars.	Wilhelms-Gym. Berlin.			City Schools, Berlin.			City Schools, Cologne.		
	Width	Depth	Area Sq. M.	Width	Depth	Area Sq. M.	Width	Depth	Area Sq. M.
VI. and V.—10 to 13 Years	.54	.61	.43	.50	.71	.35	.47	.81	.38
IV. and III.—13 to 16 Years	.59	.85	.50	.55	.73	.40	.52	.84	.44
II. and I.—16 to 19 Years	.65	.89	.58	.60	.79	.47	.58	.84	.48

But all such regulations are subject to modification at the hands of the supervising architect of the province. It is his business to see that the plans of local architects are theoretically correct and practically useful.

Duties of Supervising Architect.

He stands between the tax-payers on one side and the school children on the other, and seeks to protect both. Such an office, removed from all political influence and presided over by a master of his profession, is an inestimable boon both to the country at large and to the proper administration of school affairs.

School-houses are generally placed on quiet streets away from the stir and bustle of the city and in a locality furnishing good air and unobstructed light. If a suitable site can be found near the centre of the district population, it must be given the preference. There must be ample play-ground in connection with each school, although "ample" means little more than standing room. But as the German school-boy does not indulge in many games, he does not require a foot-ball field except for a leisurely *Spaziergang.* Each class, however, lays claim to a

The School Site.

certain portion, and it is not unusual to find these class divisions staked off or posts set up therein as rallying points. The *Turnhalle* (gymnasium), as a rule, is on the school grounds, but it is not a lounging place for pupils during intermissions. The *Turnhalle* is intended for serious work; it is the laboratory of physical culture, and as such is in charge of trained teachers who are as jealous of the honour of their department as are the teachers of Latin. The gymnastic equipment is invariably excellent and the methods of instruction all that could be desired under the prevailing system. That the system has its faults is generally understood abroad; but its faults as well as its merits are so well known that I need not discuss them here.

In recent years the problem of lighting has received especial attention. It is now recognized that the window surface of a room should be at least one-fifth of the floor space, that windows should extend to the ceiling, and that each pupil should have a view of the blue sky—the more the better. Yet there is such extraordinary increase in near-sightedness from grade to grade, and so many suicides among school children, that repeated official investigations have been made in the sphere of school hygiene. "Recent Prussian statistics have shown that in four years three hundred boys and four hundred and nine girls under fifteen years committed suicide. The near-sightedness became so serious that the Minister of Education, von Gossler, asked Dr. Schmidt-Rimpler, the celebrated oculist in Göttingen, to draw up a list of recommendations for diminishing near-sightedness, so prevalent in the German schools. The regulations were as follows: (1) Teachers must acquire a knowledge of school hygiene; (2) that a medical attendant should be attached to the school staff and practically inspect not only the school building, but the individual pupils; (3) sending practical instructions to the pupils to inform them of the position of the body in reading, writing and studying; (4) abolishing the afternoon session so far as possible and allowing greater exercise in the open air ; (5) abolishing written tasks at home ; (6) not allowing the school course to extend over too many years."[1]

Minute regulations are laid down for heating and ventilation. In almost all of the older buildings the rooms are heated separately by means of stoves, and from experience I can say that the ventilation is uniformly bad. In many of the better buildings the stoves are placed adjoining the corridors and so arranged that they may be supplied with fuel and regulated from the outside of the room. A glass-covered slit in the wall also allows the janitor to see the thermometer—an indispensable part of the furniture of every German school-room. In this way it is possible to adjust the heating and ventilation without disturbing the class. The buildings constructed within the last five or ten years are nearly all heated by steam or hot water, and every precaution is taken to secure proper ventilation. In passing, I might mention such buildings as the Weimar *Gymnasium*, *Wilhelm's Gymnasium* in Cassel and *Joachimsthalsches Gymnasium* in Berlin as being models of architectural style and hygienic precaution.

<small>Ventilation.</small>

While the foregoing regulations regarding the construction and equipment of school-houses are of a very general nature, the system of careful inspection renders impossible any serious deviation on the part of contractors or municipalities inclined to be penurious. The government has the power to compel alterations in plans or specifications when found to be defective, even though they were at first approved. In the city schools the municipality must stand the additional expense of such alterations. There is, however, a small fund at the disposal of the provincial school-board which can be drawn upon for local benefit, and in some cases the state does what it might compel the city to do.

The question of sanitary school seats is another much discussed problem. The outcome is that a few points of agreement have been reached. Especial emphasis is placed upon

---

[1] *Report of the Commissioner of Education*, 1889–1890, p. 338.

leaving very little horizontal distance between seat and desk. Five centimetres is the maximum. It is also recommended that desks be arranged in rows of two each with a narrow aisle between, and that for each school at least three different heights of seats be provided —one for the average for each of the three divisions in the school. On the whole it seems to me as if the Germans with all their attention to school hygiene had not advanced far beyond the theoretic view of the problem. Seats are fitted to the average boy of a grade whether that boy happens to be there or not; the rest must shift for themselves. The seating and ventilation of class-rooms are, it seems to me, out of harmony with the general equipment of German schools. *Seating.*

Perhaps the most unique feature of the class-room equipment, especially to an American accustomed to slate blackboards completely surrounding the room, is the little three by five blackboard—the only one in the room—which stands at the side of the teacher's platform. It is made of wood painted a dull black, and is supported on an easel; sometimes two blackboards are hung on cords running over pulleys and so adjusted that they can easily be run up or down. Damp sponges are always used as erasers, thus avoiding dust. Each room is supplied with a stand for displaying maps and charts, and an upright wooden case six feet high by three feet wide in which they are stored when not in use. This case also serves as a receptacle for pupils' note-books and other articles of use in daily work. No German class-room would be complete without portraits of the reigning sovereigns and their predecessors for a generation or two. In Prussia, Bismarck and von Moltke, Luther, Goethe and Schiller rank with the best. Pictures illustrative of the class work find a prominent place. One frequently finds displayed magnificent representations of classical subjects, photographs of works of classic art or charts prepared for special purposes. Some teachers make a practice of exhibiting large numbers of pictures and charts, which are ex- *Class-Room Equipment.*

changed for others from time to time as the work advances. This is often done to good effect in history, geography and nature study.

The corridors of a German school building are the meeting places for classes during the five-minute intermission between lessons. The flooring in all modern buildings is stone or tile. Rows of hooks are placed on the side wall for coats and caps. Lockers are too much of a luxury.

The auditorium is the pride of the building. It is large enough to give all the pupils seats and afford accommodations for a few visitors besides. Howsoever plain the rest of the building may be, there is always some artistic effort here. In the new buildings the decorations are really lavish. A grand piano is the one indispensable article of furniture.

The teachers' assembly-room is provided with a long table and a suitable number of chairs and book-shelves. The museums are fitted out with cabinets and shelves for the preservation of natural history specimens. The laboratories are each provided with a long table and seats about three feet apart. Attachments for gas and water are luxuries not always to be had. Some of the new schools have quite extensive laboratory facilities, but, so far as my experience goes, they are seldom or never used by the students.

Many of the classical schools of Germany have most excellent libraries, in some instances numbering thousands of volumes. These are supported by special endowments which occasionally provide for a care-taker as well. As might be expected, the larger libraries contain many volumes of little service at the present time. Works on classical subjects, doctors' dissertations, and sermons celebrated in their day, are as numerous as Reports of the Department of Agriculture in some American libraries. Schools dependent upon special appropriations for the purchase of books have no great collections; still every school has its library, and it is generally a good one. The wretched method of cataloguing in vogue throughout Germany, and the excessive care to exclude everyone from handling or even viewing the books in the cases, practically annuls the greater part of the benefit to be derived from the use of the books. I have but one judgment to pass upon the whole library economy of the Fatherland—public, school and university alike. It is an outrageous farce. The redeeming feature, however, is the uniformly excellent collection of pedagogical works to be found in every secondary school. These books are sometimes in charge of a member of the faculty and placed in a separate room. But they are generally to be found in the teachers' assembly-room, where they can be easily consulted without restriction. A typical collection would contain not only works on general pedagogy but all the most valuable reference books pertaining to the work of each teacher —dictionaries, atlases, gazetteers, commentaries, standard texts, leading educational journals, and pedagogical material such as can be obtained in no other country in the world. These collections are supported from special grants annually made by the city or the government but largely augmented from the income of special funds set apart in most schools for this particular purpose; scarcely a secondary school but has a library fund to which friends of the institution and graduates of the school are expected to make contributions.

No secondary school gives free tuition. The elementary schools of Germany are practically free to all and attendance is compulsory between the ages of six and fourteen. While every child in the state must attend school, no stipulations are made as to what school he shall attend. Until the fourteenth year, therefore, that is, during the first five years of the secondary school, attendance is compulsory, and the parents may be fined for any negligence on their part resulting in non-attendance of their children. But trouble rarely arises on this score in secondary schools. Regularity in attendance has become so much a matter of habit that nothing short of serious illness keeps a boy from school.

Compulsory School Attendance.

Tuition fees are exceedingly variable. According to a Prussian ministerial rescript of 1892, all royal schools under the administration of the state are subject to the following schedule :—

Tuition Fees.

Gymnasien, Realgymnasien, and *Oberrealschulen*......................120 marks ($30) annually;
Progymnasien, and *Realprogymnasien*....100 marks ($25) annually;
Realschulen............................ 80 marks ($20) annually.

An effort is being made to have all city schools adopt the government schedule. At present, however, city schools of nine years' course seldom charge more than 100 marks for the year; in some cities the rates are still lower, in others somewhat higher. For instance, in Frankfort-on-the-Main 150 marks is the minimum. Saxony maintains about the same fees as Prussia. The southern states are lower on the average, but because of an ascending scale the fees in the upper classes are high. In Bavaria there is an official regulation fixing the fees at 30, 36 and 40 marks respectively for the three divisions of the higher schools. In Würtemberg the rates in most schools vary from 10 marks in the lowest classes to 32 marks in the highest classes, and rarely in any case do they exceed 70 marks. In the city of Hamburg, on the other hand, the tuition fee at the *Gymnasium* is 192 marks. It is a general rule in most German states that foreigners and those who do not pay their full share of the local taxes shall pay extra school rates. Special consideration is shown to younger members of families already represented in the school by older brothers. The second son generally gets half-rates.

Fees in City Schools.

In the government schools ten per cent. of the places may be free. These free places are usually granted on the basis of scholarship, but deserving young men with good recommendations are given the preference. Endowed schools with home accommodations frequently have scholarships which entitle the holders to both lodging and

Free Places.

tuition. Schulpforta, for instance, grants one hundred and forty scholarships covering the entire expense for home and schooling. There are also great numbers of special foundations which provide for the partial maintenance of scholars in a certain class or in preparation for a particular profession, as sons of teachers or clergymen, boys from the donor's home or birthplace, and those fitting for the ministry. Some of the old classical schools can rival an English college in the number and value of their bursaries.

All secondary schools, as has been said, charge tuition fees, but they are by no means self-supporting. There is always a large deficit which is met by the government, by the municipality, or from private funds, according to the rights of patronage in the school. *School Maintenance.* On an appointed day near the beginning of the semester the pupils pay their dues to a teacher or to an authorized agent who turns over all collections to the school treasury if it be an endowed school having property of its own to administer, to the city treasury if a city school, or to the nearest government depository if a state school.

From statistics furnished by the Prussian government for the Chicago Exposition in 1893, we see the enormous growth in school expenses in the last twenty years. In 1871 the total expenditure for the maintenance *In Prussia.* of the higher schools in Prussia was 7,434,646 marks; in 1892 it amounted to 30,918,840 marks. Of this last-mentioned sum, 5,445,020 marks came from government grants; 1,903,304 marks, from school property; 14,327,590 marks, from school fees, etc.; 7,802,173 marks, from local rates; and the balance, from special endowments. It will be seen from this that although the government exercises full control of the *interna* of the higher schools, it pays only about one-sixth of the expenses. The tuition fees alone meet nearly one-half of the total expenditure.

That the German schools are economically administered is evident from the fact that, in 1892, 25,733,662 marks—more than five-sixths of the total cost of maintaining the higher schools—were expended in payment of teachers' salaries.

In the Empire.

The average expense per pupil in the higher schools of Prussia was 62.5 marks in 1871; in 1892 it was 184.3 marks. The total expense per thousand of the population for the support of the higher schools was 301.1 marks in 1871, and 1,032.2 marks in 1892.

Expense per Pupil.

In the meantime there has been a growth of but *four* per cent. in the population of Prussia. In the face of such proof no words need be wasted in adducing evidence of Prussia's interest in secondary education.

The Report of the *Schul-Deputation* of Berlin for 1893–1894 gives a good idea of the cost of the city schools. There was an attendance of 4,107 pupils in 114 classes of the 11 *Realschulen*; and in these schools 162 regular and 51 special teachers were employed.

School Expenses in Berlin.

The expense account was as follows:—

```
Ordinary expenses...................... 608,427 M.
Income from school fees............... 295,788 M.
     Deficit.................. ..................  312,639 M.
Extraordinary expenses :—
     Salaries of special teachers.....................   43,188 M.
     Care-takers ..................................   10,750 M.
     Supply teachers.... ........................    1,408 M.
     Teachers of religion for non-protestants........    1,200 M.
     Printing annual announcements...............    2,569 M.
     Building and repairs........................   12,218 M.
     Teachers of gymnastics.......................   23,564 M.
                                                   ─────────
     Total expense to city..................... 407,526 M.
```

The six *Höhere Mädchenschulen* had an attendance in 1893–1894 of 4,297, divided among 95 classes and in charge of 132 teachers. The total income was 410,334 marks, of which 407,715 marks came from tuition fees. The ordinary expenses were 484,648 marks; supply teachers, 2,331 marks; religious instruction for non-protestants, 6,480 marks; printing annual announcements, 1,247 marks; building and repairs, 13,141 marks; supervision of play-grounds, 1,832 marks. This gave a total expense of 509,679 marks, and left a deficit of 99,345 marks to be borne by the city.

The city of Berlin also supports 201 elementary schools, a school for the blind, a school for the deaf, and several nine-year higher schools which are under the jurisdiction of the provincial school-board. The cost to the city in 1893-1894 of the schools under the administration of the *Schul-Deputation*—making allowances for items placed in two accounts—may be summarized as follows :— Berlin City School System.

Kinds of Schools.	Number of Schools.	Number of Classes.	Attendance.	Income: Marks.	Outlay: Marks.	Expense to City: Marks.
Realschulen	11	114	4,107	295,788	635,297	339,509
Höhere Mädchenschulen	6	95	4,307	410,334	484,648	74,314
Volksschulen	201	3,371	179,621	121,844	9,420,149	9,298,305
School for Deaf	1	....	148	719	56,261	55,542
School for Blind	1	....	53	53,198	82,310	29,112
Totals	220	3,580	188,236	881,883	10,678,665	9,796,782

Berlin is exceptionally liberal in the support of girls' schools, but Americans or Englishmen will find it hard to understand the reason for expending 150,000 marks more on the boys than on the girls, when the girls pay nearly twice as much in fees as the boys pay. But girls grow only into women; boys become citizens and soldiers.

GENERAL REFERENCES: Wiese, *Das höhere Schulwesen in Preussen;* Wiese-Kübler *Gesetze und Verordnungen;* Rethwisch, *Deutschlands höheres Schulwesen in neunzehnten Jahrhundert*, Berlin, 1893; Kehrbach, *Monumenta Germaniæ Pædagogica*, Vols. I., VI., and VIII.; *Statistisches Jahrbuch der höheren Schulen Deutschlands*, 1897-1898; *Centralblatt für die gesammte Unterrichts-Verwaltung in Preussen*, Berlin.

CHAPTER VIII

RULES, REGULATIONS AND CUSTOMS

The School-Year. THE school-year in Prussia and in the other northern and central German states is from Easter to Easter, the semesters beginning at Easter and Michaelmas. Large institutions with parallel classes from top to bottom frequently admit new pupils both in the spring and in the fall. This gives them two sets of classes a half-year apart—the one designated Easter classes (*Oster-Oberprima, Oster-Untersecunda*, etc.); the other Michaelmas classes. But in Baden, Alsace-Lorraine and Würtemberg the school-year begins the middle of September and extends to the middle of July; in Bavaria from the 10th of September to the 14th of July.

Vacations. The historic connection of church and school is clearly evidenced in the modern custom of having school vacations at the time of the chief church festivals. In Prussia and most of the northern states two weeks are given at Easter, about one week at Whitsunday, four weeks in the summer—mostly in July—two weeks at Michaelmas, and two weeks at Christmas. Bavaria has no vacation at Whitsunday, and only one week at Christmas. This makes possible eight weeks of rest in the summer. The precise dates of vacations are set by the school authorities in each state at the beginning of each school-year. The convenience of the scholars and avoidance of the heat of summer are the main considerations. In northern Germany it is no hardship to continue school work into August; the universities uniformly require it. In South Germany the heat is more intense and of longer duration. But everywhere it is left to the discretion of head-masters to excuse classes when from excessive heat or cold some injury might result to the pupils. Most schools, on this account, are closed afternoons four or five times in the summer.

The general ministerial orders are to the effect that the year's vacations should not exceed ten and one-half weeks, exclusive of special holidays, such as the church festivals of Epiphany, Candlemas, Annunciation, Corpus Christi, *Peter-Paulstag* (June 29th), All Saints, Conception of the Virgin (December 8th)—all of which are observed in Roman Catholic schools; the *Reformationsfest*, which is observed in all protestant schools; the birthdays of the reigning sovereigns, Sedan day, and school celebrations.

The morning session in the secondary schools begins regularly at seven o'clock during the summer and closes at eleven. In the afternoons, except Wednesdays and Saturdays, which are entirely free, the session is from two to five. *Daily Sessions.* During the winter the morning session begins at eight o'clock and continues until twelve. This gives seven fifty-five minute periods a day besides intermissions. The long afternoon session is much disliked; and in many schools there is a disposition to lengthen the morning session and do all of the heavy work before noon, thus leaving for afternoon the lighter work such as drawing, singing, gymnastics and free electives. The school authorities, however, are not disposed to favour this plan, believing that continuous work for five hours makes too serious demands upon the strength of the scholars. As a result compromises are frequent. For example, the *Thomasschule* in Leipsic leaves four afternoons of the week practically free, following five hours of work in the morning. On the other two days there are four hours of work in the morning and three in the afternoon, beginning at three o'clock. The city *Gymnasium* of Frankfort-on-the-Main makes Wednesday, Friday and Saturday afternoons free, following five hours of work in the morning.

Pauses. It is required that at least forty minutes of the day shall be given up to pauses. Ordinary pauses are five minutes, but one of fifteen minutes' duration must be given at the end of every second hour. During the longer intermissions all scholars must leave the rooms so that there may be a thorough ventilation by the opening of the windows. Pupils generally pass out into the school-yards during the longer intermissions, where they walk about spending the time in conversation. Seldom, indeed, is it that one sees any games or play indulged in. Teachers are appointed for the supervision of the corridors and school-grounds as regularly as for class recitations. This is the more necessary inasmuch as teachers exercise no supervision in their own rooms or classes. In fact, the rooms belong to the classes, not to the teachers; it is only for drawing, singing and science work that the class seeks the teacher. At assembly, order is expected upon the ringing of a warning bell; the second bell is the signal for the entrance of the teacher, who generally spends the intermission in the teachers' assembly-room. As he appears the class immediately rises and remains standing until the command to sit down is given. This little act of courtesy does not seem to be performed perfunctorily and is so much a matter of habit that classes instinctively stand when anyone enters the room, no matter if a recitation be in progress. Teachers seldom occupy their class-rooms during intermission. Pupils who desire special information must make known their wants before the class is dismissed, or else seek the teacher during office hours. The teacher is generally the first one out of the room.

Home Study. The consequence of the rigid class system in vogue in all German secondary schools is that each pupil has a lesson every hour of the school-day. No time for study is allowed during the school hours, and it is an easy matter for teachers to assign so much work to be done at home that the strength of the pupils may be overtaxed. For more than fifty years this problem of the overburdening of scholars has been uppermost in the minds of both educators and parents. An article entitled *Zum Schutze der Gesundheit in den Schulen,* published in 1836 by an eminent physician (Dr. Lorinser), called attention to the matter. So much discussion ensued that the Minister of Education was obliged in the following year to issue a rescript, which was supported by a special order of the king, materially reducing the amount of home study.

Twenty years later the question again arose and a still further reduction was made. In the Prussian Parliament of 1883–1884 the question came to open debate and in consequence it was thoroughly considered from all sides. The government found itself an interested party since in some provinces eighty per cent. of secondary-school graduates were said to be unqualified for military service. Subsequent investigation proved that this percentage was placed too high; nevertheless it was clear that the secondary schools were making serious inroads on the health of their charges. In Prussia the number of suicides of males between the ages of ten and twenty years increased from one hundred and sixty-five in 1869 to two hundred and sixty in 1881. Although it was shown that the rate of increase was not disproportionate to the increase in the school population and to the total number of suicides, nevertheless so large a number gave sufficient cause for apprehension. The question of insanity among students was also raised, but no satisfactory statistics could be had in the matter. Near-sightedness was found to be the one especial evil that could be attributed directly to the schools. Many investigations were undertaken definitely to learn the extent of the evil, which everyone knew existed in a serious form.

<small>Overwork.</small>

It was found that near-sightedness increased not only from class to class but that its increase could be noted from the beginning of a school-year to its close. In the Frankfort *Gymnasium* four per cent. of the scholars were found to be myopic in the lowest class and sixty-four per cent. in *Prima.* Of 1,000 newly enlisted soldiers examined in Munich only two per cent. of the

<small>Effects on Eye-Sight.</small>

country lads from the *Volksschulen* were found to be nearsighted. Common labourers trained in the city schools showed from four to nine per cent.; clerks, merchants, bookkeepers, etc., forty-four per cent.; graduates of *Realschulen*, fifty-eight per cent.; and graduates of *Gymnasien*, sixty-five per cent. Careful investigation did not substantiate all the charges that had been made against the secondary schools, but it was clearly demonstrated that of all institutions the classical schools were the greatest sinners in this respect. It was found, too, that the number of scholars subject to headache, nose-bleed, and general anæmia was remarkably abnormal.

The careful attention given to this matter by the Prussian Parliament again gave it national importance. Elaborate reports were made by the Medical Department on ways and means of improving the conditions of the school work. Need of better lighted class-rooms, proper ventilation and sanitary precautions, were emphasized. The main pedagogical problem, however, was left for the Education Department to solve. Excessive home study was everywhere thought to be the main cause of the trouble. A ministerial rescript of 1883 prescribed the limits of home study for *Sexta* and *Quinta* at one hour per day, or six hours per week; for *Quarta* and *Untertertia*, two hours per day, or twelve hours per week; for *Obertertia* and *Untersecunda*, two and one-half hours per day, or fifteen hours per week; for *Obersecunda* and *Prima*, three hours per day, or eighteen hours per week. The new *Lehrplan* of 1892 adopts this schedule and cautions the teachers not to overstep the bounds. Inasmuch as scholars must spend on an average from five to six hours a day in recitation, this gives a total day's work of six to nine hours according to age. The preparation of lessons, therefore, in the American fashion is utterly impossible. In fact there is no such thing as a recitation in our sense of the word in a German school. What we call recitation periods they speak of as *Unterrichtsstunden* (Instruction hours). The teacher must lead; the pupils follow.

Limits of Home Study.

According to the latest Prussian *Lehrplan*, home work should consist principally in rearranging and rewriting notes taken in class, memorizing material indispensable for class work, and reviewing and fixing in the mind what has already been learned in class. As a matter of fact, custom varies widely concerning the nature and amount of home study. Teachers who are not wholly in sympathy with modern notions continue to assign supplementary work to be done at home, and so long as parents do not complain there is little probability of its reaching the ears of the head-master. A special book is kept in every class-room in which the lessons assigned in each subject are noted. This was hit upon as a method of giving precise information on what is actually required from the various classes. These books are at all times open to the inspection of the directors and the teacher who is especially charged with the supervision of the class. The influence exerted by these regulations upon methods of teaching the various subjects will be treated of later in separate chapters.

<small>Control of Tasks.</small>

Every effort has been made of late years to control pupils by moral suasion. So far as possible the individuality of the teacher is given full play. There is no doubt that since 1870 a new type of school-master has come in, due in great measure to the military spirit that is in the air. Young men now are desirous of becoming officers, and the presence of teachers having the military training and the ability to command men gives great leverage for good discipline.

<small>Discipline.</small>

Every inducement is offered the intending teacher to qualify himself in military tactics. The time that must elapse before a certificated teacher can receive an appointment is ample for performing the extra military duty required of those who aspire to become reserve officers. Those who show marked proficiency in their first year of service are permitted to advance. They are given special advantages if they desire promotion, and are allowed to demonstrate their ability to command. After two years

<small>Reserve Officers.</small>

of intermittent practice, candidates may present themselves to the officers of some regiment for election. Everything is taken into account—education, training, appearance, character, family, along with military ability. If chosen, the young man is at once admitted to the most select circle in German society and the one most jealous of its honour.

To have officers of the Reserve or *Landwehr* in a school is equivalent to saying that there are just so many able disciplinarians, perfect gentlemen, men of high moral character and ambitions, in the teaching corps. They give tone to a school and set up a standard of discipline that bids fair, in a few years, to become the ideal type. The five or six thousand military officers in the German schools are not there to no purpose; they indicate a new tendency—one that will put the teacher's profession alongside of any in the land. The military circles and the clergy may no longer consider the school-master beneath their notice, for the school-master of to-day may be the leader of a company in the war of to-morrow. This new spirit is the surest guarantee of a new system of discipline in the schools. It is indeed, military—sharp, quick, incisive—but the teacher has learned to obey and to be obeyed; he knows how to control himself, and his control over his pupils is a matter of course. He is always clear and pointed in his teaching. There is nothing uncertain in anything he does. An extended acquaintance with German teachers and personal observation of class-room methods lead me to the conclusion that the proverbially stern discipline and apparent lack of sympathy on the part of the teachers are really not burdensome from the stand-point of the students. In fact, these characteristics are distinctly the right thing in the eyes of the German school-boy, who, as I have already said, is thoroughly imbued with the military spirit and consequently is not averse to having it manifested in the school-room.

All this pertains to the younger generation of teachers. The older teachers are oftentimes careless and easy-going; sometimes cross and irritable. I have seen a master leave

<small>The Military Type.</small>

the rostrum two or three times during a single recitation to box the ears of ten-year-old boys with the teacher's book because of their inability to analyze rapidly enough problems in percentage. I have seen, too, the whole front of a large iron stove and all the window-shades in the class-room leave their places in a manner seemingly quite accidental during the process of a single recitation. I afterwards observed, however, that the shades had very suspicious-looking strings tied to them, and I more than suspect that the stove had been previously trained to perform its part. It is my opinion that school-boys in Germany have about the same motives to mischief as boys in other countries, and that the incompetent teacher is perhaps more inclined to be brutal in his treatment of a class than would be possible in an American school. *The Older Type.*

The supervision of pupils and their discipline is not confined to conduct on the school premises, but has to do with their entire life outside of school; nor are parents permitted to interfere to any considerable extent. A parent has no right to remove a child from school simply because the regulations do not suit him. It is presumed that the school is in charge of men who know better how to train children than parents do. The school-master is in possession of professional knowledge, and the whims of parents are not allowed to militate against him. *Supervision out of School.*

Each pupil on entering a secondary school is placed in charge of a teacher, usually the one who has most to do with the instruction of the class (*Ordinarius*). The pupil is expected to consult his class-master in all matters pertaining to his school work and to follow his advice at all times. Non-resident students must live in families or boarding-houses approved by the director of the school, and the director reserves the right to make such changes in the location of students and the conduct of boarding-houses as may seem desirable to him at any time. Non-residents may not change their lodgings without the approval of the director. They are not permitted to live at *Non-Resident Students.*

public-houses or to dine at hotel tables. The school is expected to look after the conduct of pupils at all times out of school. Teachers have the right, and it is expected they will perform the duty, of making special investigations of the habits of students whom they suspect of being faithless to the regulations of the school. In extreme cases the police are required upon notification from the director to report on the habits of those under suspicion.

Every pupil must be at school at least fifteen minutes before the beginning of each session, and in his seat at the first stroke of the bell. In case of illness he must at once notify his *Ordinarius* either by mail or by special messenger of his absence, and when he returns to school he must present to his *Ordinarius* and to each of his teachers a written excuse from his parents. The *Ordinarius* may excuse the pupil for an occasional lesson, but permission for an absence of a day or more must be obtained from the director.

<small>Excuses for Absence.</small>

Pupils are required to attend all religious exercises in the school, such as morning exercises (usually held in the larger schools only on Mondays), and the communion service, which is administered in all evangelical schools once or twice a year. Church attendance on Sundays is also obligatory for all, whatever may be the inclinations of parents. For pupils of about fourteen there is a special confirmation class which is taught by the village pastor or some clergyman appointed for the purpose, and at Easter all members of this class are expected to be publicly confirmed. It is not absolutely obligatory, but the custom is so general that it may be said to be universal. The festivities connected with the event are sufficient inducement to win over those not otherwise persuaded. For the *Volksschüler* it means that the school-days with their accompanying prohibitions and restraints are over. Good Friday is the last day of the old *régime;* the Saturday before Easter, the first of the new order. It is a novel experience for a foreigner to see these boys on a Saturday, dressed in their best and for

<small>Church Attendance.</small>

the first time sporting gloves and cane, streaming out to suburban beer-gardens to spend the day in mild carousal. It means, too, for the secondary-school pupil greater freedom than he has hitherto enjoyed; he may now smoke to his heart's content. The casual observer finds it difficult to see much that is religious in the German mode of confirmation, and I much doubt if the average German school-boy finds in it more than the removal of certain scholastic disabilities.

The use of tobacco among pupils of the four lower classes is altogether prohibited; upper-classmen may smoke, but not on the streets or in public places. Scholars must not loiter on the way to or from school, and must avoid excessive noise or disturbance on the streets. They are not allowed to visit public-houses, confectionery shops, beer-gardens, theatres or balls, except in company with their parents. Non-residents must secure permission from their tutors or school principals before going to public resorts. <small>Conduct of Pupils out of School.</small>

The opinion is growing in Germany that excessive beer drinking, especially as indulged in by university students, is a dangerous custom. Experts pronounce it the most prolific cause of insanity among young men, and a whole train of other diseases follows in its wake. And it is no wonder that health is endangered where the custom prevails of putting down ten or fifteen quarts of beer at a sitting—a not unusual practice of the university student—even though no intoxication results. But university students know no law but that of tradition. With the pupils of the secondary schools it is different; they are under the control of masters. Students above the age of fifteen, however, may congregate at a respectable house without supervision, but must not remain later than nine o'clock in summer or eight o'clock in winter. On special occasions the whole evening may be spent in such merriment with the permission of the faculty and under the supervision of the director or one of the teachers. Wine, beer and coffee are the only drinks in which they are supposed to indulge. It is <small>Drinking Customs.</small>

the constant care of teachers and directors of the secondary schools to see that their scholars do not fall into the company of bad women—a task that is by no means easy anywhere on the continent. Hence there must be no loitering on the streets, and attendance at legal trials and public meetings is forbidden.

Students may not use the public libraries, or receive papers and magazines in their own names, or publish any school journal. No pains are spared that students read only that which will be of advantage in their school work. For three-quarters of a century it has been the policy of German educators either to refuse students admission to the circulating libraries, or else to exercise strict control over what may be loaned them. Hidden in this desire to control the outside reading of pupils there is a two-fold purpose: first, that their minds may not be poisoned by trashy literature; and second, to prevent young people from imbibing political, social or religious heresies. In view of the demonstrations of the last few years indicating socialistic tendencies among university students, is it problematical as to which of these aims is looked upon as the more important? A university student is a free lance over whom it is difficult to exercise any control. But the pupils in the secondary schools are completely in the hands of the government throughout what is considered their plastic age, and the discipline of these schools is regulated quite as much with regard to the avoidance of all influences tending to undermine the patriotic and religious character of school instruction as to the suppression of positive evils.

Libraries and Reading.

The rule forbidding student publications was directed originally against a paper started in 1875 which was intended to have a wide circulation among secondary-school students, and in which they might air their grievances and express opinions on matters pertaining to school life. Since German teachers are state officials and the school a state institution, it is readily seen that political complications might easily arise. The paper

Student Publications.

was promptly suppressed, and though attempts have since been made to evade the ministerial edict, student journals are unknown except in the form of an occasional bulletin published for some school festival. There is great temptation on the part of students in the upper classes of the secondary schools to ape university customs in forming clubs and societies, but no such organization can be legally established without the approval of the school authorities. The university fraternities have given the government trouble enough, I take it, to prevent the hatching of a younger brood.

The impression is abroad that German teachers are severe disciplinarians. That severity is tempered with mercy and judiciously administered will be apparent, I think, to all who note the following official gradations in punishments :— *Punishments in Schools.*

1. Warnings to the pupil (a) in private, (b) before class, (c) from the faculty.

2. Assignment to a special place in the class-room or otherwise degrading the pupil in class work.

3. Detention after school, which occurs under supervision and in order to make up deficiencies (but the pupil must not be deprived of his midday intermission). The director is informed in every instance.

4. Incarceration, always with a definite amount of work to do which must have a direct relation to the class work. This punishment can be assigned only by the faculty in conference and for a period not exceeding six hours. Most of the schools have cells for this purpose; but nearly all of the new buildings are constructed without them, thus showing the decadence of the practice.

5. Corporal punishment, which is not to be regarded as proper, but is allowable in three lower classes in cases where immediate action is necessary. In every instance the teacher must announce it the same day to the director. Fines are under no circumstances allowed in higher schools.

If these punishments do not suffice to bring recalcitrant scholars into line, nothing else remains but removal from the school. In this case the various methods employed are: (1) *Consilium abeundi* which is to be communicated to the pupil in the presence of the assembled teachers, a parent or guardian being at once notified; (2) quiet suspension, in which the pupil's father is advised to remove him at once for a definite time; (3) public expulsion, whereupon the provincial school-board must be immediately informed. Dismissal from the school is in the hands of the faculty as a whole. In case of public expulsion all the higher schools of the province are officially notified that the pupil concerned must not be admitted to any school in good standing. In case of the suspension or expulsion of a non-resident the police department is also notified at once that the pupil is no longer under the supervision of the school. The certificate, which every pupil must be given on leaving school, will also state the fact that he has been removed for cause. This of itself is generally quite sufficient to prevent admission to another school. In case of suspension no notice of any kind is given—not even to classmates unless they have a knowledge of the offence.

<small>Suspension and Expulsion.</small>

The annual program of the *Friedrichs-Gymnasium*, Berlin, for 1895–1896 contains the following summary of rules for the guidance of parents:—

"Applications for admission of new pupils at Michaelmas, 1896, will be received on and after May 1st; for admission at Easter, 1897, on and after November 1, 1896. The application fee is three marks, which will be deducted from the tuition of the first quarter if the pupil enters on time; in case there is no vacancy in the class for which the pupil is found to be fitted, the fee will be returned; but should the pupil not enter the class to which he is assigned, or fail to appear at the opening of the semester, the fee will be turned into the fund for poor scholars.

<small>Typical School Regulations.</small>

"The pupil will bring with him on the day of his admission to the school, (1) the certificate of his application, (2) certificate of birth, (3) baptismal certificate (if pupil is a Protestant), (4) certificate of vaccination (if pupil is over twelve years old, also the certificate of revaccination), (5) certificate of honourable dismissal from school previously attended, and (6) the tuition fee for the first quarter. *Admission.*

"The tuition—27.5 marks for the *Volksschule*, 32.5 marks for the *Gymnasium*—is payable strictly in advance. Herr Nautsch, Collector, will be at the *Gymnasium* on a day to be announced to receive the fees.

"Applications for free schooling must be addressed to the city council (*Magistrat*) and handed unsealed to the director of the *Gymnasium* before the first day of March or of September. If a free place is desired for a third or fourth son, it will be necessary to show, besides the need of assistance, that the other sons are students in good standing of Berlin secondary schools. *Free Tuition.*

"Scholars are not permitted to appear at unseasonable hours or to congregate on the streets. The class-rooms are opened fifteen minutes before the opening of the session.

"All scholars must be revaccinated when twelve years old. If the operation is unsuccessful, it must be repeated each year until the certificate of the physician shows three successive failures. The free services of the school physician are recommended for this purpose. *Vaccination.*

"Parents of our scholars are requested to give careful attention to the following official regulations relative to contagious diseases, and to observe them implicitly in case of need: *Contagious Diseases.*

"The diseases which, because of their infectious character, are specially to be guarded against are: (1) cholera, dysentery, measles, scarlet fever, diphtheria, smallpox, typhus and intermittent fever; (2) typhoid, contagious eye diseases, itch and whooping-cough (so long as it is spasmodic).

"Scholars suffering with the above diseases are excluded from the school. Children in the same family with persons suffering from a disease included in the first list, (1), must have a physician's certificate to the effect that they are in no danger of infection before they will be received in school.

<small>Exclusion from School.</small> Scholars thus excluded from school will not be re-admitted under the normal period for each disease (scarlet fever and small-pox, six weeks; measles, four weeks), nor without the statement from a physician that all danger is past and the proper disinfection completed.

"Scholars are forbidden to leave school at holiday periods (especially before the summer vacation) before instruction closes, without permission of the director.

"Parents should countersign the weekly reports sent them and take note of their sons' work.

"Parents are requested not to send anonymous communications to the director, but to consult with him personally on all matters pertaining to the welfare of the school and its pupils. Promotions are made by vote of the entire faculty, and the results are under no circumstances subject to change.

"Visiting of beer-gardens, confectioners' shops or similar resorts is not permitted to scholars, except in company with responsible guardians. <small>Public-Houses.</small> Smoking on the streets or in public places is unconditionally prohibited. Parents will be notified of infractions of these rules; and in case of repetition the pupil will be immediately dismissed from the school.

"A written notice of the intention to withdraw from the school should be given to the director before the end of the semester; otherwise the parent will be holden for the tuition of the following quarter. At the same time the director should be informed of the school the boy will next attend, or of his future occupation.

"Vacations for 1896 are appointed as follows:
Easter—Saturday, March 28th, to Tuesday, April 14th.
<small>Calendar.</small> Whitsunday—Friday, May 22d, to Thursday, May 28th.
Summer—Friday, July 3d, to Tuesday, August 11th.
Michaelmas—Saturday, October 3d, to Tuesday, October 13th.

Christmas—Saturday, December 19th, to Tuesday, January 5th."

Pupils nine years of age are admitted to the lowest class of the secondary school upon examination in (1) reading and writing the German and Roman scripts; (2) spelling; (3) parts of speech and analysis of simple sentences; (4) simple arithmetical operations involving the four fundamental principles—addition, subtraction, multiplication and division of simple numbers; (5) important Biblical stories.   *Preliminary Training.*   No restrictions are placed either by state or city upon the selection of the school which a boy will attend; that is regulated entirely by the wishes of his parents and the accommodations of the school. But, on the other hand, neither royal nor municipal authorities are bound to provide facilities for the secondary education of all who may desire it. A certain number of secondary schools have been founded. They are provided with a certain number of teachers, and are intended for a certain number of pupils; but, if these do not satisfy the requirements, there is no redress for those excluded. Applications for admission to some of the larger city schools must be made long in advance. The less fortunate—sometimes because less influential—must put up with what can be had.

The schools of Germany, from the *Volksschulen* to the university, are open to any person of good character who can satisfy the conditions for entrance. But the reader should not make the mistake of inferring that class distinctions are of little importance.   *Class Distinctions.*   Social rank is by no means a dead letter in the Fatherland. The young man or woman who enters into manual service is enrolled as a servant on the books of the police and of the state insurance department. Henceforth there is no breaking with the past; to rise above the present rank unaided is well-nigh a social impossibility. And in the schools class distinctions, while not obtrusive, are nevertheless closely drawn. I have seen the Crown Prince of Weimar occupying a place on the benches of *Prima* in a public *Gymnasium;* but on the books of that school his name appeared as a prince of the royal blood. Some of his classmates were set down as peasant born. Until a student has attained a profession of his own, the *Stand* of his father follows him everywhere he goes. When he enters school his social rank is noted first of all; in every certificate of merit it appears again; it is demanded on admission to the university, and comes up again even in the *Vita* attached to his doctor's dissertation. And every time he changes his residence, or stops at a hotel; whenever he pays his taxes, or gives his signature to any official document; in short, when he is born, marries or dies, or does aught else between times, somebody's *Stand*, if not his own, must be sponsor for him.

I have not been able to get statistics of the social rank of the scholars in the secondary schools; but the records of the Prussian universities will show, I think, the general make-up of the *Gymnasien*. During the five years preceding 1891, according to official reports, there were 12,630 German students in the Prussian universities; of these, 3,244 were sons of university graduates. The following table throws additional light on the professions chosen by gymnasial graduates, as shown by their university studies:

Social Rank of Students.

University Departments.	Number of Students.	Number Whose Fathers were University Graduates.	Per Cent. from Learned Class.
Theology (Protestant)..............	2,562	709	27.67
Theology (Catholic).................	581	22	3.79
Law................................	2,348	873	37.18
Medicine...........................	3,471	831	23.94
Philosophy.........................	3,668	809	22.06
(a) Philology and History...........	1,622	327	20.16
(b) Mathematics and Science........	1,076	230	21.38

It is evident that the future officials and jurists of Prussia, more than other professions, are to be influenced by family tradition. On the other hand, the clergy and leaders of the catholic church will enjoy less of inherited strength, or more of independent thought—as one prefers to consider it—than their associates. The philosophical department, from which the secondary teachers are recruited, stands lower in point of social rank than any of the other leading faculties.

In a country where church and state are so closely united as in Prussia, and where besides the state church there are one or two other important religions, the attitude of these bodies toward the schools is always a grave consideration. The Prussian constitu- *Religious Preferences.* tion guarantees freedom of religious belief and denies to no one the privileges of schooling. There are schools for the Protestants, schools for Catholics, schools for Jews and mixed schools. The secondary schools of Prussia in 1891–1892 had an attendance divided as follows among the various confessions:—[1]

KINDS OF SCHOOLS.	SCHOLARS.					
	Protestant.		Catholic.		Jew.	
		Per Cent.		Per Cent.		Per Cent.
Höh. Bürgerschulen............	6,901	75.0	1,527	16.6	751	8.2
Realschulen...................	4,295	67.2	1,155	18.1	913	14.3
Oberrealschulen	3,497	78.4	629	14.1	299	6.7
Realprogymnasien............	7,076	76.2	1,482	16.0	494	5.3
Realgymnasien	19,035	78.1	3,146	12.3	2,358	9.2
Progymnasien	2,282	49.9	1,948	42.6	337	7.4
Gymnasien.........	52,800	67.8	17,918	23.0	7,015	9.0
Totals....................	96,786	70.5	27,805	20.3	12,167	8.9

The population of Prussia, according to religion, is 19,232,-449 Protestants (67.2 per cent.), 10,252,818 Catholics (34.2 per cent.) and 372,059 Jews (1.24 per cent.). From a comparison of these percentages with the figures above given, it is clear that the Catholics are least interested in the higher education. The astonishing persistency of the Jews, however, in pushing their way into the high places is a source of much anxious thought in the kingdom. In com-

---

[1] Arranged from statistics given in the *Centralblatt*.

parison to their numbers, they send to the universities eleven times as many students as the Catholics send, and six times as many as the Protestants. This, unquestionably, is a serious problem, since race hatred is growing constantly more menacing, and one that some day will cause a deal of trouble, if the present system is maintained.

There is another way of getting at the character of the students who attend the secondary schools. It is well known that graduates of the *Realschulen*, as a rule, enter business or some phase of commercial or technical life. With graduates of the *Gymnasien* it is otherwise; of the 83,880 graduates of Prussian *Gymnasien* and *Realschulen* between 1868 and 1891, 62,236 (74.2 per cent.) entered the learned professions. Gymnasial graduates numbered 71,226; and of these 58,373 (81.95 per cent.) entered the learned professions, 2,498 (3.51 per cent.) the technical professions and 10,355 (14.54 per cent.) other professions. Of the realgymnasial graduates 30 per cent. entered learned, 19 per cent. technical and 51 per cent. all the other professions. These figures exhibit conclusively the aim of these schools. Not all who enter, to be sure, ever see the end. More than four-fifths of those who begin fall by the wayside; forty in every one hundred are satisfied with the privilege of one-year military service; the remainder (39 per cent.) do not reach that standard. It remains to be said, therefore, that while the chief aim of the secondary schools is preparation for the university, they are really fitting the great majority—85 per cent. and more—of their pupils for a practical life. And a doubtful preparation it is.

<small>Future Occupation.</small>

GENERAL REFERENCES:—*Centralblatt für die gesammte Unterrichts-Verwaltung in Preussen; Statistisches Jahrbuch der höheren Schulen Deutschlands,* 1897–1898; Wiese-Kübler, *Gesetze und Verordnungen; Lehrpläne und Lehraufgaben für die höheren Schulen,* Berlin, 1893; *Instruction für die Directoren der höheren Unterrichtsanstalten der Provinz Brandenburg (amtlich),* Berlin, 1868; *Instruction für die Lehrer und Ordinarien an den höheren Unterrichtsanstalten der Provinz Brandenburg (amtlich),* Berlin, 1868.

CHAPTER IX

EXAMINATIONS AND PRIVILEGES

THE aim of the higher schools in Germany is to give an *Allgemeine Bildung*, but it should be clearly understood that this liberal education is intended at the same time to be the first stage in a practical preparation for life. Every higher school is at once a place of liberal culture and a fitting school for some specific vocation or profession. The union of these two ideals has gradually come in the course of the present century to be well understood and everywhere recognised as inevitable. This fact is responsible for much of the confusion and uncertainty to be met with in the educational system.

Aim of Higher Schools.

Theoretically and historically, too, in a degree, the secondary education of Germany is absolutely divorced from the practical affairs of life. "First make a man, and let the man look out for himself," is the motto that perhaps best expresses the idea of the old school-masters. "In making a man, make one that will be good for something," is the principle underlying the administration of the higher schools at the present time. School curricula and pedagogical theories, as a rule, emphasize the cultural side; governmental regulation and the official management of school affairs emphasize the practical side.

Unites Theoretical and Practical.

The system of examinations and privileges in operation in all Germany bears striking testimony to the fact that the higher schools have a special mission in combining liberal culture and practical ability.

In the first place, the very method of conducting examinations is designed to test the power to use knowledge rather than the extent of information. It is not so much what a pupil has learned that counts,.as what he can do with it; not *Wissen,* so much as *Können.* That incubus of written examinations, which weighs so heavily on British schools, and which is so popular in some parts of America, particularly in the State of New York and some Canadian provinces, would never be tolerated for a day in Germany, not even by the most conservative pedagogue of the old school. They would say that by such means you may gauge more or less accurately of a pupil's knowledge and skill in displaying it, but it leaves untouched the very facts which an educator most wants to know—the desire for further study, power of will, love of home and country, religious feelings and the appreciation of the good, the true and the beautiful. Not what a man has, but what he is, is the true test of educational progress. "As a man thinketh in his heart, so is he."

<small>Purpose of Examinations.</small>

Next, it will be observed that with the completion of successive grades in the higher schools certain privileges are granted which determine admission to all the higher vocations and professions. This makes not only each school, but each grade, a step in a general course of professional or business training. The successful working of such a plan requires that young men on leaving school shall know something of practical worth and that they have the ability to use it in further preparation for their respective careers in life. The student who completes a gymnasial course must have definite knowledge of those subjects which he will need in the university; all students, no matter what their future occupations, need to be put in touch with the best that the national life and thought has to offer. The schools are confined to a definite curriculum, which is prescribed by the state; its workings are supervised by the state; and the state examines the results, and points out the possible lines of future advancement. But the way in which this is done is specially instructive.

<small>The Practical Side.</small>

EXAMINATIONS AND PRIVILEGES 177

A pupil's promotion within the school depends upon (1) the quality of his daily work, (2) private and public examinations and (3) the judgment of his instructors. The kind of school in which he is entered and the length of his course therein determine the possibilities of future study and occupation.

Conditions of Promotion.

A teacher is required to note the daily work, conduct, industry and attention of his pupils, and from time to time to grade them accordingly. This should be done whenever the teacher has seen enough of his pupil to enable him to form sound judgment, say, daily in the lower classes, where the teacher has better opportunity to judge, and at least once a week in any case. No checking of errors as they occur, and no marking by percentages, is allowed under any circumstances. The teacher who should attempt to note in class each mistake made by his pupils, as though his business were to find errors rather than give instruction, would be excluded from a German school as unfit for his office. The designation of grades which are officially recommended for use in the higher schools is as follows: "Very Good," "Good," "Satisfactory," "Barely Satisfactory," "Unsatisfactory." The value of written work, as class exercises, notes and essays, is estimated in the same way and noted in the class records. At the end of each quarter, as a rule, and necessarily at Easter, Michaelmas, and Christmas, the reports of all teachers are gathered in and entered in the individual record-books of the pupils. The pupil's book gives the name of the pupil, the class to which he belongs, the number of pupils in the class, his industry and attention, his marks in the various studies, list of punishments received, notice of promotion and a space for remarks, followed by the signatures of the director and class-master (*Ordinarius*). After this report has been countersigned by the parent or guardian of the pupil, it is returned to the school, and placed among the school archives. It belongs to the school, and not to the pupil. The parent's signature is evidence that he has seen the official record of his son's work, and is fully acquainted

The Marking System.

with the school's estimate of his progress. On leaving school a pupil receives a certificate showing his standing at the time; his record-book, as I have said, remains in the school. And under no circumstances is it permissible to give a pupil his relative standing in class. Each person is entitled to a certificate showing what he has done, but he may not receive any information concerning the work of others.

At the close of the school-year, in faculty meeting, the standings of all pupils are considered, with a view to promotion. Inasmuch as a strict class system prevails in German schools, individuals must be promoted with the class or remain where they are at least another semester. Occasionally a pupil will be allowed to make up some deficiencies during vacation. As a rule, however, pupils are promoted on the basis of a "Satisfactory" standing in the more important subjects. Under this category are to be understood, of course, in the *Gymnasien*, German, Latin and Greek.

Promotion in Course.

Examination in the higher schools are of two kinds: (1) private, (2) public. The private examinations include the entire round of individual and class tests which are considered in the reports to parents, and which have any bearing on promotion. Public examinations are for the sake of appearances—a concession to the curiosity and pride of parents. The aim is thereby to give parents, patrons and friends of the school some idea of school life and school work. These exhibitions are given at the end of semesters, the one at Easter being of chief importance. The director's report of the work of the past year, the *Schulprogram* or *Jahresbericht*, extends a formal invitation to the *Schlussfeier*. The public examinations are conducted by the regular teachers of the various classes, and continue about half an hour each. Drawings, note-books, and other handiwork of the class are on exhibition. Then follows a program of declamations, readings and music, in which the entire school takes part.

System of Examination.

These public tests are generally severely criticised as being superfluous and an unnecessary strain upon pupils. But, on the other hand, it is conceded that the school owes something to the patrons, as well as to its pupils. The schools are public institutions, supported by public funds, and the public has a right to know something of the inner workings of the system. It should be remembered, too, that these days are the only ones in the entire year when parents, or anyone else except state officials, can gain admission to Prussian schools, except by special permission of the Minister of Education. But such an argument does not appeal strongly to a Prussian school-master. Many schools—the city *Gymnasien,* of Berlin, for example—have abolished the public examinations, and others are contemplating similar action. In the *Karolinenschule* of Eisenach no public examinations have been held since 1890. Instead, one entire week toward the end of the last quarter is set aside, during which parents are invited to hear instruction in all classes which their children attend. The plan has met with marked success in Eisenach; but Eisenach is not in Prussia. *[Public Examinations.]*

Private examinations in course are conducted by the teachers at their discretion. For these each school is free to make its own regulations. The only ones of exceptional significance are the intermediate examination (*Abschlussprüfung*) at the end of the sixth school-year, and the leaving examination (*Abgangs-, Abiturienten-, Reife-* or *Maturitätsprüfung*) at the end of the ninth year. *[Private Examinations.]*

The *Maturitätsprüfung* was introduced in Prussia in 1788, reaffirmed in 1812, and made obligatory for admission to the university and the learned professions in 1834. The plan has subsequently been adopted by all the German states. The far-reaching consequence of this examination made it necessary that it be conducted with extreme care, and according to an approved norm. It should be remembered that while the state exercises strict control over the higher schools, *Lernfreiheit* *[Introduction of the Final Examination.]*

rules in the universities. A university student may study what he will, when he will, or need not study at all. If he registers for one lecture a week, pays his fees and conducts himself with ordinary propriety, no questions will be asked. He may spend one semester, or twenty, in the university; it is nobody's business but his own. It not infrequently happens that students, especially of the wealthier class, spend two or three years in idleness bordering on dissipation. The strict discipline of the *Gymnasium* and the long and continuous course of study are frequently urged as an excuse for license in the university. The state, however, relies for support upon its educated youth. Social influence and political intrigue would soon sap the vitality of the entire civil service, were not bulwarks erected by the state itself to withstand the tides of incompetency. These safeguards are, first of all, the leaving examination, and, in the second place, special examinations before royal commissions, for entrance to the various professions and administrative posts.

The *Maturitätsprüfung* is the first real test of individual ability. The *Staatsexamen* comes, in the ordinary course of events, after about five years of professional study. The one discloses signs of promise in the youth; the other tests the strength of manhood.

It has been urged, inasmuch as the teachers in the higher schools are state officials—men well educated and profession-
<small>Point of Contact between State and School.</small> ally trained, and on the grounds, too, that the schools themselves are state institutions, therefore the state should accept the leaving examination as evidence of fitness for admission to professional study. In answer, it has been pointed out that school-masters belong to a single profession, and that they are presumably unacquainted with the inherent needs of the other professions, much less familiar with the essential requirements of the practical administrative affairs of the state. Common sense, accordingly, demands that the state be represented in the examination, to offset local influences. The representative of the state on these occasions does not usurp the functions of

the school, but appears rather as a counsellor and friend. Very considerable power is given the school faculty, both as to who shall be admitted to examination and what shall be the character of the examination itself. In this way there is secured a happy blending of local government and state control.

The purpose of the leaving examination is to ascertain whether the candidate has accomplished the work of *Prima*. All *Gymnasien* which have been approved by the Minister of Education have the right of holding this examination. The subjects for examination are religion, German, Latin, Greek, French, history and geography, mathematics and physics. English and Hebrew are optional subjects. The examination committee consists of a commissioner appointed by the provincial school-board, who is chairman, the *Director* of the *Gymnasium*, and the regular teachers of *Oberprima*. The representative of the provincial school-board is usually the *Oberschulrat*, who is inspector of the school. In case he cannot act, the *Director* of the *Gymnasium* is usually commissioned to fill his place. Patrons of city and endowed schools also have the right to name one member of the examining committee. Their representative is generally elected for a term of years, and has a vote on all matters. *[The Examining Board.]*

Absolute secrecy is enjoined on all members of the examining board. Admission of a scholar is seldom permitted earlier than the second semester of *Oberprima*. Application for examination is to be made in writing three months before the end of the semester. The director then places before the committee these applications, together with a complete record of all candidates from the date of their admission to the school and such other information concerning their work, character and future occupation as may seem to him desirable. The committee is empowered to recommend for admission to the examination all those whom they unanimously find to be "satisfactory" in scholarship and morals. This *[Admission to Examination.]*

report is thereupon transmitted to the provincial school-board. It must show with regard to each candidate: his name, age and place of birth; the religion, occupation and residence of his father; his deportment, industry and standing throughout his school course, and his choice of future occupation. Notice must be given at the same time of all cases rejected by the committee, and the reasons for such action. This done satisfactorily, the provincial school inspector designates those applicants who may come up for the final examination.

The final examination is both written and oral. As required in the *Gymnasium*, the written examination in-
<small>Subjects of Examination in Gymnasium.</small> cludes (1) a German essay; (2) a translation from German into Latin; (3) a translation from the Greek, and (4) from the French into German; and (5) four problems in mathematics—one each from plane geometry, solid geometry, trigonometry and algebra. The oral examination includes Latin, Greek, religion, history and mathematics.

In the written examination all candidates in the same subject are examined at the same time. The questions set must
<small>The Written Test.</small> be of a nature familiar in *Prima* and of no greater difficulty. They must not, however, be so like those already studied that the test would lose the character of independent work. Passages for translation are to be taken from works similar to those read in class, but previously unseen by the candidates. The examination paper as a whole is made up after the following fashion: Each teacher of *Prima* gives the director a list of three questions in each subject. These, if approved by the director, are then sent to the provincial school inspector, who makes up the paper from the questions submitted. But if the questions proposed do not seem adapted to the purpose, if they are not up to the standard, or if there is any other reason why they should not be used, the inspector may alter them or replace them entirely. The director and the teachers are placed upon their honour not to disclose the questions

for the examination or take unfair means to prepare their classes for them.

The examination is held in a room of the *Gymnasium* and under the supervision of a member of the examining committee. The time allowed is five (morning) hours for the German essay; five (morning) hours for mathematics; three hours each for Greek and French; two hours for Latin. No intermissions are allowed except in case of the mathematical examination, which may be cut in two. In translating from a foreign language, lexicons are allowed; and for the mathematical work, a table of logarithms. All papers, whether complete or not, scrap-work included, must be handed in at the expiration of the period. Any attempt at deception during the examination is severely punished, even to the extent, if necessary, of exclusion from all future examinations. The extreme penalty, however, requires the approval of the Minister of Education. *How Conducted.*

The papers in each subject are read by the teachers concerned, errors are noted, and the grades "Very Good," "Good," "Satisfactory," "Barely Satisfactory" or "Unsatisfactory" assigned, according to the merits of the papers. All marks are then brought together, and a decision is reached by the committee in conference on the admission of candidates to the oral examination. A detailed report is then made to the provincial school-board. The original papers and each set of answers are sent in, together with a statement from the director of the reference books used, and that further than this no assistance of any kind has been given. The papers are then examined by the inspector, who approves the markings or makes such changes as seem to him necessary. *Marking Papers.*

Candidates who are not excused on account of very superior work in the written test are now required to take the oral examination in the presence of the provincial school inspector, who sets the day to suit his own convenience, and the assembled teachers of the school. All the records of the candidates during *Prima*, *The Oral Test.*

their note-books, essays and other written work, are on exhibition, and may be made the basis of examination. Ten candidates at a time is the usual number admitted to examination. Classes above ten are divided and the groups examined on different days. The inspector, who is chairman of the committee, arranges the order of subjects and designates the time for each. No helps of any kind are allowed. The teacher of any subject is the chief examiner in that subject; after him, anyone may continue the test. The inspector may interject questions at any time, or take the lead himself in case of necessity. In Latin and Greek, candidates are expected to read at sight ordinary prose of a kind similar to the readings in *Prima*; the verse which is called for is generally that studied during the last semester. Criticism and exegesis are always in order. The examination in history is confined to the later periods, especially the development of Prussia. Physics is not prescribed for examination, but it is recommended that it be treated incidentally in connection with mathematics.

The examination in each subject is graded by the chief examiner (*i.e.*, the regular teacher of the subject), with the approval of the other members of the committee.

The Final Standing. The committee then goes into executive session, and considers in detail all matters pertaining to the examination, both written and oral, of each candidate. Three factors enter into the final decision: the candidate's record in the school; the results of his written examination; and his standing in the oral test. The passing mark in all three is "Satisfactory." High standing in some subjects, however, may atone for slight deficiencies in others; but no candidate will be passed who is deficient either in German or in both the classical languages. The grade "Unsatisfactory" in one of the classics may be offset by a standing of at least "Good" in the other ancient language, in German or mathematics. In the same way, "Unsatisfactory" in mathematics requires at least "Good" in Greek, or Latin or German. All members of the committee have a right to vote, the youngest member voting first; and in case of a tie the provincial inspector casts the deciding ballot. The formal report is then signed by all members of the committee, and the inspector announces the results to the waiting candidates.

Successful candidates receive a diploma (*Reifezeugnis*) signed by the provincial inspector of schools and other members of the examining committee. This diploma certifies to the character, conduct, attention and industry of the holder; to his standing in each subject of the examination, and to the quality of his work in *Oberprima*. It also designates his rank, all things considered, as "Very Good," "Good" or "Satisfactory." In case of failure the candidate may have two more trials, whether he attends school in the meantime or not.

The Diploma.

Persons who have not taken a regular gymnasial course, but who wish to enter the university and enjoy the privileges attached to the leaving examination, may apply to the provincial school-board for assignment to the *Maturitätsprüfung* of some *Gymnasium*. In the same way, graduates of a *Realgymnasium* or an *Oberrealschule* may be admitted to the gymnasial examination in subjects which they have not already passed.

The general regulations for the conduct of leaving examinations are the same in the *Realgymnasium* and *Oberrealschule* as in the *Gymnasium*. In each case the work of the last year of the course indicates the character and scope of the examination.

The *Realgymnasium* and the *Oberrealschule* require in the written examination (1) a German essay; (2) a French or English essay; (3) a translation from German into French or English; (4) four problems in mathematics — one each from algebra, plane geometry, solid geometry, trigonometry or analytical geometry; (5) one problem in physics or chemistry; and, in the *Realgymnasium*, (6) a translation from Latin into German. The oral examination is confined to religion, French, Eng-

Examination in Other Higher Schools.

lish, history, mathematics and either chemistry or physics, according to which is called for in the written test.

The candidate is not passed if his rank in German, or in both modern languages, is "Unsatisfactory." If "Unsatisfactory" in one modern language, he must be at least "Good" in the other, or in German or in mathematics. A realgymnasiast ranking "Unsatisfactory" in mathematics must be at least "Good" in the modern languages or in German; a candidate from the *Oberrealschule* who is "Unsatisfactory" in mathematics must be at least "Good" in physics or chemistry.

The *Progymnasium* includes in its written examination (1) a German essay; (2) a translation from the German into Latin, (3) into Greek and (4) into French; (5) two problems from geometry and algebra, and one in mensuration of solids. The oral examination comprises religion, Latin and Greek, history, geography and mathematics, including physics.

<small>Final Examination in Six-Year Schools.</small>

In the *Realprogymnasien* the written examination includes (1) the German essay; (2) a translation from the German into (3) Latin, (4) French and (5) English; (6) two problems from algebra and geometry, and one from the elementary mensuration of solids. The oral examination includes religion, French and English, history and geography, mathematics and science. In the *Realschulen* and higher burgher schools the written examination comprises (1) a German essay; a translation from German (2) into French and (3) into English; (4) two problems in algebra and geometry, and one from the elementary mensuration of solids. The oral examination is the same as in the *Progymnasien*.

No one can be graduated from any secondary school who is deficient in the mother-tongue. This is a result of the regulations and *Lehrplan* of 1892, in which special stress is placed upon the language, literature and history of Germany. Some of the standard subjects of the old examinations are no longer found; for example, the Latin essay and the Greek *scriptum*. While not

<small>General Requirements.</small>

all such changes are agreeable to teachers trained under the old dispensation, the younger men as a rule cordially support the new order. There can be little doubt that the writing and speaking of Latin as formerly taught in the schools was more an end in itself than a means to an end. The aim of modern methods is to give a liberal education that shall be as practical and useful as possible. And in the supreme test, as has been shown, no attempt is made unduly to test a candidate's memory. The only person who knows what a scholar is worth and what he can do, his teacher, is his chief examiner.

The *Abschlussprüfung*, which comes at the end of the first six school-years in the nine-year schools, and which corresponds to the leaving examination of the *Progymnasien*, the *Realprogymnasien* and the *Realschulen*, is of recent introduction. From the official statistics of the school-year of 1889–1890 it was found that, out of a total attendance of 135,357 in the secondary schools of Prussia, 20,038 left at the end of the year. Of these, 4,105 completed the course, 8,051 left at the end of six years, and 7,882 dropped out of the lower classes. It is seen, therefore, that of those leaving school forty per cent. were satisfied with a six years' course, while only twenty per cent. secured the *Reifezeugnis*. The important fact to be noted is that only 368 (from higher burgher schools) of those who left school at the end of the six years went out with a theoretically complete education. All others were in schools whose curricula required three years longer in attendance. This was one of the problems which engaged the attention of the Berlin School Conference of 1890. Up to that time all of the secondary schools, with the exception of the higher burgher schools, were organized for the express benefit of those who completed the nine years' course. It was recognized that nothing could be done for the thirty-nine per cent. who left school during the first five years, but for the forty per cent. who remained only long enough to secure the certificate for one year's military service

The Mid-Course Examination.

Reasons for Its Establishment.

it was felt that some reform was necessary. The curricula of 1892, therefore, were so arranged that those leaving at the end of *Untersecunda* would have a well-rounded training, at least in religion, German, history and geography, and mathematics. Opponents of the new order object to this measure on the grounds that it amounts practically to converting the nine-year institutions into six-year schools, with a three years' continuation course. That there is some ground for this view of the matter is evident from the especially marked tendency in the *Lehrplan* to go over in the last three years much the same ground as that already covered, but in a more thorough and intensive way. This theory of working in concentric circles has been attacked as contrary to the best pedagogical thought of the times. Nevertheless, the stern fact remains, and it is one with which there is no compromising, that more than twice as many students leave school from *Secunda* as finish the course. The practical necessity of assuring so large a percentage of high-school pupils a tolerably complete education has rendered imperative an awkward division in the curriculum at the end of the middle grades of the nine-year schools.

The *Abschlussprüfung* has been introduced, therefore, as a leaving examination at the end of the *Untersecunda* for all those who do not intend to continue their studies. It is of the same rank as the *Reifeprüfung* in six-year schools, and is conducted by an examination committee, under the direction of a school inspector, in precisely the same way as the other leaving examinations. But as yet few of the German states have adjusted their courses to it; Prussia is content to await their pleasure. In the meantime she is incurring the enmity of some well-meaning educationists, who would hold steadfastly to the highest pedagogical ideas regardless of the needs of a majority of higher-school pupils.

Its Comparative Rank.

There could scarcely be a better system of examinations for secondary schools than that which has been worked out in Germany. If one does not find himself in full sympathy with it on its theoretical side, he is forced to acknowledge its superior excellence in its practical workings, especially when it is contrasted with the prevailing systems in England and America. It is not a lash held over scholars to make them work the harder, nor does it convert a youth into a mere machine for grinding out facts on demand. It allows full play to the individuality of pupil and teacher, and gives both every opportunity for performing the best possible service. It leaves the teacher free to devote his best energies to the mental-spiritual development of his charge, without the suspicion that someone may come in, wholly ignorant of the character of his pupils and of his course of instruction, to test them on what might be the veriest non-essentials. It gives free scope for the best teachers to work out their problems in their own way; it sets a standard below which the poor teacher dare not fall; in short, it accomplishes all that any system of examinations could be expected to do, while it is free, at least in its practical workings, from the evils incident to the popular methods of this country.

Merits of the System.

It has been repeatedly pointed out in this essay that the higher schools of Germany serve purposes other than merely giving a liberal education. It is inevitable that a state system of education should be controlled in the interests of the state, but under a bureaucratic government there is danger of using the schools in the interests of the class that happens to be in power. The tendency in Germany to regulate everything that can be regulated applies to the control of public education as to everything else. Little chance is allowed anywhere to individual initiative; small credence is given to the ability of the masses to act aright. The German theory is that it is better to avoid mistakes than to make them even for the sake of gaining experience.

The System of Privileges.

It is with reluctance that I turn to the system of privileges so intimately associated with the examination system. It is at this point that the grip of the government is most seriously felt. The state is not content to give to youth a liberal education which he can use in the service of the state, but it must compel him to conform to a prescribed form if he would succeed. Thus it happens that each higher school, almost each year in school, has its cash value. It is a load which the schools can ill afford to carry. It mars what otherwise might be the most nearly perfect educational system in the world. It distorts educational progress, and bids fair ultimately to give an advantage to the enemies of the Fatherland, the value of which they seem thoroughly to appreciate.

There are three groups of privileges which may be distinguished: First, the right of one-year volunteer service in the army; second, the admission to the university and the learned professions; third, preparation for various posts in the civil and military service. The first two are of special interest in this connection.

Three Main Divisions.

1. The privilege of one-year volunteer service in the army (*Einjährig-freiwilliger Dienst*) is granted upon the successful completion of a six years' course of study in any recognized higher school in any German state, and to those persons not being pupils in a higher school who are fitted privately or by study in a school not officially recognised and succeed in passing a special examination similar to the *Abschlussprüfung*.

1. Military Service.

In the last century, when the army was recruited by conscription in the various cantons, university students were free from military service. So many accordingly entered the university for no other purpose than to avoid army service that a special examination was instituted in 1793 to determine who might take up university work with a profit. At first the examination was restricted to gymnasial students fourteen years of age. With the introduction of universal military service, in 1814, an exception was made in the case of young men of the upper classes who desired to devote themselves to professional study whereby they were given the privilege of but one year

Origin of One-Year Service.

of army service. Only those who gave promise of special ability were awarded the privilege. Students in the higher classes of the *Gymnasien,* even down to *Tertia,* who satisfied these requirements might receive the recognition. In 1822 the completion of *Tertia* was required, and since that time the standard has been gradually raised until, in 1868, the minimum requirement was set at the end of the *Untersecunda,* where it has since remained. Other changes have also been made. The privilege was granted first only to those who gave special promise of professional success. For thirty years, however, it has been held up as a prize for all who could pass a definite examination, notwithstanding that some might not intend to enter upon professional study at all, or even remain longer in school. As a matter of fact this latter class now includes more than one-half of all those who secure the privilege. Present Conditions.

With the foundation of the North German Confederation and, later, of the Empire, the system introduced by Prussia was adopted by the other states. In order to secure a greater uniformity in methods and an approved standard, an Imperial School Commission (*Reichs-Schulcommission*) was appointed in 1875, whose chief function is to advise the imperial chancellor as to what schools may with propriety be granted the privilege of awarding the certificate which frees its holder from one year of military service. This commission consists of six members : Four represent Prussia, Bavaria, Saxony, and Würtemberg ; a fifth member is chosen biennially from Baden, Hesse, Alsace-Lorraine and Mecklenberg-Schwerin in turn ; the sixth member represents the other German states, likewise in terms of two years. This is the only attempt made to unite the different states of the empire in any matter pertaining to school affairs. The members of the commission are all teachers, or officers in the Education Departments of the different states. The Imperial School Commission.

2. Admission to any faculty of the university, and ultimately to the learned professions, is unconditionally permitted

only to those who hold a *Reifezeugnis* from a *Gymnasium*. Graduates of a complete course in the *Realgymnasium* may pursue such courses in the university as will fit them to become teachers of mathematics, natural sciences and modern languages, but they may not study theology, law or medicine. A *Reifezeugnis* from an *Oberrealschule* grants the privilege of university study only in mathematics and natural sciences.

<small>2. University Study.</small>

The leaving examination which was introduced in Prussian schools in 1788 carried with it the privilege of admission to the university, but not until 1834 was the test of much practical importance. In the latter year it was made an essential prerequisite to all professional advancement. During the following generation the *Gymnasium* had a monopoly of all university preparatory work. In 1870, by the recognition of the *Realgymnasium*, Greek was made optional for entrance upon the courses in mathematics and modern languages. Finally, in 1892, the privileges mentioned in the preceding paragraph were granted to the higher schools. It has been a long struggle, the end of which is not yet in sight.

<small>Present Conditions.</small>

3. Graduates of *Gymnasien, Realgymnasien* and *Oberrealschulen* alike have the privilege of continuing their studies in higher technical schools in architecture; in civil, mechanical, electrical and mining engineering; in art, in agriculture—in short, in all lines which lead up to the state examinations for admission to all posts in the civil and military service not included in the learned professions.

<small>3. State Examinations.</small>

The privileges attached to certificates of completion of courses less than nine years in length will be found in full in the appendix to this volume. An examination of this table will show that the higher schools are the only gateways to positions of honour and trust in the state. Industrial and commercial occupations alone are freed from official interference; but with state control of the railways, telegraph and postal systems, of bank-

<small>Scope of the System.</small>

ing and certain industrial interests, even freedom in business is not altogether assured. Bureaucracy is omnipresent, and almost omnipotent; the higher schools, unfortunately, are a chief means of perpetuating its power.

GENERAL REFERENCES:—Wiese, *Das höhere Schulwesen in Preussen;* Wiese-Kübler, *Gesetze und Verordnungen; Centralblatt für die gesammte Unterrichts-Verwaltung in Preussen;* Encyclopedias of Schmid and Rein; Phillip, *Das höhere Schulwesen im Königreiche Sachsen,* Dresden, 1889.

13

CHAPTER X

STUDENT LIFE IN THE HIGHER SCHOOLS

THE school life of the average German boy, estimated in English or American terms, is rather tame and uninteresting.

Schooling a Serious Business. There is little of the dash and vigour, little of the vivacity and buoyancy of spirits, which we consider essential to the normal development of a healthy boy. Carelessness and indifference, where they exist, are evidences of laziness rather than of perverseness. The German school-boy has no time for sports; family pride and personal ambition keep him incessantly at his tasks. The good time that he looks forward to, the time of his freedom from bondage, comes with his admission to the university. "Then," he resolves, "I will do as I please."

This getting of an education is a serious matter to the German youth, and he looks every inch the martyr that he really is. He has no interest in outdoor games,

No Time for Play. no especial fondness for indoor gymnastics; he is practically denied what every American boy considers an inalienable birthright, the privilege of joining with his fellows in societies for moral, intellectual and social purposes; an ardent admirer of all things military, yet military drill forms no part of his physical training until his school-days are over. The inevitable consequences are clearly to be remarked in the middle and upper grades—great unevenness in form and stature, sallow complexions and general lack of animal spirits. Skating seems to be the one form of popular recreation. The recent revival of gymnastics may have done much, it may yet do more, for the physical well-being of the German schools; but I have serious doubts of the complete success of the system so long as it provides for no spontaneous outdoor sports.

The *esprit de corps* of the public day-schools is, in my opinion, weak and uncertain. Too many pupils regard themselves deprived of harmless liberties, many others have no thought except to get through and away; there is far too little personal contact of teacher with pupil, too little love and devotion between pupil and teacher. A strong sentiment of loyalty to the school and its traditions cannot thrive in such atmosphere. It would be erroneous, however, to conclude that because school loyalty is not strong, therefore disloyalty and anarchy prevail. To all appearances German school life is neither the one nor the other. It has always impressed me as being almost entirely devoid of sentiment, good or bad. The average boy seems to consider schooling a necessary evil—something to be endured patiently, resolutely, thankfully, if only thereby he escape social damnation. _{Little School Spirit.}

So far as I can judge, the little effervescence to be found in the day-schools is allowed to work off in harmless public entertainments, to which the parents have a special invitation. At the close of the year it is customary for the director to issue the program of the year's work, including list of graduates, important announcements and an invitation to all interested to attend the closing exercises. These consist (1) of public examinations; (2) of rhetorical, musical or gymnastic exhibitions, and (3) of public lectures. _{Public Exercises.}

The examinations are purely formal in character, as has been already stated, and are of comparatively little interest except to parents. The Berlin city schools have done away with them altogether; many others would like to, but the time does not seem to have come for severing another link that binds the present to the past.

The rhetorical and gymnastic entertainments are always liberally interlarded with excellent musical selections. The very lack of an inspiring school life sends German boys to their homes for amusement and recreation. And the cultured home is certain to be musical. It is an open question whether the love of music is cause or effect of the prevailing disregard of outdoor sports; at any rate, the two interests do not seem to thrive well together. There is devotion to music in the home, and there is a love for it in the school. The result is plenty of good musicians, few good athletes. Elocution is little practised; the ability to write clearly and to read well is everywhere considered an essential element in education. Public exercises, therefore, are most popular in which music and essay reading predominate. The patriotic theme is the prevailing one for public occasions; panegyrics on William I., Bismarck and von Moltke are good stock in trade. Hero-worship is a settled policy of the Fatherland; from it patriotism is born.

Music and Readings.

The birthdays of the reigning sovereign and the anniversary of the victory at Sedan are occasions of special rejoicing, of speech-making and of freedom from lessons. On these days all public buildings are decorated; bunting, flags and streamers are flung out from every house, and at night illuminations are visible on every hand. In school all work is suspended. The boys gather early to hear an oration from some one of the masters on the significance of the day; after this short exercise there is freedom for all.

Public Celebrations.

The German boarding-schools, some of them at least, occupy an honourable place in the school system. The gymnasial schools are as proud of their records as Eton, or Harrow or Rugby. The cloistral schools of St. Afra in Meissen, Schulpforta and Rossleben are the most famous of the gymnasial boarding-schools. The two former were founded in 1543, and Rossleben is only eleven years younger. St. Afra has an income of 125,000 marks, of which more than one-half is from its original endowment. Besides running expenses, this provides

Old Boarding-Schools.

free places for 105 scholars, and 25 more receive some aid. The Saxon Minister of Education grants 65 of these scholarships, 11 of which must be given to sons of clergymen; 20 places are at the disposal of certain noble families, and the remaining 45 belong to some 26 cities of Saxony. Only boys of thirteen, or those prepared to enter *Unterter-* *tia,* are admitted. That the St. Afra boys are kept busy is evident from the following order of the day: 5 A.M., rising bell; 5.20, prayers and first breakfast; 5.40, study; 6.30, free; 7, lessons; 9, second breakfast; 9.15, lessons; 11, free; 12, reading; 12.45 P.M., dinner, afterward free; 2, lessons; 4, free; 5, study; 7, supper; 8.15, busywork; 9, prayers; 9.15, younger pupils retire; 10, lights out.

Meissen.

Rossleben, with an income of 129,000 marks, is distinctly a school for noblemen. It has about eighty pupils in seven gymnasial classes; boys are taken first in *Quarta.* The thirty free places provided for in the endowment are awarded by four members of the Witzleben family, direct descendants of the founder of the school. The discipline at Rossleben is truly Prussian. The extreme penalty, removal from the school, is attached to the violation of many rules. Typical prohibitions are the following: gambling in any form, having playing-cards in one's possession, all aping of university societies and customs, having or drinking wine, beer or liquors on school premises. No sweetmeats may be brought to the school; visits to the confectioners', as to beer-gardens, are regulated by the teachers in conference. The *Rektor* inspects all correspondence in which the boys are a party.

Rossleben.

Schulpforta—income, 273,000 marks—is perhaps the finest type of upper-class school. Its situation, midway between Kösen and Naumburg, on the banks of the Saale, is especially charming. The gray stone walls of the old cloister, the ivy-covered towers, the soft colourings of the tiled roofs and the Gothic spires of the newer buildings combine harmoniously to produce an effect quite in keeping with the beauty of the natural surroundings. The

Schulpforta.

grounds, several acres in extent, are walled in as they were, I suppose, three hundred and fifty years ago. At the entrance stands an imposing building belonging to the administration department; for one must know that Schulpforta is a considerable village of itself—at least, it provides employment to the usual number of government officials. Near by are the barns connected with the agricultural domains of the institution. Farther down the avenue and directly facing it stands the main group of buildings, consisting of the cloister, which is used as a school-house and boys' home combined, library, chapel and gymnasium. The houses of the *Rektor* and the married masters, the hospital and home of the school physician, stand by themselves apart. The class and study-rooms are dull and unattractive; the chapel, *aula* and library have recently been modernized, but without violence to the spirit of their mediæval architecture. In the rear of the buildings is a spacious play-ground—such as would delight the hearts of the most fastidious foot-ball team—while several pieces of outdoor athletic apparatus and a bowling-alley for each class do not lessen its attractiveness for the German school-boy. Of the one hundred and eighty places in the school, one hundred and forty are free. The Prussian Government awards half of these, and the remainder are distributed among certain Prussian cities and the church. Even the casual visitor to Schulpforta must be impressed with the beauty of the place and the wealth of its historic traditions. Who can tell what events occurred here, what tragedies were enacted, before the quiet convent of Luther's time was transformed, under the influence of his teaching, into the protestant school that Maurice of Saxony made it! A portrait of the founder hangs on the chapel wall; and a kindly face it shows, too, but his full coat of burnished armour bespeaks methods not wholly peaceful in the accomplishment of his purposes.

The modern boarding-school is of a different type. In so far as the modern spirit is commercial are these schools adapted to that end; but there are many learned men in Germany who deprecate the hard and fast lines of the public schools, and accordingly seek out for their sons a more elastic curriculum. Such a school must necessarily be private, though privileged to prepare for the volunteer army service. The *Stoy'sche Erziehungs-Anstalt* in Jena, which I choose to describe at length, is one of the best of its kind. For the student of education it has an especial interest in that it embodies to the very detail those ideas which made Professor K. V. Stoy one of the most famous educators of the last generation. The world already knows of his early struggles to found a truly educational institution on the Herbartian principles, which should at the same time be a training-school for his university students in pedagogy. From the small beginning in 1843 there developed eventually the original Stoy School. But when Stoy was called to Heidelberg, in 1866, the school in Jena passed into strangers' hands. Fourteen years later the old banner was again raised over a new institution bearing the name of the old master, but with a son of the former one, Dr. H. Stoy, as the new *Direktor*. The pupils of the old school transferred their allegiance to the new, and the friends of the father became supporters of the son. Its success was assured from the start.

<small>The Stoy School.</small>

The school property, situated on the rising ground in the northern part of the town, is some two or three acres in extent. A large piece of land on the heights a mile below Jena is also in the possession of the school, and there the head-master has a summer cottage where the boys find entertainment on many of their country excursions. The school buildings, four in number, are in the Swiss style of architecture. The school-house, a three-story building completed in 1892, is admirably arranged for class purposes, well lighted and ventilated and heated by steam. In addition to class-rooms, it provides a large room for drawing, another for the very large collection in natural history, besides chemical and physical laboratories; another building serves for gymnasium and workshops; a third is the hospital, which is fitted up for ten patients. The boarding-

<small>Equipment.</small>

hall, an imposing three-story structure, is the home of the *Direktor*, the unmarried masters and seventy boys. On the first floor are the head-master's rooms—eight in number—the kitchen, dining-room and lower class study-rooms. The entire second floor, save for teachers' conference-room, seniors' study-hall and a servants' work-room, is divided into four dormitories, each with fifteen to twenty beds. The third floor is arranged for teachers' rooms and rooms for music, school library and housekeeper's appointments.

The army life, which the average German boy looks forward to with pleasure, predisposes him to regard favourably the barrack system in his boarding-school. The dormitories of the Stoy School are scrupulously clean, but absolutely wanting in those conveniences which American boys consider indispensable. The single pair of hooks at the head of each bed and the row of towels surrounding the general wash-stand were the sole articles of use or luxury that I could detect. The bedsteads are of iron, single, and without springs. Each boy provides his own mattresses and bedding, as well as towels, napkins, spoons and personal clothing. The requirements in these respects are unusually large, and bespeak a good class of patronage. A boy's school expenses vary from 1,200 to 1,500 marks yearly.

Dormitories.

The household management is exceptionally good. In systematic precision it is truly German—and Prussian at that. The housekeeper, besides the customary duties of such a position, takes entire charge of the boy's wardrobe and keeps it under lock and key. Except at stated times, a boy may not have even a change of handkerchiefs without a written order from the *Direktor*. Twice a week clean underwear is given out, and the soiled articles gathered up from the dormitories the next day. In the linen-room there is a case for each boy's clothing; every article, even to the shoes, must be marked with the boy's number. Special requests for clothing may be made to the head-master after supper; the orders are written in the housekeeper's book, and the articles, as ordered, are delivered in the sleep-

Regulations.

ing-rooms before the boys go to bed. Orders for the shoemaker and tailor are taken in the same way, by number, and the record is retained by the housekeeper, through whom all such business is transacted. In this work the housekeeper is assisted by a maid ; she has, too, under her direction a cook, two waitresses, who also do the chamber work, and two resident porters and their wives. The laundry work is done in town, the housekeeper being responsible merely for the mending.

The school is a *Realschule* with six classes. In addition there is a lower school of three classes, for boys from six to nine years, which is intended to fit for any kind of higher school. The school usually numbers about one hundred and fifty pupils, most of the lower school and some of the older boys being day pupils. French is taught from the beginning of the course, and English the last three years. Latin and Greek may be had only in private lessons. Mathematics and the sciences are especially emphasized. Elective subjects are quite unknown, as indeed is the case in all German schools. Six Classes.

The masters, twelve in all, are appointed by the *Direktor*, subject to confirmation by the state department of education. The qualifications are the same as for the public higher schools, *i.e.*, university training followed by the state examination, and then a year in a pedagogical seminary and another year as trial teacher in a higher school. The assistant city pastor gives lessons in religion, and there are two special music teachers. The salaries are practically the same as for the public schools, 1,800–4,000 marks. New appointees, beginning at the minimum, are advanced annually 100 marks for the first ten years, after which private arrangements are made. The ordinary supervision of the hall is divided among the masters, whether resident or not, each taking a day in turn ; and a day means twenty-four hours ! At Schulpforta the masters serve a week about, taking the entire discipline, day and night. On Sundays and half-holidays extra supervision is required from the younger masters. Three conferences a week are held—two on house matters and one for the school. Subjects for discussion arise from the written reports of the supervisors and from the class-books, in which are noted the main points of every lesson and the progress and deportment of the pupils. Aside from these conferences, the masters not on duty are entirely free. In view of the fact that the average teacher gives not more than twenty lessons a week, it must be acknowledged, I think, that a master's position in a German boarding-school is not only more secure but less irksome than usually obtains in American schools. The difference in the national customs and modes of life is undoubtedly the prime reason; but, whatever be the causes, the fact remains that the German is more independent and can less justly complain of the never-ending round of extraneous duties incident to boarding-school life.

By courtesy of the head-master I was enabled, on March 5, 1894, to spend an entire day with the boys of the Stoy School.

A Day's Experience. It was not yet daylight when I began my rounds with the teacher in charge. At six o'clock the boys are called. One sleepy lad fumbles around for a bit of paper, and when it is found he brings it to the master for his signature. It is explained to me that the poor fellow has the pernicious habit of sleeping a little late in the morning—and you know Germans must never be late—hence this collection of teachers' autographs. Half an hour is allowed for dressing, turning down the beds and putting all in order; at 6.30 the sleepiest boy of the lot must leave the room, not to return till 9 P.M. The dormitories are then carefully inspected by one of the boys, who notes in a book the numbers of those luckless chaps that have forgotten to hang up their towels, to open the windows, or otherwise have done offence to the letter of the law. In the meantime the boys are exchanging, in the corridor below, their house-slippers for shoes, which have been carefully polished for them overnight and placed by the porter in the numbered compartments of a large case. Next they line up on each side of the hallway, where they are inspected by the master; the roll is called by number, each boy speaking out his own. The monitors—the *Helfer*, so called—one for the sleeping quarters, another for the study-rooms and boot-case are appointed by the faculty from the upper classes and serve for one week; then give their report. Delinquents must at once make good their failures; then breakfast is announced. Before taking places at the tables all gather about the piano to sing the *Morgenlied;* to-day it is a single stanza of one of Luther's hymns.

The breakfast would scarcely satisfy an American boy—two small rolls (no butter) and a cup of tea for the elder pupils, hot milk for the younger ones, is the entire bill of fare. But it is the German custom to breakfast on coffee and rolls. The room is of ample size, finished in dark woods and ornamented with the ever-present signs of German patriotism—the busts of the recent Emperors, Bismarck, Moltke, Schiller and Goethe. I remark that the circle is incomplete, as the Grand Duke and Duchess and the Empress are wanting; but I am told that it is for lack of room, not of loyalty, that it so happens.

<small>Breakfast.</small>

After breakfast comes an hour of study. There are four rooms for this purpose, three of them connected and under the supervision of a teacher; the first class and a few selected from the second enjoy the privilege of a separate room under the guidance of a monitor. Each boy has a table with drawer, and woe to him who lets confusion enter here; besides this he is allotted a shelf in the general bookcase and a small cupboard, which is under lock and key. This last is the boy's own, his sole possession that escapes inspection. I got a glimpse of the contents of one compartment belonging to a twelve-year-old : a pair of skates, a ball, an old cap, a handkerchief or two that had escaped the housekeeper—so much was on the surface, the rest must be left to imagination. At eight o'clock we go to the schoolhouse, where we assemble in the drawing-room to sing the morning song. Recitations begin at the first quarter of the

<small>Study-Hours.</small>

hour and last forty-five minutes each. According to the German plan each class, with the exception of the *Vorschule*,
<small>Lessons.</small> recites every period. The schedule for the upper classes, therefore, calls for some thirty-three to thirty-five periods a week, but naturally little outside preparation is expected.

At ten o'clock comes the second breakfast. Each boy gets a generous slice of black bread with butter, which he eats <small>Second Breakfast.</small> while at play in the yard. And here let me remark, parenthetically, that the second breakfast is even of more consequence than the first ; the roll and coffee may be dispensed with, but not so with the *Butterbrot*. In the *Volksschulen* the pupils generally are equipped with two huge slices of very black bread and a minimum of butter. At this mass the child gnaws away during every intermission of the morning, and notwithstanding the size of the piece—often eight to ten inches long by two thick—I have seldom seen a division made of the lunch for the different periods. Sufficient unto the day is the bread thereof !

The work of the morning is finished at twelve, save on Wednesdays and Saturdays, when it runs till one o'clock, be-<small>Dinner.</small> cause of the afternoon half-holidays. At 12.15 the study-tables and bookcases at the hall must be in perfect order. The boys then line up in the corridor, as in the morning, for inspection, rollcall and the report of the *Helfer*. By eights they go to the lavatory to make ready for dinner, which is served promptly at 12.30. It consists to-day of boiled rice and beef, prepared, I am told, according to a recipe brought by one of the pupils from his home in Greece. It appears to be relished by the boys, who return their plates for two or three extra portions. Black bread completes the list. There is no butter, nothing to drink— not even water. The hour after dinner most of the boys spend in play about the yard. In the meantime I am initiated into the mysteries of the higher circle. The masters gather in the room of one of their number, who serves us with coffee, cakes and cigars. Thus a pleasant hour is spent before the afternoon work begins. From two o'clock till four recitations are held, as in the morning; the *Vorschule*, however, is free. From four until five the masters are in conference over the final examination papers of the first class. A little before five the boys again put on their slippers, and are then admitted to the dining-room, where they find slices of black bread spread with *Pflaumenmuss*, a sort of prune marmalade. A few, by order of their parents, get also a bowl of hot milk. No especial order is kept during this afternoon meal—*Vesperbrot*, so-called; some sit at the tables or in the window-seats, others walk about the hallways. Soon the bell sounds for study. At 6.45 there is another roll-call, inspection, etc., in preparation for supper.

Vesperbrot.

The evening meal is the most interesting one, perhaps because the most elaborate of the day. We find at each table a large platter piled high with sandwiches of black bread and smoked herring. Tea and milk are served, and there is plenty of butter. In an astonishingly short time the platter is cleaned and replenished again, but this time with corned-beef in place of herring. Whether or not the change is a concession to my American stomach I cannot say, but I have no doubt that the original package bore the brand, "Chicago Corned-Beef." At the end of the meal the head-master notes the wants of the boys: first in the tailor's book—No. 15 has torn his coat, 33 wants buttons on his vest, while nothing short of cleaning and pressing will suit the fastidious taste of 47; next is the shoemaker's turn, and various are the orders for new soles and patches that he gets; in yet another book are noted the numbers of those who last night disturbed the peace of one sleeping-room, and in consequence are sentenced to do special tasks in the study-room for an hour after their peaceful comrades are in bed. Special requests from the first class are granted those who wish to be called an hour earlier to-morrow morning—the dreaded "final" is only one week distant. Still another book goes to the housekeeper.

Supper.

Wants.

Ten minutes are thus spent and no end of annoyance saved for twenty-four hours to come.

At 7.30 all boys go to the shops. Here they work in five divisions, corresponding in general to the school years: the beginners are busied with paper work—box-making, bookbinding, etc.; the second division uses hand fret-saws; next come classes in wood-carving, carpentry and wood-turning in order. This work, which is in charge of master workmen from the town, is carried on only during the winter on Monday, Tuesday and Friday evenings. Some good pieces are turned out; but on account of the short time of training and the somewhat cramped quarters, the results are mainly beneficial by way of diversion for the pupils. I doubt not that the dormitories will be the more quiet tonight in consequence of the evening's employment, and the poor lads who must put in an extra hour of penance will find their tasks the more trying. The bell rings at nine o'clock for *Abendlied*. Again all gather about the piano in the dining-room, and, under the leadership of the head-master's wife, sing the evening song, a single stanza of a well-known hymn. The boys then pass in single file before Frau Stoy and the teachers present, shaking hands with all and wishing all good-night. Fifteen minutes later the peaceful part of the community is in bed. The work of the day is completed with the final inspection of the dormitories by the two teachers who sleep with the boys tonight. We pass from room to room, turn down the lights and say "*Gute Nacht*," the signal for quiet. That the average boy will gladly heed the injunction I am persuaded no less by the drowsy replies that reach our ears than from my own feelings at the prospect of coming rest after a long day of interesting and novel experiences.

<small>Manual Training.</small>

<small>Good-Night.</small>

The order for Sunday is varied by rising an hour later, church from 9.30 to 11.00, after which a period is set apart in which letters must be written home. At dinner beer is served to those who wish it, all getting one glass, the older boys two glasses. Sunday after-

<small>Sunday.</small>

noons, as on the Wednesday and Saturday half-holidays, the entire school, in charge of one or two masters, takes a long walk; on week days the excursion rarely lasts longer than two hours, but on Sunday it is customary to prolong it to three or more. In summer the first order for Sunday morning is a swim in the river at six o'clock; on week days the bathing hour is 4 P.M., and every boy in the school must join in the sport under the eye of the master and the teacher in charge. On Wednesday and Saturday evenings, when swimming is not possible, the boys go to the bath-room dressed in bathing-suits and there enjoy a shower-bath *en masse*. The head-master takes special supervision of this hour. On retiring each boy finds on his bed a complete change of linen and underwear, which he must wear on the morrow. Once a month on a half-holiday there is a general hair-cutting, the barber coming to the hall, after which each boy takes a warm tub-bath.

The Stoy school has been distinguished from the days of the "old doctor," as I hear him called, for especial attention to bodily development, even making the physical training as important an item in the curriculum as any other. The long walks above mentioned on three days of the week tend directly to this end. The summer trips, of which I shall speak later, are not only valuable from a general educational point of view, but they serve to test the bodily vigour of the boys. The preparation, however, which enables even the youngest boys to undergo long tramps for twenty days in succession consists mainly in class exercises in gymnastics. The gymnasium (*Turnhalle*) is fitted up with parallel and horizontal bars, and such apparatus as is necessary for vaulting, jumping, etc. In comparison with an American gymnasium of the better class the outfit is scanty, but the deficiency is in large part made good by outdoor apparatus. Poles and ladders for climbing, all framed together, and bars of various kinds, find a place here. It is needless to say that the boys appreciate most what is at all times accessible to them. I

Physical Training.

have seen a dozen of the smaller lads, bareheaded in midwinter, climbing around like monkeys on the highest framework and apparently enjoying the fun to the utmost, despite the slippery rods and the flying snow. Once a week the entire school has a class exercise in gymnastics (*Turnen*), and on two other days the juniors and seniors exercise separately. For this purpose the scholars are divided into groups of six or eight, each with a leader, or so-called *Vorturner*. In a special hour on Sunday the *Vorturner* receive directions and drill in new movements which, with the master's help, they are expected to carry out in the exercises of the week.

It was my pleasure to attend the Stoy *Turnfest* held in August, 1893, on the last Sunday of the semester. The student body marched into the play-ground in column of fours, headed by a drum corps and buglers. Following some evolutions, a hearty song was sung and an exhibition given on the parallel bars by ten of the older boys. The upper school then separated into squads of eight, each of which had a special task, *e.g.*, vaulting, jumping, exercise on horse, buck and bars. Calisthenics and games by the lower school called out some applause. But to an American the striking feature was the lack of all competition; and, indeed, not till toward the end of the program was any spirit manifested, and that only in running and pole-climbing. Nevertheless, it would be an error to conclude that the boys found little pleasure in the performance; on the contrary, the winners received as hearty congratulations as one could wish, and the prizes and laurel wreaths were as proudly displayed as if won in that heroic struggle miscalled foot-ball. The pent-up enthusiasm of the day seemed to find full expression at the close of the singing of "*Deutschland, Deutschland, über alles.*"

I am told that there are field-sports; but I have seen none of them save a flimsy attempt at foot-ball, a recent importation from England. The fact is, there is no time for sports as we know them; there are no two hours of the week in succession not provided for in the school schedule. The theory that short periods of alternate work and rest produce the best results is characteristically German; but, as one of the boys remarked to me, "two 'works' to one 'play' is nearer the truth." There is as little time for indoor diversion as for sports. The absence of a boys' parlor or reading-room testifies to this. But in music they find a solace quite unknown in American boys' schools. There are three music teachers: one gives his entire time to the violin, piano and orchestra; a second conducts the singing, and a third gives private lessons on the 'cello. Twice a term there is a private musical recital, followed by dancing, to which the boys' friends are invited; every other year in midwinter a public recital and ball are given in the town opera-house; in alternate years a large masquerade ball is held, to the great satisfaction of the boys. The birthdays of the Emperor, the Grand Duke and Luther are also publicly celebrated—generally by speeches interspersed with music.

Field-Sports vs. Music.

The great event of the year, however, the one around which all extraneous interest centres, is the *Schulreise* of the summer holidays. More than forty years ago Professor Stoy undertook, with the boys of his training-school, his first trip into the Thuringian forest. Thenceforth it was made a veritable part of the curriculum, and many and strange are the stories told of incidents connected with these early tours. In these days the journeys are more pretentious, owing to the greater depth of the patrons' pockets. Early in July the boarders, with the entire corps of teachers, spend four days in the Thuringian forest. In 1893 the region between Blankenburg and Coburg, including the Schwarzerthal, was explored. On the way glassworks and stone-quarries were visited, and a day was spent at the famous old castle in Coburg. But the real pilgrimages come in August. The hall is divided into three parties, according to age and strength of the pupils, and to each party three or four teachers are assigned. The first division, led by the head-master, usually goes to South Germany; a few

School Journeys.

days are spent in Munich, with the special view of studying architecture and the rich collections of the city museums, after which the Bavarian Alps are visited. Last August the route included Nuremberg and Augsburg; thence through Switzerland into Tyrol, and on to Venice; thence back to Munich. During this trip of three weeks, the boys were most of the time on foot; travel by rail was of course necessary, but was indulged in sparingly. The total expense per boy was 140 marks.

The customary routes for the second division are (1) the Harz Mountains and the Rhine Valley; (2) Dresden, Prague and Bohemia, or (3) the Bohemian forest, along the Danube to Passau, Nuremberg, home. The third party goes to the upper valley of the Saale, and thence through the forest to Eisenach.

Routes.

The educational value of these journeys lies chiefly in the fact that, inasmuch as the entire hall must join them, a general preparation can be made a part of the school-work for a year in advance, and the results summed up afterward in permanent form. The routes are carefully planned from the beginning of the fall term by the masters in conference. Accurate maps are drawn by the boys, and every effort is made to arouse the scientific imagination. The history of art, especially in architecture, is studied, and the lessons in general history are made to supplement the special means of preparation. On the trip each boy makes notes and sketches of the chief points of interest; these are worked over immediately at the end of the trip, that nothing be lost. Before Christmas it is expected that he will write a complete history of his journey, and, as this is a part of the essay writing for the fall term, the pupil profits from suggestions from his teacher, and has the additional stimulus of writing on his own experiences and making a book for himself. Some of these accounts are most interesting. I have seen one of some three hundred octavo pages, bound in two volumes, written by a member of the second division; with its tasty head-lines, initial letters and numerous

Educational Value.

pen-and-ink sketches, it is really artistic. To be sure, not all the boys are artists; but most of them can show a good account of what they have seen.

To promote good fellowship among the students, the school is divided into five clubs, *Kameradschaften*, to each of which belong two or three teachers. The older members of a club are in a way responsible for the conduct of their fellows. Comrades are expected at all times to be mutually helpful, and it is a point of honour that the strong should aid the weak. Pin-money for the boys is deposited with the senior masters, according to *Kameradschaften*; cash-books must be kept by all, and those of the juniors are left with the masters. The usual allowance varies from one mark fifty a month for the youngest to three marks for the seniors. *Student Clubs.*

There is little need, as we have seen, for boys to go into town on errands, and the permission is rarely granted. The desire for sweetmeats, no less strong here than elsewhere, is scarcely considered a legitimate excuse; but with true Yankee ingenuity a young friend of mine —I hope he will not count me an informer, after such a lapse of time—is doing a flourishing business as a result of the ban. These operations, confined as they are to imports—whether on the theory of free-trade or tariff for revenue only, I am not informed—undoubtedly contribute not a little to the commercial training of all concerned. But mischief is not rampant among the Stoy boys; indeed, one must look long and closely to detect signs of the ordinary human weaknesses. This is due in part to the thorough supervision, but a still more potent cause is that these boys are Germans—and Germans are born to obey. *Side-Lights.*

No feature of German school life calls out more criticism from foreigners than the seemingly exacting discipline, especially of Prussian schools. Good masters have remarked to me—and I am inclined to credit the statement—that the average school-boy considers an amiable teacher as a prodigy fit only for girls' schools. The all- *Discipline.*

pervading military spirit tends in a different direction. Most boys are anxious to serve in the army, if they can do it as volunteers. Something by way of a uniform and brass buttons is the delight of the youngsters, and as they grow older their favourite game of "war-play" is barely left off before the days of actual service. But there is a wide difference between a conscript and a volunteer: the one serves two years at no expense to himself; it costs the other at least fifteen hundred marks for the privilege of wearing the "Emperor's coat" one year. It is not the difference in length of service that begets the eager volunteer, nor yet the desire to expend a sum greater than is necessary for a year's attendance at the university; but above all considerations stands social rank. To have had ten years of successful schooling counts for nothing when reckoned with that higher distinction of belonging to a family that can afford the ten years of training and the fifteen hundred marks besides. There it is in a nutshell! Not only the boy himself, but his entire family as well are concerned in his success at school. The final examination *must* be passed at all hazards, and no means thereto, however severe or exacting, if successful in the past, will be repudiated by the patron. The boy can afford to take no chances. The result is an obedience bordering on servility. It is a factor of prime importance in estimating correctly the peculiarities of German schools, and especially must it be reckoned with in the boarding-school. The original causes are to be sought in the social and national life rather than in the personality of the teacher.

GENERAL REFERENCES:—*Jahresberichte* and announcements of Schulpforta, St. Afra in Meissen, Grimma, Rossleben and the *Stoy'sche Erziehungs-Anstalt* in Jena.

CHAPTER XI

INSTRUCTION IN RELIGION

"See to it that your children above all things are instructed in divine things, that you first dedicate them to God and then to worldly matters," was Luther's advice to the German people. And down to the present century the chief end of all school teaching was the training of young men for the ministry and of a laity that would accept their leadership. Even under a national school system the principal function of the German school is officially declared to be the making of "God-fearing, patriotic, self-supporting citizens." It is recognised that the harmonious development of the human mind means more than merely intellectual acuteness; the heart must grow with the head, if the whole man is to be developed. A character lacking religious knowledge, principles and ideals is not an ideal character. Too much of our modern civilization is founded on Judaism and Christianity to make it possible to dispense with a knowledge of these religions, and too much is involved in the religious life to make it safe for the state to disregard spiritual training. On utilitarian grounds, therefore, if there were no better reasons, the German states insist on the teaching of religion in all elementary and secondary schools. *Luther's Advice.*

It never occurs to a German that there could be a valid reason for excluding religious instruction from the public schools. He would as soon think of eliminating the entire national literature, as the Bible, from the school curricula. As literature, if nothing else, he would accord it a prominent *Religion an Essential Part of German School Training.*

place. But in protestant Germany the Bible, Luther's Catechisms and Luther's Hymns are reverenced above all books; to the masses they are constant reminders of their religious liberties. And Luther's words are words of life to his people.

The fact that there are fewer religious sects in Germany than in America accounts in part for the retention of religious instruction long after the separation of school and church. There are practically only three denominations: Lutheran, Catholic and Jewish. Nearly two-thirds of the total population are adherents of the Evangelical Church; roughly speaking, they make up all central Germany. The Roman Catholics are next in importance, and are to be found especially in Bavaria, along the Rhine and in the extreme eastern part of the empire. Jews are everywhere, but particularly in the cities.

Three Religious Denominations.

The historical relations of church and school can still be traced in the designation of every public secondary school as protestant, catholic or jewish, according to the confession of the majority of the scholars.

Schools and Teachers.

In a protestant school, for example, the director and most of the teachers will be members of the Evangelical Church, and the instruction of the classes in religion will be given by the regular teachers. But in case there are at least twenty-five children of another faith in the school, a class must be formed for them and a teacher engaged who belongs to their church. The teacher may be a member of the regular staff, if he has a certificate for the subject; or, what is more likely, a local minister will be called in and installed as special teacher, in the employ of the state. In the large cities it generally happens that one higher school will be jewish, another catholic and the rest protestant. Whenever there are two or more higher schools of different confessions, the dissenting pupils in one will be sent to another school for instruction in religion.

It is the constitutional prerogative of every parent that his children shall not be compelled to attend religious instruction contrary to his own belief, and that no child shall be denied admission to the public schools on religious grounds. On the other hand, every child in the secondary schools must receive some instruction in religion; if not received in the schools, the parents must provide for it privately in a systematic way and from regularly authorized instructors. *Religious Training Required.*

General-superintendents of the Evangelical Church, catholic bishops and jewish rabbis are permitted at stated times to inspect the religious instruction of their respective confessions, but they have no right to interfere in any way with the work of the teachers. *Ecclesiastical Supervision.* If they have criticisms to offer, they must address them to the provincial school-boards, who are authorized to take such action as may seem expedient. While the church has no direct control of religious instruction in secondary schools, this right of supervision puts the church in a position to know what is being taught and indirectly to direct its course. Moreover, one school inspector in each province is generally a catholic, which insures a respectful hearing of the views of the minority. Inasmuch as the state church of Prussia is evangelical, it follows that the religious instruction in the protestant schools is more directly under state control than is the teaching in other schools. But no instruction is given without official sanction. The government appoints all teachers, prescribes the courses of study, approves the text-books and tests the results by examination.

Teachers of religion are trained, certificated and appointed like all other teachers; they enjoy the same rank, honours and emoluments as other teachers. In fact, unusual significance is attached to these positions. *Duties of Teachers.* Instructors in religion must not only be scholars and skilful teachers, but they must also possess high moral character and gentlemanly bearing, such as will exercise an unconscious influence for good over the young. The examining boards and school inspectors are specially warned to pass no candidate who does not possess these characteristics in an eminent degree. The ability to lead and inspire boys and young men is the essential prerequisite to this office. A ministerial rescript of 1826 admonishes all teachers of religion not to forget the responsibilities of their position. They are not merely to train the intellect, but to educate their pupils to high Christian citizenship; it is their duty to inculcate not simply a pleasing theory of morals, but faith in the living God and in Christ as the Saviour of men. The text-books used must express correctly the doctrines of the Evangelical Church, which make religion the basis of all morals, and which represent a living faith in Jesus Christ and salvation through Him as the end to be attained.[1]

Teachers of religion are not confined to this subject alone. Religion may be taken as a major or minor in the state examination, like other subjects, and the certificate received determines the grades in which instruction may be given. In the *Friedrichs-Gymnasium* in Berlin, nine out of twenty-four members of the faculty teach religion; two of the nine have made religion their major subject. The subjects which are naturally allied with religion are German, the classical languages and history.

Certification.

The following is the course in religion, as outlined in the program of the *Friedrichs-Gymnasium* in Berlin, for the year 1895-1896:

Prussian Course of Study.

Sexta: 3 hours. Selections from the Old Testament, especially the early history, the patriarchs, Moses, David, Elias and Elisha, according to the Schulz-Klix, *Biblisches-Lesebuch*. Selections from the New Testament relating to the birth, resurrection and ascension of Christ. Explanation of the Christmas, Easter and Whitsuntide holidays. Learning of the first part of the Catechism, with Luther's exposition. Drill on biblical quotations and four church hymns (Nos. 6, 1, 33, 35 in *Lesebuch*).

Quinta: 2 hours. Selections from the New Testament relating to the life of Christ. Learning of second part of Catechism, with Luther's exposition. Biblical quotations. Review of the Catechism and hymns learned in *Sexta*, and the learning of four new hymns (Nos. 8, 30, 22, 25 in *Lesebuch*).

---

[1] Wiese-Kübler, *Verordnungen und Gesetze*, I., pp. 162-3.

Quarta: 2 hours. Winter—Reading of the more important parts of the New Testament : The Sermon on the Mount, Parables (Matt. xiii., Luke xv.). Travels of the Apostle Paul. Review of the life of Christ, at the holiday time. The books of the Bible. Practice in quotations. Summer— Reading of more important parts of the Old Testament, with especial reference to the prophets, and part of Apocrypha. Geography of Palestine. Throughout the year a study of the third part of Catechism, with Luther's exposition ; memorizing of Parts IV. and V. Review of the Catechism and hymns learned in *Quinta* and *Sexta*. Drill on four new hymns (Nos. 2, 15, 18, 24 in *Lesebuch*), and Psalms xxiii., xlvi. and cxxxix., 1–12, 23–24.

Untertertia: 2 hours. Reading of selections from the Old Testament relating to the history of the Israelites ; also from the Psalms and Job. History of the church calendar and the significance of the church festivals. Review of the Catechism and biblical selections, and memorizing of hymns (Nos. 12, 28, 26, 21 in *Lesebuch*), scriptural texts and Psalms xc., ciii., 1–13, and cxxvi.

Obertertia: 2 hours. Selections from the New Testament, especially the Sermon on the Mount and the Parables. The history of the Reformation, in connection with the life of Luther. Review of the Catechism, biblical quotations and hymns already learned. Discussion and explanation of the sacraments, in connection with the history of the Reformation.

Untersecunda: 2 hours. Exegesis of the Gospel according to St. Matthew. Biblical antiquities and literature. Reading of selections from the prophets, Job and Psalms, and the story of the crucifixion according to Mark, Luke and John. Comprehensive review of the Catechism and of the selections and hymns already learned.

Obersecunda: 2 hours. Apostolic history. Epistle to the Philippians. The church calendar. Review of the Catechism, biblical selections, hymns and Psalms previously memorized.

Unterprima: 2 hours. Summer—Chief epochs in church history. Christianity and the heathen powers. Dissension in the Apostolic Church. The most important Church Fathers—Augustine and Pelagius and Boniface. Rise of the Roman Catholic Church. Scholasticism and mysticism : their bearing on the Reformation. The most important tendencies in the subsequent development of the Evangelical Church.

Pietism (Spener and Francke), the Moravians, home missions, sects. Winter—Exegesis of the Gospel according to St. John.

Oberprima: 2 hours. Winter—Exegesis of the Epistle to the Romans. Summer — Dogmatic Theology and Christian Ethics, in connection with Art. i.-xvi., xviii. and xx. of the Augustinian Confession. Outline history of the church hymns.

The course of study is so arranged that in the lower classes special attention is given to Bible stories, mostly biographical, and to memorizing church hymns, the catechism and selected scriptural texts. The middle grades aim to present a tolerably complete notion of the Christian religion, as expounded by Luther, some church history and the significance of the forms and ceremonies of the church. Although after *Untertertia* no more formal memorizing is required, frequent reviews help the pupils to retain what they have previously acquired. In the upper grades the character of the work is somewhat changed. A general study of the history, antiquities and literature of Holy Writ and a history of the Christian Church are introduced. Special attention is given in all classes to broad reading, research and exegesis, not of isolated passages, but of complete parts and books.

[Contents.]

The methods of teaching religion are practically the same as those employed in teaching German and history. The teacher tells the story of the lesson, or has it read by the class. Then follows a discussion by question and answer of the chief points, with a view to bringing out clearly the ethical or religious truths involved. The lesson generally centres around some scriptural text, which is committed to memory as an index of the whole. This practice accounts for the great amount of memorizing generally required in the lower grades. In 1871 the department of education recommended the following list of scriptural texts, to be learned in connection with Luther's Catechism:[1]

[Methods.]

Sexta: 2 Tim. iii. 15-17; John xvii. 17; Matt. xxii. 37-

---

[1] Wiese-Kübler, *Verordnungen und Gesetze*, I., pp. 165-6.

40, x. 28; 1 John v. 3; Ps. xxxvii. 5; Jas. iii. 9–10; Matt. v. 37; Gal. vi. 7–8; Ps. l. 15; Ex. xx. 9–10; Luke xi. 28; Eph. vi. 1–2; Prov. xxx. 17; Rom. xiii. 1; Hebrews xiii. 17; Eph. v. 3–5; Matt. v. 8; 1 Tim. vi. 9–10; Hebrews xiii. 16; Eph. iv. 25; Matt. xii. 36; Jas. i. 13–15; Gal. v. 24; 1 John ii. 15–17; Matt. xxvi. 41. *Selections to be Memorized.*

Quinta: Eph. ii. 8–9; Hebrews xi. 1; Rom. i. 19–20; Rom. ii. 14–15; John. iv. 24; Ps. cxv. 3; Ps. xc. 2; 1 John iv. 16; Rom. xi. 33–34; Ps. cxxxix. 1–4; Ps. v. 5; Jer. ii. 19; 2 Cor. xiii. 13; Ps. civ. 24; Ps. xxxiii. 13–15; Matt. x. 29–31; Isa. xlv. 7; Hebrews i. 14; 1 Peter v. 8–9; Rom. v. 12; Gen. viii. 21; Eph. iv. 18; John iii. 16; 1 Tim. i. 15; Acts iv. 12; John x. 30; Matt. xxviii. 18; Matt. xxviii. 20; Isa. liii. 4–5; 1 Peter i. 18–19; 1 Cor. xv. 17; Rom. iii. 24–25; Phil. ii. 12–13; Ps. li. 5–6; Acts xvi. 30–31; Gal. v. 6; 1 Tim. iv. 8; John xv. 26; Ps. cxliii. 10; 1 Cor. xii. 3; 2 Cor. v. 17; John iii. 3; Hebrews ix. 27; 2 Cor. v. 10; John xi. 25–26; 1 Cor. xv. 42–44; 1 John iii. 2.

Quarta: 1 Tim. ii. 1–2; Ps. ciii. 1–4; Ps. cvi. 1; Matt. xv. 8; John xvi. 23; Rom. xiv. 17–18; Matt. vi. 33; Matt. vi. 14–15; 1 Cor. x. 13; Rom. vi. 3; Gal. iii. 26–27; Acts ii. 38; 1 Cor. x. 16; John vi. 53; 1 Cor. xi. 27–29; Ps. cxxxix. 23–24; 1 John i. 9.

The first period of the school-day is regularly given up to the classes in religion; in case of conflict, the director may use the succeeding period. In 1826 a prayer was ordered at the beginning and end of every school session, but in practice the morning prayer is all that is required. Prayer is offered at the opening of all special exercises, and once a week, generally Monday mornings, the entire school assembles in the auditorium for religious exercises. The directors of all private schools are required to hold morning and evening prayers, say grace at meals, attend public worship with their pupils and join with them in the church sacraments. *Classes.*

When pupils reach the age of fourteen or fifteen years, it is expected that they will present themselves for confirmation at Easter time. For some time previous to this important step each pupil receives special instruction from his pastor, as well as that prescribed for the school. A rescript of 1838 declares that a candidate for confirmation should be familiar with (1) the first five parts of the Small Catechism, the Ten Commandments, the Apostles' Creed, the Lord's Prayer; (2) the titles, order and principal contents of the books of the Old and New Testament; (3) the parts of the Bible upon which the important doctrines of the Christian religion are founded, and (4) the more common church hymns. The special instruction preparatory to confirmation is not a part of the regular school work; nevertheless, directors are expected to keep free for this instruction in the middle grades the hour from eleven to twelve on two days of the week, and teachers are required to reduce the amount of home study in these grades during the four weeks preceding Easter. It is at this point where church and school come into closest touch; through the confirmation class, the local clergy learn more of the religious instruction given in the schools than from any amount of official inspection.

Confirmation.

The subject-matter of instruction in religion is mainly from the Bible, Luther's Catechism and the church hymns. No text-books in German schools have been so long in use as these, and no others are considered so important to-day. It should be noted, however, that an expurgated edition of the Bible is always used—never a complete edition. But even with the youngest children whatever is used is kept in Luther's own words. A Child's Bible, or Family Bible, is always Luther's Bible with certain passages omitted. Educators believe that the child and youth are not prepared to understand the significance of all Holy Writ; the selections used, therefore, must be adapted to the pupil's mind, and arranged in such a way as will best serve the ends in view.

Subject-Matter of Instruction.

There are many comprehensive text-books in use which seek to place before the learner all the material for his study of religion. I have before me the Schulz-Klix *Biblisches Lesebuch*, which is referred to in the outline above given, and which is perhaps the most popular of all such books. Its popularity is seen in its enormous sale; up to 1896 it had passed through fifty-three stereotyped editions. Twenty editions have been issued since 1879.

Text-Books.

This book is divided into three parts: (1) Selections from the Old Testament, 141 pages; (2) selections from the New Testament, 64 pages; (3) general commentary, which includes (a) biblical information, 4 pages; (b) chief facts in the geography and history of the Holy Land, 6 pages; (c) history of the Old Testament, 10 pages; (d) history of the Jews to 70 B.C., 6 pages; (e) summary of New Testament teachings, 18 pages; (f) church history, 6 pages; (g) Luther's Small Catechism, 15 pages; (h) the church calendar, 5 pages; and (i) thirty-six church hymns, 20 pages.

The selections from the Bible are intended to present a continuous narrative from Genesis to Revelation. The list of topics is in itself so instructive that I present herewith, as an example of the whole, a complete outline of the New Testament selections:

Biblical Selections.

The Birth of Christ, Luke ii. Infancy of Christ, Matt. ii. The Boyhood of Christ, Luke ii. The Baptism by John, Matt. iii. Testimony of John, John i. The Temptation, Matt. iv. Jesus Begins His Ministry, Mark i.–ii. The Sermon on the Mount, Matt. iv. 23–25, v.–vii. The Centurion, Matt. viii. Nicodemus, John iii. The Samaritan Woman, John iv. The Woman of Canaan, Matt. xv. The Woman's Faith, Luke vii. The Disciples, Matt. ix., x. John the Baptist, Matt. xi., Mark vi. The Parables: (1) The Sower, Luke viii.; (2) The Tares, Matt. xiii.; (3) The Labourers in the Vineyard, Matt. xix., xx.; (4) The Prodigal Son, Luke xv.; (5) The Lost Sheep, Matt. xviii.; (6) The Rich Man, Luke xvi.; (7) The Pharisee, Luke xviii.; (8) The Good Samaritan, Luke x.; (9) The Great Supper, Luke xiv.; (10) The Wedding Dress, Matt. xxii.; (11) The Ten Virgins, Matt. xxv.; (12) The Talents, Matt. xxv. The Sayings of Jesus: (1) Who is the Greatest in the Kingdom of Heaven? Matt. xviii.; (2) Jesus, the Children's Friend, Mark x.; (3) The Rich Young Man, Matt. xix.; (4) The Worthlessness of Earthly Goods, Luke xii.; (5) Warning against Arrogance, Luke xiv.; (6)

From the New Testament.

The Fig Tree, Luke xiii.; (7) Martha and Mary, Luke x.; (8) Christ, His Mission, Matt. xx.; (9) The Kingdom, Luke xvii.; (10) The Widow's Mite, Luke xxi.; (11) Zacchæus, Luke xix. The Miracles of Jesus: (1) The Marriage, John ii.; (2) The Draught of Fishes, Luke v.; (3) Jesus Stills the Tempest, Matt. viii.; (4) The Healing of the Dumb, Mark vii.; (5) At the Pool of Bethesda, John v.; (6) The Feeding of the Four Thousand, Mark viii.; (7) The Feeding of the Five Thousand, John vi.; (8) Restoring the Blind to Sight, John ix.; (9) Raising the Widow's Son, Luke vii.; (10) The Daughter of Jairus, Mark v.; (11) The Outcasts, Luke xvii.; (12) Lazarus, John xi. The Pharisees and Sadducees, Matt. xv., xvi., xxii. The Entry into Jerusalem, Matt. xxi., Luke xix. Jesus Purges the Temple, Luke xix. Jesus and the High Priest, Luke xx. The Last Supper, Luke xxii. The Washing of the Feet, John xiii. The Designation of His Betrayer, John xiii. Jesus in Gethsemane, Matt. xxvi. Before the High Priest, Matt. xxvi. Before Pilate and Herod, Luke xxiii., John xviii.-xix. Crucifixion, Luke xxiii., John xix. Jesus' Words on the Cross, Luke xxiii., John xix., Matt. xxvii. The Burial of Jesus, John xix., Matt. xxvii. The Resurrection, Mark xvi. The Journey to Emmaus, Luke xxiv. Jesus Appears to His Disciples, Luke xxiv. The Doubting Thomas, John xx. The Last Words of the Lord to His Disciples, Mark xvi. The Ascension, Acts i. The Outpouring of the Holy Spirit, Acts ii. Peter's Wonderful Work, Acts iii. Persecution of the Apostles, Acts iv. Ananias and Sapphira, Acts iv., v. The Apostle in Prison, Acts v. Stephen, Acts vi., vii. Mission of Paul, Acts ix. Cornelius, Acts ix., x. Meeting of the Apostles, Acts xi., xv.

Under the title *Die Christlichen Confessionen*, Schulz-Klix gives a short sketch of the origin of the Christian Church; its divisions into the Greek Catholic, the Roman Catholic and Protestant branches; the history and contents of the Apostolic, the Nicean and the Athanasian creeds; the doctrines of the Reformed and Lutheran denominations; their origin, development and union in the Evangelical Church; and the principal articles of the Augsburg Confession.

Church History.

But what of the results? Six years of such a book as I have been quoting, and three years besides in a study of church history, dogmatic theology and Christian ethics, ought to bear magnificent fruit. Undoubtedly in many cases the results are all that should be expected, but this cannot be said of all. The government is undoubtedly right in seeking to attract to this work men of striking personality and deep religious faith. But it need not be said that this ideal is hard to realize. And when teachers are at fault, one must expect to find faults in their work. *Results.*

A well-known provincial school inspector stated the case to me somewhat in the following manner: It is certainly true that a very great change has come over the country in the last twenty years. The theory of evolution in the natural world has given rise to critical schools in history and theology. Young men have been leaving the universities for years with these critical notions in their heads, and the definite amount of religious knowledge which was once supposed to be essential to every man's education has been steadily growing less. Not a third as much is required to-day as was insisted on thirty years ago. The teachers are not so certain in their beliefs; the feeling of uncertainty in the teacher begets uncertain results in the class-room. Pupils consequently do not take the same interest in the subject. Many of them say openly that the teacher is obliged to teach them what he himself does not believe. At any rate, the results are unfortunate and are not growing better. It is the outcome of a bad philosophy which has been abroad in the land for the last half-century. *Criticisms.*

In the *Kreuzzeitung* of November 25, 1894, I find this scathing arraignment of German religious life: "As matters stand at present," it was said, "we have a double-entry system of spiritual book-keeping. For the masses, so far as they attend the elementary schools, and, theoretically, for pupils of secondary schools as well, we have instruction in religion on the lines of positive Christianity, in the name and by the authority of the state. In the universities, on the contrary, where the young men are being educated who will in time succeed to the leader- *Defects in German Religious Life.*

ship in church and state . . . something entirely different is put forward in the name of science; doctrines are preached which stand in sharpest contradiction with those given to the people. . . . This is excused on the ground that religion is for the people, and for them it is good enough as it is; science, however, occupies another field and seeks a different patronage—the two do not come in contact."

The church also is far from being satisfied with the religious education in the secondary schools, and some influential churchmen have attempted to bring about a reform which should give more time to religion.

Position of the Clergy.

This is strongly opposed by school-men, on the ground that not more time, but better men and better methods, are wanted. The prevailing opinion is that there is far too much formal memorizing. It is a good thing to know the catechism, most of the Psalms, many hymns, and a large part of the Bible; but if the religious life of the child is to be stunted thereby, it were better to let some things pass. It is said that some text-books give as many as three hundred and fifty disconnected scriptural texts to be learned by heart. It is no wonder that the letter kills the spirit. The school-men complain also that their scholars know the history of the Jews better than the history of the Germans. The remedy, they say, is not more formal study; for pupils might spend all their time on religion, memorize the entire Bible, and yet come out irreligious. Better no catechism than so many tears in learning it.

Professor Kirchner, of Berlin, speaks for the majority of his colleagues when he says: "If the religious feeling is not revered, awakened and fostered [in the home], the school can do very little. As a rule, the yearning toward God in a child's soul is very slight. A surfeit of religious doctrines, maxims, hymns, forms, ceremonies, prayers, as experience proves, often produces a result precisely opposite to the one intended. Not the school, but the church, has the largest share in fostering the increase of piety. Least of all should the school be

Views of Educators.

pressed into the service of a rigid orthodoxy; it should not forget that the educational point of view must be its standard. Lessons in religion ought not to be hours dedicated to devotion, but give instruction in a grave, cheerful manner. The school must be content to establish in its pupils genuine religious feeling and sound morality. The means of doing so is on the one hand instruction, and on the other the teacher's example. Hypocritical sanctimoniousness, external attention to church forms, nay, even polemics against those who hold a different faith, will have no good result. In the choice and treatment of subjects the standard must be genuine religious stimulation, rather than dead knowledge, scholastic erudition or barren forms."[1]

The ministry has now come around to this idea. The new curricula lay special stress on the spirit of instruction. "The religious instruction is to be so imparted that emphasis shall be laid upon the living acceptation and the inward appropriation of the facts of salvation and the Christian duties, and especial attention be given to the apologetic and ethical side. Along with considerable diminution in the amount taught, especially by cutting out the history of the church and dogma leading to the taking sides in religious controversies, the instruction, so far as it is based on history, is to be limited to the occurrences of enduring significance for the ecclesiastical and religious life." <small>Governmental Instructions.</small>

Still, it is better to have some religious instruction to complain of than none at all. The situation is not as bad as the doubters think. There is a vast deal of excellent work being done, and I am convinced that students who are seriously entering into their school work in other lines are as seriously studying the facts and principles of their religion. I rarely found a school-boy, whose judgment I considered of value in other matters, who was not deeply impressed with the worth of his religious train- <small>The Present Situation.</small>

---

[1] *Educational Review*, I., pp. 479-80. See also his monograph: *Zur Reform des Religionsunterrichts*, Berlin, 1876.

15

ing. There is much doubt, much senseless criticism, abroad in the land, but its sources are not to be sought in the schools. On the contrary, the religion of protestant Germany, as it is presented in the schools, is one of the most powerful forces making for unity in German life.

GENERAL REFERENCES :— Schüren, *Gedanken über Religionsunterricht*, Gütersloh, 1888; Wiese, *Der evangelische Religionsunterricht*, Berlin, 1891; Meyer, *Der evangelische Religionsunterricht an die höheren Schulen*, Hanover, 1876; Gottschiek, *Der evangel. Rel. Unt. in den oberen Klassen höh. Schulen*, Halle, 1884; Schrader, *Erziehungs und Unterrichtslehre für Gymnasien und Realschulen*, Berlin, 1893; Schiller, *Handbuch der praktischen Pädagogik für höhere Lehranstalten*, Leipsic, 1890; Encyclopedias of Schmid and Rein; Wychgram, *Handbuch des höheren Mädchenschulwesens*, Leipsic, 1897; Frick, *Pädagogische und didaktische Abhandlungen*, Halle, 1893.

CHAPTER XII

INSTRUCTION IN GERMAN

THE question of how to teach the mother-tongue, and of what to teach, and for what ends, is not new to German educators. For a generation it has arisen in one form or another to vex the devotees of the old system, and with each reappearance it has won increased favour from the public. It has been discussed scientifically on its own merits; it has been an important factor in the wider problem of the national policy in education; it has been invoked as the bulwark of the fatherland against the rising tides of social democracy. That there should be unanimity of opinion is scarcely to be expected. My purpose in this chapter is to extract from the mass of material at hand what seems to me of value to English readers, and at the same time to represent as faithfully as I can the essentials of theory and practice from the German point of view. *[sidenote: Its Purpose.]*

Instruction in the mother-tongue, it is generally conceded, should occupy a central place in the curriculum; it should be treated directly as an independent subject, and indirectly in connection with all other subjects of the course; it should introduce the pupil to the national history and literature; and its especial aim should be to beget a readiness in the correct use of the oral and written language. While there are few dissenters from the first proposition, a glance at the program of a Prussian *Gymnasium* shows sixty-two week-hours assigned to Latin and twenty-six to German. This would be contradictory were it not possible to teach the mother-tongue in- *[sidenote: Central Subject of the Course.]*

directly. The weight of departmental rulings favours this
plan. If the *Gymnasien* need for Latin more than twice the
time that is given to German, they must make the use of
good German an essential part of the training in Latin. A
sensible pedagogics bases this demand on higher motives:
All instruction may not be restricted to the subject in hand;
it should also contribute to the general culture. As new
ideas are acquired words must be found to match them. If
the pupil is allowed to speak in his vernacular, if his use of
language is not extended beyond the range of his provincial
dialect, it is safe to say that the new ideas will lose half their
value because inadequately expressed. With clearness and
correctness of expression comes a keener insight into the
mental content. And when every recitation is made indirectly an exercise in the right use of the mother-tongue;
when the pupil is taught to appreciate the value of concise,
correct and suitable language as the exponent of his ideas;
when every sentence written for a teacher's criticism is tested
not only for content but for form; and, above all, when the
teacher is always careful not to offend in written or spoken
word—when all this is carried out faithfully and cheerfully,
then is the difficult part of the training already accomplished.
And, further, if the mother-tongue is not taught indirectly
in connection with every other subject, the hours specially
devoted to it—be they never so many—will be disappointing.
It is not possible, if success would be attained, to have our
speech on parade certain hours of the week and off duty the
rest of the time.

The reading of good literature is its own reward; but when,
as in Germany, the literature breathes the national life and
spirit, the reader catches an added charm. If
Emphasis on Literature. he be a school-boy, he lingers long over the
tales of wonderful adventure and stirring pa-
triotism so characteristic of the fatherland, and thereby becomes—a German. Not only does he imbibe new feelings,
new ideas, but unconsciously his tongue acquires something
of the richness of the language in which he reads—a language

new, but yet his own. And the study of foreign classics, ancient and modern, gives him a deeper insight into the nature of the mother-tongue; the points of comparison not only fix the limits of his speech, but suggest greater freedom within its bounds. With right, then, is the study of literature emphasized in German schools.

Historically, German is one of the most modern subjects in the German schools. From the time of Comenius, and even earlier, there have been occasional advocates of German instruction; but in schools given over primarily to Latin there was small place for the mother-tongue. *Historical Development.* Moreover, it was not till late in the eighteenth century that there was such a thing as German literature, in the modern sense of the term; and it was wellnigh a century later before it gained admission into the school curricula. The first half of the present century was so overshadowed by formalism in all matters educational that what little attention was given to German was mainly the study of grammar and rhetoric. It is only in the last generation, almost in the last decade, that instruction in German has become respectable; and since 1892 it has advanced to first place in the estimation of the government. It is the beginning of a new era, in which the chief aim is to reveal to youth the wealth of their national inheritance and, through its literature, to inspire them with a deeper patriotism and a more abiding faithfulness to the German spirit. In the Berlin Conference of December, 1890, the Emperor placed himself frankly on the side of the nationalists. His declaration that the schools were making of their pupils young Greeks, young Romans, anything but young Germans, put the problem squarely before the people from a statesman's point of view. The result has been a thorough revision of the curriculum for Prussian schools, and a similar change in the school program of most of the smaller German states.

The new Prussian program went into effect at Easter, 1892. It has been severely criticised in many particulars, but I have not learned that the course in German has met with serious opposition. To be sure, there are those who say that, granting the wisdom of the general aim, the means prescribed are not calculated to attain those ends; but a teacher who accepts the fundamental principles will find, I think, small excuse to complain of official strictures. First, the time for German is increased—in the *Gymnasium* from 21 to 26 week-hours, in the *Oberrealschule* from 30 to 34, and in the *Realschule* from 21 to 28 for nine and six years' courses respectively. No distinction in aim or methods is made between the classical and the non-classical higher schools. The new program differs from the old one (1) in the increased attention to the national literature, (2) in the demand for more practice in composition, and (3) in a decided restriction of the time formerly given to the study of grammar.

<small>Recent Reforms.</small>

For the lower classes, in which the boys range in age from nine to twelve years, the new course is as follows:

<small>Course of Study.</small>

SEXTA.

Gymnasium and *Realgymnasium*, 4 hours weekly; *Oberrealschule*, 5 hours. (1) Grammar: Parts of speech; the simple sentence; strong and weak declensions. (2) Exercise in writing from dictation once a week. (3) Readings: fables, legends, stories from the national folk-lore and history. (4) Oral reproduction of stories told in class. (5) Recitation of poems committed to memory.

<small>Lower Grades.</small>

QUINTA.

Gymnasium and *Realgymnasium*, 3 hours; *Oberrealschule*, 4 hours. (1) Grammar: The simple and compound sentence; elements of the complex sentence. (2) Exercise in writing from dictation; punctuation. (3) Readings from the ancient legends and history. (4) Oral reproduction; first attempts at composition. (5) Recitation of poems, etc., as in VI.

QUARTA.

Gymnasium and *Realgymnasium*, 3 hours; *Oberrealschule*, 4 hours. (1) Grammar: The complex sentence; word-building. (2) Writing from dictation, to alternate with exercises written on what is heard in class; composition every four weeks. (3) Readings from prose and poetry. (4) Oral reproduction of what is read in class. (5) Memorizing and recitation of poems.

An outline of the entire grammar course may be found in Hopf and Paulsiek's reading-books for the lower classes. In this bare sketch of ten pages are given typical examples of the parts of speech and their uses, *Grammar.* the formation and development of the sentence and rules for punctuation. The declensions of nouns, pronouns and adjectives are illustrated by appropriate sets of endings. Six classes of strong verbs are distinguished according to change in root-vowel, and lists of each class are given; the formation of the principal parts of weak verbs is noted; a list of irregular verbs is added, but receives no comment. Prepositions are grouped according to the cases which follow them. In the treatment of the sentence few definitions are formulated; the peculiar uses of compound and complex sentences are classified according to the usual method of Latin grammars, and the Latin terminology is used throughout.

The above outline, or a similar one, I have found in use in several schools—but for teachers' use only. The education department positively prohibits the teaching of the German grammar as if it were the grammar *How Taught.* of a foreign tongue. So far as it is necessary it must be taught indirectly and inductively, but it should lead up to a clear understanding of grammatical theory. To illustrate, I once visited a recitation in *Sexta* in which attention was turned indirectly to the parts of speech. From occasional questions of the teacher I could see that certain parts were already known to the class. The adverb, however, was new, but from the material of the lesson words were found which answered to the questions, *how? when? where?* These were written on the board and names given to the groups. The use of the adverb and its forms of comparison were easily deduced. In a subsequent lesson I saw the preposition studied in the same way. On inquiry I found that the class was not so backward as the apparent ignorance of grammatical terms seemed to indicate. The teacher, who also had Latin in *Sexta*, preferred to make the one study supplement the other. From the beginning of the course declension and conjugation in Latin furnish ample drill in German forms, and the treatment of the sentence makes comparison of idioms fruitful. To systematize in the German recitations what is learned with the Latin costs small labour, and is the more likely to be of interest to the pupils because of the association. This teacher followed the new program to the letter, and were the results universally so good as in his class there could be no question of the wisdom of the measure.

The parts of grammar assigned to *Quinta* and *Quarta* are very difficult. Young boys, even natives, are not likely to find the intricacies of the German complex sentence easy. They do not use subordinate clauses in simple conversation ; and while they may understand, it is quite another thing to speak the language idiomatically. This must be learned for the most part in school. What with declension for everything declinable, genders that know no law and a phraseology doubly compounded, the masters of the lower grades see sorry times. English teachers may find comfort in knowing that fate has not exhausted all its woes in imposing on them a wretched orthography. Foreigners underestimate, I am sure, the hindrances met with by Germans in fixing the elements of their language. The training in Latin clears up many difficulties for gymnasial scholars, and for this advantage the *Realschulen* have a partial recompense in the larger number of hours assigned to German. The weekly exercise in writing from dictation is always connected with a recitation in the literature, and contributes to its review. In *Sexta* five or six simple sentences—usually selected to illustrate some grammatical principle as well—are deemed sufficient. The pupils' books remain with the teacher, who returns them with errors indicated in time for the next exercise. The

Difficulties in Syntax.

more common faults of writing and spelling are then discussed in class. In *Quinta* and *Quarta* the same methods prevail. The use of the extended sentence gives rise to difficulties of punctuation to which special attention must be given.

The real basis of all the work is the literature. The Prussian program requires that the reading be in line with the history for the corresponding grades; in the schools of central Germany I have noticed a disposition to join it with the instruction in religion as well. Hopf and Paulsiek's reader for *Sexta* (I quote this series because it is one of the most popular in use in German schools) has seventy-two pages of legends, fables and tales from the national folk-lore, of which fully one-half is from the Grimm collection; thirty pages contain historical sketches from the lives of the German emperors from Charlemagne to Frederick III.; and in the remaining forty-six pages of prose is to be found a variety of selections relating to animal life, nature, etc. Then follows some sixty pages —eighty selections—of poetry in which the historical element predominates. Many of the finest lyrics of the language are in the list. In fact, the book within its limits contains the best the language affords. The editors assume that the best is none too good for school use, and that boys of nine and ten years can appreciate it. Such a book is not read from cover to cover; for lack of time a large part must be excluded. Freedom of choice, therefore, is the teacher's privilege in the interest of his class.

<small>Literature the Basis.</small>

The readings for *Quinta* stand in close relation to the course in history for the same class : "Stories from the legendary history of the Greek and Romans." Tales from Germanic history of a corresponding era naturally find an important place. The same line is followed in *Quarta,* save that the legendary makes way for the historical.

The striking peculiarity of the instruction in the lower grades is the great emphasis put upon oral work. Reading-books are little used in *Sexta;* the teacher tells the story, after which the main points as they occur to the pupils are written on the board. This is a chance for skilful questioning, and it tests directly the pupils' attentiveness. The story is then reproduced orally by several pupils in turn; correctness of expression and completeness of detail are especially considered. The reading-books, if used at all, are brought out after the oral exercise, that the selection may be read aloud. Such comparison as naturally arises between the forms of expression used by the pupils and those of the author makes the work interesting and profitable. Often, however, the entire exercise is oral. I recall having once heard stories of the adventures of Ulysses related in order during an entire hour, the only advance being the account of the shipwreck and the landing on Calypso's isle. No text-book had been used during the semester; the only record was the outlines put on the board from day to day, which the boys copied into note-books. Frequent reviews kept the connection fresh in mind. Through *Quinta* the reader becomes gradually more used, till in *Quarta* the pupils read the advance lessons at sight. A thorough understanding of the piece must result from the written analysis and the oral reproduction which follows.

[margin: Oral Work.]

No writing, except from dictation, is expected in *Sexta*. During the first semester in *Quinta* the reproduction of the lesson is frequently in writing; in the second half-year the pupil occasionally writes his account at home. In *Quarta* he is asked for the first time to use his own words in the oral and written class exercise. Heretofore the aim has been to reproduce the exact form of his model. Theoretically, the memory is foremost up to the twelfth year. In a lower school I have heard an hour wasted —as it then seemed to me—in the endeavour to have reproduced exactly a dozen sentences related by the teacher descriptive of the Luther-room in the Wartburg. A picture of the room hung before the class, but notwithstanding the frantic efforts of the teacher not more than two or three of his pupils succeeded in the task. The boys took no interest

[margin: Writing.]

in the exercise, and failure was inevitable. The method, however, may be most successful, as I have since observed, in the hands of a good teacher; but I also note two conditions essential to success: (1) an interesting story; (2) reasonable freedom to the pupil in relating it.

The Germans recognize that the surest way of creating in a boy a love for good literature is to let him read it for himself. Desultory reading is time wasted; only in so far as the reader makes what is read a part of himself is it of value to him. *Memorizing.* The memorizing of choice selections, therefore, is an important feature of the entire course. From three hundred to five hundred lines are usually required in each of the lower classes. It is unnecessary to enumerate the selections; suffice it to say that the gems of the language are found therein.

The program for the middle classes is as follows:

UNTERTERTIA.

Gymnasium, 2 hours; *Realgymnasium* and *Oberrealschule*, 3 hours. (1) Grammar: Comprehensive review of the most important rules peculiar to the German. (2) Composition to be written out of school once a month. (3) Readings from prose and poetry. *Course in Middle Grades.* (4) Study of poetic forms, so far as necessary, in explanation of what is read. (5) Memorizing and recitation of poems as in lower grades.

OBERTERTIA.

Gymnasium, 2 hours; *Realgymnasium* and *Oberrealschule*, 3 hours. (1) Composition as in III*b*, to which is added reports on personal experiences in letter form. (2) Readings: lyric and dramatic poetry; some prose. (3) Rhetoric and prosody treated inductively. (4) Recitation of memorized poems and of selections from the dramas.

UNTERSECUNDA.

Gymnasium, *Realgymnasium* and *Oberrealschule*, 3 hours. (1) Instruction in essay writing through practice in selecting the material and arranging it in class; critical essay monthly. (2) Readings: *Jungfrau von Orleans* (in schools without

Greek, *Wilhelm Tell*), *Minna von Barnhelm*, *Hermann und Dorothea*. (3) Memorizing of selections from the dramas; first attempts in recitation of pupils' own productions.

The study of grammar is completed with the review prescribed for *Untertertia*. Custom varies widely, but my observation is that most teachers accomplish this review indirectly in connection with the reading. The study of syntax, together with continued practice in word-building (begun in *Quarta*) and in the use of synonyms, makes a good introduction to the later study of the science of the language.

Grammar.

The formal composition, which now appears in the program for the first time, is mainly descriptive; but translations from Latin or French are often accepted as equivalent. Such written work as obtains in the lower classes aims at exact imitation of what is heard or read; in *Untertertia* the pupils are expected to abstract from a more extended reading the important facts and relate them within smaller compass in their own words. The exercise is similar to what in American schools is sometimes called "paraphrasing." It has especial value in the study of poetry, both as an exercise in composition and in the elucidation of the text. The almost daily practice in oral and written reproduction of what is read in class prepares the way naturally for the more formal monthly composition. Besides these formal exercises in composition, each instructor assigns once a quarter-year a special task in his own subject to be written up in class. This work serves the dual purpose of an examination in subject-matter and in writing German.

Composition.

It is quite impossible to give here a comprehensive review of the development of the German methods of teaching composition. The subject is so interwoven with the development of the entire curriculum, and has passed through so many changes incident to the progressive educational ideas of the country, that it may not be explained apart from its wider environment. Composition in some form

Essay Writing.

has always held a prominent place in linguistic instruction; it is not so long ago that the writing of Greek and Latin was the highest test of scholarship in Germany; and, in fact, it is only since the promulgation of the new Prussian curriculum that the Latin and Greek essays have retired to a subordinate place. In proportion as less stress has been put upon composition in foreign tongues has the German essay advanced to a front rank. But a lingering prejudice among the older masters does not hasten the modern reforms. If anything were ever damned by faint praise, it is the German essay in the hands of some of these erudite classicists. The younger teachers are not so; their minds are not fixed by long years in a single class-room, and the spirit of the new program finds its fullest and heartiest expression in their work.

The "practical teaching of essay writing" prescribed for *Untersecunda* is too often, I fear, a mockery. The theories of ancient rhetoricians, as cut-and-dried by tradition in Germany, are not conducive to the highest results, especially with men who write almost any language better than their own. *{Methods of Teaching It.}* But I have seen most excellent results in the upper classes, and there is no reason why it should not be the rule. The preparation afforded in the lower grades is certainly of a high order, and if properly continued should produce telling effects. The main difficulty is that inasmuch as only eight or nine essays are prescribed for the year, the practice in writing will be left to these supreme occasions. Those who are really in sympathy with the new reform insist on a little writing every day, and so arrange this practice work that when the time comes for the formal essay the student already has his ideas well fixed, and knows almost to a certainty what form the expression should take. In other words, the theory is that it is infinitely better to avoid errors by previous careful training than to correct them after they are made. To this end the "practical instruction" above mentioned is no more nor less than almost daily drill in arranging logically a train of ideas with which the students are already familiar. It is in this connection that translations from the foreign languages may be made most valuable ; here the ideas are given, and in logical order, according to the spirit of the original. The test is to express the same ideas and arrange them according to the recognised laws of the mother-tongue.

The history course for *Untertertia* traces the political changes in western Europe from the death of Augustus to the end of the Middle Ages ; so far as possible, the readings for the year are intended to illustrate this period. The Scandinavian tales and the old Germanic legends of the *Nibelungenlied* are prominent; epic poetry and ballads receive particular stress. From *Tertia* on, dramatic poetry becomes foremost in the course. So, too, the reading of entire works in place of selections becomes more and more characteristic of the higher classes. Schiller's *Glocke* and *Wilhelm Tell* are commonly read in *Obertertia ;* but in schools without Greek, translations from Homer may take the place of *Tell*. The list of poems—according to Hopf and Paulsiek—to be committed to memory includes *Die Kraniche des Ibykus, Der Ring des Polykrates, Der Handschuh* and *Die Glocke*, by Schiller, *Der Erlkönig*, by Goethe, and seven other selections—in all, about 1,200 lines during the year. These selections are not, of course, officially required, and it will seldom happen that this precise list will be memorized. Custom decrees, however, that at least six or eight such poems shall be made the pupils' own.

<small>Literature.</small>

It must not be forgotten that young men who complete *Untersecunda* in a higher school are privileged to serve only one year in the army. In 1889-1890, 8,051 Prussian students left school after winning the coveted military boon ; only 4,105 finished the entire nine years' course. For German schools, therefore, it is highly important that something like completeness should be attained in the course, exclusive of the last three years. That this is attempted is evident in the abrupt change in the character of the work after *Secunda* is passed. But under the most favourable interpretation it must be said that the Prussian schools are designed for the four thousand who complete the course, instead of the eight thousand who find it convenient or necessary to drop out three years before the end.

The arrangement of the course in the upper classes is as follows:

OBERSECUNDA.

Gymnasium and *Realgymnasium*, 3 hours; *Oberrealschule*, 4 hours. (1) Composition at home and in class; shorter essays on topics drawn from the general instruction; about eight essays in the school year. (2) Introduction to the *Nibelungenlied* in the original text; the courtly epic and lyric. (3) General review of styles of poetry. (4) Reading of dramas: *Wallenstein, Egmont, Goetz*. (5) Occasional committing to memory of selections from the reading; original discourses by the students upon the contents of the more significant poems of the middle-high German and of modern dramas.

<small>Course in Upper Grades.</small>

UNTERPRIMA.

Gymnasium and *Realgymnasium*, 3 hours; *Oberrealschule*, 4 hours. (1) Composition as in IIa. (2) History of the literature of the sixteenth, seventeenth and eighteenth centuries, treated biographically. (3) Readings: Selections from Lessing's *Laokoon*, etc.; a few odes of Klopstock; lyrics of Schiller and Goethe; dramas—*Iphigenie, Braut von Messina* (in schools without Greek, Sophocles' dramas in translation); selections from the later poets. (4) Discussions by the students on the lives and works of the poets.

OBERPRIMA.

Gymnasium and *Realgymnasium*, 3 hours; *Oberrealschule*, 4 hours. (1) Composition as in IIa and Ib. (2) History of the literature from Goethe to the present time in biographical form. (3) Readings from the *Hamburgische Dramaturgie*; dramas, especially Shakespeare's, in translation (in *Gymnasien*). (4) Original discourses by the students on the lives and works of the poets.

The dangers incident to the composition work in the middle grades are likely to increase in the higher classes, but it is not my purpose to write on the shortcomings of individual teachers. I accept without question the Prussian program as it stands. But there is a real danger, as confessed to me more than once, even for the ablest teachers, that they will make the composition too much an exercise in literary criticism. The more enthusiastic the instructor is, the more familiar he is with the deeper significance of the literature, the more likely is he to overestimate the mental calibre of his class.

<small>Composition.</small>

A teacher of many years' experience in the schools of Cassel recently placed in my hands some half-dozen volumes devoted to critical exposition of the readings, with full outlines of essays for the upper grades of higher schools. I have met with many such books for teachers' use, which give hundreds, if not thousands, of composition themes, with appropriate outlines. The mass of material is really bewildering, and, were not the national passion for book-making generally understood, one might infer that the average German teacher has no ideas of his own. But such helps may be used advantageously by earnest teachers, and it is to be hoped that one day in America there will be a choice of as rich material.

As an indication of the trend in essay writing I give herewith two lists of themes actually used in *Prima:*

<small>Essay Themes.</small>

Unterprima, Jena *Gymnasium*, 1893–1894:
(1) What were Hagen's motives in murdering Siegfried? (2) Brunhilde as portrayed by Geibel and in the Nibelungen legends: a comparison. (3) Explain and justify Schiller's distich:

"Euch, Ihr Götter, gehöret der Kaufmann:
   Güter zu suchen,
Geht er, doch an sein Schiff knüpfet das Gute sich an" (class essay).

(4) Would not Shakespeare's *Julius Cæsar* have been better entitled *Brutus?* (5) The virtues and vices of the Germans, according to Tacitus' *Germania*. (6) What share had the Prince in Lessing's Emilia Galotti in Marinelli's deed?

Oberprima, Wilhelms-Gymnasium, Cassel, 1892–1893:
(1) In how far is the second Punic war a decisive turning-

point in Roman history? (2) The development of the dramatic action in the third act of Shakespeare's *Coriolanus*. (3) (a) Causes and significance of the revolt of the Netherlands; (b) The consequences of the discovery of America (class essay). (4) Epaminondas and Gustavus Adolphus: a comparison. (5) The historical importance of the Great Elector of Brandenburg. (6) The historical significance of Greece, Rome and Palestine, with particular relation to Germany. (Eleven other essays were written during the year, of which nine were composed in class.)

The reading of entire works finds its fullest scope in the upper classes. In proportion as the mechanical use of the language becomes familiar is the reader enabled to consider more the content of what he reads. *Literature.* At first the form is all-important, and in a measure the form conditions the idea; but with time the highest art of expression becomes subservient to the intellectual content. In the writings of Schiller and Lessing, Goethe and Shakespeare, the German school-boy has a wealth of material unsurpassed in variety of treatment and in richness of meaning. And when we consider his readings from the ancient and modern classics, his studies in the history of Greece and Rome and of the fatherland, it will be noted with what a liberal training he approaches the study of master-pieces of his own literature.

But is Shakespeare German? The answer must be that if sympathetic renderings on every stage, if a general and appreciative reading in the schools and in the home, can naturalize a man's work, then is Shakespeare German. *Shakespeare.* A German teacher of English recently told me of his experiences of a vacation in England. He wanted especially to hear Shakespeare played in English by English actors. And his experience? Not once during the summer did he have the chance. Light comedy he could hear every night, and silly operas. This is not true even of small towns in Germany. And I know that during the few months I spent in Jena more of Shakespeare's plays were given in that quiet Thuringian town of 13,000 inhabitants than have been played in most American towns of the same size in as many years.

In Germany the theatre supplements the school; once a year all the gymnasial students of Saxe-Weimar are invited to a classic drama in the Court Theatre. Other states have similar customs, and everywhere students may attend the best plays and hear the finest music at greatly reduced rates. In some of the larger cities special arrangements are made whereby secondary-school pupils may hear the best dramas for about twenty pfennigs—*five cents*—each. No school-boy will be admitted without the permission of the director of his school. Under such conditions the teacher of literature is indeed fossilized who cannot inspire his scholars with a loftier patriotic and moral ideal.

The readings for the lower and middle grades have no regard for the historical development of the language or the growth of the literature. Scientific methods are first employed with *Obersecunda*. A short introduction shows the place of German in the Indo-European family, after which the peculiarities of the middle-high German are learned inductively from the *Nibelungenlied* in the original text. Many selections from the early writings are read, and care is taken to classify them historically. In *Unterprima* the development of the new-high German is traced in the literature from Luther to the end of the eighteenth century. The historical study of the literature depends not upon names, dates and titles, but upon the relation of influences to results. Shakespeare finds a place in the curriculum primarily because of his influence upon a later school of German writers. In *Oberprima* a critical study of Schiller and Goethe rounds out the course to perfection. It has been my pleasure to hear a series of lessons in this class on Goethe's *Iphigenie auf Tauris*, conducted by a live teacher of a live *Gymnasium*. Under his skilful leading I could feel the interest of the class increasing daily, till the height was reached in Iphigenie's monologue in the fifth scene of the fourth act. The pent-up emotion of all that had preceded found expression here. No member of that class was unresponsive. I am certain, to those agonizing words which mark the climax:

[marginal note: History of Language and Literature.]

"*Rettet mich, Und rettet euer Bild in meiner Seele.*" And at the next lesson I was gratified to hear the monologue—seventy-six lines—repeated from memory with scarcely an error. After such exhibitions I needed not be told that for gymnasial students the *Iphigenie* stands without rival in the literature.

The German course, as I have tried to show, is designed as a unit from first to last. It recognises two principal means of teaching language: (1) through the ear, and (2) through the eye; first hearing with speaking, and then seeing with reading and writing. *The Course a Unit.* If at some time in the course one method is emphasized more than the other, at no time must one exclude the other. "It is fortunate that so much stress is coming to be put on the spoken language in our schools," said a university professor to me once; "we are naturally a race of readers and writers, and are prone to forget that language may be something apart from books." And "reading" is not skimming over printed pages for the sake of the story. The reader, if he would master what he reads, must read not once, but many times; must ponder well the contents; and no harm is done if he commit a goodly part to memory. But I repeat again: the course is a unit. There are no tests in "grammar," or "spelling" or "rhetoric;" no division into "elementary" and "advanced" German; no chapters on "prefixes, suffixes and stems;" no course in "literature," national or otherwise. But there is most emphatically a *course in German.*

This is the German point of view. And, if I mistake not, it is the ideal toward which American educators have been tending for many years. Such a course reads well on paper, and theoretically meets with general approval. *Ideals and Results.* The practical workings, however, do not furnish grounds for unmixed praise. The important factor in this, as in all school problems, is the *teacher;* if he is all knowledge, all skill, all tact, all perfection, the highest results may be reached. But he is not to be found in every German school, and I am yet to be convinced that his species is more common there than in America. He is a rare man who can be at once a specialist and a successful all-round teacher, according to these later-day notions. Indeed, the first requirement of the aspirant for tutorial honours in the mother-tongue is not that he shall be a specialist, but a form-master. The Berlin conference recognized this fact, and gave it the prominence it deserves. But, with all deference to the superior learning and skill of German school-masters, I am of the opinion that the conditions of highest success in teaching the mother-tongue will be met quite as readily on American soil as in the fatherland. American teachers are to-day perhaps no nearer being form-masters than are German teachers, but a generation at least of gymnasial specialists must pass away before the spirit of the new program will find expression in true heart service.

The key of the situation is admirably put in the closing paragraph of the official instructions accompanying the Prussian syllabus : "The instruction in German, joined with that in religion and history, is ethically the most important in the organism of our schools. Its tasks are extraordinarily difficult, and can be fully discharged only by that teacher who—supported by a thorough understanding of our language and its history, upheld by an enthusiasm for the treasures of our literature and dominated by a deep sense of patriotism—knows how to enkindle the susceptible hearts of our youth with a passion for the German language, the German life and the German spirit."

GENERAL REFERENCES :—Hiecke, *Der deutsche Unterricht auf deutschen Gymnasien*, Berlin, 1852; Laas, *Der deutsche Aufsatz in der oberen Gymnasialklassen*, Berlin, 1877; Laas, *Der deutsche Unterricht auf den höheren Lehranstalten*, Berlin, 1872; Hildebrand, *Der deutsche Sprachunterricht in der Schule*, Leipsic, 1887 ; Müller, *Quellenschriften des deutschsprachlichen Unterrichts*, Gotha, 1882 ; Kern, *Zur Methodik des deutschen Unterrichts*, 1883; Völcker, *Aufgaben des zu verstärkenden deutschen Unterrichts*, Schönebeck, 1892; Nagel, *Der deutsche Unterricht in den unteren Klassen der höh. Bürgerschulen*, Berlin, 1892; Schmidt, *Der deutsche Unterricht in der Obersecunda*, Borna, 1892 ; Müller, *Der deutsche Unterricht auf Realschulen*, Envlen, 1892; Hand-Books of Baumeister and Wychgram; Encyclopedias of Schmid and Rein.

CHAPTER XIII

INSTRUCTION IN GREEK AND LATIN

"THE classical literature is, and will continue to be, the source of all our culture. It must remain, therefore, not only an indispensable, but by far the most important, study in our higher schools." This thought, expressed a century ago by Frederick Gedike, the first *Oberschulrat* of Prussia, has been the guiding principle of the *Gymnasien* to the present time. Through Winckelmann, Lessing, Herder, Goethe and Schiller the German mind was made ready for humanistic training. The ideals of the new humanism were embodied by Frederick August Wolf in his *Science of Archæology*—a science which included not only the classical languages and literatures, but all that was concerned in the civilizations of Greece and Rome. Its highest aim was "the knowledge of the classical humanity itself." In Wolf's *Seminar* in Halle the men were trained "who, in the higher schools, universities and educational councils of a great part of Germany and of Switzerland, exerted an unparalleled influence upon the subsequent development of the higher culture."

<small>Centre of Gymnasial Training.</small>

The influence of Wolf and his school, powerful as it was, was insufficient to preserve the spirit of the new movement from violence at the hands of those who were determined to nationalize the school system, and make a knowledge of Greek and Latin the condition of admission to the learned professions and to all positions of honour in the civil service. That classical study should serve other ends than those of pure culture was a

<small>Greek at First Optional.</small>

proposition abhorrent to the new humanists. Gesner, the founder of the movement at Göttingen, considered Latin and Greek quite unnecessary for the ordinary trades and professions and for civil and military service. Gedike based his hopes of true educational reform on the conversion of all so-called Latin schools in the smaller cities into genuine *Realschulen,* and the reception into the *Gymnasien* only of such pupils as were destined to become learned men. Even Wolf held that the classics were valuable only to the learned; Latin should not be required of candidates in medicine, and Greek should be obligatory only for gymnasial teachers and students of theology.

The place of the ancient languages in the curriculum of the German schools during the greater part of this century has been determined by the shifting of opinions between these two extremes—between that view which makes the study of the classics purely a formal discipline, and that other view which bases the worth of such study on the acquisition of humanistic culture, on contact with "the best thoughts of the best men of antiquity." In the one case it is considered of equal value as a means of preparation for all trades and professions dependent on intellectual acumen; in the other case it is of worth only for those who can practically apply the technical knowledge thereby acquired, or who may have sufficient leisure to enjoy its æsthetic qualities. It is a question of making the ancient literature a means to an end or an end in itself.

Aims of Classical Study.

With the introduction of the state system of education the courses of study of all schools fitting for the universities became practically uniform. The reforms were carried out by men friendly to the humanistic party, but they encountered strong opposition. Not only were a majority of the classical teachers unable or unwilling to follow the new ideals, but a considerable party in the state was barbarous enough to think that what the nation most needed was an education capable of producing more patriotic citizens. The Napoleonic wars were a rude shock to

Reforms of this Century.

INSTRUCTION IN GREEK AND LATIN   247

Goethe's universal *Humanitätsideal*, and gave decided impetus to all reactionary influence. The gymnasial program of 1816 put much emphasis on mathematics to the disadvantage of Latin, which was reduced *Lehrplan of 1816.* to 76 week-hours in a ten years' course, and made Greek obligatory with 50 week-hours. After the entrance of Johannes Schulze into the Education Department in 1818, Latin was again gradually advanced to first place. A plan of supplementary reading followed in the *Gymnasium* of Dantzic was officially recommended to all directors, the time of mathematics being soon afterward reduced a half in order to make it possible. In this way the schools were able to read the following works : " The entire *Iliad* and *Odyssey*, several dramas of Æschylus, Sophocles and Euripides, four books of Herodotus, two books of Thucydides, the *Anabasis*, several of Plutarch's *Lives*, Demosthenes' *Oration on the Crown*, Plato's *Phædo*, all of Vergil except the *Georgics*, Horace complete, Ovid's *Metamorphoses* complete and selections from other poets, Cæsar's *Gallic War* and *Civil War* complete, five or six books of Livy, all of Sallust, Tacitus' *Annals*, many of Cicero's *Orations* and *de amicitia, de senectute, de officiis, de divinatione* and *de natura deorum*." The speaking of Latin, which was in common use in the schools at the beginning of the century, gradually fell into disuse. In 1834, however, it was ordered that the final examination in Latin should be conducted in Latin.

In response to a popular demand that the gymnasial requirements should be reduced, a new program was announced in 1837, according to which the seven lower classes had each 10 hours of Latin a week and *Lehrplan of 1837.* the two upper classes 8 each—total, 86 week-hours. Greek was taught during seven years 6 hours a week. Pupils were not admitted to the *Gymnasien* until ten years of age. The prescribed number of weekly lessons—in all, 32—was under no condition to be increased, and compulsory private reading was abolished. The program of 1856 emphasized still more strongly the formal side of classical training. Four to six

Latin essays were required each semester. Greek prose composition was included in the final examination. The oral test in both Greek and Latin was to be conducted in Latin. German literature, French, natural science and philosophy were omitted entirely from the final examination. Until the founding of the German Empire Latin was the main part of the gymnasial course; everything was subsidiary to the classics. The aim was to afford a formal training without any regard whatsoever to the pupil's future position in life. A thorough knowledge of Latin, ability to read, write and speak it with ease, was the one thing necessary.

In the 70's forces which had long been dormant or held in check began to be felt. The needs of a great nation made new demands on the educational system. *Lehrplan of 1882.* Baden and Hesse were the first to respond by giving more time to science, mathematics, German and French, at the expense of the classics. The literature was made the central point of the work in Greek and Latin. The Prussian program of 1882 reduced the week-hours of Latin from 86 to 77, and postponed the beginning of Greek to *Untertertia* with a total of 40 week-hours. The literature was mildly emphasized, but much stress was still put upon the writing of correct Latin. The formal educational value of Latin was specially recognised in the transformation of certain *Real*-schools into *Realgymnasien*, i.e., *Gymnasien* without Greek. During the succeeding decade two important tendencies became more strongly developed: (1) the modern side of education was evidently growing in public favour, stimulated by rapidly increasing industrial needs; and (2) in the reaction against formalism in the teaching of the classics, the revival of new humanistic ideals was becoming more apparent. The reforms of 1892 were, indeed, radical. Emphasis was placed upon the need of a national education *Lehrplan of 1892.* in practical lines, as distinguished from the theoretical training of the mental faculties. A patriotic citizenship became the chief end of all school work. Vigour of mind and right conduct are conditioned by health of body;

physical exercise, therefore, was encouraged, and all undue pressure in school work prohibited. The national history and literature were given a prominent place; classics were set back. Prussia reduced the week-hours in Latin from 77 to 62, and in Greek from 40 to 36. Bavaria placed Latin at 66, and Greek at 36. Both Saxony and Würtemberg made reductions, but the hours still remain much above the average, *viz.*: Saxony, Latin 71–73, and Greek 40–42; Würtemberg, Latin 81, and Greek 40 (classes II.–X.). The most significant general change was in the emphasis put upon the literature and its humanistic content. Formal drill in grammar and the Latin essay were abolished. "Take warning!" says an opponent of the reforms, "nothing but financial considerations keeps the schools from having veritable museums of classic art. They would apparently make the literature a basis for applied archæology and the essential subject in a course in art history."

The trend of the opposition to the formal educational value of classical study was clearly manifest, too, in the attempted overthrow of the *Realgymnasien*—an abortive attempt, to be sure, but nevertheless indicative of the reaction against formalism and of the increasing importance of practical education. *Latin in the Realgymnasium.* While Latin is still retained in the Prussian *Realgymnasium*, its efficiency is endangered by the manifest hostility of the government. Students no longer feel that Latin is of supreme importance in the final examination, and numerous petty official acts show all too clearly that the authorities do not consider the Latin instruction in the *Realgymnasium* of much account. In fact, one can find very little spirited Latin work in these schools. The attitude of the government may be largely responsible for the results, yet there is another not unimportant reason. The teachers of Latin in these schools are, as a rule, elderly men. They belong to a generation which looked upon the study of the classics purely as a formal discipline; and notwithstanding the fact that they find themselves in a modern environment, it is with great difficulty that they adjust themselves to the practical needs of the *Realgymnasien*. Furthermore, one often hears it said that the less promising candidates for teachers' positions are "steered" into the *Realgymnasien*. At any rate, an influential *Gymnasium* not infrequently finds a means of having an undesirable member of its staff transferred to some less favoured school. The relatively large number of *Realgymnasial* teachers who once held posts in *Gymnasien* suggests that the *Realgymnasium* is the chief sufferer.

Were it not for the far-reaching system of privileges connected with graduation from classical schools, Latin would speedily disappear, no doubt, from the *Realgymnasien*. But as long as admission to higher courses in the university and appointment to the better places in the civil service are conditioned by the study of Latin, so long will the ambitious spirit of the German middle classes insist on the retention of the *Realgymnasium* at any cost. And, besides, there are such men as Professor Paulsen, of Berlin, who maintains that a knowledge of the Latin language is an essential element in a practical education—that the man, as Schopenhauer says, who knows not the influences of Rome on our modern civilization is like a traveller in a beautiful country enveloped in a dense fog. Merely as an information subject, therefore, Latin deserves a place in every school that leads to the university and to the higher positions in the state.

The Outlook for Real-Schools.

What the outcome will be of all this discussion cannot be predicted. This much at least seems assured, that the middle classes will insist on a fair representation in the government and in the civil and military service. If Latin is a *conditio sine qua non*, then Latin will be kept in the higher schools ; if the training of the *Oberrealschulen* is considered sufficient for all purposes, save for entrance upon certain lines of professional study, then we may expect the gradual extinction of the *Realgymnasien*. In short, it would seem that the future of classical study were more dependent upon social ideals and economic conditions than has hitherto been the case. It is not in accord with German imperialism to concede much to the demands of the industrial classes, but the time is not far distant when certain new and rapidly increasing forces in the German social life must be recognised. And when that time comes it will bring with it greater reforms in the school system than we have yet seen.

A significant movement looking to a compromise between the factions warring over the place of classical study in liberal education is that for the *Reformschule.* One of the severest charges brought against the old *Gymnasien* is that parents must practically decide the future career of their sons when first they are sent to school. What father knows the bent of his son at nine years of age? How can he intelligently mark out a course of study before he knows anything of the boy's aptitude in studies? Not long since I heard a prominent physician of Leipsic enter a most emphatic protest to an assembly of teachers against the responsibility placed on him in the selection of a course of study for his nine-year-old boy. "I have carefully studied the child," said the father, "since his birth, but I feel that I am in no position to decide the matter. The boy himself is uncertain whether he wishes to become a street-car conductor or a general in the army." The gymnasial pupil at fifteen is debarred from choosing a technical profession; the *Real-*school boy at fifteen finds it a thorny road that leads to the university. There are, indeed, a few notable exceptions to the rule, but the obstacles which the few succeed in overcoming suffice to dissuade the many from the attempt.

<small>The Reformschule.</small>

For several years Director Schlee, of Altona, has had royal permission to begin the course in his *Realgymnasium* with French instead of Latin, and later on to give to Latin some of the time that would ordinarily go to French. In this way the curriculum for the first three years is made to accord with that of the *Realschule.* Pupils, therefore, can pass easily from one school to the other so late as *Untertertia.* At fifteen years of age a pupil would have no greater difficulty in making a change than at twelve under the old plan. The success of the Altona experiment was so

<small>In Altona.</small>

marked that at Easter, 1892, the plan, in a slightly modified form, was introduced into all the higher schools of Frankfort-on-the-Main. Latin is begun in the *Gymnasium* in *Untertertia* with ten hours a week. The total week-hours for the six years' course amount to fifty-two. Greek is begun two years later with eight hours a week—an allotment that is maintained during the four years. In the *Realgymnasium* English takes the place of Greek. In other respects there is no great divergence from the governmental program.

<small>In Frankfort.</small>

The Frankfort plan is vigorously championed by a party of reformers not only for its practical advantages, but for pedagogical reasons as well. They claim that the only rational method of teaching language to children of nine and ten years of age is the inductive, all the time using the language so far as possible as if it were the mother-tongue. Habits of speech, rather than thought and judgment, should be the chief aim at first. Latin was once so taught because Latin was then a popular tongue. Times have changed, and it is now little short of farcical to insist on treating Latin as a spoken language. Still, it is recognised that a humanistic training is desirable. Some language should be begun when a child enters school. It should be a living language. French, therefore, satisfies the theoretical conditions, and besides has a practical value that commends it to the German people. The training in French during the first three years of schooling should lay such a foundation, should cultivate such linguistic sensibility, that better work can be done in Latin in the succeeding six years than has formerly been possible in the full nine years' course.[1]

<small>Pedagogical Considerations.</small>

Here, then, there is an attempt at sailing a middle course between the old order and the new. If it succeeds, it will be proclaimed a rational solution of a difficult problem. Whether, as a compromise—for that is really what it is—it will please either party, will depend largely upon the outcome of the

---

[1] See: Reinhardt, *Die Schulordnung in Comenius Unterrichtslehre und die Frankfurter Lehrpläne*, Leipsic, 1894.

more radical plans now being urged. If the Frankfort plan fails, it is safe to say that the fault will not lie with Director Reinhardt and his associates, who have entered upon the work with unbounded faith in its possibilities, and who are eminently qualified in every way to realize its highest ideals. The experiment in Frankfort will be watched with increasing interest for three years to come. In 1901 the first class to make the trial will be graduated; the attainments of this class will have an important influence in shaping the future curriculum for the German higher schools. *Practical Significance.*

The present, it is apparent, is a period of transition in the instruction in Greek and Latin. Uncertainty and confusion are to be found in most schools; and not a few teachers openly assert their disdain of the new order, and express a determination to cling to their old methods till the curriculum shall again be revised. Uniformity in method or in scope of work cannot be expected until time shall remove or harmonize the multiplicity of disturbing elements. *The Present a Period of Transition.*

The official syllabus allows considerable freedom of choice in the matter of text-books and subject-matter. For this reason one rarely finds precisely the same work being done at a given time even in the schools of the same city. Then, too, there is a variation from year to year in the selections from the literature, in order to avoid repetition for pupils set back. The plan gives zest to the teacher's work as well.

In giving the course of study for a particular school, it should be borne in mind that it can at best be only a type. No other school may be doing precisely the same work; the differences, however, are of minor consequence. For purposes of illustration, I present herewith an outline of the work in 1894-1895 in Latin and Greek in the *Städtisches Gymnasium*, Frankfort-on-the-Main. This school is noted not only for the excellence of its classical instruction, but also for its general progressive spirit. In 1894, when I visited the school, it had about six hundred *Course of Study.*

pupils in nineteen classes under thirty-two teachers. In reality, however, there are two schools of about three hundred pupils each, united in name and under one general management, but essentially distinct in internal arrangement and methods of work. The program given below is from the division which is following the prescribed governmental curriculum. (I have already referred to the plan adopted by the other division.) For the sake of comparison, I give also the Latin course of the *Dorotheenstädtisches Realgymnasium*, Berlin. The differences in time and amount in the last six years correspond to the official requirements.

GYMNASIUM (AND REALGYMNASIUM).

SEXTA. *Latin*, 8 hours. Perthes' *Reader* for VI. and the corresponding vocabulary and forms. Written class exercise once a week.

QUINTA. *Latin*, 8 hours. Review of regular forms; deponents; common irregular forms; memorizing of selections and vocabulary from Perthes' *Reader* for V. Study of *acc. c. inf.* and *abl. abs.;* construction of city names. One written class exercise and one home task a week.

QUARTA. *Latin*, 7 hours. Reading (4 hrs.): *Nepos*, 12 *vitæ*. Grammar, (3 hrs.): review of forms; essentials of case. Latin composition. Translation into Latin as class exercise once a week; two written translations into German each half-year.

GYMNASIUM.

UNTERTERTIA. *Latin*, 7 hours. Reading (4 hrs.): Cæsar, *Gallic War*, I.–IV. Grammar (3 hrs.): Review of case; main rules of mode and tense; oral and written translations; textbook, Ostermann's for III. Class exercise in writing Latin once a week; written translation into German every six weeks.

UNTERTERTIA. *Greek*, 6 hours. Regular Attic forms up to and including liquid verbs. Memorizing of words; textbook, Wetzel's *Uebungsbuch*. Translation from *Wetzel*, §§ 1–90. Written translations every two weeks.

REALGYMNASIUM.

UNTERTERTIA. *Latin*, 4 hours. Reading (2 hrs.): Cæsar, *Gallic War*, I., II., III., 7–19. Grammar (2 hrs.): Review

INSTRUCTION IN GREEK AND LATIN

of case and mode as far as learned in IV.; further study of case. Written and oral translation from and into Latin, one exercise every two weeks.

GYMNASIUM.

OBERTERTIA. *Latin*, 7 hours. Reading (4 hrs.): Selections from Ovid's *Metamorphoses;* Cæsar, *Gallic War*, V. (from ch. 38), VI., VII. Grammar (3 hrs.): Review and continuation of mode and tense; main rules of verb-syntax; text-book, *Gillhausen*. Oral translations from *Ostermann*. Each week a translation into Latin based on Cæsar; every six weeks a written translation from Cæsar.

OBERTERTIA. *Greek*, 6 hours. Grammar (3-2 hrs.): Verbs in μι and the most important irregular verbs. Review and extension of forms; text-book, *Römer*. Greek composition for practice in forms; text-book, *Wetzel*. Every two weeks a written class exercise or home task based on the reading. Reading (3-4 hrs.): At first from *Wetzel;* later, Xen., *Anab.*, I.-III., selections. Practice in retranslation and narrating contents.

REALGYMNASIUM.

OBERTERTIA. *Latin*, 4 hours. Reading (2 hrs.): Cæsar, *Gallic War*, IV., 1-3, V., VI., 11-24 and parts of 25-51, VII.; Ovid, III., 1-137. Grammar (2 hrs.): Review of case; essentials of tense and mode. Written exercise once in two weeks.

GYMNASIUM.

UNTERSECUNDA. *Latin*, 7 hours. Reading (4 hrs.): Livy, XXI. (selections) and XXII.; Vergil, VI. Training in preparation of lesson. Practice in sight translation and retranslation. Memorizing of selections of poetry. Study of style and synonyms based on reading. Grammar (3 hrs.): Reviews and advance. Every week a translation into Latin as class exercise or home task; every six weeks a written translation from the Latin.

UNTERSECUNDA. *Greek*, 6 hours. Review of forms. Case-syntax. Essentials of mode. Reading: Xen., *Anab.*, IV., and *Hellen.*, VI. and VII. (selections); Homer, *Odyssey*, V. and VI. Written class exercise every two weeks.

REALGYMNASIUM.

UNTERSECUNDA. *Latin*, 3 hours. Reading (2 hrs.): (Only one author read at a time, hence not prose and poetry together; one-third of the time given to poetry) Curtius, *Bks.* III., IV., VI.-VIII.; Ovid, *Metamor.*, I., 1-4, 89-112, I., 253-312, IV., 663-772 (Andromeda), IV., 773-789 (Medusa), V., 385-408, 438-445, 505-538, 564-571 (Ceres), IX., 98-153 (Nessus), VI., 146-312 (Niobe), VIII., 159-182 (Ariadne), VIII., 183-236 (Dædalus and Icarus). Study of hexameter. Grammar (1 hr.): Reviews of forms and syntax. Every two weeks a translation from the Latin or into Latin.

GYMNASIUM.

OBERSECUNDA. *Latin*, 6 hours. Reading (5 hrs.): Livy, XXII.; Cicero, *Sex. Roscius ;* Vergil, *Æn.*, IV. and VI. and selections from the remaining books; study of the Epic. Every two weeks written class exercise based on reading or home task from dictation; every six weeks a translation from the Latin as class exercise. Grammar (1 hr.): Reviews in connection with the written exercises.

OBERSECUNDA. *Greek*, 6 hours. Reading (5 hrs.): Xen., *Memor.*, III. and IV. (selections); Herodot., VIII. (selections); Hom., *Odys.*, VII., VIII. (selections), IX.-XII., XXI. and XXII. Written translations from the Greek once in four weeks. Grammar (1 hr.): Syntax of mode and tense; infinitive, participle. Review of forms.

REALGYMNASIUM.

OBERSECUNDA. *Latin*, 3 hours. Reading (2 hrs.): Sallust, *Jugurtha, Catilina ;* Ovid, *Metamor.*, VI., 146-312 (Niobe), VIII., 611 ff. (Philemon and Baucis). Review of grammar and metric; occasional retranslation.

GYMNASIUM.

UNTERPRIMA. *Latin*, 6 hours. Reading (5 hrs.): Tacitus, *Hist.*, I., 1-51; selections from Cicero's letters; Horace, *Carm.*, I.-IV. (selections); *Epod.*, 2 ; *Epist.*, I., 2 ; Cicero, *Manil.* Translation at sight. Private readings from Livy, Curtius, etc. Memorizing of passages, mostly from Horace. Every two weeks a translation into Latin—often based on reading—as class exercise or home task; translations from the Latin and critical exposition of same. Drill in grammar, synonyms and style.

UNTERPRIMA. *Greek*, 6 hours. Reading: Thucydides, I.; Plato, *Kriton ;* Homer, *Iliad*, I.-XVI. (selections); Sophocles, *Antigone.* Memorizing of selected passages. Written translations from the Greek and critical exposition. Occasional reviews of grammar.

REALGYMNASIUM.

UNTERPRIMA. *Latin*, 3 hours. Reading (2 hrs.): Livy, I. (selections); Vergil, *Æneid*, I. and II. (in part); Cicero, *in Catilinam*, I. and IV. (in part). Every two weeks written exercises (usually in class); translations from Livy and Cicero. Grammar (1 hr.): Reviews; occasional drill in retranslation from German.

GYMNASIUM.

OBERPRIMA. *Latin*, 6 hours. Reading (5 hrs.): Tacitus, *Annal.*, I. and part of II., *Germania;* Cicero, *P. Sestius;* Horace, *Epist.*, I., 17–20, II., 1–3, *Satires*, I. (selec.), II., 6 and 8. Private readings from Sallust (*Catilina*), Livy, Curtius, etc. Translation at sight. Memorizing of passages from Horace. Written translations and exercises as in *Unterprima*.

OBERPRIMA. *Greek*, 6 hours. Reading: Plato, *Phædo* (introd. and conclusion); Protagoras (selections); Demosthenes, *Olynth.*, III., *Phil.*, I., III.; Homer, *Iliad*, IX., XI., XII., XIV.–XXII., XXIV.; Sophocles, *Antigone;* selections from lyric poets (Stoll's *Anthologie*). Memorizing of select passages from the poets. Occasional grammatical reviews as needed. Written translation from the Greek each month.

REALGYMNASIUM.

OBERPRIMA. *Latin*, 3 hours. Reading: selections from Catullus, Horace, Ovid and Vergil (Mann's *Anthologie römischer Dichter*); Livy, XXIII. and II. (in part). Occasional reviews of grammar. Written exercise once in two weeks.

The prominence given to the thought-content, intellectual, æsthetic and moral, in all classical study is everywhere apparent in the new program. It decides what authors are to be read, and the relative worth of each ; *Present Ideals.* it gives a new view-point for estimating the value of grammatical rules, composition and the oral use of the classic tongues. Pupils are to study Latin and Greek, not for a mental discipline which will enable them to solve any intellectual task no matter how difficult or disagreeable, but for the purpose of bringing into their lives the noblest and best influences of the spiritual life of classic antiquity. The ability to understand and interpret the literature, rather than facility in using the language, is the chief end. It is this view, emphasized so strongly in the Conference of 1890, that is responsible for the present uncertainty in methods of teaching Latin and Greek. Each teacher who accepts the dictum of the government is obliged perforce to readjust his methods to the new conditions. Formal grammar is ruled out. The Latin essay is banished. Composition in Latin and Greek may no longer be practised for the sake of style. No time is allowed for drill in speaking Latin. Cicero, the Latinist, is dethroned, and Cicero, the statesman and moralist, exalted in his stead. No wonder the scholar of other days sees only ruin ahead. His idols have fallen, and with them his hope for the future.

A generally accepted norm in methods, therefore, cannot be found. Not a few teachers, disdainful of the new-fangled notions and devotedly loyal to that form of training which has created for them a second mother-tongue, hold to the pedagogical omnipotence of the Latin language. The man that exercises his intellect, it is claimed, in thinking, writing and speaking Latin becomes thereby twice a man. With this class of teachers memory is the dominant faculty, and methods of instruction are chiefly designed to exercise this faculty. Repetition is the means to the end. There is another class of teachers who accept the new doctrine theoretically, but for lack of adaptability are practically unable to lift themselves out of the old ruts. They do as they always have done, but hope for different results. Lack of confidence in themselves and want of ability to adapt means to ends limit their success. There are teachers, however—many of them—who, knowing what is wanted and heartily sympathizing with its objects, throw themselves unreservedly into the work of establishing order amidst the prevailing confusion. It is this party, I believe, that repre-

Difficulties.

sents the latest, and what bids fair eventually to become the
prevailing mode of thought. Their practice, varied as it is at
present, tends toward uniformity along certain lines. These
lines I shall attempt to follow.

The subject-matter of instruction in all classes is selected
with a view to its thought-content, rather than as a means of
exercising the linguistic faculty. Forms and
expressions of rare occurrence are avoided. The *Emphasis on Content.*
logical development of the language, while not
put prominently forward by way of grammatical formulæ, is
nevertheless not neglected. At the beginning the teacher
pronounces a Latin sentence, translates it, writes it on the
board. The class reads it and gives the German equivalent,
at first singly and later in concert. A series of such sentences are learned, giving several forms of the first declension.
Next follows the explanation of case-endings of familiar
words and drill on the complete declension. The same plan
is followed in the matter of conjugation, all the time avoiding
irregular and uncommon forms. Paradigms are thus built
up, and for each form the pupil has a sentence at command.
The same holds true of rules of syntax; by induction the
rule is formulated, and for illustration of its use several examples are already at hand. Further, a careful record is kept of
each new word as it occurs. Thus vocabulary, forms and syntax keep even pace.

During the first three years there is little change in method.
Teachers are often promoted with their classes, in order to
avoid all possible disturbing influences. In
time, short, detached sentences give way to *Methods in Lower Classes.*
connected discourse; a text-book is depended
upon for new material; more and more time is given to oral
and written translation. Incessant drill and repetition, often
conducted with surprising rapidity, are the means employed
to fasten it in the pupil's mind. And aside from a well-
learned vocabulary, forms and rules of syntax, the method
familiarizes the pupil with a large number of common phrases
which enable him, even in *Quarta*, to retranslate sentences

into Latin with surprising skill. Nepos is "read at sight," as it would be called in most American schools. New words and constructions are explained by the teacher; the rest must be done by the pupils in class. Home study, for which only about twenty minutes are allowed, is mainly given to writing up the note-book, or reviewing a bit of translation already done in class.

One point deserves notice here. Whereas the inductive method is in high favor with the best classical teachers, they Grammar. do not, so far as I know, ever go to the length of depending upon some standard text for all the material used in the introductory course. Two reasons are urged: in the first place, Nepos (much more then Cæsar or Xenophon) gives too many irregular and unusual forms for the beginner, and, besides, such an author does not facilitate the building up of a symmetrical body of grammatical knowledge. And without a thorough knowledge of grammatical forms and principles, no foreign language can be learned from a few recitations a week. Hence, Latin for beginners must be Latin written or selected for the purpose. Some schools—Jena, for example—use Latin stories written expressly for class use. A commoner practice, however, is to make selections from standard authors, eliminating undesirable parts. Careful editing will, with few changes, give a continuous narrative, which is generally preferred after the first few weeks.

Retroversion, so-called, is an exercise much used in all grades. One pupil reads a Latin sentence slowly; another Translation. repeats it with book closed; a third translates it; a fourth puts it again into Latin. Variation, which is begun in the lower grades, comes increasingly into prominence. Here the teacher gives a thought in German; a pupil is asked to recast it in better German form; the next pupil construes it in German; and another puts it into Latin. The reading of the day furnishes the material. In the lower grades the variation is mainly in tense, number, person, use of interrogatives, etc.; in the upper grades paraphrasing comes into play. Until all danger of misapprehension of the thought has passed, the German forms are always given and carefully construed. In this respect, perhaps, as much as in any other, is seen the tendency of the modern methods. Formerly the custom was to have memorized large amounts of the text, putting the main stress on vocabulary; translation was avoided as much as possible. To-day translation is to the front; the emphasis is placed on the thought-content. In order to understand the thought the pupil must associate it with what he already knows, *i.e.*, with the mother-tongue.

The division between the *Gymnasium* and the *Realgymnasium* comes with *Untertertia*. The program above given shows the lines of cleavage. The formal grammar of the middle grades is practically completed with *Untertertia*, but until the end of the sixth school-year full one-half of the time is given to exercises involving an application of grammatical principles. The aim, however, as I have tried to make clear, is the understanding of the literature; grammar is an important means to that end. Hence, it rarely happens that an hour is given up to drill on grammar alone. The periods scheduled for grammar in the middle grades are employed in construing parts of the text already read and in preparing for future translation. Incidentally, much grammatical drill is given; but the immediate end is a better understanding of the text, in order to facilitate translation. Since the Latin essay and verse-making are done away with, the only test of the student's appreciation of the classic language is in the skill he displays in retroversion and the excellence of his translations. The Latin composition formally prescribed in the program is merely a summary of the "grammar" work of the week. [sidenote: Literature.]

The work of the lower and middle grades is but a preparation for the real work of the course, which is to be found *par excellence* in the upper classes. This is divided into three main lines—poetical, historical and philosophical. The reading of poetry which is begun in *Untersecunda* culminates in Vergil, Ovid and Hor- [sidenote: Methods in Upper Grades.]

ace, and in Homer—beginning with the *Odyssey*—Æschylus and Sophocles. Here, in addition to a thorough understanding of the text, an appreciation of its æsthetic qualities is insisted upon. A taste for the beautiful in literature grows by what it feeds on. Mere admiration of the beautiful is not sufficient. Full possession demands that the student memorize choice selections—make them his own. A German *Primaner* has at his tongue's end many Odes of Horace and much of Æschylus and Sophocles. Aside from the pleasure which such possession gives, it has a pedagogic value in the interpretation of new material. A student knowing half of Horace by heart has not merely a wealth of apperceptive material for the other half, but a command of phraseology, metre and happy turns of thought which must needs make new translation a pleasure.

Poetry.

With the Greek dramatists the acme of poetic style is reached, and in them the great problems of human life confront the student. Nowhere in the course is the poet's art at better advantage ; nowhere is the ethical content so prominent. The true teacher—he who believes in teaching men, not books—finds in the pages of Sophocles opportunities unparalleled in the ancient literature. With a class thoroughly at home in the *technique* of the drama, knowing pages of it by heart, what cannot a teacher accomplish ! I have heard such masters as Directors Muff of Cassel, Reinhardt of Frankfort and Richter of Jena—not to mention others—teach Sophocles in a way to make one uncertain which to admire most, the marvellous beauty, depth of emotion and ethical content of the tragedy, or the artistic power of the teacher in making every scene pulsate with life and every sentence speak straight to the hearts of his students. The ethical, the æsthetic and the patriotic blend in one.

The Latin historians have something definite to tell the German student of his country's historic past. Tacitus and Cæsar are but a step farther removed from his present than Charlemagne. Livy, Sallust and Thucydides are connecting links with antiquity. They give

History.

the setting, too, for much of the literature read in the upper classes. Hence, if there were no direct arguments for placing historical prose in the curriculum, it would still find a place because of its indirect value.

The philosophical readings are mainly from Cicero and Plato. Formerly an introductory course in philosophy was given in all *Gymnasien;* the practice has long since been abandoned, except as it is incidently the outgrowth of class work with Cicero and Plato. In many schools to-day so good a beginning is made that philosophy may be said still to have a place. And just to the extent that attention is directed to the thought, rather than to the linguistic forms, is Plato made worth reading. The new program will, I think, give considerable impetus to philosophic study; at least, it will serve to arouse an interest in philosophy at the university. *Philosophy.*

It may be presumptuous to say it, but the tendency in Germany to-day is away from those methods which have come to be looked upon as peculiarly German, and toward what has long been the ideal of the best American schools. The movement for the *Reformschule* is essentially an attempt to preserve the classical training, and at the same time provide a means of easy transition from lower schools to the classical school so late as the twelfth year of age. Stating it in another way, it means a six-year Latin course instead of a nine-year course. Again, the reduction of time given to classics has eliminated much of the formal drill in linguistics which formerly characterized the instruction. The increased pressure put upon the teachers to secure as good results as before is having the effect of making method more prominent. But the most American characteristic of all is the impetus given to annotated and illustrated text-books. The old idea was that the barest outline should be placed in the pupil's hands—in language work, merely the text. The teacher was the source of all inspiration and information. Within five years there is a marked tendency to give the class text-books with introductions, out- *Present Tendencies.*

lines, explanations and notes. As I write I have before me copies of the *Œdipus Rex* and the *Antigone*, prepared by Director Muff of Cassel. These books are each in two small volumes. One contains an introduction treating of the Greek Tragedy before Sophocles, the life and work of Sophocles, an analysis and criticism of the theme of the drama, explanations of the theatre, of the chorus and the action of the play. Then follows the text, with a short introduction to each scene. The companion volume is a commentary on the text. This series of texts, which is edited by Directors H. J. Müller, Berlin, and Oscar Jäger, Cologne, and published by Velhagen and Klasing, Leipsic, is one of the latest and most popular undertakings in the line of school-books. It aims to supply texts for the entire course; the names of the editors are evidence that the work will be scholarly; the plan is American, but bids fair to become German as well. But even though the tendency in Germany is to seek the ideal in our direction, we have still a long way to go before arriving at the meeting point.

Some criticisms of this paper which have reached me since it was first published in the *School Review* furnish an illustration of the difficulties one encounters in attempting such a task. Mr. B. G. Teubner of Leipsic is unwilling that I should give others the sole credit for the new text-books, especially as he says he was the first to hit upon the idea. On further investigation, I find that Teubner's *Schülerausgaben Griech. und Latein. Schriftsteller* are in the same style and are intended to serve the same purpose as the other series. The matter of priority I cannot determine from the conflicting evidence. "It is of small moment anyway," so I am told by a gymnasial teacher whose judgment I much respect, "inasmuch as these books are the invention of the devil, and are calculated to destroy all genuine interest in classical study by depriving the pupil of the pleasure of independent research." The very fact, he declares, that there is a demand for such books shows that a period of decadence in classical scholarship has set in. This is one side. The other side is represented, fortunately for the sake of the antithesis, by the school inspector who is officially responsible for the supervision of the work of the teacher above quoted. The inspector, who is well known throughout Germany for his classical scholarship and professional skill, writes that I have truthfully given the views of the progressive teachers and most loyal supporters of classical training in Germany. "The future success of humanistic studies," he adds, "depends upon the acceptance of these ideals and methods." These two men represent what I have called the antagonism between the old humanism and the new.

GENERAL REFERENCES :—Eckstein, *Lateinischer und griechischer Unterricht*, Leipsic, 1887; Berger, *Stilistische Vorübungen der lateinischen Sprache*, Coburg; Jäger, *Aus der Praxis: Ein Pädagogisches Testament*, Wiesbaden; Schiller, *Handbuch der praktischen Pädagogik*, Leipsic; Schrader, *Erziehungs- und Unterrichtslehre*, Berlin; Baumeister, *Handbuch der Erziehungs- und Unterrichtslehre;* Encyclopedias of Schmid and Rein; Rethwisch, *Jahresberichte über das höhere Schulwesen*, Berlin.

CHAPTER XIV

INSTRUCTION IN THE MODERN LANGUAGES

THE modern languages taught in the secondary schools of Germany are French, English, Italian and Polish. Of these, French easily holds first place; Italian and Polish are offered in a few schools, and only in response to local needs. In this sketch, therefore, I shall consider merely the teaching of French and English.

Mainly French and English.

Historically considered, there has been some demand for a knowledge of the French language since the twelfth century, but in early times this need was felt only by the nobility and the commercial classes. For the one, the services of private tutors and foreign travel sufficed; to others the way was pointed out through the exigencies of trade and barter. The surpassing brilliancy of the French political constitution and social order, the superiority of French art, literature and science, began to dazzle the eyes of the German aristocracy toward the end of the sixteenth century. Finally, with the end of the Thirty Years' War sentiment passed over into conviction. A knowledge of French was an indispensable part of a gentleman's education. Special schools (*Ritterakademien*) were founded for noblemen's sons in which the French language and literature had a prominent place. But as yet French was not admitted to classical schools of the country; the function of the *Gymnasien*, it was agreed, was to give instruction in the humanities, not to provide for the practical needs of any class. In some schools, however, French was offered as an

Early Development.

elective study even as early as 1700, and fifty years later it was not an uncommon thing to find Frenchmen installed in German schools as teachers of their mother-tongue. Local considerations, of course, induced this innovation; but in Strasburg, for example, no instruction was given in French as late as 1730, notwithstanding the city had been for half a century under French control and more French than German was spoken by the inhabitants.

The growth of utilitarian ideas in Germany in the eighteenth century which resulted in the founding of *Real*-schools also promoted the study of French. Under Frederick the Great, the first definite movement was made to establish French in the curriculum of the Prussian *Gymnasien*. *Encouraged by Frederick the Great.* The ministerial rescript advised a restricted use of the grammar, and that the main emphasis be placed upon the reading of the literature, coupled with a speaking knowledge of the language. The works of Fénelon, Molière and Voltaire were recommended as reading material. Whenever possible, native Frenchmen should be employed as instructors in the upper grades. That French soon became an important study in some secondary schools is evident from an order of government in 1812, making an essay in French one of the requirements of the final examination; yet it is equally patent that French was not universally taught, inasmuch as substitutions could be made for the French essay.

The school program of 1816 ignored the subject altogether —a politic expression of the popular hatred of France. Indeed, there was excuse for the feeling that the humbling of Germany in the Napoleonic Wars was the result of too great deference to French ideas. *Obligatory since 1831.* In time, however, this spite exhausted itself, and in 1831 French was made an obligatory study in all Prussian *Gymnasien*.

A circular rescript of 1837 assigned to French 2 hours a week during the last six years of the gymnasial course. The first official program of the *Realgymnasium* (1859) gave to French 5 hours a week in *Quinta* and *Quarta,* and 4 hours a week throughout the upper six classes. English (now for the first time made an obligatory subject) was begun in *Tertia* with 4 hours a week, and continued throughout the four succeeding years 3 hours a week. The revision of school programs in 1882 left the *Gymnasien* with 21 week-hours of French in an eight years' course, and English elective. In the *Oberrealschule* French was required throughout the course, with a total of 56 week-hours, and English during the last six years, with a total of 26 week-hours. As matters stand at present, since the reforms of 1892, 19 week-hours are given to French in the *Gymnasien,* beginning with *Quarta;* 31 week-hours in the *Realgymnasien,* beginning with *Quarta;* and 47 week-hours in the *Oberrealschule,* beginning the first year of the course. English is still elective in all *Gymnasien,* but required in the last six years in the *Realgymnasium* and *Oberrealschule,* with 18 and 25 week-hours respectively.

Lehrplan of 1837.

From the very beginning of modern-language instruction in the public schools, there has been continual controversy over the methods to be employed. The private tutor lived with his pupil, and in a natural way the latter acquired the language of the former. Habits of speech were of major importance. In class teaching the instructor found himself overloaded with pupils, and master of altogether too small a portion of their time to permit of success by the natural method. Moreover, few teachers were fluent in the use of the foreign tongue. Trained in the *Gymnasien* and universities, they were far more familiar with the classical than the modern languages. Their only experience in language teaching had been gained from training in Latin and Greek. What wonder, then, that they should seek to teach French as though it were a substitute for Latin? Ought not the methods perfected by centuries of practice with one language be equally applicable to any other language? Considerable facility was often acquired in writing and speaking Latin; why should not the same effort be pro-

Early Methods.

ductive of even better results with so simple a language as French or English?

The outcome of such questions was the adoption by the great majority of teachers of the methods in vogue in the teaching of Latin. This meant that a good vocabulary of isolated words, paradigms, rules of syntax and prosody, were the essential con- *The "Natural" Method.* siderations in the early part of the course; and in the upper classes success was measured in terms of translation and prose composition. But the especial advantage claimed for this kind of work was not so much the learning of the language as the mental discipline thereby gained. It was argued that anyone could learn to use a modern language, provided he could hear enough of it and get sufficient practice in speaking it, and yet be none the stronger from a mental point of view. In fact, the less thought given to the process involved the better. Nothing so hampers a speaker in his use of the mother-tongue as self-consciousness. The person who is most fluent in the use of a foreign tongue is he who has lived from childhood in the foreign environment, and has learned it by the most *natural* method. On the contrary, if the pupil be taught to analyze the foreign language, to understand the principles upon which it is constructed and to translate its thought into precise, idiomatic, vernacular terms, he will thereby acquire the intellectual power necessary to cope with the higher problems of life. It means the development of the faculties of observation, memory and reason.

In a word, the modern-language teachers of Germany down to very recent times have been divided into two hostile parties—the one advocating the tutorial, or so-called "natural," method, for the sake of its practical advantages; the other favouring the classical "translation" method, because of the implied mental discipline.

With the political and consequent social advancement of Germany in the past quarter of a century have come many important changes of pedagogical belief; and in no field is this more apparent than in that of modern languages. The initial impulse was unquestionably given by the increasing commercial demands of the empire. Real-schools grew in numbers and in influence, and in this growth the modern languages came in for a large share of attention. This was partly due to the belief that they were worthy of study along with the great languages of antiquity, but more especially was it the outcome of a desire to promote closer commercial intercourse with neighbouring countries. As trade increased there was greater demand for young men who could speak the modern languages. This demand, however, could not be supplied by the secondary schools. Their graduates knew only the literary French and English; and what with their outrageously bad pronunciation and almost total ignorance of the life and customs of foreign peoples, they were seriously hampered in their business careers.

<small>Recent Changes.</small>

This condition of affairs was the making of the private schools which depended for patronage on the larger cities. The popularity of such institutions was a standing criticism of the secondary-school system, a measure of the practical worth of the secondary school in public opinion. In 1882 the Prussian government, yielding to this criticism, attempted in the school program of that year to reform the modern-language work. Not more work was called for, but better work and more practical. Many teachers, too, were becoming sceptical of the old order, and were beginning to contrast the time and energy expended in instruction with the results attained. The suspicion that something was radically wrong with modern-language teaching paved the way for reforms.

<small>Popular Demands.</small>

Popular criticism was focussed by an essay that appeared in 1882, under the pseudonym of *Quousque Tandem*, entitled *The Teaching of Languages must Start Afresh*. This proved to be a veritable firebrand. Educators ranged themselves for or against the views presented by this anonymous writer, and

<small>Quousque Tandem.</small>

for several years there was heated discussion and bitter controversy.

The new ideas, in part originated by *Quousque Tandem,* who proved to be none other than Dr. Wilhelm Vietor, Professor in the Marburg University, and in part the outcome of subsequent discussion, were formulated as follows: "First, foreign languages should, primarily, be taught by means of connected types, the grammar being kept in the background; second, imitation and thought should be encouraged, instead of translation; third, pronunciation should be taught upon the basis of scientific phonetics; and fourth, living languages should be learned before dead ones." The new movement from its inception was in opposition to the long accepted "translation" method. A modicum of grammar, connected discourse and mastery of the language by its use were all notions contrary to former belief.

<small>Principles of the Reform Method.</small>

Insistence upon correct pronunciation, and scientific methods of teaching it, would of itself exclude many modern-language teachers from the profession. This proposition alone sufficed to arouse relentless opposition to the new school. But the science of phonetics would not down. Several new books on the subject met with a warm reception from the champions of the new movement and materially strengthened their cause.[1]

<small>Correct Pronunciation.</small>

The immediate effect of this unwonted attention to pronunciation not only furnished a stimulus to the scientific study of the language as a whole, but also led directly to its practical use in idiomatic form. The movement had from the beginning the cordial support and sympathy of those

---

[1] The most important of these were the following: Sievers, *Grundzüge der Phonetik*, Leipsic, 1876 (2d edition, 1886); Sweet, *Handbook of Phonetics*, London, 1877; Trautmann, *Die sprachlaute im allgemeinen und d. Engl., Französ u. Deutsch.*, Leipsic, 1884; Vietor, *Elemente der Phonetik und Orthoepie d. Deutsch., Engl. und Französ.*, Heilbronn (2d edition, 1887); Schröer, *Uber den Unterricht in der Ausprache des Englishen*, Berlin, 1884.

who were looking for practical results from instruction in the schools. Some of the younger modern-language teachers began practical tests of the reform theories, and published the results of their experiments. Had it not been for the indefatigable labours of Klinghardt, Kühn, Quiehl and Walter, it is doubtful if Vietor's ideals would ever have become realized. His own attempts at class instruction in Marburg were disappointing; teachers of exceptional ability and good judgment, more interested in the progress of their pupils than in proving the truth of every letter in the theory, were needed to put the new movement on a working basis. Contributions to the practical solution of the problem began to flow in, and ere long the reformers were in a position to support their claims in a most convincing way. In the meantime opposition from the university professors and gymnasial teachers was becoming increasingly vehement and acrimonious. The breach was still further enlarged by the formation, in 1886, of a Modern Language Association, distinct and separate from the modern-language section of the general Philological Congress. Membership in the new organization rapidly grew, and sentiment was constantly tending in the direction of the "new school." The climax was reached in the fifth meeting of the Association, held in Berlin in 1892, when Dr. Waetzoldt, well known to many Americans as the affable director of the German educational exhibit at the Chicago Columbian Exposition, took the meeting by storm in charging the universities with perpetuating antiquated methods, and by advocating the need of reform in high places in the teaching of modern languages. In the vote which followed, the mind of the meeting was expressed in no uncertain way. Feeling ran so high that the minority, made up for the most part of university professors and gymnasial teachers, felt constrained to withdraw, thus leaving a free field to the reformers.

Period of Controversy.

It amounts to saying that at present there are two associations of language teachers in Germany: one of teachers of the modern languages, according to the new methods;

the other of teachers of the classical languages, including such modern-language teachers as cannot affiliate with the new school. The line is definitely drawn between adherents of the "translation" method and those who advocate the new, or "direct," method.

Two Parties.

At about the time the Modern Language Association separated from the general Philological Congress, Dr. Paul Passy was effecting an international organization, with head-quarters in Paris, for promoting the teaching of modern languages according to the phonetic system. German teachers of the reform school eagerly welcomed the proffered assistance from France. A triad of scientific leaders was thus recognised: Sweet, in English phonetics; Vietor, in German; and Passy, in French. The organ of the French society, *Le Maître Phonétique*, has tendered invaluable assistance to the promoters of the reform movement in Germany, both in promoting the science of phonetics and assisting in reducing it to a practical basis.

Leaders of the Reform Party.

Thus it appears that there are now two principal schools of language teachers in Germany, diametrically opposed in doctrine. The representatives of the old school are firmly intrenched in the *Gymnasien* and universities, where scholastic ideas largely predominate, and classical training, with a view to mental discipline, receives the first consideration. The reformers count among their numbers a few of the younger university professors and *Privat-Docenten* and the majority of instructors in the *Real*-schools and *Höhere Töchterschulen*. A sketch of the gymnasial course, therefore, will represent the ideals of the one party; the work of a typical *Real*-school will embody the views of the other.

Gymnasial vs. Real-School Training.

In the *Gymnasien* the study of French is begun in *Quarta*, with four hours a week. There is some practice in pronunciation, but at first the main effort is directed to learning the grammar and the manipulation of sentences based on a set vocabulary. Later comes translation of connected discourse and the writing of themes in French. The all-but-universal text-book is by Ploetz and Kares. The literature read in the *Thomas Gymnasium* of Leipsic is, I think, fairly typical of the best classical schools. The books are changed from year to year, but the average amount of work does not vary. The first connected reading is in the fourth year of the course, from Thier's *Expédition de Napoléon en Egypte*. The following year Molière's *l'Avare* is introduced, and in the last two years four books are read: Thierry's *Guillaume le Conquérant*, Racine's *Britannicus*, Molière's *les Femmes Savantes* and Taine's *les Origines de la France contemporaine*. English is offered in the *Gymnasien* as an elective for two hours a week in the three upper classes. The method of teaching corresponds closely to the work in French. The course as a whole, even at its best, does little more for the pupil than give the ability to translate literary English with the help of a dictionary. In general, there is good reason why gymnasial students have no knowledge of the spoken language and no acquaintance with English lands and English customs: the average gymnasial teacher never goes beyond the borders of the fatherland.

<small>The Gymnasial Course.</small>

The best that can be said for the modern-language teaching in the *Gymnasien* is that it is neither better nor worse than the corresponding work in American high schools. It is an open question which party is most complimented by the comparison. Notable variations are to be found among German gymnasial teachers, but I believe that every divergence from the norm can be matched from the list of American teachers. The aim and methods of both are essentially the same. Even our most popular American text-books might well be considered translations of manuals used in the German *Gymnasien*.

<small>Results.</small>

Modern-language instruction in the *Real*-schools is quite another thing. Here is life and vigour and ability—and, of course, most excellent results. The province of Hesse-Nassau seems to be a luminous centre; but superior teaching can be found in Berlin, Altona, Leipsic, Carlsruhe, Munich, and also, I have no doubt, in many other cities which I was unable to visit. The course of study in French and English in one of these schools gives a very imperfect idea of what is done; but for sake of comparison I give herewith an outline of the work in 1892–1893 in these languages in the *Realschule* in Bockenheim, a suburb of Frankfort-on-the-Main.

<small>The Real-School Course.</small>

SEXTA.

French, 6 hours weekly. (a) Oral exercises: Exercises for ear and tongue; phonetic charts and phonetic spelling are used exclusively during the first months; special stress laid upon clear and correct pronunciation. In the second quarter, beginning of orthography. Learning by heart and singing of easy poems. Thorough explanation of the reading material; home and school life are subjects for conversation, in connection with Hölzel's *Pictures* (*Anschauungsbilder*). The most important grammatical laws (numerals, possessive and personal pronouns, plural of substantives, feminine forms of adjectives, declension of nouns, *ce qui, de qui, à qui, que avoir, être*—indicative, indicative of *-er* conjugation, agreement of subject and predicate with *être*) were taught inductively from the material used in conversation and reading, and fixed by independent exercises. (b) Written exercises: Beginning with the second quarter, weekly exercise in class—dictation, writing from memory, arithmetical problems, answers to questions in French and simple descriptions. Grammatical exercises: Text-book, *Französisches Lesebuch* by Kühn. (The following poems from the reader were committed to memory: Nos. 1, 3, 8 (a), 8 (b-c), 9, 12, 28, 29, 33, 44, 48, 55. The selections for reading were as follows: Part I., Nos. 15, 17, 18, 21, 49, 50, 51, 85; and from the small reader, Nos. 21, 25, 32, 36, 40, 41, 42, 52, 60 (c), 62 (a-b).)

<small>Outline.</small>

QUINTA.

French, 6 hours. (a) Oral: Readings from Kühn's *Lesebuch*, in connection with practice in hearing and speaking. Conversational exercises on affairs of daily life, the weather, seasons, geography and history. Memorizing from prose and poetry and practice in singing. Grammatical exercises according to Ploetz's *Elementarbuch*, in connection with readings, pictures and conversation. The reading material of *Sexta* was extended. One dialogue was learned. (b) Written: Daily exercises in class. One theme each week. Further practice in writing from dictation, answering questions, grammatical exercises and letter-writing.

QUARTA.

French, 6 hours. (a) Oral: Repetition of conversational material of VI. and V. The study of a large number of poems and selections from Kühn's *Lesebuch* (I. *Contes*, II. *Histoire*, III. *Leçons de Choses*). Conversational exercises in closest connection with this material, and, further, in connection with life of the pupils at home and in school, in city and country (Hölzel's *Pictures*). Practice in repetition of simple stories and descriptions of historical and geographical facts. Irregular verbs were studied systematically, as met with in reading or needed in conversation. (b) Written: Class exercise weekly—dictation, answering of questions, simple descriptions, free reproductions of stories told in class. Grammatical exercises with regular and irregular verbs, in connection with reading and conversation.

TERTIA.

French, 6 hours. Three stories were read from Souvestre, *Au Coin du Feu* and *Les Clairières*. Conversation on the contents of the readings, and practice in speaking in connection with Hölzel's *Pictures* and the daily experiences of the pupils. Repetition of previously learned poems and songs. Memorizing of new poems. Grammar: Review of the irregular verbs and syntax of substantives, adjectives, adverbs, numerals and prepositions; use of modes and tenses. Two written exercises in class each month—conversations, descriptions, dictations, translations. Text-books: Ploetz's *Schulgrammatik der französischen Sprache*.

English, 5 hours. (a) Oral: Phonetic exercises in connection with the *Lauttafel* and *Lautschrift*. In second quarter, beginning of orthography. Memorizing of poems, some of which were sung. The study of selections through question and answer. Further exercise in speaking concerning the surroundings and life of pupils at home and in school (Hölzel's *Pictures of the Seasons*). Simple grammatical exercises; the most important rules of syntax were learned inductively, and fixed by practice in the foreign tongue. (b)

INSTRUCTION IN THE MODERN LANGUAGES 277

Written : After the first quarter, one class exercise each week —writing from memory, simple description, answering of questions put in English, dictation and grammatical exercises. Text-books : Gesenius, *Elementarbuch der Engl. Sprache;* Victor and Dörr, *Engl. Lesebuch.*

SECUNDA.

French, 6 hours. (a) Readings : Guizot, *Récits historiques,* I.; Souvestre, *Au Coin du Feu* (five stories). Several songs were learned and sung; former ones reviewed. Free oral and written exercises, in connection with the readings and Hölzel's *Pictures.* A written exercise bi-weekly. (b) Grammar : The most important rules on order, modes and tenses, articles and adjectives, in connection with Plöetz's *Schulgrammatik, Lekt. 39–68.*

English, 4 hours. Stories, poems and songs from Victor and Dörr's *Englisches Lesebuch.* Memorizing of poems and songs and practice in singing. Exercise in speaking about reading materials, pictures and the pupils' surroundings. Review of poems. A written exercise bi-weekly. Systematic study of grammar, in connection with Gesenius' Text-Book, chaps. 1–22.

PRIMA.

French, 5 hours. Readings : *Tartarin de Tarascon,* by Daudet ; *L'Avare,* by Molière. Free oral and written exercises, in connection with the literature and object-lessons ; transposition and repetition of stories read or recounted in class ; exercises in dictation, condensation and translation. Class essays and letter-writing. One written exercise bi-weekly. Drill in grammatical forms.

English, 4 hours. Reading : *Jackanapes,* by Mrs. Ewing ; *Sketches,* by Dickens. A few poems learned and sung. Constant practice in speaking and writing, in connection with the reading material, the daily life of the pupils in home and school and Hölzel's *Pictures.* Practice in rapid reproduction of passages of read or spoken English and in letter-writing. Writing of English essays ; dictation and translation. A written exercise bi-weekly. Systematic study of grammar, according to Petry's *Die wichtigsten Kapitel der englischen Syntax.*

Nothing that I can add to this outline will show more clearly the scope and contents of the courses in modern languages. In this respect the schools themselves have no choice; the course is prescribed by the government. But there is much to be said concerning the ways and means of reaching the ends that are officially prescribed.

Dr. Quiehl of Cassel is one of the most successful teachers of modern languages in Germany. In the spring of 1894 I had the pleasure of spending several days in his school (the *Neue Realschule*), where I was given every opportunity to observe his methods. Inasmuch as the first lessons present the greatest difficulties and show the widest divergence from the gymnasial type, I will give here a transcription of my notes on an exercise with a class of forty boys who had been studying English one week.

The Reform Methods.

A phonetic chart (*Lauttafel*, by Victor) hangs on the wall before the class; it gives a schematic arrangement of all the vowel and consonant sounds in English, French and German. The class has already made its acquaintance, and knows the value of most of the characters. The teacher's first words are: "We will take the sounds to-day. What is the first sound in 'sounds'?" A boy is directed to point out the *s* on the chart; the boy repeats it, and the class gives it in concert. This process is continued with the remaining sounds of the word. It presents great difficulty to most of the pupils, and much drill is needed to make it clear. Other vocables previously studied are reviewed with the same precision; each sound is pointed out on the chart, and practised singly and in combination. The boys are already quite familiar with the chart; they run it over rapidly and skip about, following the master's pointer, very much as would be done in learning the musical scale. Next comes the use of numerals. They count (with the master's assistance) up to fifty. Special attention is given to pronunciation; each new difficulty is referred to the chart, and rapid drill follows individually and in chorus. The teacher, I notice, does not attempt to confine himself to English; his chief object is to make these

Lesson by Dr. Quiehl.

boys produce the right sounds and understand what is wanted. If German is necessary, they get it. The advantage in the use of numerals is that they already know the symbols; the figures can be written on the board as the words are pronounced without distracting the attention from the sounds. Particular stress is put on the correct English idiom. Over and over again come such expressions as the following: "Give me the stick [pointer]." "I have the stick." "He has the stick." "Can you count?" "Yes, I can count." The teacher writes 123, 1,456, 2,789 on the board, and asks a boy to read them. Others try it. Then comes practice in addition. Such examples as "$8 + 1 = ?$" and "$9 + 5 + 12 = ?$" are written on the board, read and solved. Boys set similar tasks for each other, and stir up a good deal of rivalry. The advance for the day now begins. A boy goes to the board and writes a number of six places. As he writes he names the figures; the class watches critically. "Is that right?" "Is that the right figure?" "Is that the right sound?" "Point it out on the chart"—such questions are being rapidly put at each step (with the help of German, if necessary) and as rapidly answered by simply changing the order and making necessary insertions. "Yes, that is right," or "No, that is not right." Other boys try their hands—and voices. This leads up easily to a series of sentences, with appropriate actions, like the following: "Take your seat—crayon—book—pencil." Boy: "I take my seat, crayon," etc. Class: "He takes his seat," etc. Teacher: "Put your book on (under, into) your desk (chair, table)." Boy: "I put my book on (under, into) my desk (chair, table)." Class: "He puts his book on (etc.) his desk (etc.)." Other sentences used in the same way are: "Open your book (books);" "Shut your book;" "Open the door;" "Shut the door;" "Enter the room;" "Go to your seat;" "Take your penholder;" "Write on your paper;" "Put down your penholder." All possible variations in the present tense are tried again and again. The equivalent German expression is called for whenever a boy seems not to understand or becomes confused. Next, plural forms are used. Two boys do as directed, and accompany their actions with appropriate responses. The class addresses the actors in the second person, and repeats it to the master in the third. This occupies several minutes, and is enthusiastically entered into by all. Everybody wants to take part, and few if any of the forty fail of an opportunity. Eight verbs are designated for practice at home, in preparation for the next recitation. "Shut your books"—"Put your books away"—"Stand up"—"Take the sponge"—"Wipe out the words on the blackboard"—"Open the window"—"Open the door"—"March." Time: fifty minutes.

The chief end of the lesson was to afford practice in using English sounds, particularly those not found in the Hessian dialect. Not a slip in the whole hour but was corrected by the master, and during the review the chart was in constant use. Yet incidentally a surprising amount of English was learned: idiomatic expressions involving some twenty new words; the use of four or five prepositions; the present indicative plural of eight or ten verbs; several pronouns, together with constant drill in the grammatical forms previously given. Not a letter had been written; probably no member of the class could have recognised a single word of all those he used so glibly, even if he had seen it in print. I need not say that the teacher was a master of his art; he knew English, and he knew how to teach it. And this kind of lesson, as I repeatedly observed, was an every-day occurrence. His scholars in the upper classes were reading and speaking French and English with ease. They had unbounded confidence in their ability to use what they knew, and, for school-boys, they knew a deal.

Aim of Lesson.

A lesson which I attended in the Bockenheim *Realschule* gave me some idea of the results of this method in the upper classes. The school had been for some time under the directorship of Professor Walter, who shortly before my visit had been transferred to the *Musterschule*, a *Realgymnasium*, in Frankfort. Professor Walter's reputation as a master of modern languages had been presented to me in such eulogistic terms that I was very desirous of learning something of his methods, but I was totally unprepared for the surprise that awaited me. Here was a class of thirty boys, about fourteen years of age, who had been studying English two years. They were just taking up *Jackanapes*, by Mrs. Ewing, having had perhaps ten lessons in the book. At the beginning of the lesson the boys were called upon to give a *résumé* of that part of the story which they had already read. The master then read a selection in advance; the class followed him with open books. One of the pupils then read the same passage, with scarcely a mispronunciation or false inflection. The grammatical construction was critically discussed, difficult words picked up and new ones pointed out, and the precise meaning of the author carefully analyzed—all in precise and idiomatic English. Other passages were treated in the same manner, but during the first two-thirds of the hour no attempt was made to give a literal translation. The story itself was the all-important thing; and, to make this more certain, variations in the text and in the syntactical construction were freely introduced, and as freely explained by the pupils—all in English. There could be no doubt of the complete mastery of the lesson by every member of the class. There was constant drill in speaking, in grammar and in composition. To make sure that nothing was being lost, the last few minutes of the hour were given up to idiomatic translation into German of the more difficult parts of the text, and to free reproduction in English of the story as contained in the day's lesson.

Lesson in Bockenheim.

It was all so skilfully done, and such perfect English used throughout (I was deceived into thinking the teacher an Englishman, but I afterward learned that his fluent speech and perfect cockney accent were the result of laborious study of Sweet's *Handbook* and the patient instruction of an English wife), that I was inclined to set it down as a "show" lesson for my especial benefit. The fact was, however, as I afterward convinced myself, that not

Results.

a boy in the class had had any chance whatever to make special preparation for it. The reading of these boys from start to finish was at sight. And I could well believe it possible from my experience with them after the hour was over. The master asked me to speak to them in English. I complied with some trepidation, lest I should be the means of marring an otherwise perfect exhibition. Imagine my surprise, therefore, when, at the teacher's suggestion, six of these boys in turn reproduced in their own words and in almost faultless English the gist of all I had told them. They were perfectly at home in English, so far as their studies had led them, and had no fear of conversation if restricted to their own vocabulary. And all this the result of two years of class instruction in English four hours a week!

After this experience in the Bockenheim school, I was the better prepared to appreciate Director Walter's work in Frankfort. The first lesson which I heard him give was to a class of thirty-seven boys in *Sexta*. They were just beginning French, and the lesson turned on the pronunciation of sounds which had no equivalent in their speech. The *s* in *maison* and *son* gave them much trouble. The chart was at hand, but it could not tell them how to pronounce what they could not hear. But a beginning was made by imitating the buzzing of bees and escaping steam; and when everything else failed the boys were requested to feel the teacher's throat and nose, even look into his mouth to see the position of the tongue, while he gave the sounds. After patient drill some progress was evident, but it was slow work. Everything was sacrificed to this one aim of clear and correct vocalization. It was a fine illustration of the theory underlying the phonetic method that everything starts with the sound; once right, always right; it is easier to teach the correct pronunciation than to correct a pronunciation that is bad.

[Margin note: Lesson by Professor Walter.]

And yet the lesson was not all phonetic drill. Words designating objects in the class-room were being used as illustrative material; a few common substantives, pronouns and verbs came in incidentally, and were put at once into use. Books, desks, windows and doors were opened and closed. The adjectives red, brown and black were freely used, to show their order in the sentence. The exercise shifted rapidly from individual attempts to concert recitation, and back again to action. Difficult words were analyzed, the sounds referred to in the chart, new combinations presented, and finally everything gathered up in a bit of verse which appealed to the children's fancy. Two little songs had been already learned, the words and music of each being the work of Director Walter; and thus many difficulties in vocalization disappeared in the musical tones. By drill in the production of single sounds and of sounds in combination, by individual practice and concert recitation, by intonation and chorus singing, these small boys were being introduced to the mysteries of spoken French. It was a purely formal exercise. I can imagine that the same work in the hands of a less skilful teacher might become an intolerable bore, but not so in this case. There was the greatest enthusiasm throughout the hour; and if at any time the attention was inclined to flag, the signal for a song would quickly revive it. But, on the whole, I agree with the verdict of an able American teacher of modern languages, whom I had advised to visit the Frankfort schools: "Director Walter's teaching is marvellous; but he would succeed with any method, or with none." Nevertheless, he protests that the "direct" method is everything to him. *[margin: The Purpose and Results.]*

"*Erst der Laut, dann der Schrift!*" It is a first principle of a direct method that the sound should precede the symbol, and that the sound should be learned by imitation of the teacher. The peculiar sounds incident to most dialects are quickly picked up by children long before they come to school. No one will pretend to say that there is any reflective thought involved; it is imitation pure and simple. The child of foreign parentage, other things being equal, learns the French sounds as readily as native children. Yet this natu- *[margin: Principles of the Direct Method.]*

ral process is impossible in school work. Imitation alone will not suffice, as many teachers have erroneously believed, because the linguistic environment is opposed to the introduction of sounds foreign to the mother-tongue. The learning of foreign sounds, therefore, must at first be a conscious process. Ordinarily, a child can imitate anything he can hear; and so long as he cannot hear the vocalized *s* or the French *u*, to say nothing of nasals, there is little probability of his giving the right vocalization, no matter how faithfully he tries. For this reason the science of phonetics must be applied to the work of the class-room. The child can sometimes feel the difference between the "hisses" and "buzzes" in English by placing his hands on the throat or covering his ears when by no means could he hear them. The application of phonetics, a physical science, to the production of sounds is possible just because voice culture is a physical process.

Phonetic Drill.

Furthermore, the number of sounds in French or English is limited, and the few not found in the mother-tongue can be learned in the first two or three lessons. In another lesson or two the pupil can be made so familiar with the phonetic chart that the gamut of sounds can be run over as easily as the notes of the musical scale. It is only by such training, founded on the science of phonetics and aided by exact phonetic symbols, that a correct pronunciation can be acquired.

The process at first may be a matter of knowledge, but unless it becomes a habit the knowledge may soon be lost. The next step, therefore, is to take up combinations of sounds to which the child can attach some meaning, preferably short sentences which by frequent repetition become well-fixed in the memory as indicative of certain ideas. Longer sentences, or several of them, may be easily learned, if there be some rhythm in them which tends to fix the habit. Hence, short poems are memorized almost from the beginning of the course. I have already referred to the excellent use made of music by Director Walter,

Correct Pronunciation.

not only as a means of acquiring vocabulary and its proper pronunciation, but also as delightful recreation in the midst of hard work. The little poem beginning *"Cherche, cherche, papillion; Tu es bien loin da ta maison!"*[1] and the songs *"Le bon camarade"* and *"Ma Normandie,"* are the first to be memorized—selected perhaps as much for their stock of nasal vowels as for their simplicity.

A song or poem learned, the next step is to refer every sound to its appropriate symbol. It is written out verse by verse in the phonetic characters, and copied into the pupils' note-books for practice at home. *Phonetic Script.* The phonetic is the only written form that the pupils see for months. At first the work is altogether oral; later, for the sake of precision, the phonetic script is introduced; and, finally, short pieces written in the phonetic characters are used for reading exercises in class. Walter and Quiehl recommend that the phonetic script be used exclusively for four months, at least, in French, and one month in English. It is said that Passy has used it successfully in the Paris *École Normale* during the first year and a half of class instruction.

Advocates of the direct method differ among themselves in regard to the use of the phonetic system in place of the ordinary spelling. Some go so far as to use the phonetic characters almost as diacritical marks. *How Used.* But I have observed that the best teachers make exclusive use of the phonetic system for a longer or shorter period. The natural query is, how do these German boys ever learn two spellings for every French or English word? The reply invariably made is that no confusion whatever results; the regular form is learned quite as easily, as it would have been at the beginning—yes, more easily, because knowing the precise pronunciation the learner has to grapple with but one difficulty. It is merely the elaboration of the maxim, "Do one thing at a time." A close examination of hundreds of copy-books convinces me that for some reason the spelling of

---

[1] No. 14, Kühn's *Lesebuch*.

English presents no more difficulty to the German than to the American school-boy; nor have I been able to observe any disadvantage in using the phonetic system while learning the pronunciation, even though it extends over several months.

One thing is perfectly apparent: isolated words are never used. In declension and conjugation, as well as in the earliest conversation in class, the complete sentence is spoken, and especial pains are taken that it be pronounced fluently. In this way a vocabulary is built up which consists not merely of words, but also of idiomatic phrases and sentences. Perhaps the most apparent effect of this plan is to be seen in the translations. Never dealing with words alone, but always with combinations of words the significance of which is understood as a whole, the pupil will be led to translate idiomatically and precisely, but not word for word. The pupil knows the meanings of words only as they stand in sentences: a word-for-word translation seldom conveys the meaning of a sentence. The direct method, therefore, can lay claim to the most direct route to idiomatic literal translation, the *summum bonum* of the old school.

<small>Always Complete Sentences.</small>

The needs of conversation finally transcend the school-room and actions that can actually be performed in class. With young pupils something objective is necessary to retain their attention. The *Pictures of the Seasons*, by Hölzel, serve this purpose excellently. They are large wall pictures, brightly coloured and mounted on stiff cardboard, and depict various phases of city and country life at different seasons of the year. In the hands of some teachers these pictures afford excellent material for conversation; and conversation rightly conducted means the acquisition of vocabulary, training in grammatical forms and syntax and a lively appreciation of the meaning of the foreign language.

<small>Object-Lessons.</small>

The first impulse of the advocates of the direct method was to make the study of grammatical principles a secondary affair; what are popularly termed the laws of grammar are merely the forms of expression adopted by the users of language. If, therefore, the right use of language be taught, what need is there of spending time in memorizing a fund of lifeless knowledge? But in practice it has been discovered that lifeless knowledge may not be useless. The child that learns a language in the natural way may have little need of formal grammar; not so the school-boy who hears the language only in class. Practice may fix habits of simple expression, but connected discourse must be ordered according to conscious principles, even more than pronunciation needs be referred to a system of phonetics. Hence the leaders of the new movement have come to make almost as much of formal grammar as ever did the most zealous supporters of the old *régime*. But with this difference: the one party will arrive at a systematic knowledge of grammatical forms inductively, as a result of language study; the other will deduce the right use of language from a study of grammatical laws. In practice at least, grammar is as much emphasized by one party as by the other. And it is just at this point where the advocates of the direct method part company with those who rely on most so-called "natural" methods. There must be a basis of conscious knowledge in the acquisition of any language that is not learned as the child learns his mother-tongue; such a basis is grammar for the psychical side and phonetics for the physical —both are indispensable.

Study of Grammar.

The writing of French and English is an important feature of the work throughout the course. It begins in the lowest class with writing simple sentences in phonetic characters; when the regular script is introduced, practice in spelling is given in writing from dictation; later on paraphrasing is a regular exercise, which finally merges into free composition. In the earlier part of the course the pupil writes only that which he has learned in class, but when he has gained more power and understands better the grammatical forms he is allowed more freedom. But at all stages of progress prose composition is

Prose Composition.

the immediate outgrowth of reading, and is never dissociated from it.

The literature is the centre of instruction; but as every teacher knows, much depends on what is selected for class use. The classic writers of a language may not always be best suited to enlist the sympathy and interest of foreign school-boys. It is characteristic of the new school that *Jackanapes*, *Tom Brown's School Days* and Irving's *Sketch Book* should be preferred to Emerson, Macaulay or Shakespeare. A rational understanding of a foreign literature must grow out of a comprehensive knowledge of the national life. The history, geography and social customs of the country must be studied along with its language. The school courses in history and geography can be so correlated with the language work as to be of great assistance. If the literature is properly selected, it will reflect the social life and personal characteristics of the people in a way to command the attention of any class, and give pith and point to conversation and prose composition. Hence I found Dr. Quiehl using in his highest French class Bruno's *Le Tour de la France par deux Enfants;* and in Berlin Dr. Hausknecht, whose teaching I much admired, was using as the basis of his second-year English a book of his own composition on the school life of an English boy. Such material is easily supplemented, and is a constant incentive to conversation and oral reproduction.

<small>The Literature.</small>

This method of language teaching requires specially trained teachers. In the first place, they must be thoroughly familiar with the foreign tongue, must know it idiomatically and be able to use it fluently; secondly, they must understand its phonetic peculiarities and grammatical construction; and in the third place, they must have a comprehensive knowledge of the culture and customs of the people whose language they will teach. In fact, this kind of teaching is more than instruction in language and literature; it is training in foreign culture through language and literature. It is closely correlated at

<small>Need of Trained Teachers.</small>

all points with the course of study in history and geography, and re-enforces both at every step. This is what gives it life and vigour, and makes the results so eminently superior to any method that deals exclusively with language and literature.

The Prussian *Lehrplan* of 1892 gave the adherents of the Vietor school precisely the support they wanted. It set as the aim of modern-language teaching, familiarity with the living tongue and an intimate acquaintance with the life of the people who use it. Re-enforced by the Prussian Government. The idea of making French and English a *Real*-school substitute for the classical languages was intentionally abandoned; instead of formal discipline of the mental faculties, the government set as the standard of excellence the ability to use the modern language and the knowledge of modern literature and social life. Not power in general, but power in special directions, was made the end of all such instruction.

The government understands full well that this end is beyond the reach of most teachers. Few of them have enjoyed the advantages of residence in France or England, and not many have been trained in phonetics or have any acquaintance with the methods of the reformers. Holiday Courses. Holiday courses, therefore, have become a practical necessity, and the government is heartily supporting them. The intention is to give teachers a two weeks' leave of absence once a year, if they will attend these courses Such a subsidy, it is thought, will make the attendance sufficiently large to warrant the engagement of able instructors, and to arouse a permanent interest in distinctly modern-language teaching.

It remains to be seen whether the rank and file of modern language teachers can be brought to an intelligent appreciation of the new methods and trained to make good use of them. A "deductive" The Outlook. method they can understand, an "inductive" method they can understand; but it is an open question whether many of them can make the combination of the two, on the modern social basis which is the secret of all the success of the Victor school. This is, however, no argument against the reformers. Some teachers cannot make a conspicuous success of any method; some are bound to win under any circumstances. But given a good teacher, the training of the Victor school will make him a better teacher.

GENERAL REFERENCES :—Walter, *Entwurf eines Lehrplanes für den französischen Unterricht*, Marburg; Quiehl, *Franz. Aussprache und Sprachfertigkeit*, Marburg; Hano, *Anleitung zur Erlernung der franz. Umgangssprache*, Frankfort; Hölzel, *Bilderbuch für Schule und Haus*, Vienna; Wieke, *Einführung in die Engl. Sprache*, Leipsic; Ohlers, *Methodische Anleitung zur Unterricht im Französischen*, Hanover; Wilke, *Anschauungs-Unterricht im Englischen*, Leipsic; Beyer and Passy, *Elementarbuch des gesprochenen Französischen*, Cöthen; Sweet, *Elementarbuch des gesprochenen Englischen*, Oxford; Walter, *Anfangs-Unterricht im Englischen* (program of *Realschule*), Cassel; Klinghardt, *Ein Jahr Erfarungen mit der imitativen Methode; Drei Weitere Jahre*, etc., Marburg; Junker, *Lehrversuch im Englischen nach der neuen Methode* (*Realschule* program), Bockenheim; Zergiebel, *Grammatik und natürliche Spracherlernung* (*Realschule* program), Cassel; Breymann, *Die neusprachliche Reform-Litteratur von 1876-1893*, Leipsic, 1895; Waetzoldt, *Die Aufgabe des neusprachlichen Unterrichts und die Vorbildung der Lehrer*, Berlin, 1893; Baumeister, *Handbuch der Erziehungs- und Unterrichtslehre*, Munich.

CHAPTER XV

INSTRUCTION IN HISTORY AND GEOGRAPHY

"It has to be remarked," says Comenius, "that in every class, history, as the eye of life, should find a place, so that all that is most memorable in the past, both in deed and word may be known. This, so far from increasing the burden on pupils, will lighten their labours. Little text-books should be written, *viz.*, one on biblical history; one on natural things; one on inventions and mechanical arts; one exhibiting the most illustrious examples of virtue; one on the various customs of nations; and, finally, one containing all that is most significant in the history of the world and especially of our own country." *Comenius on History.*

It is remarkable that, notwithstanding the high regard in which the study of history was held both by Luther and Melanchthon, no serious attempt was made to introduce it into the secondary schools before the time of Comenius. The Jesuits were early impressed with the correctness of Comenius' ideas, and gave history a place in their curriculum. Others, notably Francke and Leibnitz, did something for the teaching of history in the secondary schools; but so little time was given to the subject that the work degenerated into the mere memorizing of historical facts. Frederick the Great, in the truly rationalistic spirit, severely criticised the pedagogues of his day for stuffing the memories of the pupils, giving no heed whatsoever to the development of the powers of judgment. In his instructions to the Berlin *Ritterakademie* (1765), he said: "It *Early Development.*

is no longer permissible for a young man who will live in the great world not to know the events which belong in the chain of European history." In his opinion, a knowledge of the history of the classical world was of little value without the ability to apply it to modern conditions. The immediate outcome of the rationalistic movement was a change in the method of treating history, as well as a decided increase (four to six hours) in the number of week-hours devoted to the study. In the upper classes of some schools, the method now frequently recommended could be found even then in actual operation. A whole semester, and in some instances an entire year, was devoted to an intensive study of special topics.

At the beginning of the present century, when things were shaping for the subsequent development of the German school system, the influence of F. A. Wolf was such as to retard the study of history. In his opinion, nothing should be taught in a *Gymnasium* that did not serve directly as a preparation for the learned professions. Little can be gained from a study of modern history, he urges, that does not tend to narrow and pervert a young man's judgment. Mediæval history can contribute little, because the events of that period are not such as to elevate or inspire. In fact, ancient history is the only history of any value, because in it we learn of the motives and acts of the greatest people the world has ever seen, of the causes that made them great and of the errors which brought about their ruin. Such knowledge must be not only a desirable, but also an essential element in a well-rounded education. With Herbart, history received a prominent place in the curriculum. He considered a knowledge of what man has done and suffered, of what he has tried to do and the reasons for his failures, as the surest means of rousing a pupil's interest in the past and inspiring him with lofty sentiments. History becomes, therefore, a study of particular value. Its object is not only intellectual, but moral development. Old Testament history deserves a place beside that of Greece and Rome. Schleiermacher, too, called history the picture-book of ethics.

Recent Progress.

It will be seen that in the humanistic schools, where the chief end of education was a familiarity with classic authors, and where the whole course of training was purely formal, there was no place for history. But with the introduction of realistic notions, through Comenius, Locke and Rousseau, together with the utilitarian ideas which characterized the period of enlightenment, the study of history and geography was recommended for its practical worth. "A man," said Frederick the Great, "who does not imagine himself fallen from heaven, who does not date the history of the world from the day of his birth, must be curious to know what has taken place in all ages and in all lands." But neither Frederick the Great nor the educators of his time believed that a mere knowledge of useful facts is the chief end of the study of history. On the contrary, it was held that the study of history offers the best opportunity for the development of the discriminative judgment. Properly presented, it teaches the pupil to pass over the unessential, and fasten upon the important links in the chain of causes. It affords scope for common-sense comparison, and aids in the formation of judgments which have a practical bearing upon the affairs of every-day life. History has never been so strongly emphasized as in the latter half of the eighteenth century. In the opinion of von Zedlitz, minister of education under Frederick the Great, six or seven hours a week were not too much time to give to historical studies. With the reorganization of the Prussian school system at the close of the Napoleonic wars, three hours a week were assigned to history and geography (program of 1816). As the schools came more and more under the influence of the humanistic leaders, and education became increasingly formal, history fell into the background—if not in theory, at least in practice. As taught in the schools, it amounted to little more than sketches of military campaigns and the memorizing of dates.

The new Prussian *Lehrplan* of 1892 lays great stress upon the language, literature and history of Germany. These

Influence of the Realists.

must be the centre to which all else tends. The secondary schools are looked upon as the mainstay of the throne, and the supreme authority has declared that these schools shall turn out patriotic citizens. To this end, nothing should be left undone to give the youth of the fatherland a critical insight into the history of the German empire. As Goethe puts it, the best that we get from history is the enthusiasm which it arouses. With this in mind, the education department of the Prussian government has set a new stamp on the educational value of history. It is held to be of worth primarily for its ethico-religious influence in the development of character.

Lehrplan of 1892.

Granted that history shall have a place in the curriculum, what kind of history should it be—political history? or something more comprehensive? national, or general history? Obviously, the gymnasial policy has been to consider political history as of little worth in comparison with the broader and more comprehensive history of civilization, and national history as narrow and one-sided when viewed in the light of general history. Prior to the reform of 1892, the secondary schools of Prussia accepted history as an end in itself, without reference to its practical bearing in the training of citizens. "The object of historical instruction in the *Gymnasium*," according to the rescript of 1882, "is to arouse in the pupils a respect for the moral greatness of individual men and nations, to make them conscious of their own imperfect insight, and to give them the ability to read understandingly the greatest historical classics." The *Lehrplan* of 1892 brings prominently to the front the necessity of understanding the events in German and Prussian history. It is the national history rather than the universal which is emphasized: the political which has culminated in a new and regenerated German empire, rather than the general which deals with the salient points in the progress of civilization.

Subject-Matter of Instruction.

It shows clearly the determination of the government to make use of the schools in stemming the tides of socialism and liberalism. History is to be taught, not altogether as a means for intellectual training, nor as an essential part of a liberal education, nor yet as an independent science, but pre-eminently with a view to the making of patriotic citizens.

The new syllabus also shows a change in the arrangement of the course in history. Formerly there were two years of mythology and biography in the first part of the course, beginning with the legendary history of Greece and coming down to the early history of Germany. The new *Lehrplan* provides that in *Sexta* scenes in the national history shall be described, beginning with the events which are closely related to the pupils' own environment, and working from the present back into the past. This regression continues throughout the first year, and in *Quinta* it reaches the legendary history of Greece and Rome. The chief events of Grecian history to the death of Alexander the Great, and of Roman history to the death of Augustus, are taken up in the following year (*Quarta*). In *Untertertia* the chronological order is followed to the end of the Middle Ages. *Obertertia* continues the work to the accession of Frederick the Great, with special reference to the history of Brandenburg. *Untersecunda* fills out the course to the present time. Up to this point the course is the same for both six-year and nine-year schools. The three upper grades of the latter begin again with an intensive study of Grecian and Roman history in *Obersecunda*, of the mediæval and modern history to the end of the Thirty Years' War in *Unterprima* and of the later developments down to the present time in *Oberprima*.

Prussian Course in History.

The introduction of the *Abschlussprüfung* at the end of *Untersecunda* determined the allotment of the work in the middle and upper grades. The course as a whole, however, has thereby been cut up into three distinct parts: the first of these proceeds from the present back to the legendary history of the Greeks; the second begins with early Grecian history and traces the casual series, so far at least as the German people are concerned, down to the present; the third is but a larger circle drawn around the other two.

Teachers of history who believe in maintaining a strict continuity, and who think that the explanation of present events is to be sought in causes lying in the past, have no faith in the manner of treatment suggested for the first and second years in the Prussian course; and least of all will they tolerate the division in the courses at the end of the first six years. Another class of educators is unalterably opposed to the allotment of only two years to ancient history, one year of which (*Quarta*) is at the very beginning of the true historical course. Furthermore, it has been pointed out that, inasmuch as the leaving examinations are based solely upon the work of *Untersecunda* and *Oberprima* respectively, no direct tests can be made of scholars' attainments in either Grecian or Roman history, and that this applies no less to the *Gymnasien* than to the *Real-* schools.

Objections.

Prussia may change her course of study as often as she pleases, she may dictate what shall be taken up in each class; but she cannot change the views of her teachers by a ministerial rescript. To all appearances, the new order has served to introduce only confusion into the history teaching of most schools. The veterans educated and trained under the old dispensation are not anxious, as a rule, to adapt themselves to the new requirements, which have all the appearance of using the teachers as props for bolstering up the throne. I regret to say that I was unable to find in any Prussian school what might be considered as a typical illustration of the Prussian program. Furthermore, very few of the German states have followed Prussia's lead in the matter of teaching history.

There are those who maintain that the emperor's idea of making the special aim of historical study the fostering of a national spirit, while in theory perfectly correct, is nevertheless pedagogically short-sighted. They maintain that patriotism should be more than mere enthusiasm, more enduring than the frothy exuberance of spirits that arises from the contemplation of great deeds; that love of country and of king depends upon a firm and unchangeable character. It follows, therefore, that character-building must at least go hand in hand with the development of the patriotic spirit. The best representatives of this school are unquestionably the Herbartians.

The lamented Dr. Frick, of Halle, untiringly advocated more rational methods in the teaching of history. Probably no man in Germany has done more than he in working out a course of study closely correlated with the work in German, the classical languages, geography and religion. He had great influence in the Berlin conference, and his views were largely instrumental in effecting some of the more important changes there made. It is to be regretted, however, that other interests interfered with the complete expression of his views.

The teaching of geography in the German schools has become a highly perfected art. I am not sure but geography is the best taught subject, on the whole, of all the subjects of the curriculum. At any rate, one sees less of offensive formalism and more of intelligent freedom in the treatment of geographical topics than in almost any other sphere. In its present form geography is a very modern subject. It took its rise from Karl Ritter, who acknowledged his indebtedness to Pestalozzi for suggestions as to natural methods of teaching. And from that day to this there has been no lack of university instruction for the teachers of the secondary and normal schools. The influence of a few such men as Ratzel, of Leipsic; Kiepert, of Berlin; Kirchhoff, of Halle; and Sievers, of Giessen—all interested in the training of teachers—is sufficient to give geography a high rank in the schools.

Geography.

But geography, so far as it has to do with the earth as the abode of man, is inseparable from history; and in the secondary schools of Germany history and geography keep even step. Except possibly in the first two years of the course, geography is nowhere an independent study in the higher schools. The study of topography and of political and commercial geography and the drawing of maps are closely correlated with the work in history. The general truths of mathematical and physical geography which have no direct bearing upon the events of history are taught incidentally, one might say, in the lower grades. On the other hand, the more important facts of physical geography, meteorology and geology are generally carefully expounded in the best German schools as a partial explanation of political and social conditions. It is for this reason that in nearly all secondary-school programs of Germany history and geography are classed together as a single subject. In so doing, to be sure, geography loses some of the characteristics which would naturally place it among the natural sciences; but as the object both in history and geography is not so much to develop an accurate scientific knowledge of these subjects as the formation of certain habits of thought and feeling, the correlation is a distinct gain for both studies. The union is made still closer by placing the instruction of both in the hands of the same teacher.

Relation to History.

As a typical example of those schools in which history and geography seem to have a place commensurate with their value as an educational means, and in which the problems of historical and geographical teaching are being solved in the best pedagogical manner, I select the *Gymnasium* of Jena. The *Director* of the school, Dr. G. Richter, was an intimate friend of Dr. Frick and for several years co-editor with him of the *Lehrproben und Lehrgänge,* in which some of the best pedagogical work of the secondary schools has been published. Dr. Richter, however, is more than an expounder of the views which have made Dr. Frick famous. He has associated with him in his school faculty several able young men who are in entire accord with the Herbartian views as modified by Drs. Frick and Richter. It is to their united efforts that success is due.

Jena Program.

The program for history and geography in the first two classes of the Jena *Gymnasium* is as follows:

SEXTA.

History and German, 3 hours. Stories from the *Odyssey* and selections from German legendary history. *Geography,* 2 hours. (a) Simple geographical notions to be gained from Jena and the surrounding country. *Course in Lower Grades.* Eleven excursions to various points of interest in the neighborhood. (b) Thuringia — (1) The map ; (2) course of the Saale, as far as Halle ; (3) Ilm ; (4) Unstrut ; (5) Elster ; (6) Werra, as far as Eschwege ; (7) Itz ; (8) railroads. Chief topics : elevations, climate, products, industry, trade, religion and political divisions. Throughout the entire year observations of the temperature, winds, position and movements of the sun and moon—all of which are entered in a note-book.

QUINTA.

History and Geography, 4 hours. (a) German mythology and history, chiefly Thuringian ; selections of typical scenes. With the extension of the history proceeds the gradual development of the geography, until it includes all Germany. Map-drawing, at first of Germany ; then a gradual extension to all other European countries.

The Jena program of the work for the first two classes differs from the Prussian syllabus in that comparatively little attention is given to classical mythology. In fact, stories from the *Odyssey* are about all that are not German. In *Sexta* there is very little of what could be called under any stretch of imagination historical work ; and, contrary to the Prussian plan, the entire time of *Quinta* is devoted to a systematic description of the chief events in German history.

In *Sexta* the geographical instruction is particularly interesting. The *Gymnasium* is situated on ground once occupied by the city walls. The broad street now separating the old city from its modern suburbs *Study of Home Region.* gives a starting-point for a map of the town.
It is linked, too, with historical associations that easily arouse the interest of the pupils. Pictures of the old town before

the walls were removed are still to be had. An occasional watch-tower yet remains standing as a monument of former times. A few minutes' walk brings the teacher with his class to one of a dozen points of interest in the town. The river Saale, with its tributaries, can be traced for fifteen or twenty miles from the heights. The location of a dozen villages can be indicated on the map as a result of a single excursion to a neighbouring hilltop. In fact, the excursions which are always made by teacher and pupils during this first year furnish the fundamental concepts necessary at the beginning of geographical study; and the observations taken day by day of the movements of heavenly bodies, fluctuations in temperature and changes of the wind are the basis of all future work in mathematical geography and meteorology.

The work of *Quinta* is divided into some thirty or forty topics, the most of which can be centred about some illustrious man or great event. These embrace a description of the Cimbri and Teutons, their subjugation and liberation; stories of Drusus, Germanicus and Armin, together with the geography of western Germany; the Slavic invasions of eastern Germany; the coming of the Christians; Charlemagne and his times; the building of the Wartburg; the Crusades; great Thuringian rulers; founding of the universities; Hussites in Thuringia and the Reformation; the Thirty Years' War; Brandenburg and Prussia; Karl August, Goethe and Schiller; Napoleon, and the battles of Jena and Leipsic; Stein, Blücher and Scharnhorst; the new German Empire; Wilhelm I., Bismarck and Moltke.

<small>Local History.</small>

The Jena *Gymnasium* is peculiarly fortunate in having some of the best teachers which it has ever been my privilege to hear. The younger members of the faculty in particular have given much time and labour to the development of rational methods in the teaching of history and geography. In the lower grades a typical recitation begins with a review of such parts of previous lessons as may be necessary for the proper understanding and assimilation of the topic about to be presented. From

<small>Methods of Teaching.</small>

five to ten minutes of the hour may pass in this way. Then comes the narration of the new story, with particular emphasis upon certain important events, personages and dates. As the teacher proceeds with the story, he develops an outline on the board which he has previously carefully prepared. As he places this upon the board, point by point, the pupils enter it into their note-books. Historical pictures are freely used, to bring out clearly references made to the military, social, family or industrial life of the times.

This use of illustrative material, be it said, is more common in German schools than in American. It may be in a large measure due to the lamentable fact that we in America are at a serious disadvantage in this respect. Our pictures, charts and maps are decidedly inferior to the German in point of accuracy, execution and artistic merit. The German teachers of *Sexta* and *Quinta* have at command an elaborate series of pictures and charts illustrating almost every phase of national life from the earliest times to the present. What cannot be obtained by reproduction of famous works of art is supplied in the form of ideal illustrations executed in accordance with the best scholarship obtainable.

Illustrative Material.

The pedagogical value of such use of pictures in class work, so Germans maintain, is very great. It is said that the child living in the present and thinking in the terms of the present is unable to adjust himself to the past without great efforts of the imagination. It is peculiarly the function of pictures to assist the mind of the child in grasping the real significance of past events. They are of particular importance, too, in the teaching of geography. At first the child acquires a store of geographical ideas from observation of his local environment. The moment he is asked to go beyond his actual experience, he must draw upon his imagination. It is too much to assume that he will grasp the full significance of geographical facts which are totally unconnected with anything already known; but pictures properly executed may be of the greatest service in the

Its Educational Value.

development of the constructive imagination, provided care be taken that the child interpret correctly what the picture presents.

In the presentation of the lesson the teacher will of necessity often be obliged to consider the topography of the country in which the scene of the story is laid. This involves an elaboration of the geographical knowledge of the class. It may happen that a halt must be called in the development of the historical side, in order that maps of the region may be drawn and the physical characteristics of the country carefully studied. In general, it is expected that the equivalent of one or two hours a week will be given to this phase of the work during the first four or five years of the course. If no such interruptions are necessary, the teacher will give not more than half of the hour to the presentation of new material.

Division of Time.

The next step in the lesson is the oral reproduction by the pupils of what has just been told them, according to the outline as it stands before them on the board. No one who has observed this part of the recitation in the Jena *Gymnasium* can fail to be impressed with the intense interest manifested by the pupils, as shown in their eagerness to tell what they know and to discuss its consequences.

Excellent Results.

There is a life and vigour to be found here, which, I regret to say, I rarely saw elsewhere. One pupil begins to tell the story, and at a convenient resting-point he is succeeded by another; and so on in regular order, until perchance some wrong impression calls up a more general class discussion. Whenever an important name or date occurs, the pupils rise and repeat it in concert; thus the attention of all is fixed more closely upon the topical outline of the lesson.

It would hardly be doing the Herbartian teacher justice to say that the oral reproduction is the final step of the lesson. He would certainly consider his work very much of a failure if, in addition to proper preparation and presentation, he did not proceed to generalize and to make application of the truth of the lesson to the every-day life of the scholars. A Jena teacher will rarely fail in this respect. The lesson is a work of art.

The program for the second part of the work in history and geography is as follows:

QUARTA.

History and Geography, 4 hours. (a) Geography of the Balkan Peninsula, the Carpathian countries and Asia, particularly Asia Minor; Grecian history to 146 B.C. (b) Geography of Italy, Spain, France and Africa, especially northern Africa; Roman history to 476 A.D. Course in Middle Grades.

UNTERTERTIA.

History and Geography, 3 hours. (a) Geography of central Europe, with special reference to physical characteristics and political history; German history to 1096 A.D. (b) German history from 1096 to 1555; outlines of American geography, in connection with the history of discovery.

OBERTERTIA.

History and Geography, 3 hours. (a) Modern history from 1555 to 1700; the geography of Great Britain, the Scandinavian Peninsula, Denmark, France and Russia; review of European geography. (b) Modern history from 1700 to 1815 and from 1864 to 1871; geography of America and Australia and of the German colonies.

The most important deviation from the Prussian course that appears in the Jena *Lehrplan* is in the amount of time devoted to the history of Greece and Rome. The Prussian plan, as has been stated, gives but two years to this work—one in *Quarta*, when the pupils are but twelve years old, which covers the whole field of classical history in a single year of two lessons per week; the other year is in *Obersecunda*, during which all of Greek and Roman history to the fall of the Western Empire is done in three lessons per week. Further than this there is nothing of classical history, not even a review in the last year of the course. The Prussian *Lehrplan*, as has been previously mentioned, has been arranged with a view to the practical needs of those who leave school at the end of a six years' course (about forty per cent. of the entire number); and it has been considered especially desirable, therefore, that they should take with them a well-rounded training in the language, literature and history of Germany and in religion. Hence, the Grecian history formerly taught in *Untersecunda* has given way to an additional year of modern history. Few other German states have adopted the Prussian plan to this extent. There are undoubtedly certain practical advantages connected with it, both in the emphasis placed on modern history and in the division of the work made for the benefit of those who do not intend to complete the school course. Still, the classical schools feel that in the time allowed it is impossible to teach Greek and Roman history satisfactorily. From a pedagogical stand-point there is no doubt that the Jena plan, which is the one generally followed in the other German states, has superior advantages for the classical schools. Although the second part of the course is completed with *Obertertia*, it provides for a more intensive course in the upper classes, one-half of which is devoted to the history of Greece and Rome.

The work of *Quarta* begins with a review of the most important Greek legends. Nearly all schools give a year to the mythology of Greece and Rome—in Prussia, *Quinta*, and in other states, generally *Sexta*. In Jena, however, the work is confined for the most part to stories from the *Odyssey*, which also form a part of the German reading course. The wanderings of Ulysses demand a careful study of the geography of Grecian lands. Maps are drawn of the Balkan Peninsula and Asia Minor; the islands of the Ægean are located, and the classic routes of travel compared with those of modern times. Then follows an outline history of the political events in Greece between 1104 and 500 B.C., together with the necessary changes in the geographical divisions. The study of the Persian wars brings in the geography of Asia and Egypt, and the biographies of Cyrus, Cambyses, Darius and Pericles. The account of the Peloponnesian War is accompanied with a study of the geography of Sicily. Then follows a narrative of the events clustering about the lives of Socrates, Agesilaus, Epaminondas and Pelopidas, Demosthenes and Philip of Macedon. The story of Alexander the Great, the division of his empire and its subsequent subjugation to Rome completes the historical course in Grecian history, and also furnishes an opportunity for a review of the geography of southwestern Asia. The work of the second semester is Roman history, and a study of the geography, ancient and modern, of the countries included in the Roman Empire. The class, at the same time that it is studying the history of Greece and Rome, has the geography of Palestine in connection with religion, and is reading in German the Theban legends, stories from Greek history, Schiller's *Cranes of Ibycus*, stories from Roman history and travellers' descriptions of Italy and Athens.

In *Untertertia* the history of the Holy Roman Empire is traced down to the year 1555. So far as possible the social and political changes are treated with reference to the fortunes of the city of Jena, which lies *In Fourth Year.* at the crossing of the two great highways contended for both by the Germans and the Slavs. Within sight of the town are a dozen castles and strongholds, each of which has a story to tell of the struggles of these races for supremacy. The history of the city church and cloister, of the city hall (*Rathaus*) and of the market dates from early times, and illustrates the gradual development of local self-government. The founding of the university and its later history afford a natural means of introducing the study of the Reformation. The political and physical geography of central Europe affords important contributions for the understanding of the course in mediæval history. The period of discovery brings in America, South Africa and Asia.

In *Obertertia* the chief events of modern history from 1555 to the present time are considered. It is the period of colonization, in which England takes a leading part. Queen Elizabeth is portrayed, and the geography of Great Britain is studied. The Thirty Years' War brings in Sweden and Denmark, under the hero Gustavus Adolphus.

<small>In Fifth Year.</small>

The French influence in the seventeenth and eighteenth centuries necessitates a study of the history of France as it centres in the career of Louis XIV. Russia, as represented by Peter the Great, is given some attention. The second semester is devoted to the history of the eighteenth century, and the culmination of events in the overthrow of Napoleon and in the final restoration of the German Empire. A study of the German colonial possessions, and of those countries enriched by German immigration, gives ample opportunity for a review of the geography of the world. During this year the class reads in German selections from Schiller's *History of the Thirty Years' War* and from his *Wilhelm Tell*, both of which are side-lights on the work in history.

There has been much discussion concerning the best methods of teaching history in the middle and upper grades. Teachers have pointed out the defects of the narrative method, and maintained that thereby scholars attain no power of independent investigation; that even the faculty of discriminative judgment is not properly cultivated, and that few pupils ever acquire a love for historical reading. Professor Schiller, of Giessen, a noted writer on gymnasial pedagogics, still holds that it is highly desirable to assign readings to be done out of school and to devote the lesson period to a discussion of the topic. The Prussian regulations, however, distinctly prohibit the general adoption of this method, because of the restrictions it places upon the free time of the pupils. From twenty minutes to half an hour a day is all that a teacher has a right to expect of his pupils by way of home study, and this is hardly sufficient for the correction of notes and the making of such maps as are necessary in class work. In fact, there is but one method possible for the German teacher. He must himself

<small>Methods of Teaching.</small>

narrate the stories, make outlines and do the reviewing in the class.

The method of presentation in the middle grades does not differ materially from that already described in the lower grades. First, there is a review of the important events of past lessons; then the telling of the new story, and its oral reproduction by the class according to the outline which the teacher has developed and placed upon the board. Text-books are commonly used, of which there are many excellent varieties. They are, however, mere outlines, which by no means usurp the function of the teacher. They are hand-books for consultation in review and for fixing lessons already elaborated in the class. A text-book that presumes to give a complete account of the historical development of the period studied would be worse than useless to the pupil. He would not have time to do the required reading, to say nothing of sorting out the important facts. For pupils' use a concise reference book rather than a text-book is required.

Use of Text-Books.

The Jena program for the final course is as follows:

UNTERSECUNDA.

History and Geography, 3 hours. (a) Review and continuation of Grecian history down to 338 B.C., with reference to the ancient geography of Greece and Asia Minor. (b) Alexander the Great and the Hellenistic Empire down to its subjugation by Rome, together with a geographical review; then a review of Roman history to 133 B.C., and of the geography of ancient Italy. Geographical reviews of Asia and Africa.

Course in Upper Grades.

OBERSECUNDA.

History and Geography, 3 hours. (a) Roman history from 133 B.C. to 375 A.D. (b) Mediæval history to 1056 A.D. Geographical reviews. Review of important dates in the world's history.

UNTERPRIMA.

History and Geography, 3 hours. (a) History of the period from 1056 to 1555. (b) Modern history from 1555 to 1786. Geographical reviews.

OBERPRIMA.

History and Geography. Modern history from 1786 to 1888, with special attention to geography. Comprehensive *résumé* of the historical development of modern civilization.

The methods to be followed in the upper classes do not differ essentially from those already outlined. The pupils are more mature; they have read more exten-
<small>Methods of Teaching.</small> sively from both classical and modern authors, and have greater power in abstract thought. Nevertheless, the same general plan of presentation must be followed as in the lower classes, the only difference being that less effort is required to make the work interesting, and more attention can be given to the relations of cause and effect. In fact, this final course does not cover much more ground than the one just finished; but it is treated in a more general way, and the causes of political changes are emphasized to the exclusion, in a degree, of the descriptive work which characterizes the earlier course. The pupils already know the more important facts; the main thing now is to search out the reasons for their being. In *Untersecunda*, while the history of Greece and Rome is being studied, the class work in religion is concerned with the apostolic history and the founding of the Christian church. In Greek, Xenophon's *Anabasis* and selections from the *Odyssey* are being read; and the connection is maintained throughout the following year by readings from Herodotus. Early Roman history is supplemented by reading Cicero's *de imp. Cn. Pompeii* (alternating with *pro Roscio*), Vergil's *Æneid*, Books I.–III., and selections from Livy, Books I., II., III., V., VI., VII. and IX.

In connection with later Roman and mediæval history to 1056, the *Obersecunda* class reads in Latin several books of
<small>Correlation with Other Subjects.</small> Vergil and selections from Livy, Books XXI., XXII., XXV., XXVI., XXVII. and XXX. The work in religion is confined to the apostolic period of the church and the mission of Paul, which

afford excellent opportunity for bringing together important facts in history and geography.

In *Prima*, the course in religion develops the history of the church through the Reformation down to modern times. The class, by the study of *Nibelungenlied* in the original text and the middle-high German literature, which is a part of the work in *Obersecunda*, is now ready to read the *Germania* of Tacitus. And with this course the climax of interest in German antiquities is reached. The gulf between the present and the past is effectually bridged over; the German school-boy henceforth feels that ancient history is very real.

The course as outlined for the Jena *Gymnasium* is perhaps the best illustration of recent attempts to correlate the instruction in the humanistic subjects in the secondary-school curriculum. The Prussian *Lehrplan* is by no means so carefully adjusted in this respect; nevertheless, it would be difficult to devise a curriculum for the German schools, considering the available material, in which one subject did not bear some relation to the other subjects of the course. In Jena there is not only the external correlation, but there is an even more serious attempt to make the instruction of the class-room effective in more directions than one. The Jena curriculum as it now stands is the result of many years of study on the part of a large number of school-masters. In this work, as has been said, Dr. Frick was the leader; and the Jena curriculum is to-day perhaps the best example of the fruit of his work and the labour of his colleagues.

In conclusion, I find it difficult to estimate the worth of the German methods of teaching history. The geographical instruction has always seemed to me most excellent, but there is room for wide differences of opinion with regard to the work in history. In certain schools which I could mention the work is undoubtedly of a high order; the scholars are deeply interested, and the results are eminently satisfactory. Still, it must be remembered that in many schools—I fear in the great majority of them—the work is purely formal and disconnected, unrelated and exceedingly

Criticisms.

uninteresting. The successful teacher, according to the German method, must be an able story-teller, and have the power to stir the emotions of his pupils by the narration of historic events. He must be enthusiastic, and possessed of encyclopedic information. When these conditions are not fulfilled there is a dry recital of events, which is followed by a still drier recitation by the pupils. A few facts may be learned, but so long as they are not related to other facts they are lifeless. I confess to having heard lessons—many of them—which were soporific in the extreme; and so unusual was it in my experience to find a good teacher of history, that I often despaired of seeing the German system at its best. Teachers continually complained to me, by way of excuse for a poor showing, that no time was allowed for outside study; and that with only two or three lessons a week, it was impossible to get good results when everything depended upon the teacher in the class.

On the whole, I was greatly disappointed in the practical working of the German methods. Comparatively few teachers, it seems to me, have the ability or the disposition to treat the subject in the only way that can bring success. Germans are not natural story-tellers; as a rule, they are too phlegmatic. Success for the average teacher, therefore, depends upon his ability to systematize and arrange his material in such a way that at the end of the course the pupil has a definite, closely related body of knowledge. Lack of interest on the part of some and lack of methodical arrangement are, it seems to me, the two great factors which account for the unsatisfactory results in the teaching of history in the secondary schools.

<small>Defects in Narrative Method.</small>

It is still a fact, however, after all is said, that the German students who do their work at all satisfactorily generally have upon the completion of their course a very comprehensive view of the world's history. They are familiar with the chief events in history from the Trojan war to the accession of William II.; they have traced the development of political geography for some three thousand

<small>Results.</small>

years up to the present; they know the topography of the countries in which the great historical scenes have been enacted; they know something of the physical conditions which have determined the economic characteristics of various nations; they have been led to notice the changes that have taken place in historical times in the relations of the industrial life to the family, of the family to the community and of the community to the state. Finally, the influence of art and literature upon the development of civilization is tolerably clear in their minds. They may be deficient in the ability to make independent historical investigations, or even be unable to read intelligently certain historical works of a technical nature; but they have, nevertheless, what may be called a historical instinct. They may not be able to account for the faith that is in them, but they have the faith notwithstanding. Such students, when they go up to the university, very quickly become acquainted with the methods of doing research work; they easily adapt themselves to circumstances, and become what may be rightfully termed students of history. It should be understood, however, that the patient industry, the dispassionate judgment and breadth of scholarship that are exhibited by the typical German historians can scarcely be credited to the study of history in the secondary schools. I am disposed to believe that the courses in Greek and Latin, in German and in religion, furnish the muscle and sinew; the historical course builds merely the skeleton.

GENERAL REFERENCES:—Richter, *Systematische Gliederung des Unterrichtsstoffes in der neueren Geschichte*, in *Lehrproben und Lehrgänge*, 1897; Haunak, *Methodik des Unterrichts in der Geschichte*, Vienna, 1891; Jäger, *Bemerkungen über den Geschichtlichen Unterricht*, 2 ed., Wiesbaden, 1887; Peschel, *Die Erdkunde als Unterrichts-Gegenstand*, in *Deutscher Vierteljahreschrift*, 1868; Delitsch, *Beiträge zur Methodik des geographischen Unterrichts*, in *Neue Jahrbücher für Philologie und Pädagogik*, 1881; Matzat, *Zeichnende Erdkunde*, Berlin, 1879; Oberländer, *Der geographische Unterricht nach den Grundsätzen der Ritterschen Schule*, 5 ed., Grimma, 1893; Tromnau, *Der Unterricht in der Erdkunde in seiner geschichtlichen Entwicklung, unter Berücksichtigung der neueste Reformbestrebungen*, Halle, 1893; Hand-books of Baumeister and Wychgram and Encyclopedias of Schmid and Rein.

CHAPTER XVI

INSTRUCTION IN MATHEMATICS

THE school reforms consequent upon Prussia's defeat in the Napoleonic wars mark the beginning of serious mathematical study in the *Gymnasium*. Hitherto, two to three recitations a week had been considered ample time for a subject so little in harmony with humanistic ideals; 10 to 14 hours weekly were not too many for Latin and Greek. But in the program of 1816 mathematics was made a main subject alongside of the ancient classics and of equal worth with them. The course led up to and included theory of equations, chance, the elements of analytic geometry and mechanics. In zeal to outdo France, the reformers had been too radical for the schoolmen. In 1827 the time was reduced from 6 hours a week to 4. The programs of 1837 and 1856 were still less liberal, allotting to *Quinta*, *Quarta* and *Tertia* only 3 periods. In 1882 only two classes were left with so few as 3 recitations a week; the total week-hours were 34. The program of 1882 decreased the week-hours for mathematics in the *Realgymnasium* from 47 to 44, and in 1892 a still further reduction of 2 hours a week was made. The *Oberrealschulen*, with French and English in place of the classics, but with a nine-year course as in the *Gymnasien*, have at present 47 week-hours of mathematics.

<small>Historical Development.</small>

Mathematics as taught in the best German schools is a unit. If I refer to the sub-courses independently, for convenience's sake, it must be remembered that they are more than parallel—they are interlaced and interwoven to a degree that makes it difficult to separate them. A further difficulty arises from the differences in the secondary schools themselves. They have not the same courses, nor a common aim. From a quantitative point of view, the *Realgymnasium* stands midway between the two extremes; qualitatively, it may be questioned if it does not rank at the head in mathematics. But for the sake of a norm, it may be well to take a middle ground. I have chosen, therefore, to describe the course of the *Realgymnasium* in Cassel, Dr. Wittich, director—one of the best schools in the kingdom, and renowned as the *Alma Mater* of Prince Henry of Prussia. For illustrations of method I shall draw freely from my experiences in all sorts and conditions of schools, and it goes without saying that whatever of criticism I may indulge in should not be construed as reflections on the Cassel institution. Indeed, I am obliged to go elsewhere for my material, as during my stay in Cassel the celebration of the twenty-fifth anniversary of the founding of the school was of greater interest to the pupils (and to the visitor?) than the daily routine of the class-room. Its curriculum follows necessarily the last Prussian program; and so far as this discriminates against *Realgymnasien*—and it has cast a cloud over them all—in so far does this school suffer with the rest. For this reason one often finds the best results in mathematics in other German states. Prussia is not altogether Germany in educational matters; yet, from force of circumstances, the smaller states follow her leadership, though at a respectful distance. The course of 1882, which was willingly adopted in the southern states, gave advantages which non-Prussians are loath to yield; and while the Prussian reforms have been followed to a certain extent, it has been done under protest. The attitude of the southern leader is happily put in the following words, addressed to me in criticism of recent changes: "I cannot bring myself blindly to admire a thing merely for the sake of its coming from Berlin." The Saxon ministry has especially favoured the *Realgymnasium*, and so have most of

Unity of the Course.

A Typical School.

the duchies. The Weimar *Realgymnasium* has a most enviable reputation, and to its director, Dr. Wernekke, I am indebted for many favours. Here the good points of the German system are to be found at their best, and the course is not too much "reformed."

A boy on entering *Sexta* at nine years of age is expected to bring with him from his three-year preparatory course the ability to add, subtract, multiply and divide simple whole numbers. For the lower grades the Cassel course is as follows:[1]

SEXTA.

Rechnen, 4 hours. Extended knowledge of numbers from 1–100, especially division of numbers by smaller numbers and factoring. System of tens. Numeration. Repetition of the four fundamental principles, with abstract whole numbers. Weights, measures and money. Reduction of complex numbers, and in connection therewith the simplest tasks in decimal fractions. Text-book, Böhme's *Uebungsbuch*, VIII.

[Course in Lower Grades.]

QUINTA.

Rechnen, 4 hours. Preparations for study of fractions. Common and decimal fractions. Rule-of-three. Text-book, Böhme's, IX.

QUARTA.

I. *Rechnen*, 2 hours. Review of fractions. Rule-of-three with whole numbers and fractions. Profit and loss. Interest, discount and partnership. Text-book, Böhme's, XII.

II. *Plane Geometry*, 2 hours. Introductory course in object-lessons. Angles, parallel lines, triangles, quadrilaterals. Simple constructions. Text-book, Koppe's *Planimetrie*.

Arithmetik, the theory of numbers, includes both reckoning with definite numbers (*Rechnen*) and with numbers in the abstract. *Algebra* is the theory of equations. The work of the lower grades, therefore, is with *Rechnen*—practical arith-

---

[1] The Weimar *Realgymnasium* has *five* periods a week in *Sexta* and *Quarta*. By teaching simple rule-of-three in *Sexta*, time enough is gained for one hour a week of geometrical object-lessons in *Quinta*.

metic. The aim is to secure "accuracy and facility in operations with figures," and to lay the foundation for future study. The first desideratum is favoured by extraneous circumstances. Classes usually number thirty to forty pupils. Recitation-rooms are comparatively small. One blackboard, and that a small one behind the teacher's desk, must suffice for the needs of the class. An exceptional arrangement is to have two such boards balanced on pulleys, or a second board mounted on an easel nearer the pupils. There are neither slates nor paper for rough work. All reckoning must be done on the board, in the exercise books which are inspected by the teacher or —in the head. The last, as the path of least resistance, is followed by the average boy, notwithstanding his natural prejudices against thinking for himself. Whether these circumstances be cause or effect, I cannot say; but I suspect they are partly both. The German teacher will tell you, however, that "years ago" it was the custom to assign long lessons to be worked out at home; that, to secure a reasonable percentage of correct answers, rules and copies were invented; but, he will add, the process was purely mechanical. To-day the ideal is that every step in advance shall be taken in the class-room; that there shall be but one step at a time, and that all shall take that step at the same time. This forbids independent home study; it limits the master's work to teaching.

<small>Methods of Teaching.</small>

A recitation opens with questions, rapidly put, on the review leading up to the work of the day. Answers must be short, concise and complete sentences. New principles are developed inductively, if possible. A boy goes to the board—why more than one board?—and writes a problem as read to him by another boy or by the teacher. Then more questions to the class. The pupil at the board merely registers the progress; he may be quizzed with the rest, and if he has suggestions to make he may volunteer in the usual way—by raising the hand—and await the master's recognition. Sometimes, if the problem is important,

<small>Oral Work.</small>

the work is erased and another boy performs the same operation, recounting each step aloud while the class copy it into their exercise books. So goes the hour. The proportion of time given to written work as compared with the questions asked and answered is not far from 1 : 5, so great is the stress put upon oral demonstration. The home work is of the same nature—generally the identical problems, if not already written out; but the task must not take more than half an hour of the pupil's free time. A special exercise to be done at home may be required not oftener than once a month. If new problems are set, all inherent difficulties must be previously cleared up and sifted in class. The pupil is not to experiment, nor work in the dark.

From the beginning of the course particular stress is put upon facility in mental calculation. Practice is daily afforded in the ordinary work of the class-room, but special drill is given with each lesson in the lower grades. At first simple whole numbers are employed, but in *Quinta* the work has so far progressed that numbers of two and three digits are freely used. Such work, to be of value, must be done quickly; the answer should be ready immediately on conclusion of the statement. From twelve such problems given in one recitation, I select at random three: (1) $4,1+0,9-4,9+0,9=?$; (2) $1,2+3,4 \times 10=?$; (3) $0,9+2,4+3,1 \div 8=?$ Such tasks are rendered the more difficult by the German way of reading decimals—thus in (1): "Four-comma-one, plus naught-comma-nine, minus four-comma-nine, plus naught-comma-nine," etc. This reading of figures and points in succession, though not expressly sanctioned, seems to be connived at in all parts of Germany from the common schools to the universities; illogical as it may be, it seems to the foreigner a sensible reaction against the laws of the grammarians. The next step brings in the blackboard; the problem is written out, thus: $(25,5+27,45+31,55):5=?$; but the solution is given orally. How far and in what lines these methods shall be developed lies wholly with the teacher. In geometry, too, there is ample

Marginal note: Mental Calculation.

field. A good *Tertianer*, I am told, should be able to demonstrate the Pythagorean proposition in his head, following any designation of lines and angles that may be given him. In arithmetic, the multiplication table may be taught as high as the 20's, after which it is comparatively easy to make all necessary combinations. But in explaining his methods to me an excellent teacher made this remark: "It is well that a pupil should be familiar with short methods, and be able to reckon rapidly in his head; but it is better to know that 18 times 27 is the same as 18 times 20, plus 18 times 7, than to perform the operation mechanically." Whatever the methods in mental arithmetic may be, the results in most German schools are admirable.

Some of the best schools are making a trial of the so-called "Austrian methods" of reckoning. Illustrations follow (the figures here given I have copied from actual class work; no others were used): Austrian Methods.

(1) Subtraction—

$$\begin{array}{r}954\\-761\\\hline 193\end{array}$$

Boy says, "One and *three* make four (writes 3); six and *nine* make fifteen (writes 9); one (to carry), seven and *one* make nine (writes 1)."

(2) Multiplication—

225,67 . 875 = ?

$$\begin{array}{r}180536\\157969\\\hline 197461{,}25\end{array}$$

Multiply first by 8, then by 7, and then by 5, adding to this product the partial products already found; write only complete sum in last case. The final operation is as follows: $5 \times 7 = 35$ (write 5); $5 \times 6 + 3$ (to carry) $+ 9 = 42$ (write 2); $5 \times 5 + 4 + 6 + 6 = 41$ (write 1); $5 \times 2 + 4 + 9 + 3 = 26$ (write 6), etc.

(3) Division—

427654 : 145 = 2949,3.
$$\begin{array}{r}1376\\715\\1354\\490\\\hline 55 \text{ rem.}\end{array}$$

First figure of quotient is 2. Then $2 \times 5 + 7 = 17$ (write 7); $2 \times 4 + 1$ (to carry) $+ 3 = 12$ (write 3); $2 \times 1 + 1 + 1 = 4$ (write 1). Bring down next figure (6) of dividend, and continue as before.

(4) Square-Root—

$\sqrt{42 \mid 76 \mid 54} = 653,9.$
$$\begin{array}{r}6\quad\; 76{:}125\\5154 : 1303\\124500 : 13069\end{array}$$

The methods, as will be seen, are the same as in division.

After a close inspection of pupils' exercises, I cannot say that the chances of error are greater than with the usual way. It reduces the written work to a minimum, and decidedly increases the rapidity of computation. It is well worth a trial. Schools which have adopted it show no inclination to go back to the old methods.

The rule-of-three plays an important part in *Quinta* and *Quarta*. The easier problems are stated and solved as follows:

(a) *Statement*—

If 25 *kg* of *x* cost 53,45 m., what will 155 *kg* cost?

(b) *Solution*—

$$\begin{array}{r}
25 \text{ kg cost } 53{,}45 \text{ m.}, 155 \text{ kg cost}? \\
\hline
150 \text{ `` } \text{ `` } 320{,}70 \text{ ``} \\
5 \text{ `` } \text{ `` } 10{,}69 \text{ ``} \\
\hline
155 \text{ kg cost } 331{,}39 \text{ m.}
\end{array}$$

Rather more is made of compound proportion than might be expected from the practical nature of the course; the method most frequently used is as follows:

(a) *Statement*—

A canal 245 *m* long, 3,3 *m* deep, 7 *m* wide, is built by 140 men working 546 days, at 7½ hours a day; what is the length of another canal, 5 *m* deep, 8,2 *m* wide, on which 182 men are employed 324 days, working 8⅕ hrs. a day?

(b) *Solution*—

140 men in 546 d. of 7½ h. make 3,3ᵐ d. 7ᵐ w. 245ᵐ l.
182 `` `` 324 `` 8⅕ `` `` 5 `` 8,2 `` x.

$$x = \frac{245 \times 182 \times 324 \times 50 \times 33 \times 70}{140 \times 546 \times 45 \times 50 \times 82}$$

Say,—If 245 *m* be done by 140 men, one man will do the 140th part, 182 men will do 182 times as much; *viz.* in 546 days—hence in one day the 546th part, in 324 days 324 times as much; *viz.* in 7½ hrs. (45-6)—hence in 1·6 hr. the 45th part, in 8⅕ hrs. (50-6) 50 times as much; viz. 33-10 *m* deep—hence if 1-10 *m* deep 33 times as much, if 50-10 *m* deep the 50th part, etc.

The problems of commercial arithmetic are solved in the same form. Here is a task in interest:

(a) *Statement*—

What is the interest on 450 m. for 2 yrs. 3 mos. and 10 ds. at 5 per cent.?

(b) *Solution*—

   100 m. give 5   m. int. in 1 yr.
   450 "   " 22,50 " " " "

   450 "   " 45,00 " " " 2 yrs.
   " "   "   5,625 " " " 3 mos.
   " "   "   ,625 " " " 10 ds.

450 m. give 51,25 m. int. in 2 yrs. 3 mos. 10 ds.

Fractions. The greatest difficulties of the lower grades are in common fractions; but from the start every effort is made to keep within the pupils' sphere. When a boy knows what the division of a unit means, the term "fraction" has for him a tangible reality, a definite value. Beyond this limit the German teacher hesitates to go. The theory may best be taught with numbers not too large; and as for pure practice, there is enough of that in other connections. The main thing is to know the value of a fraction both in concrete terms and in its decimal form, and to realize that in its treatment only familiar principles are employed. The prevailing use of the decimal system of weights, measures and money makes the transition comparatively easy. By far the greater part of the work is done orally, *i.e.*, without book, paper or blackboard.

Inventive Geometry. The introductory course in geometry is given by most non-Prussian schools in *Quinta*, one period a week. The object is to familiarize the pupils with the essentials of geometrical form—"enough to get them looking at things from a geometrical point of view." The object-lessons begin with solids, which are handled, described and measured. Thus arise correct ideas of surfaces, lines and points and their relations. It is but a step to the drawing of figures, and this in turn forms a basis for the systematic study of plane geometry. Formal theorems are unnecessary. A long series of constructions follows the demonstration of such statements as these : "The base angles of an equilateral triangle are equal"; "The angles of a triangle make two right angles"; "Diagonals of rectangles are equal"; "A tangent stands at right angles to its radius," etc. Such are the concrete methods of the common schools (*Volksschulen*); and there is a party of schoolmen, including the Herbartians,[1] who would carry them still further in the secondary schools. Their success is not marked, but to the movement may be accredited certain tendencies which are becoming apparent even in the most conservative circles. The school that would *educate* its pupils, it is said, has no use for what is purely theoretical or abstractly mathematical. The universities are for specialists; the higher schools stand for general culture. "Were Shakespeare, Schiller and Goethe skilled in logarithms and equations of the third degree?" The mathematician may be Jew or Gentile, materialist or idealist; it is not *what* he thinks, but *how* he thinks, that is of concern.

I have sketched the mathematical work of the secondary schools to a point commensurate with the beginning of the American high-school course. The next step, following the standard of the Cassel *Realgymnasium*, is as follows :[2]

UNTERTERTIA.

I. *Geometry*, 2 hours. Theory of the triangle, polygon and circle. Equality of figures. Constructions. Text-book, Koppe's *Planimeterie*.

<small>Course in Middle Grades.</small>

---

[1] See Shultze's *Deutsche Erziehung*, pp. 278-79.

[2] The Weimar course is as follows : *Untertertia*, 5 hours. Commercial arithmetic. Theorems of sum, difference and product. The circle. Equality of figures. Proportion.—*Obertertia*, 5 hours. Compound division. Factoring. Equations of 1st and 2d degree with one unknown. Square-root. Similarity and measurement of figures. Algebraic geometry.—*Untersecunda*, 5 hours. Plane geometry concluded. Solid geometry. Powers, roots and logarithms. Equations of 1st degree with more than one unknown quantity, and of 2d degree with one unknown. (Special tasks monthly.)

II. *Arithmetic*, 2 hours. Reckoning with abstract quantities. Equations of first degree with one unknown quantity. Text-book, Heis's *Sammlung von Aufgaben aus der Allgemeinen Arithmetik*, §§ 1–25; 61–63.

III. *Rechnen*, 1 hour. Commercial arithmetic continued.

OBERTERTIA.

I. *Geometry*, 3 hours. Reviews. Proportion. Similarity of figures. Relations and contents of rectilinear figures and circles. Pythagorean proposition. Text-book, Koppe's.

II. *Arithmetic and Algebra*, 2 hours. Review and extension of work of III*b*. Theory of proportion, powers and roots. Equations of first degree with more than one unknown quantity, and simple quadratic equations with one unknown. Text-book, Heis's.

UNTERSECUNDA.

I. *Geometry and Trigonometry*, 3 hours. Elements of trigonometry; computation of triangles. The most important propositions. Solid geometry of the plane and straight line; simple bodies and computation of dimensions, surface and contents.

II. *Arithmetic and Algebra*, 2 hours. Theory of logarithms, with practice in logarithmic reckoning. Quadratic equations. Text-book, Heis's.

Geometry. The geometry of the middle grades presents no striking peculiarities of method, as I have observed, beyond those common to the mathematical instruction in all classes. Euclid seems to find no greater recognition here than in America; the German explanation is that the great Alexandrian wrote for men, not boys. The four years' course in plane geometry gives ample time, not only for thorough grounding in the theory, but also for a variety of practical applications impossible in a shorter course or under a plan which does not provide for simultaneous exercise in arithmetic, algebra and elementary trigonometry.

The course in arithmetic and algebra is practically a course in Heis's *Collection*. The book seems to be everywhere used, either as text-book or for reference. Since its first appearance, in 1837, there have been some ninety editions, in all over 270,000 copies. The influence of this book—the work of a noted mathematician and astronomer—upon the teaching of two generations is clearly demonstrable, and to it may be ascribed many of the peculiarities in German methods. It contains no definitions, no rules and but very few typical solutions. Its strength lies in the systematic gradation of examples and problems, from the rudiments of addition to the involved types of equations of the higher degrees. The world over one will scarcely find four hundred pages of material more suggestive in treatment or richer in detail than this collection for use in the secondary schools of Germany and Austria. There are many other text-books, some of them most excellent, as Bardey's, for instance — perhaps better than Heis's—but to a striking degree they are all modelled after the master-work. In describing the first 215 pages of the book, the work of the middle grades is described. Its richness and variety is apparent from the presentation in this space of over 2,700 examples, of which some 700 are practical problems. The number actually used by any one class is relatively very small.

[margin: Arithmetic and Algebra.]

[margin: Text-Books.]

The needs of the many who do not continue their schooling beyond *Untersecunda* demand a wider range of study in the middle grades than would doubtless be the case were *Oberprima* the Mecca for all. Yet at every step the ideal is that theory and practice shall be united; neither factor may be sacrificed to the other. The conceptions underlying the theory of logarithms are not less important than skill in manipulating them; the ability to *think* even a short problem clearly to its conclusion is better than occasional success in finding "the answer" to problems intricate and confusing to the last degree. There is no greater danger in teaching than in overestimating the pupil's strength. Accuracy and facility in calculation and inference depend far more upon right thinking than upon correct writing. The mechanical skill necessary to note properly on paper or blackboard the essential headings of a

[margin: Aim is Right Thinking.]

mathematical demonstration is easily acquired, when it is clear what is to be done. It is right thinking, then, that is to be emphasized ; correct writing follows as a result. Every task that invites purely mechanical treatment, every problem too difficult for oral analysis, is a step in the wrong direction.

For the upper classes of the Cassel *Realgymnasium* the following courses are prescribed : [1]

OBERSECUNDA.

I. *Geometry and Trigonometry*, 3 hours. Plane trigonometry and plane geometry reviewed and concluded. Solid geometry. Practical applications. Text-books, Koppe's ; Gauss' *Logarithmic Tables*. <small>Course in Upper Grades.</small>

II. *Arithmetic and Algebra*, 2 hours. Arithmetical and geometrical series. Compound interest and annuities. Quadratic equations with more unknowns. Permutations and combinations ; binomial theorem applied to positive whole exponents. Text-book, Heis's.

UNTERPRIMA.

I. *Geometry and Trigonometry*, 3 hours. Solid geometry continued. Theory of plane and spherical angles. Spherical trigonometry and its application to mathematical geography. Conic sections. Text-book, Koppe's.

II. *Arithmetic and Algebra*, 2 hours. Continued fractions and applications. Arithmetical series of second order. Cubic equations. Problems of *maxima* and *minima*. Reviews. Text-book, Heis's.

OBERPRIMA.

I. *Geometry*, 3 hours. Solid geometry reviewed and concluded. Analytic geometry. Problems in mathematical geography. Geometrical drawing.

II. *Arithmetic and Algebra*, 2 hours. Functions and ap-

---

[1] Weimar course: *Obersecunda*, 5 hours. Solid geometry. Equations of 1st and 2d degrees with more unknowns. Determinants. Arithmetical and geometrical series. Compound interest and annuities. (Special tasks monthly.)—*Prima*, 5 hours. Permutations and combinations. Chance. Binomial theorem. Series—exponential, logarithmic, sine and cosine. Analytic geometry of the plane. (Special tasks monthly.) Perspective drawing and shading. Map projection.

plications to higher equations, especially those of third degree. Exponential, logarithmic and sine and cosine series. Practical applications. Text-books by Koppe, Heis, and Gauss.

It is not my purpose to dwell on details which may be found in practice in any good American school. For this reason the mere statement of what is done in the upper grades is sufficient. It is of more interest to know in how far these courses are actually followed, and with what success. And here's the rub. No one school, no single type of schools, can adequately represent the work of all; and yet a norm of some kind is necessary. The *Oberrealschulen* are too few in number to set a standard; and, besides, their material is not the best. The ambitious parent is prejudiced in favour of the *Gymnasium*—the door to all that is desirable in civil and professional life; but if the boy cannot get on there, the *Realgymnasium* and *Realschule* are next on the list. And, on the other hand, many classical schools make a farce of mathematics; the better the classics, the worse the mathematics. The gymnasial course is concluded with quadratics and binomial theorem, the elements of solid geometry and plane trigonometry. But, other things equal, the demands on the gymnasial master are as great as in the *Real*-schools, owing to the restricted number of recitations—four a week, save in *Tertia*, where only three are given. To overcome this difficulty, some teachers prefer to divide the time of *each* recitation equally between algebra and geometry. The objections are at once apparent. But, hampered as the gymnasial teachers are in many ways, I have been surprised to see how successfully the best of them master their environment. I am convinced, however, that the conditions which determine the highest results in mathematics are to be found in the *Realgymnasium* of *non*-Prussian states.

<small>Extent of the Course.</small>

Pupils are promoted from class to class on the advice of the teacher. He has for his guidance the marks of the regular recitations, the pupil's note-books and the monthly tasks done at home. Written examinations are held in some schools about once a month, the regular recitation period being used for the purpose; but, so far as I have learned, the practice is not general. The final examination of the course is both written and oral,[1] the latter being held by the master in the presence of a committee of his colleagues and the inspector, *Oberschulrat*, of the province. In both the written and the oral examination mathematics is considered a main subject. In *Real*-schools the test is undoubtedly efficacious, and the results accepted as they stand; but everywhere gymnasial teachers are outspoken against the slight put upon their efforts under cover of these examinations. I am told that it really makes little difference whether or no a boy is proficient in mathematics, if he knows his classics. The absence of an exact marking system forces the teacher of mathematics to join issues of judgment with his philological colleagues; in questions of pupils' maturity his opinion has small weight. The average boy

Promotion and Examination.

---

[1] I give herewith the final written tests for the *Realgymnasien* of Cassel and Weimar at Easter, 1894:

CASSEL: *Time, five hours.*—(1) A sphere with radius $r = 15$ is cut by a plane a into two parts, so that the entire surface of the one holds the relation to the other of m : n = 3 : 2. What is the height of the smallest part? (2) Two stars appear to be at a distance of 17° 15' from each other. The declination of the one is 21° 9', of the other 35° 8'. What is the difference in right ascension between the two? (3) A parabola and a straight line have the equations, $y^2 = 4x$ and $y = x - 3$. How large is the segment of the parabola which is intersected by the straight line? (4) $x = 3 + \sqrt{\frac{10}{x} + 2}$.

WEIMAR: *Time, six hours.*—(1) Find a circle touching two given circles, one of them in a given point. (2) Given the longest side of a triangle equal to 25 cm, and the ratio 2 : 3 : 5 of the radii of the three circles touching externally, find the other two sides, the angles and the radius of the inscribed circle. (3) A cone made of pine wood (sp. gravity $\frac{1}{2}$), whose radius and altitude are the same, has had $\frac{1}{4}$ of its volume cut off at the top. How far does it, with its base turned upward, go down in water? (4) Two elipses, whose minor axes are as 1 : $\sqrt{2}$, have each the end of its major axis coinciding with the centre of the other. Find the co-ordinates of their points of intersection, and the condition of their being of the same length.

is not slow to take advantage of all that comes his way. Indirectly, therefore, the best interests of a department are jeopardized; weakness is introduced where there should be strength.

Not only have examinations no terrors, but it is not generally recognised that a knowledge of mathematics increases one's chances of success in professional life. *Mathematics Discredited.* These factors all tend to make a complicated problem the more involved. And not all masters are teachers. The results in such cases are deplorable in any event, but especially so under German methods. When all depends upon the teacher and he fails, what is to become of the pupil? He has no incentives, ideal or material, to spur him on; and if he be a genius, the very text-books discourage independence. The pupil must follow; he can neither lead nor go alone.

The German ideal is very high, though possibly none too high. But for ideal methods you must have ideal teachers, and no one will say that Germany has too many *Effects on Teachers.* of such. Indeed, I am told that it is more difficult to find *good* teachers of mathematics than of any other subject. One cause is not far to seek. The German universities are founded on the classics. For three centuries, and more, a knowledge of Greek and Latin has been the *conditio sine qua non* of admission to university privileges; and to-day only graduates of the *Gymnasien* have full rights. Popular demands of the last few years have secured some concessions for the *Real*-schools, but in each step the intellectual monopolists have fancied an encroachment on the dignity of learning. The medical fraternity, as individuals, would be glad of more and better training in science and the modern languages; but the pride of the profession demands Greek and Latin instead. What wonder, then, that questions of caste have arisen from the partisan strife over the rights of the secondary schools! It even enters the university, and casts a shadow upon those courses that are "fit only for *Real*-school graduates." And what are these courses? *Mathematics* and *Natural Sciences!*[1] The moral is plain. The teacher of mathematics has not the social standing of the philologian. Caste enters into school life, and the students see it. Nothing but the force of personality can break these bonds—a personality stronger than most men have. Or, stated in another way, there is nothing inherent in the office of the mathematician to gain for him a social rank equal to that indissolubly connected with the humanistic studies. I speak especially of the mathematical post in the *Gymnasium;* in the *Real*-school there may not be the same internal gradations, but the school itself stands on a lower level. The outlook discourages the best candidates; and, as a result, the mantle too often falls on men who have not the keen, clear-cut intellects so essential to success under the German system.

Despite these defects in particulars, there are advantages in the German plan which no thoughtful teacher, no one charged with school management, can afford to disregard. The teacher is always a *trained specialist.* No man finds a post in a German school nowadays who is not master of what he purposes to teach; he has had, moreover, two years of professional training in theory and practice. And, on the other side, there are (1) the unity of the course, which is rendered still more effective by the interlacing and blending of the subordinate lines; (2) the emphasis put upon mental operations, and (3) the supreme end toward which all aims—*logical thinking.* These, at least, can be unreservedly commended. As for the German methods, the final question is, Does the pupil become an *independent* thinker? Granting good teachers, my answers are: *No*—so far as the poorest are concerned; *Very doubtful*—for the average; but emphatically *Yes*—for the best in the class. To the earnest student, the very consciousness of increasing strength and clearness of vision is of itself an incentive to mastery. He feels that he is getting something better than skill in the manipulation of symbols. The external operation is for him merely the record of his own thought—convenient and useful

Merits and Defects.

---

[1] Realgymnasiasts may also study the modern languages.

for the time being, but relatively unessential. "The life is more than meat, and the body is more than raiment."

GENERAL REFERENCES :—Meyer, *Mitteilungen aus dem mathematischen Lehrplan des Stadtgymnasiums zu Halle*, program of 1891; Becker, *Zur Reform des geometrischen Unterrichts*, Wertheim, 1880; Wernicke, *Die Grundlage der Euklidischen Geometrie des Masses*, Brunswick, 1887; Schellbach, *Über den Inhalt und die Bedentung des mathematischen und physikalischen Unterrichts auf unseren Gymnasien*, Berlin, 2d ed., 1884; Kehrbach, *Mon. Ger. Pæd.*, Vol. III.—*Geschichte des mathematischen Unterricht im deutschen Mittelalter bis zum Jahre 1525;* Beier, *Die Mathematik im Unterricht der höheren Schulen von der Reformation bis zur Mitte des 18. Jahrhunderts*, Krimmitschau, 1879; Schellbach, *Der Zukunft der Mathematik*, Berlin, 1887; Baumeister, *Handbuch*, Vol. IV.; Schiller, *Praktische Pädagogik ;* Encyclopedias of Schmid and Rein.

CHAPTER XVII

INSTRUCTION IN THE NATURAL SCIENCES

IN the early days of the German schools the classical languages and literatures formed substantially the entire curriculum. The Reformation induced some minor changes and gave a new impulse to educational activity, but we are told that in Sturm's school in Strasburg—the most famous and influential school of the sixteenth century—neither history, nor mathematics, nor the natural sciences, were considered of any consequence; that for thirty years even the elements of arithmetic were not taught, and that throughout Sturm's long tenure of office arithmetic and geometry, geography and astronomy, were never much in evidence except on paper. *In Early Protestant Schools.*

The Jesuits did little more in science; *pietas et boni mores*, their great aim in education, seems to have been conceived of as independent of the physical world. But with the advent of the seventeenth century a new view of the world was promulgated, and the necessity of man's knowing the significance of his environment became obvious. The ideas of Bacon were domiciled in Germany by the teachings of Ratke and Comenius, but it would be erroneous to suppose that the ideals of these advanced thinkers were speedily realized in the fatherland. Not even in the *Ritterakademien* of the following century did the natural sciences have any important place; nevertheless, the secondary schools of the eighteenth century, influenced doubtless by A. H. Francke's experiments in Halle, recognised for the first time the utility of certain forms of *In the Schools of the Jesuits.*

scientific knowledge. Utilitarian considerations, pure and simple, determined the admission of *Heimatskunde* into the curriculum of the first *Real*-schools. As these institutions became more clearly differentiated from the humanistic schools, the practical advantages of the natural sciences were the more apparent; and in place of the desultory work in general science, systematic study of particular sciences was introduced.

The natural sciences have been prescribed as an integral part of the curriculum of all Prussian higher schools since 1816. The southern states did not recognise the innovation for several years; and when they did, less time was given to the sciences than in Prussia. This distinction is still maintained in respect to the comparative time allotment. The Prussian *Gymnasium* has eighteen week-hours in the sciences, an average of two hours a week for each class; Bavaria gives but five hours to natural history, as compared with eight hours in Prussia, and does not yet recognise physics as a subject independent of mathematics; Würtemberg prescribes a total of fourteen week-hours for natural history and physics, an average of one and four-tenths hours a week.

Lehrplan of 1816.

At the present time the biological sciences are everywhere completely separated from physics and chemistry. The course in natural history begins in *Sexta* with children of nine years of age, and is continued in the Prussian *Gymnasien* during the succeeding four years, in the *Realgymnasien* and *Oberrealschulen* for six years. Physics and chemistry are taught only in the upper classes.

The chief aim of all instruction in the natural sciences is to cultivate the habit of keen and accurate observation, to strengthen the pupils' reasoning powers and to increase his ability of expressing clearly what he sees and thinks. The acquisition of a fund of systematic knowledge or useful information is a secondary consideration. Pedagogical writers and practical teachers are agreed in this; furthermore, there is general unanimity of opinion touching

The Chief Aim.

the subject-matter and methods of instruction. So far as is possible, the material used should be taken from the pupils' immediate environment; the order of progression should be from the near and simple to the more remote and difficult. In methods, it is generally agreed to be advisable to work inductively rather than deductively. A revolution in methods of teaching is even now taking place.

A few years ago the ideal was to give a systematic presentation of each science; the subject-matter might come from near or far, providing it satisfied the general scheme. The leaders in theory and practice of the present day have no hesitation in throwing over any scheme that early takes the child out of his local environment and substitutes for his own observation, crude though it may be, the ready-made reflections of the text-book or the opinions of the teacher. As between a little of all that can be known and all that can be known of a little, there can be no doubt in the German mind; to drink deep or not at all is surely a German characteristic. Nevertheless, it is impossible to follow out all lines that have their origin in the home environment; a selection must be made, and the government allows absolute freedom of choice to schools and teachers as to what shall be taught within the limits above mentioned. Success or failure, therefore, in science work reflects directly upon the teachers and the management of schools. *Former Ideals.*

The first steps in natural history lead the child to observe the simplest and most familiar forms of plant and animal life in his home region. The wisdom of the teacher is manifested in the selections he makes for class instruction; not all groups are represented in the local flora and fauna, and consideration of too many representatives from any one group is precluded for lack of time. Training in observation demands that the pupil handle the specimens studied and report his own opinions. In botany this can be easily managed, but in zoology it becomes a different problem. No laboratories are provided for individual work in natural history, and consequently from the very be- *School Equipment.*

ginning the opportunity for individual observation is greatly restricted. To overcome this obstacle, magnificent collections illustrating almost every department of natural science have been gathered by many of the leading schools. In botany, most schools will have a complete herbarium of domestic plants and many specimens of foreign flora. Besides this, models are commonly used for class demonstration, and excellent charts of foreign plants supplement the illustrations of text-books.

Mounted animals, skeletons and preparations in alcohol are found in large numbers in some schools, and are put to good use in the class-room; but without laboratory work there is small chance of promoting those habits of "keen and accurate observation" everywhere demanded of instruction in science. Again, the teacher must rely largely on models and charts. And although the German teacher is fortunate in having his choice of the best models and charts in the world, yet there is an obvious contradiction between the demands of theory and the results of practice. In other respects, too, practice often lags so far behind theory, that one is inclined to doubt the all-sufficiency of high ideals even in Germany.

It is with no little hesitancy that I attempt an explication of the prevailing methods of teaching the natural sciences in the German schools. So much of the instruction to which I listened was unpardonably bad, that I much distrust my ability to present clearly that which is obviously commendable. Fortunately, my experiences were not always disappointing; and, on the whole, it may be quite as well for the reader to know that German schools and German teachers are not always the paragons of excellence that some would have us think.

We have seen that more time is given to the sciences in the *Real*-schools than in the *Gymnasien*—in Prussia, a total of thirty week-hours in the *Realgymnasien* and thirty-six in the *Oberrealschulen*, as compared with eighteen in the *Gymnasien*. Furthermore, the science

Time Allotment.

work in the *Real*-schools is taken more seriously than in the *Gymnasien*. In consequence, I have selected as a type of what is done in Prussia the course of study prescribed in the *Königstädtisches Realgymnasium* of Berlin. This is one of the oldest *Real*-schools of the city, founded in 1832, and now attended by nearly six hundred students. For the fifteen classes there are twenty *Oberlehrer* and six *Hilfslehrer*, besides four teachers of drawing, music and gymnastics. Three *Hilfslehrer* and six *Oberlehrer* teach natural science—no one, however, devoting himself exclusively to science work. The most frequent combinations are natural history, geography and arithmetic; natural history, geography and German; physics (or chemistry), algebra and geometry; chemistry, natural history and arithmetic. The *Direktor* teaches physics, natural history and religion.

The course followed in this school comes near the high-water-mark in Prussia. Such differences as exist in other schools are chiefly due, as I have shown, to the preferences of individual teachers. The teacher who delights in field work will arrange for class excursions, not merely for the sake of securing botanical specimens, but with a view of interesting his pupils in nature and nature study. Another teacher may have a genius for class-room demonstration, and succeed thereby in arousing the right form of scientific curiosity. A third may know how to utilize the laboratory and make it an efficient instrument in promoting inductive research. The *Königstädtisches Gymnasium* has such teachers, and we find represented here all phases of scientific work to be found in any secondary school.

The Course of Study.

The course in natural history, as outlined in the program of 1895–1896, is as follows:

Sexta: 2 hours. Summer—Description of various plants with large and simple flowers. Explanation of morphological principles. Winter—Description of various mammals and birds and their habits. Explanation of the most important zoological principles and laws.

Natural History.

Text-book, Vogel, Müllenhoff, Kienitz-Gerloff, *Botanik und Zoölogie, Teil I.*

Quinta: 2 hours. Summer—Comparative description of plants of simple structure, with a view to their classification according to common and differential characteristics. Study of morphological principles continued. Winter—Comparative description of mammals and birds, with special attention to scientific classification. The skeleton of man, of other mammals and of birds. Text-book, same as in *Sexta.*

Quarta: 2 hours. Summer—Comparative description of related plants and species, with special attention to various representatives of families of highly developed plants (*Umbelliferæ* and *Compositæ*). Extension and classification of the principles of morphology. Toward the end of the semester practice in plant analysis according to the Linnæan system. Winter—Comparative study of mammals and birds continued. Description of various representatives of reptiles, amphibians and fishes. Principles of the skeleton of vertebrates. Classification of vertebrates. Text-book, same as in *Quinta.*

Untertertia: 2 hours. Summer—Comparative study of compound flowering plants, *e.g.*, *Amentaceæ* and *Graminaceæ*. Characteristics of the most important families of uncultivated plants. Study of plant morphology continued. Study of plant growth. Analysis of plants. Winter—Comparative study of the anatomy and growth of articulates. Characteristics of insect species Review of the system of vertebrates. Text-book, same as in *Quarta, Teil II.*

Obertertia: 2 hours. Summer—Study of gymnosperms and cryptogams, and the most important of cultivated foreign plants. Explanation of the chief morphological, biological and anatomical characteristics of the same. Arrangement according to the natural system of all plants thus far studied. The simplest principles of plant distribution. Practice in plant analysis. Winter—Description of certain representatives of the lower animals. Review of all animals thus far studied, according to types and classes of the natural system. Fundamental principles of palæontology. Text-book, same as in *Untertertia.*

Untersecunda: 2 hours. First semester—The anatomy and physiology of plants and animals continued and extended. Anthropology. Second semester—Physical and chemical peculiarities of water, air, fire and earth. Text-book, same as in *Obertertia, Teil III.*

The instructions of the Prussian department of education emphasize observation and description of natural objects. The importance of accurate description is seen in the terms everywhere used in Prussia designating the first division of science work, *Naturbeschreibung;* the older designation, *Naturgeschichte,* is still used in Hamburg and some of the southern states.

A necessary prerequisite to observation and description is that the child shall have something to observe and describe. Specimens of plants may be put in the pupil's hand for this purpose, and the entire work restricted to the class-room. Such a plan may give practice in description, but intelligent observation of nature can be taught only by going to nature herself. The structure of plants and animals may be learned in the class-room and laboratory ; but the significance of plant and animal life, the interdependence of the lower and higher orders and the influence of climate, soil and moisture upon all forms of life are to be seen only out-of-doors. For this purpose class excursions are usually arranged on half-holidays. The *Königstädtisches Gymnasium* arranges for one excursion a week. Pupils of any class in natural history may take part, but the participation is optional. The success of the undertaking is entirely dependent upon the teacher. As may be imagined, some teachers have more followers than they can readily manage ; others, after making a few trials, conclude that field work is a farce.

<small>Observation and Description.</small>

These excursions are generally of a half-day's duration, but in some schools there is a midsummer outing of a week or two. The pupils visit various places of interest pertaining to some particular study or line of work which they are about to begin. Geographical points are located, and historical events impressed upon the children's minds by perceiving the actual places of their occurrence. Botany, zoology, geography, geology and mineralogy are thus studied objectively, and much material is collected for use in the class-room. The appearance and habits

<small>Class Excursions.</small>

of various birds and animals are discovered by experience; the life and habitat of many plants are made known; and all this, scientifically conducted and explained by the teacher, serves not only to increase the knowledge but also the interest of the pupil in the pursuit of his studies. The main object, that of increasing the power of observation, is certainly accomplished. It is a difficult matter in the large cities to arrange for excursions far enough into the country to see nature at her best, but parks and zoological gardens offer a fair substitute. It must be said, however, that a trip through a city park does not furnish much material for class use. To offset this difficulty, many city schools have adopted the charming expedient of maintaining flower-gardens of their own. The children plant the seeds and tend their growth, labelling each specimen in true botanical fashion. I have observed, too, that in some of the smaller towns the schools have not only beautiful gardens of flowering plants, but miniature parks, set out with trees and shrubs of rare beauty. A more effective means of awakening an interest in botany, I think, would be hard to devise. Here is a suggestion of what might be done with the spacious grounds of our American public schools.

I have already spoken of the part played in instruction by the school museum. Considered as a means of elucidating obscure problems incident to class teaching, these collections are very valuable. In this respect some secondary schools rival the smaller universities. The danger is that, so long as somewhere in the school there is a chart, model or mounted specimen of each object studied in class, the museum will be drawn upon for its stores to the neglect of almost all field work. Precisely this state of affairs exists in the majority of schools that I have visited. My own experience would lead me to say that the average teacher relies almost exclusively upon accumulated stores of past years. While in theory each pupil is expected to have in his hands a specimen of all the common plants as they are discussed in class, I have seen the pea studied by a class of

School Museums.

thirty boys from a model that was not taken from the teacher's desk during the hour; and at the close of the lesson not a word was said about noting the plant in its cultivated state, although acres of it were growing within a mile of the site, but, on the contrary, the home task as assigned was *to copy the drawing given in the text-book.* I still have my doubts whether the majority of the class did not conceive of the true flower as being about a foot in diameter.

Such an instance as the one just related is, of course, an extreme case. The teacher, if he had any object other than drawing his salary, was aiming at systematic botany. And, notwithstanding the efforts of recent years, many of the science teachers are still engaged in teaching botany and zoology, physics and chemistry. There is plenty of evidence of this in almost every school. Even the course of study outlined above seems to emphasize at every turn the systematic presentation of the subjects. In the last resort, we must turn to the methods employed in instruction rather than the material of the course in order to evaluate correctly the work in natural history.

Observation, inference and description go hand in hand. Assuming that a class is provided with something to examine, it is a teacher's business to see that right observations are made. Nothing is gained by puzzling the child or allowing him to waste time and energy in a fruitless search for something he might find instantly if properly guided. As if anyone ever learned to see by groping in the dark ! This conception of teaching is characteristically German. One of its principal advantages is that it permits the teacher to lead his pupils quickly and easily to an understanding of some general principle which might otherwise be misinterpreted or overlooked entirely. The course of study, therefore, outlines the general principles which are to be arrived at ; the teacher alone is responsible for the methods of procedure.

Methods of Teaching.

I find among my notes a fairly typical lesson in zoology with boys of ten years of age (*Quinta*). The school is a private institution in central Germany; the topic, "The Seal." The lesson opened with a review of the families of animals already studied, a few individuals being cited as characteristics of each group. Next followed a brief summary of the previous lesson, on the means of identifying animals by the teeth and skull. Specimens of these parts were distributed among the class, and each boy was requested to name the animal to which his specimen belonged and state the grounds on which he based his inference. Great interest was manifested in this part of the work, which was continued for about twenty minutes.

A Typical Lesson.

The teacher next directed their attention to a finely mounted seal standing upon his desk. His questions ran somewhat as follows: "What is it? Who has seen one? Where? What did it do? How long can it stay under water? What does it do when it comes again to the surface? How is it able to stay so long under water? Why does it go under water? What does it get there? What else will it eat? Will it eat fresh-water fish? (Several boys are called up to examine its nose and feet.) What about his legs—number, shape—fingers, etc.? How can it close its nostrils? What can you say of its coat? How does the fur lie? What advantage is it to the animal? How long are its whiskers? What are they for? How long is this seal? (Boy measures it, and reports to class.) How broad? What is the shape of its body? Why does it not freeze in the ice-cold water? Is the body of the living seal of the same temperature as the water? What is the temperature of this room? What is the temperature of your body? What enables the seal to keep so warm amid such cold surroundings?"

From the trend of these questions, it is easy to infer the answers given by the class. In regard to the habits and habitat of the seal, the teacher had to supplement the knowledge of the class. The main purpose of the lesson, apparently, was to emphasize the difference in temperature between the animal's body and its surroundings. The subject of food assimilation and oxidation of tissue was treated at length. The recitation, measured both by the interest manifested by the pupils and the skill with which the teacher brought the lesson home to them, was a decided success.

An essential part of the descriptive work in science is the making of a detail drawing of every object studied in class. In general, this is the only home task in science work. The care exercised in writing up the note-books and in making the drawings is everywhere apparent; sometimes, I suspect, teachers of doubtful ability cover up their own sins by fine displays of note-books on all public occasions. But, whatever the motive may be, it is certainly true that drawing is of most effective service in all science teaching. *Drawing.*

Laboratory work, as has been said, is practically unknown in natural history. The nearest approach to it is in plant analysis, but the methods employed preclude the possibility of independent work. The process is precisely the same as is followed in the solution of mathematical problems. Pupils are not given a number of specimens and told to work them out previous to the next lesson. Having learned inductively the main principles of the Linnæan system from the classification of individuals studied, this knowledge is applied in the process of identifying new specimens. The teacher asks for each of the essential characteristics. The responses of the class are based on strict observation of the specimen in hand. At each step the teacher reviews past observations and calls up the peculiarities of the various classes, orders and families. Under such leadership, it would be strange if any pupil should fail in identifying his specimen. Notwithstanding the great stress put upon observation and description in natural history, one is forced to the conclusion that there is little independent observation or unbiased description. *Laboratory Work.*

There is something to be said for the teacher who is unable to make his work popular and successful. The residuum of many conversations with science teachers and others is to this effect: In the first place, the universities, where all secondary teachers must get their training, give no heed whatsoever to the needs of the schools. The sciences are taught in the most thorough and intensive manner possible. In other words, the man who after five years of advanced study in the university, the greater part of the time devoted to independent research, can adapt himself to the needs of nine-year-old children is a genius. It is too much to expect of the average man till the university offers training courses for teachers. In the second place, the government, while apparently expecting field work from the fact that botany is regularly put in the summer semester, makes absolutely no provision for it and allows no credit for what may be done. It means, too, that teachers and pupils must give up their half-holidays to outside work. Furthermore, the government makes no allowance for the extra demands made upon the science teacher in the collection and preservation of material, the preparation of objects for demonstration and the supervision of the laboratory work; he must put in full time—twenty to twenty-four hours a week—the same as his colleagues. And, finally, the excuse is often urged that in the *Gymnasium* the pupils feel it is of small consequence whether they are proficient in the sciences or not; there is no final examination, and even the indolent and dullards will be promoted if only they know some Latin, Greek and German. The science teacher, especially if he be not cast in the classical mould, sometimes is made to feel that his social and professional standing is questionable.

<small>Difficulties in Science Training.</small>

Such statements, though coming from thoughtful teachers, should not be regarded as the whole truth. It is unquestionably true that in some schools the teachers of science belong to a different social stratum from the other teachers; but the accident of birth is the important factor. A gentleman may teach science and not lose caste. Germany is far from being a pure democracy, and social distinctions are not always obliterated by recognition of personal worth. On the other hand, there is just cause for complaint from gymnasial teachers when proficiency in other

<small>Class Distinctions.</small>

subjects will secure a pupil's promotion in science. This is a serious problem; and, so long as the government leaves it unsolved, there can be no doubt that science is really considered a second or third-rate study.

But after all the shortcomings in the teaching of natural history in the German schools are discovered, we are obliged to express high regard for what is accomplished by the leaders of the new movement. As a conspicuous instance of the acme of arrangement and method, I subjoin an outline of the course in nature study followed during the first two years in the Jena *Gymnasium*. It will be noted that the aim is not only to give the child information about nature, but to help him to see scientific facts in their interrelations. For this purpose nature study is closely correlated with *Heimatskunde*—that branch of study which aims to give the child an elementary knowledge of his home environment, physical and social. Side by side with the study of botany and zoology goes that of geography, history and the legendary tradition of the country. Few schools in Germany show such careful attention to details, and have so successfully worked out the correlations with kindred subjects.

Jena Gymnasial Course.

Nature study in *Sexta*:[1] The local environment: (a) Surface elevations; hills and valleys of the neighbourhood. (b) Water-courses and roads: formation of valleys. Neighbouring watersheds. Influence of the water-courses on the local industries; grist-mills on the smaller streams; city woollen mills on the Saale. Land, road and water-ways: paths, roads, highways, railroads, boating, rafting. (c) Climate of mountains and valleys. Influence of mountain and forest on atmosphere. Vegetation of mountain sides influenced by position, exposure, etc. (d) Plants and animals: grasses cultivated for fodder (clover, lucerne, etc.), grains (wheat, rye, oats, barley, etc.), esculent plants, plants valuable for manufacturing purposes (flax, hops, etc.), garden fruits and wild flowers (violet, rose, bell-flower, sunflower,

---

[1] See *Program* of the Jena *Gymnasium*, 1891.

crane's bill, etc.). Plant life: distribution, habitat, dependence on soil, climate and animals—these facts to be pointed out and studied on the class excursions. The animals studied are as follows: bat, porcupine, mole, shrew-mouse, field-mouse, weasel, squirrel, swine, deer, horse, duck, goose, eagle, woodpecker, song-bird, common adder, lizard, frog, carp, honey-bee, May beetle and ant. Interdependence of animals and man.

In *Quinta* the work is extended beyond the local environment, but is conducted upon the same general principles.

Nature Study and Heimatskunde. While the geography of Thuringia is being studied, the names and location of the mountains, towns, valleys and river-courses are learned. In the lessons devoted exclusively to nature study, the influences of these natural phenomena upon the climate and industrial life of the people are emphasized. Special industries and natural resources of certain towns, as glass-blowing, the making of pottery, mining of iron and coal, hot springs, etc., are carefully explained, and, when possible, excursions are made to the more accessible towns. The products of the land, its flora and fauna, are studied in so far as it is a continuation of the work in *Sexta*. In a country so diversified as central Germany, it is possible to find types of the most common plants and animals within a radius of fifty or a hundred miles. The extensive mountain forests, with their well-stocked parks (game animals) and fertile valleys, afford abundant opportunity for elementary study of forestry and the more important agricultural industries.

The excellent results obtained in the Jena *Gymnasium* in some classes, and in some schools in all classes, lead me to infer that when the sciences are poorly taught the causes are not far to seek. "Where there's a will there's a way" is certainly true in respect of this subject, as of all others. The reason why most schools have no "way" worth following is because there is no "will" worth consideration. This is conspicuously true in the case of physics and chemistry in all *Gymnasien*, and with botany and zoology in not a few.

INSTRUCTION IN THE NATURAL SCIENCES 343

Thus far I have been considering chiefly the teaching of natural history in the first six years of the higher schools. Inasmuch as the age of the pupils in *Sexta* is between nine and ten years, the greater part of the course would correspond to the upper primary and grammar school course in American schools. The work in physics and chemistry in the German schools corresponds more nearly to our high-school standards.

The following outline of the course in physics and chemistry is from the program of the *Königstädtisches Realgymnasium*, Berlin, 1895-1896:

UNTERSECUNDA.

Physics, 3 hours. First semester: Frictional electricity, and phenomena out of the domain of magnetism and galvanic electricity. Acoustics and optics. Second semester: Mechanics of solid, liquid and gaseous bodies. General properties of matter. Parallelogram of forces and of motion. Laws of falling and vertically projected bodies. The simple machines. Textbook, Jochmann, *Grundriss der Experimental Physik*.

Course in Physics and Chemistry.

OBERSECUNDA.

Physics, 3 hours. First semester: Magnetism and galvanic electricity. Second semester: Heat. Repetition and extension of mechanics, especially of oblique projection and of central motion. Text-book, same as in *Untersecunda*.

Chemistry, 2 hours. First semester: Discussion of the elements hydrogen, oxygen, nitrogen, chlorine, bromine, iodine, fluorine, in connection with experiments suitably selected. Foundation of the conception of element, compound, base, acid and salt. The law of Marriotte and Gay-Lussac [the gas law, $PV = RT$], the law of combination by weight and by volume [law of Gay-Lussac], the hypothesis of Avogadro, the molecule, the atom, valance. The regular [isometric] system (magnetite, rock-salt, fluor-spar), the quadratic [tetragonal] system (cassiterite). Angle measurement with the goniometer, the solution of stoichiometrical problems. Second semester: Discussion of the elements sulphur, phosphorus, arsenic, boron, carbon and silicon, with experiments.

Extension of the crystallographic idea. The orthorhombic and monoclinic systems (sulphur). Dimorphism, allotropism; the rhombohedral system (calcite, quartz). Angle measurement with the goniometer. Solution of stoichiometrical problems.

UNTERPRIMA.

Physics, 3 hours. First semester : Wave theory, acoustics and optics. Second semester: Mechanics. In both semesters, reviews and more thorough mathematical treatment of particular parts of the earlier work. Solution of problems. Text-book, same as in *Untersecunda*. (Physical laboratory exercises, 2 hours, optional.)

Chemistry, 2 hours. First semester : Discussion of the elements potassium, sodium, calcium, barium, strontium and magnesium, with experiments. Vapour density. Volumetric analysis. Extension of the crystallographic idea (hemihedrism, twinning, isomorphism, pseudomorphism; the physical appearance of crystals). Manufacture of gunpowder; production of salt, soda, chalk and gypsum. Angle measurement with the reflection goniometer. Solution of stoichiometrical problems. Second semester : Discussion of the elements of zinc, lead, iron, copper, manganese, cobalt, nickel, chromium. The law of Dulong and Petit. Extension of the crystallographic idea. The monoclinic system (green vitriol). The triclinic system (blue vitriol). Metallurgy of ores of lead, zinc, iron and copper. Solution of stoichiometrical problems. Technological excursions. Work in the chemical laboratory. Illustration of preparations. Qualitative analysis by the "wet" method. Blow-pipe analysis ("dry" method). Physical experiments important for chemistry.

OBERPRIMA.

Physics, 3 hours. First semester: Optics. Second semester : Mechanics. In both semesters, reviews and more thorough discussion of parts of the earlier work, especially quantitative determinations and methods of measurement. Text-book, same as above. (Physical laboratory exercises, 2 hours, optional.)

Chemistry, 2 hours. First semester : Discussion of the elements tin, aluminum, antimony, bismuth, mercury, silver, gold, platinum, with experiments. Manufacture of alum. Periodicity of the elements. Solution of stoichiometrical

INSTRUCTION IN THE NATURAL SCIENCES 345

problems. Work in the chemical laboratory. Illustration of preparations. Some quantitative determinations. Volumetric analysis. Second semester: Introduction to organic chemistry. Elementary ("ultimate") analysis. Acids, alcohols, aromatic substances, carbohydrates, fermentation, albuminates, organic synthesis. Chemical theories. Manufacture of paper, starch and sugar. General view of the natural processes of the organic world (germination, food assimilation, respiration, decomposition, putrefaction). Solution of stoichiometrical problems. Technological excursions. (Work in the chemical laboratory. Illustrations of organic preparations; determination of sugar by chemical and optical methods, 2 hours, optional.)

This outline leaves little to be said on the subject-matter of instruction in physics and chemistry. The aim in the teaching of physics, as in natural history, is not so much acquaintance with a large number of facts as the cultivation of the pupil's ability to make accurate observations and the development of his logical powers, chiefly with reference to the causal relations existing between particular natural phenomena. In this respect the *Real*-schools can show better results than the *Gymnasien*. But in all schools the government emphasizes the need of scientific observation, confirmed and strengthened by a certain amount of formal practice. *[Best Results in Real-Schools.]*

According to the Prussian syllabus of 1892, the course in physics is divided into two parts. The part first is intended to give the pupil some notion of the fundamental principles of the subject as exemplified in the ordinary and more familiar manifestations of nature; it is concluded with *Untersecunda*. The continuation of the course aims to give those who may pass on to the university a more comprehensive understanding of physical laws and their applications. This division is in strict accord with a prevailing idea of the Berlin Conference, that those leaving school at sixteen should have as symmetrical training as it is possible to provide. Only the most important principles are taught in the first part of the course, and much stress is put *[Physics.]*

upon the application of these to the practical affairs of everyday life.[1]

The advanced course is first of all a repetition and extension of the earlier work, and in the second place a more extended mathematical treatment of the subject. This latter phase of the work can be done successfully only in the *Real*-schools, inasmuch as the mathematics taught in most *Gymnasien* is insufficient for the purpose. The *Realgymnasium* of Weimar, for example, provides a special course in mathematics during the last two years devoted exclusively to mechanics. Particular attention is given to mathematical geography and the elements of astronomy.

It is only in the *Oberrealschulen* that a separate course in chemistry is given in *Untersecunda*. Other schools are requested to present a few important chemical facts in connection with the study of galvanic electricity.

Chemistry.

At best, but little can be done. Organic chemistry and its applications are practically untouched in all schools; any consideration whatever of the subject must be purely incidental, and confined to those processes of greatest practical importance.

Stoichiometry is the one branch of chemistry which is thoroughly taught, and it is the mathematical treatment of this branch which receives most attention. Mineralogy is a side issue; so far as I have observed, it amounts to little more than a formal study of crystallography.

A text-book is always employed in teaching physics and chemistry, precisely in the same manner as in teaching natural history. But, unlike the methods commonly found in American and English schools,

Text-Books.

German teachers invariably use these books for reference only. It is not expected, however, that they will take the place of the elaborate compendiums found in each schoolroom; they are mere outlines of the subject, intended to as-

---

[1] Full information of what may be accomplished in this preliminary course may be found in the *Zeitschrift für den physikalischen und chemischen Unterricht*, Jahrgang V., Heft 4 (April, 1892).

sist the pupil in making scientific classifications, not for purposes of recitation. In fact, as we have repeatedly observed, the German teacher never assigns a lesson in advance to be studied out at home. Recitations, therefore, at least in the American sense, are unknown.

A typical lesson always includes a review of the principles and experiments of past lessons which have a direct bearing upon what is next to be presented. The teacher explains the nature of the apparatus with which he is to deal, and places it upon his desk in full view of the entire class. (It may be observed, in passing, that school-houses of recent construction have a lecture-room for the classes in physics and chemistry in which the seats are elevated, generally in a semicircle about the teacher's desk.) Certain conditions are stated, and the class questioned as to what results may reasonably be expected. This preliminary discussion having carefully prepared the way for a right understanding of the experiment, the demonstration by the teacher follows. The students are required to make note of the apparatus used, the principles involved, the conditions under which the reaction occurred and the results obtained. By means of a running fire of questions, the teacher keeps himself informed in regard to the mental state of his class; for it is his duty to see not only that all understand the trend of the experiment, but also that its significance is realized. *Methods of Teaching.*

German practice is always consistent in its adherence to the idea that good teaching never leaves the pupil in doubt. In mathematics he is not assigned a problem to wrestle with by himself alone; in the early days of his language study all the translations are made in class; and even in natural history we have seen how he is guided, step by step, first in making his observations and then in describing what he has discovered. *Class Demonstration.*

We observe the same facts in the prevailing methods of teaching physics and chemistry. Every principle worth demonstrating is illustrated in class. But the teacher does more than demonstrate; he *teaches* as well. And successful teaching requires that present impressions be definitely related to past experiences. Wrong relationships, or none at all, are an inevitable consequence of misapprehension. For this reason the German teacher counts it his duty to prevent his students drawing wrong inferences. They have not yet arrived at the stage of independent study; that comes in the university. In the secondary schools no time should be wasted in beating about the bush. The ability to make an occasional lucky guess is in nowise identical with sustained logical thought.

At the conclusion of a lesson topic, the pupil is directed to consult his text-book and afterward write up his notes. This done, the teacher inspects the book at his leisure.

Laboratory exercises, if required at all, are introduced at this point, in order that students may themselves duplicate the experiment performed by the teacher or make other demonstrations putting to practical test the knowledge just acquired. The function of laboratory practice, as will be seen, is to make application of facts already learned, not at all for the purpose of presenting new truths or arriving at new deductions. Inasmuch as laboratory practice is optional, and the exigencies of the time-card usually place it out of school hours, few students enter for it.

Laboratory Work.

No harm is done, however, if only a part of the class avail themselves of the opportunity. They learn something thereby, to be sure; but their previous knowledge is intensified rather than extended. In other words, the certainty of promotion is not jeopardized by failure to elect the laboratory course.

Probably the best adducible evidence of the relative value of the various studies, as popularly estimated, is the part each plays in the final examination. Judged in this way, the sciences take low rank. Physics may be counted as a fourth part of mathematics in the gymnasial examination; in the *Real*-schools, one problem

Final Examinations.

is assigned in physics and one in chemistry.[1] The worst of it is that "nothing short of a miracle," to quote a German teacher, "can prevent the promotion of the most deficient member of the class, provided his attainments be satisfactory in other subjects."

In conclusion, it need hardly be said that the teaching of science in the German secondary schools is intended primarily to provide formal discipline of the powers of observation, of logical thought and accurate description. Evidence is not wanting to show that the sciences are not taught as distinct

---

[1] The problems in science assigned at the *Abiturientenprüfung* in the *Königstadtisches Realgymnasium*, Berlin, were as follows:

Physics, Michaelmas, 1895. "To determine the internal resistance of a Bunsen battery cell, the following experiments are made:

"(a) In one arm of a Wheatstone's bridge a resistance of one ohm is inserted; in the other arm, a rheostat. The galvanometer needle shows no deviation when the rheostat resistance, $r_1 = 4.5$ turns of the wire.

"(b) There is now introduced into one arm of the bridge a copper wire whose length, $l = 9.8$ meters, and whose thickness, $d = 1$ millimeter; and again in the other arm, the rheostat. The galvanometer needle now shows no deviation when the rheostat resistance, $r_2 = 0.84$ turns of the wire.

"(c) Through the same copper wire, and through a tangent galvanometer (joined in series), a current is led by means of the Bunsen cell under investigation. The needle of the tangent-galvanometer now shows a deviation, $a_1 = 17°\ 30'$.

"(d) A second and like Bunsen cell is now introduced into the circuit in series with the first. The needle now shows a deviation, $a_2 = 25°$.

"How great, according to these experiments, is the internal resistance of a Bunsen cell?

"Further, how great, according to the experimental results obtained, is the specific resistance of copper?

"The above experiments—especially the arrangement and mode of operation of the Wheatstone's bridge—are to be described and explained by means of a simple diagrammatic figure."

Chemistry, Easter, 1896. "The description of the most important chemical and crystallographic properties of silicic acid, and the explanation of its importance in the plant and animal kingdoms, with some examples."

subjects, but as a means of assisting the individual to a more complete realization of his environment. Pedagogic writers emphasize repeatedly the futility of attempting to give the preparatory student a thorough knowledge of the principles even of a single science; this is the work of the university. The aim of the secondary schools should be to provide such training as will enable the student when he enters upon his university career to begin the study of any science intelligently. In other words, an understanding of the relations existing between sciences is of more worth than an extensive knowledge of any one. Therefore, the principles of biology and of physics, properly taught, are the sole requisite for entrance upon university work. The physical conditions under which life develops are an important accessory to the study of biology, and the principles of chemistry supplement advantageously the teachings of physics.

<small>Pedagogical Principles.</small>

The presence of laboratories well equipped for individual work, and supported by annual appropriations, in most German schools, shows that the present method of science teaching is a reaction against earlier notions concerning the function of laboratory practice. So long as the aim was to teach the sciences *per se*, laboratory work was necessary for each individual; but with the advent of the idea that the sciences are no more to be considered independent studies than other subjects of the curriculum, and that mental development of the pupil is of more consequence than definite information in any one subject, class instruction at once comes into the foreground. Laboratory work is still counted an exercise of great value, but its aim is to facilitate application rather than to promote individual investigation. The right use of the inductive method by no means shifts the responsibility from the teacher to the pupil. The teacher must do even more teaching; in fact, the pupil can be more safely trusted to work independently along deductive lines than inductive. But as I have repeatedly cautioned the reader not to confound

<small>Recent Tendencies.</small>

<small>Value of Laboratory.</small>

class instruction with the hearing of a recitation, no one will identify the German method of teaching science with certain practices well-nigh universal in America.

We may criticise the methods of the German teacher how we will; we may disapprove of his selection of subject-matter, his apparatus, laboratory and text-book; and especially we may refuse to recognise the legitimacy of his aim and the worth of his ideals; and yet, when all is said, the German teacher has some convincing arguments in store. He can point triumphantly to a long line of German scientists, once his pupils. He will tell us that all students entering the university are familiar with at least the elements of physical and biological science; that this work has been an integral part of their school training for nine years; that the classical students are broadened by contact with the *real* studies, and that the scientific men are more liberal for having included the humanities in their education. The clinching argument, however—an argument convincing at least to the commercial world—is that the marvellous industrial progress of Germany in the last quarter-century is due ultimately to the superior skill and wisdom of the German scientists. England to-day—witness the recent action of the government in promoting the teaching of science and the resolutions of learned societies and trade-unions—is assured that the preservation of her supremacy in the markets of the world is largely dependent on her ability to train up such scientists as now direct the development of the industrial arts in Germany.

Results Attained.

GENERAL REFERENCES :—Rossmässler, *Der naturwissenschaftliche Unterricht*, Leipsic, 1860; Loew, *Die Stellung der Schule zu naturw. Unterricht*, Berlin, 1874; Schwalbe, *Geschichte und Stand der Methodik in den Naturwissenschaften*, Berlin, 1877; Baenitz, *Der naturw. Unterricht an gehob. Lehranstalten*, Berlin, 2d ed., 1882; Zwick, *Der naturw. Unterricht*, Berlin, 2d ed , 1884; Piltz, *Aufgaben und Fragen für Naturbeobachtung*, Weimar, 3d ed., 1887; *Zeitschrift für den physikalischen und chemischen Unterricht*, Berlin; Baumeister, *Handbuch*, Vol. IV.; Encyclopedias of Schmid and Rein; Schiller, *Praktische Pädagogik*.

CHAPTER XVIII

THE PROFESSIONAL TRAINING OF TEACHERS

TEACHING has been a profession in Germany since the close of the Napoleonic wars. The first decade of the century marks the turning-point from the old *régime* to the new. Up to that time the teachers had been either novices awaiting holy orders or one-legged veterans unfitted for further military service. At least, such instances were sufficiently numerous to give the impression that the schools were philanthropic institutions, designed chiefly to afford employment to those who might otherwise become public charges.

Teaching a Profession.

Early in the seventeenth century Ratke and Comenius had urged the necessity of having trained teachers in the schools.

Historical Development.

In 1707 Francke established the *Seminarium selectum præceptorum* in Halle—the outgrowth of several years of trial in the training of teachers; and under his influence more than a thousand *Volksschulen* were created in Prussia by Frederick William I., and placed under teachers nominated, as far as possible, by Francke himself. Under Frederick the Great the policy of securing trained teachers for the elementary schools was adhered to, and teachers' seminaries became a necessary part of the public school system. The next important step was taken in 1763, when Frederick the Great ordered that all teachers should be required to pass a state examination in certain specified subjects, and that only those persons who had been trained in the Berlin Seminary should be eligible for appointment as teachers in elementary schools supported by the crown. It is certain that the regulations of Frederick the Great made a great advance in the condition of the public schools and in the position of the teachers; but, so long as there were non-public schools, many of them entirely removed from government influence, whose teachers were appointed by the church or private patrons, there could be no standards applicable to all. It was the *Allgemeine Landrecht* of 1794 that finally declared all schools to be state institutions, and at all times subject to the inspection and examination of the state.

The complete secularization of the secondary schools followed tardily after the emancipation of the elementary schools from ecclesiastical control. Applicants for positions in the higher schools were required to show their fitness by examination or otherwise even prior to 1790, but the clergy still maintained the upper hand. In 1779 Frederick the Great struck the first serious blow at clerical influence; he decreed that henceforth "philosophy should be taught in the higher schools only by laymen." All during the century able schoolmasters had been trained in the *Seminarium* in Halle, and they were men of influence in the state. Many students of Göttingen, between the years 1735 and 1775, fell under the spell of Gesner and Heyne, and thereby grew into enthusiastic teachers of the classics. Indeed, the *Zeitgeist* of the last half of the eighteenth century was decidedly helpful in promoting an interest in the work of the classical schools for its own sake; and just as the work of the schools was appreciated for its own sake did the social rank of the teachers rise in importance. But still it was lamentably true that the examination for teachers' certificates was the examination for holy orders.

<small>Separation of School and Church.</small>

The death of Frederick the Great, in 1786, left many of his plans for the improvement of the higher schools unfinished. His successor, however, established in the first year of his reign an *Oberschulcollegium*, which was given the supervision of secondary education in the kingdom. A year later, in 1788, it was decreed that students should take a final examination on leaving the *Gymnasien;* in 1812 the require-

<small>Work of Frederick the Great.</small> ment was made obligatory and universal. In this way the government ascertained the quality of secondary-school work, but students might enter the university and study for the learned professions whether they passed this examination or not. Indeed, not till 1834 was it finally settled that the certificate of graduation from a higher school was an essential prerequisite for admission to the university, and eventually to the professions and the higher grades of the civil service.

By the establishment of the *Oberschulcollegium* the church was deprived of some important prerogatives; still others were taken away by the *Allgemeine Landrecht*

<small>Work of Stein and Humboldt.</small> of 1794; but the complete emancipation of the teacher from ecclesiastical control was secured in 1810, by an order requiring of all intending teachers in the higher schools an examination separate and distinct from the examination for admission to holy orders. However easy the step might be for a theological student to become a higher-school teacher, yet it was a step that he had to take; and he had to take it just as other candidates did—by examination before a board of teachers. Then teaching became a profession, and the teacher a highly honoured member of the civil service. Every subsequent enactment has been to increase the dignity of the profession, and to make its honours more difficult of attainment. Every decade has seen some additional requirement made of those who would enter the ranks; and with every decade there have come increased emoluments and social advantages of a nature to invite service. The result is the best equipped and most exclusive body of teachers in the world.

One of the striking peculiarities of German social life, as viewed from the American stand-point, is that the average boy in his teens, or even earlier, knows precisely what his life work is to be. Long before he leaves school he begins to shape his course for the profession that he has in view;

indeed, it is probable that the most important decision of his life is made when he enters school at nine years of age. And with each succeeding school year the range of possible choices steadily diminishes. It is important, therefore, that parents early decide upon the course of study best suited to their children, and that the children themselves fully realize the bearing of their school work on their subsequent careers. *(Choice of Profession.)*

The student of the *Gymnasium* knows that he has the privilege, among others, of preparing himself for any position in the higher schools ; the graduate of the *Realgymnasium* may become a teacher of the modern languages, mathematics or the natural sciences ; and but recently the privilege of becoming a teacher of mathematics and the natural sciences has been conferred on graduates of the *Oberrealschule*. *(Privileges.)*

The professional training of the higher-school teacher really begins with the university course. Although graduation from a higher school is an essential prerequisite, it is only in the university that he gets the special training required of all candidates for positions in the secondary schools. *(University Study.)* The minimum course in the university, as required in most German states, is set at three years ; but four or five years are nearer the average. The student, on coming up to the university, knows full well what profession he is to follow ; and the intending teacher has his specialties already in mind. In general, the greater part of his work is directed to those subjects which he expects to teach, or, better, to those subjects in which he will later be examined. But there is no prescribed course which he is bound to follow. For a year or two he follows his own personal inclinations, without overmuch thought of the future—sometimes without overmuch attention even to the present. In time, however, he falls into the routine which invariably marks the preparation for the state examination.

The *Staats-Examen* is the sole test of a candidate's preparation for any professional career. Neither the degree of doctor of philosophy, nor any other scholarly distinction, can exempt him from the necessity of proving himself before a state board of examiners. In the smaller German states these boards are generally located at the capital or in the university towns; some states have none at all, having delegated their prerogatives to the boards of adjoining states. Prussia maintains ten examining boards for the higher-school service, called *Wissenschaftliche Prüfungs-Commissionen*. The majority of the members of these boards are university professors; but there are usually a few prominent secondary-school men and administrative officers of the department of education among the members. They are appointed annually by the minister of education, but in practice there are few changes for years together. There is no prescribed number of members, except that there must be at least one examiner for every subject that a candidate may offer; this means, as a rule, from twenty to thirty persons.

State Examination.

The aim of the state examination is to test (1) the applicant's proficiency in pedagogy and philosophy, including psychology, logic and ethics; (2) his familiarity with the German language and literature; (3) his acquaintance with the doctrines of his religion, and (4) his knowledge of the subjects which he expects to teach. In all these lines, possibly excepting religion, he will have had special training under university professors. In philosophy and pedagogy, in German and in religion, the requirements are of a general nature, intended to disclose the applicant's breadth of training and the nature of his religious faith; it is the fourth requirement that constitutes the crux of the examination.

Its Purposes.

A certificate based upon the state examination does not by any means permit the holder to teach what he will anywhere he gets the chance. Under the Prussian system, a teacher, in addition to the requirements above mentioned, must be qualified in at least four subjects or their equivalents, and he must not presume to teach anything in which he is not properly certificated. Furthermore, he may not teach those subjects in which he is certificated beyond a certain class, that class being determined by the grade of his certificate. Three grades are recognised ; these correspond to the three general divisions—upper, middle and lower—of the higher schools. A first-grade certificate in any subject is good for any class in a nine-year school ; a second-grade is good for all classes below the three highest ; a third-grade is good only for the lower classes. Third-grade certificates are granted only in those subjects which are taught in the higher schools the full nine years. Thus, in Latin, German, French, religion, history, mathematics and geography certificates may be of the first, second or third grade ; in Greek, English, Hebrew, Polish, Danish, physics, chemistry and mineralogy, botany and zoology, of the first or second grade. Applicants for certificates may enter, under certain restrictions, for any subject and any grade in that subject. {.sidenote: Teachers' Certificates.}

The subjects which are taught in the higher schools—therefore those in which state examinations may be taken—are classed in two general groups : the language-history group, and the science-mathematics group. The former includes German, Latin, Greek, French, English and history ; the latter includes mathematics, physics, chemistry and mineralogy, botany and zoology ; geography of the first or second grade may be classed in either group. Hebrew, Polish, Danish and religion are extra subjects, properly belonging to the first group. Of the four subjects in which every teacher is examined, the first two are known as majors (*Hauptfächer*)—those which he prefers to teach ; the other two are minors (*Nebenfächer*). Now, in order that the most favourable combinations may be made—favourable both for the schools and the teachers' scholarship—certain restrictions are placed upon a free choice. The most important are the following : (1) both majors and one minor must be of the same group ; (2)

first-grade Latin goes with second-grade Greek, and second-grade Latin with first-grade Greek; (3) first-grade mathematics takes second-grade physics; (4) third-grade Latin is required with any grade of French or English; (5) third-grade geography must be taken with any grade in history; (6) a major in religion takes Hebrew as its accompanying major. Geography, placed, as it is, in both groups, is always a popular minor; it may also be counted a major in either group.

The university student who looks forward to teaching as a profession early selects the combination of subjects which he prefers to teach, or which is likely to bring most rapid promotion. To these subjects he gives his main attention for three to five years. If he can afford the luxury of taking his Ph.D.—it costs from one hundred to two hundred dollars and a good deal of time—he will, in the meantime, write a dissertation and be examined on three of his four subjects. That the degree is looked upon as a luxury, and one that can be easily dispensed with, is evidenced from the fact that less than one-half of the Prussian teachers have taken the pains to secure it. The *Staats-Examen* is not only more difficult, but more honourable, because obligatory.

University Degrees.

There are in Prussia ten State Examination Commissions,[1] located in the university towns. An applicant for examination cannot come before any of these at will. He must choose the commission (1) of the province in which he was born or in which he resides, or (2) of the province in which the university is situated where he has spent at least two semesters, including the last, or (3) of the province in which he expects to teach. All foreigners, including residents of other German states, must secure the endorsement of the minister of education to their application.

Examination Commissions.

---

[1] East and West Prussia, at Königsberg; Brandenburg, at Berlin; Pomerania, at Greifswald; Posen and Silesia, at Breslau; Saxony, at Halle; Schleswick-Holstein, at Kiel; Hanover, at Göttingen; Westphalia, at Münster; Hesse-Nassau, at Marburg; Rhine province, at Bonn.

The application itself is a serious affair. First there is the fee to be paid, which amounts to $7.50 (30 m.) for each examination and re-examination; $3.75 (15 m.) for each supplementary and extension examination. *Application for Examination.* Then there are the certificates and testimonials of the applicant's higher-school course and his university training, without which no one can hope to be admitted, unless by special order of the minister. These papers show precisely what he has done, and how well he has succeeded since he entered school at nine years of age. Next he makes known his combination of subjects which he elects as majors and minors, and the grade of examination which he desires in each. In his *Vita*, which is next in order, the applicant tells who he is, when he was born, what the rank or occupation of his father is, of what church he is an adherent, and, finally, he calls attention to special points in his preparation and any noteworthy work that he may have done. This sketch of his life must be written in Latin, if the applicant's major subjects are the classical languages; if they are the modern languages, it must be in French or English; in all other cases it is optional whether it be in German or a foreign language.

After review of the application thus made, the commissioners decide upon admission to the examination. If the applicant's preparation seems faulty, they advise him not to attempt the examination; if they have *Admission.* serious doubts as to his moral character, if they suspect him of being disloyal in religion or politics, they may refuse his application altogether, in which case an appeal may be taken to the minister—if the applicant doesn't mind courting almost sure defeat. If his credentials are acceptable, however, he is soon notified when to appear for examination.

The examination is both oral and written. The written test comes first, and consists in the writing of elaborate essays on themes assigned by the commission. One theme is on some topic in philosophy or pedagogy, and is designed to test the candidate's knowledge of the philosophical basis of pedagogy and didactics, and of the development of educational thought since the sixteenth century. The applications of modern psychology to teaching are fruitful themes for such essays. The candidate must also write essays on themes selected from each of his major subjects. When one essay will include both major subjects, the two may be combined, as frequently happens in classical and modern philology, physics and mathematics, history and geography, etc. If the applicant has published something of note, as, for instance, a dissertation for the degree of doctor of philosophy, it may be offered as a substitute for one of the essays. Essays that deal with a classical language must be written in Latin; with the modern languages, in French or English, as the case may be; and with all other subjects, in German. Six weeks are allowed for the preparation of each essay, and the commission is empowered to grant an extension of six weeks—making twelve weeks in all, if necessary, on the subject. Any further extension must be authorized by the minister.

Conduct of Examination.

At the expiration of the time allowed the essay is forwarded to the chairman of the commission, together with a complete bibliography of references consulted, and a declaration by the candidate that he has received no personal assistance in the preparation of the essay. A false declaration would disqualify a candidate for further examination; if the fraud were not detected till after the certificate had been granted, disciplinary proceedings would be instituted as against any other state official. If the essays are not comprehensive enough to satisfy the commission of the candidate's breadth of scholarship, supplementary tests may be required by way of short written examinations or laboratory work. Thus the candidate shows his familiarity with the literature of his subjects and demonstrates his ability to do independent work.

Written.

If now the written examination satisfies the commission, and the candidate appears not to be an atheist or a socialist, a day is set for the oral examination. It is an open secret that few Jews reach this stage, no matter what their qualifications may be; and those who do succeed in overcoming all preliminary hindrances are, nevertheless, quietly disposed of at a later stage in a way to minimize their influence. The Prussian examination system, as actually conducted, is designed primarily to keep undesirable persons out of the profession; there are many requirements that would not be made if the sole object were to secure the best teachers.

Oral.

The oral examination is intended to test the general culture of the candidate and his ready command of philosophy and pedagogy, and to ascertain his fitness to teach his chosen subjects in a higher school. The examination in each subject is conducted by a specially appointed examiner, in the presence of other members of the commission. Candidates for first-grade certificates in Latin or English, or for first or second-grades in French, must use the respective languages in examination, at least to the extent of showing a ready command of the spoken forms. Thus the candidate shows what he knows as well as what he can do.

The oral test concludes the examination. The commissioners now decide whether the total examination has been satisfactory or not. If any part is unsatisfactory, no certificate is granted; but, instead, a testimonial is issued to the candidate, which specifies the exact results attained in each subject, the grade secured in all subjects that were passed, and the day (never within six months) when the candidate may come up for re-examination. The second trial is his last, if he again fails to meet the minimum requirements.

Grade of Certificate.

The successful candidate not only receives a certificate of fitness to teach (*facultas docendi*) certain subjects in specified classes; but his certificate is ranked according to the grades he holds in the various subjects in which he is examined. A first-rank certificate, which renders the holder eligible at some future time for appointment to the position of head-teacher, with

Rank of Certificate.

the title of professor, indicates that the holder has secured upon examination either two majors of first-grade and two minors of second-grade, or two majors and one minor of first-grade. A second-rank certificate, which entitles the holder to the position of ordinary teacher (*Oberlehrer*), indicates the possession of two majors and one minor of second-grade and one minor of third-grade. In other words, the person holding a first-rank certificate is entitled to teach (1) two subjects in all classes and other two subjects in the lower six classes, or (2) three subjects through all nine years of the higher schools. The second-rank certificate entitles the holder to teach three subjects through the first six years, and one subject through the first three years. A certificate of the second rank, therefore, excludes the holder from teaching in the three highest classes of the higher schools, and denies him the honour reserved for head-teachers.

If the candidate has been successful in both majors, but has failed in his minors, he may be granted a second-rank certificate on condition that he secure by supplementary examination second-grade in both minors or first-grade in one. Such deficiency must be made up within three years from the date of the first examination. Supplementary examinations must be taken before the same commission as was the first examination, unless the minister of education gives the candidate permission to apply elsewhere. Only one such examination is permitted.

It will be seen that a teacher's chances of securing a position are limited (1) by the subjects in which he is certificated and (2) by the rank of his total certificate. An unfortunate combination of subjects often seriously interferes with the promotion of a candidate. It happens, therefore, that many teachers seek to qualify themselves in as many subjects as possible, and to secure the highest grades in each. Such persons are permitted to take two extension examinations before the commissions by which they were first examined, or before the commissions of the provinces in which they are teaching.

The second extension examination closes the door on further opportunity. The limit is practically fixed at four or five first-grade certificates; few teachers, in fact, ever secure more than three. The only incentive to add to the number of privileges is that thereby an appointment may possibly be secured a year or two earlier. The game is hardly worth the candle.

The intending teacher, even with his certificate in his hand, has yet other gauntlets to run. The certificate of itself confers no right to teach. Something more than general culture and minute scholarship is required. It is safe to say that Germany owes more to the pedagogical training of her teachers than to any other factor in their preparation. It is the professional spirit, which every German teacher feels, that differentiates him from his species in other countries, and this spirit is the result chiefly of his pedagogical training. *Pedagogical Training.*

When the examination *pro facultate docendi* was first established, in 1810, it was specified that all candidates should demonstrate their ability to teach by giving a lesson before the examining board. This plan was soon found to be impracticable; few candidates could make a respectable showing. Afterward the trial lesson was given in private before a school inspector, but even this was unsatisfactory. Consequently, in 1826 the Prussian government introduced the plan, which has since been adopted by all the German states except Würtemberg, of requiring all candidates, after the completion of the examination *pro facultate docendi* to spend a year as trial teacher (*Probe-Candidat*) in some approved higher school. The *Probejahr*, as we learn from a ministerial rescript of 1867, was intended to give the intending teacher an opportunity to familiarize himself with the duties of his future office, and to prove to the satisfaction of the school authorities that he had the practical ability requisite for a successful teacher. Candidates were expected to teach six or eight hours a week under the immediate supervision of the *Early Attempts. Trial Lesson.*

director or head-teachers of the school. Besides this, there were special requirements concerning the visiting of classes taught by the regular teachers, preparation of lessons, supervision of scholars, attendance at examinations and teachers' conferences and participation in all the practical workings of the school.

The *Probejahr* proved in time to be insufficient for the demands placed upon it. Too many candidates were seeking appointment to the higher schools. Something had to be done to shut out undesirable persons, and at the same time to raise the standards of professional attainments. In point of didactic skill it was recognised that the elementary teachers trained in the normal schools (*Lehrerseminarien*) were distinctly superior to the teachers of the secondary schools. It was decided, therefore, to lengthen the term of practical training rather than to increase the scholastic requirements. Following the example of Hesse, it was decreed in 1890 that intending teachers in the higher schools of Prussia should have two years of pedagogical training instead of one. The last year was to remain much as before, and still to be known as the *Probejahr*. The first year of practical training, following directly after the state examination, was intended to bridge over the gulf between the university and actual school work. Candidates were to be assigned to *Seminarien*, where they might have the advantage of superior instruction in the art of applying the general principles of education—already studied in the university—to the practical problems of the secondary schools. The bulk of the work was expected to be theoretical, but always to be presented with a view to its practical application.

<small>Trial Year.</small>

<small>Seminar Year.</small>

Such are the specific requirements at the present time of all intending higher-school teachers in Prussia: nine years a pupil in a higher school, four years of university study, one year in examination, one *Seminarjahr*, and one *Probejahr*. If to this we add the year of military service, which all able-bodied men must

<small>Present Requirements.</small>

perform, we find that the minimum requirements demand seventeen years in preparation; it is oftener eighteen or twenty years. Only a few of the German states have as yet adopted the Prussian plan, in introducing the *Seminarjahr;* but where Prussia leads the others are sure to follow—if only at a respectful distance.

The Prussian *Seminarien*, to which candidates are assigned on passing the examination *pro facultate docendi*, are of two kinds : (1) those under the immediate direction of the provincial school-boards, twelve in all— two in Berlin, and one each in Breslau, Göttingen, Königsberg, Magdeburg, Stettin, Posen, Dantzic, Cassel, Münster and Coblentz ; (2) those instituted by ministerial rescript of March 15, 1890, which are connected with the leading *Gymnasien* and *Realgymnasien*, and are each under the direction of the director and one or two associated headteachers of the school. Prussian Seminars.

The *Seminarien* of the first class are state institutions on special foundations, many of them having a specific purpose, as the training of teachers of religion, of modern languages, etc. These royal *Seminarien* admit few candidates, and, as a rule, all members receive valuable stipends. The twelve institutions together do not have more than seventy members, but all are picked men. 1. State Seminars.

For some time prior to 1890 the average number of candidates for the *Probejahr* in Prussia had been over five hundred annually. Since the introduction of the *Seminarjahr*, however, the number has steadily decreased. In 1894–1895 there were only one hundred and ninety-two persons in the *Seminarjahr* and two hundred and twelve in the *Probejahr*. Hence only about thirty gymnasial *Seminarien*, of the seventy that were planned, have been needed. These, as above stated, are under the direction of principals of higher schools, who are relieved of about one-fourth of their regular teaching in order that they may have time for this work. 2. Gymnasial Seminars.

During the *Seminarjahr* two main objects are kept always

in view—a clear understanding of pedagogical and didactic principles, and an introduction to the practical workings of a higher school. Once a week the *Director* leads a discussion on some pedagogical topic, with a view to a better understanding of its practical application to teaching. The members of the *Seminar* meanwhile are observing the teaching of various masters, and after the first three months are themselves permitted to give two or three lessons a week. The *Director*, or some member of the faculty delegated by him, hears all these lessons and guides the young teachers' work. From time to time special lessons are given, which are attended by all the members of the *Seminar*, and by the director and his associates. The teacher presents the lesson according to a previously prepared outline, copies of which are in the hands of the critics during the progress of the lesson. Then comes the criticism, in which the teacher first gives his views of his own work, followed by the other members of the *Seminar;* the director sums up the discussion, and points out possibilities of future improvement. Throughout the year the young teachers are instructed in the use of special school apparatus, books and other teachers' helps; they attend all faculty meetings, have a share in the oversight of pupils and are inducted into the mysteries of the final examinations. Three months before the close of the school-year each member of the *Seminar* hands in a dissertation on some subject closely connected with his previous work. The director thereupon makes an exhaustive report to the provincial school-board of the year's work, in which the abilities of the various candidates are passed in review. On the basis of these returns and the records of the examination *pro facultate docendi*, the inspectors (*Oberschulräte*) advance the candidates to their *Probejahr*, or refuse altogether to give them further training as men unfitted for the teachers' profession.

[margin note: The Training Course.]

Of the noted institutions of Germany designed for the training of teachers for the secondary schools may be mentioned the University *Seminarien* of Jena, Leipsic and

Giessen. The first named is well known in this country from its director, Professor Rein, and bears a deservedly good name at home because of the progressive schoolmasters that it has sent out. Unfortunately, however, its influence is more on the side of elementary education; the training school, which is also under the direction of Professor Rein, is composed of folk-school pupils; and the practical problems that come up for discussion are almost invariably the problems of the lower schools. It cannot be said, I think, that the Jena *Seminar*, at least under Professor Rein's administration, has exercised any great influence on the secondary schools. Nevertheless, the general pedagogy that is so ably presented there is now being utilized indirectly through the medium of a gymnasial *Seminar* of the Prussian type which has been recently established in connection with the Jena *Gymnasium*. In this way intending secondary-school teachers can avail themselves of Professor Rein's lectures and all the general discussion of the University *Seminar*, and at the same time keep in touch with gymnasial affairs and give practice lessons under the direction of Dr. Gustave Richter, director of the *Gymnasium*.

3. University Seminars.

Jena.

The *Seminar* in Leipsic is only remotely connected with the university. It is under the direction of Dr. Richard Richter, who is both director of the royal *Gymnasium* and professor in the university. The candidates do their general work in the university, and come to the *Gymnasium* for training in practical lines. It has only a one-year course, and, inasmuch as its members are in preparation for positions in the higher schools of Saxony, the *Seminar* has little influence beyond the kingdom.

Leipsic.

It is somewhat different with the *Seminar* at Giessen. From its beginning in 1876 it has been under the leadership of Dr. Hermann Schiller, who is at once Professor of Pedagogy in the University, director of the *Gymnasium*, and *Oberschulrat* of Hesse. It is the pioneer institution of the modern type, and has given direction

Giessen.

to the recent development of the Prussian gymnasial *Seminarien*. Schiller's *Handbuch der praktischen Pädagogik* and his *Geschichte der Pädagogik* indicate the scope of the work. By means of lectures, discussions and dissertations, the way is prepared for the practical application of the principles of psychology and ethics. Every problem is a problem of secondary education, and every member of the *Seminar* is in training for the secondary schools. An unusual amount of work is required of the *Seminar* members; but, so far as I can judge from a short visit, it is done fairly well. It is evident, however, that better financial support would work great improvements. But in theory Schiller's *Seminar* is far and away ahead of any institution in Germany designed for the training of teachers for the secondary schools. It comes near being a model training school for secondary teachers.

The honours of leading the recent movement in Germany for better pedagogical training are about equally shared between Dr. Schiller and the late Dr. Frick of Halle. The former was the pioneer; but in 1881 Dr. Frick reorganized the *Seminarium Præceptorum* of the *Franckesche Stiftungen*, and became at once a recognised leader of pedagogical thought in Prussia. Since his death, in 1892, the *Seminar* has been conducted by his successor, Dr. Fries, on the Prussian gymnasial plan.

Halle.

The *Probejahr*, as I have already indicated, has not been much affected by the introduction of the *Seminar* training. As heretofore, the candidates are told off in pairs for service in the larger schools. Their work is mostly class instruction, under the guidance of older teachers. Besides the six or eight hours a week of teaching, they may be called upon for a certain amount of supervision; they must attend all faculty meetings, and otherwise identify themselves with the life of the school. For all this they receive no remuneration whatever; but, on the contrary, if their work is not acceptable, they may, on report of the director, be dismissed from the service. But if their record is satisfactory at the end of the *Probejahr*, their

Work of the Trial Year.

names are inscribed on the list of teachers eligible to appointment in the higher schools of the province. Their period of probation is finished; they have only to wait a few years before beginning their life work. This work, once begun and attended to with reasonable diligence, will insure them a competency for the rest of their days. It is a slow process, but sure. The end, however, is a desirable one both for the teachers and for the state.

GENERAL REFERENCES :—Fries, *Die Vorbildung der Lehrer für das Lehramt*, Vol. II., Pt. I., of Baumeister's *Handbuch* (This comprehensive study was not published in time to be of service in the preparation of this chapter; I specially commend it to those who are interested in the training of teachers for secondary schools.—J. E. R.); Loos, *Die praktisch-pädagogische Vorbildung in Deutschland, Zeitschrift für österr. Gym.*, Vienna, 1893; Schiller, *Die pädagogische Vorbildung der Gymnasiallehrer*, address before the 41st *Philologenversammlung* (gives the Giessen plan); Frick, *Pädagogische und didaktische Abhandlungen—Das Seminarium præceptorum*, Halle, 1893; Rein, *Aus dem pädagogischen Universitäts-Seminar zu Jena*, Langensalza; Zange, *Gymnasialseminare und die pädagogische Ausbildung der Kandidaten des höheren Schulamtes*, Halle, 1890; Beyer, *Zur Errichtung Pädagogischer Lehrstuhle an unseren Universitäten*, Langensalza, 1895; Windscheid, *Das Lehrerinnenbildungs- und Prüfungswesen*, in Wychgram's *Handbuch des höheren Mädchenschulwesens*, Leipsic, 1897; Schiller, *Praktische Pädagogik;* Schrader, *Erziehungs- und Unterrichtslehre*, Berlin, 1893; Encyclopedias of Schmid and Rein.

CHAPTER XIX

APPOINTMENT, PROMOTION AND EMOLUMENTS OF TEACHERS

CANDIDATES for teachers' positions in the higher schools who have successfully passed the state examination and completed the prescribed course of professional training make formal application to the *Provincial-Schulcollegium* in the province where they wish to teach. In case several applicants have completed their trial year at the same time, priority is determined by the dates of the state examination. This fact is of great importance, inasmuch as teachers are appointed to permanent positions in government schools in order of seniority as determined by the official list. Each candidate, it is to be noted, is certificated only in certain subjects and for definite grades. As vacancies occur in the state schools, appointments are necessarily made from those possessing the requisite qualifications.

Appointment of Teachers.

This method of appointment was especially emphasized in the Berlin Conference of 1890 as the only satisfactory mode of checking favouritism. The plan has its advantages; it also has its defects. For example, it may happen that well-qualified men, polished gentlemen, will be sent to comparatively unimportant positions, while men of less merit fall into more desirable and more exacting berths. It is always possible, however, for a candidate to surrender his chance to the man next in order, and still retain his place at the head of the list. On the other hand, if a candidate refuses an appointment once it has been

Method of Procedure.

made, he may be set back six months, put at the foot of the list or dismissed altogether, at the discretion of the provincial school-board. Such an extremity, however, is usually avoided by a little foresight on the part of the *Oberschulrat*. A candidate holding the first place on the list may be advised by the inspector to retire in favour of the next in line, whenever it seems desirable that the first eligible candidate should not be appointed to a particular position. For example, A and B, ranking respectively first *In Royal Schools.* and second in the official list, are both qualified in the major subject required to fill a vacancy existing at some important place. The inspector knows that a place much more suited to A is likely to become vacant in a few months; he advises A accordingly to give way to B, who is immediately appointed to the inferior position. If B refuses to accept, he will be set back far enough to give no trouble for some time to come. Indirectly, therefore, the inspectors have considerable power in placing men; they use it freely to advance the interests of the best candidates and the most progressive schools. It is always the senior candidate's right, however, to demand appointment to the first position falling vacant for which his credentials qualify him. Once on the official list, nothing but gross negligence can prevent his ultimate appointment to some position.

Teachers in higher schools, of whatsoever kind, must be selected from the provincial list. Vacancies in state schools must be filled in order of seniority, as described above; but city schools and others under special *In City Schools.* patronage are free to select from the list regardless of order. The local board nominates a candidate for a vacancy, and asks the approval of the provincial inspectors. This granted, the appointment is made in regular fashion. Herein again the inspector shows his power. By refusing to confirm a nomination made by a local board, and forcing, if needs be, a series of choices, the government can determine, indirectly at least, the character of the teaching force in schools not immediately under its jurisdiction. It must be conceded, however, that the privilege allowed to the local boards of selecting teachers at will from the eligible list tends to take the best teachers away from the state schools. The cities generally pay larger salaries and take younger men—all of which is a great inducement to eager candidates. But many teachers prefer to wait their turn for appointment to a state school, because of the greater dignity attached to the government service. The civil servant enjoys a certain rank at court, and has the proud satisfaction of knowing that no favouritism or political bias enters into his appointment.

All definitely appointed teachers are required to take the oath of office, which is administered by the directors of the state schools or by the local magistracy in behalf of city schools. By order of 1848, it runs as follows: "I swear to God the Almighty and Omniscient after I have been installed as........of........to be submissive, loyal and obedient to His Royal Majesty, King of Prussia, my most gracious lord, to fulfil all the duties of my office according to the best of my knowledge and belief, and also faithfully to observe the constitution. So help me God." The ceremony closes with a formal handshake, whereupon the person is installed in the service of the crown. But lest he forget his professional duties, a special ministerial rescript reminds him that "the teacher in a public school must possess both the intellectual and moral strength which enables him to be an example in all respects to his pupils. He should recognise no higher duty than with fidelity to his self-chosen profession to avoid in instruction and association with his pupils all that might tend to disturb the natural and sound development of youth, all that cannot be conceived and rightly judged by youth, all that might tend to displace right religious feelings or reverence for what is noble and good."

Oath of Office.

The intending teacher in Germany does not expect a speedy appointment to a governmental post. In fact, he expects to wait years for it. The certificated candidates who received appointments in the province of Hesse-Nassau in 1894 had waited already an average of six years since the expiration of their respective trial years. The same test applied to other provinces gives the following results: Brandenburg, 8 years; Hanover, 5.5 years; Saxony, 3.5 years; Silesia, 7.5 years; Posen, 5.4 years; West Prussia, 8.1 years; Westphalia, 4.4 years; Schleswick-Holstein, 4.2 years; Rhine Province, 3.8 years. This makes an average period of waiting for the average candidate of 5.6 years.[1]

Waiting for Appointment.

The variation in the several provinces is due to the relative desirability of positions, the number of city schools, condition of social life as determined by large cities and personal reasons. Candidates are free to make application for a place in the official list of any province, but they are not permitted to register in more than one. Some provinces, therefore, have more eligible candidates than others; some have been so unpopular at times as not to have candidates enough to fill their vacancies. But the ministry now reserves to itself the right to permit voluntary transfers from one province to another, and in case of necessity arbitrarily to equalize the lists. Eligible candidates from other states may also be assigned by the ministry to particular provinces. A candidate who leaves his province without permission, or accepts a permanent appointment to a school not under royal patronage, or engages in an employment not approved by the authorities, loses thereby his place in the eligible list.

Causes of Delay.

An unfortunate combination of subjects in which a candidate is certificated may long defer promotion. According to the list of certificated candidates in Hesse-Nassau, above re-

---

[1] Statistics for the first half of the year 1897 show that in the province of Brandenburg, in which the city of Berlin is situated, twelve permanent appointments were made. The waiting periods were respectively 11, 10.5, 10, 9.25, 9, 8.5, 8, 8, 7.5, 7.5, 6 and 5.5 years—average, 8.33 years. The ages of the teachers thus first appointed to their life work were respectively 36, 34, 42, 41, 41, 36, 35, 38, 43, 33, 36 and 31 years.—*Pädagogisches Archiv*, Vol. XXXIX., p. 176.

ferred to, the distribution among major subjects was as follows: Religion and Hebrew, 7; Latin and Greek, 54; French and English, 15; mathematics and physics, 32; chemistry and natural sciences, 2; history and geography, 8; gymnastic training, 9. If there were the same number of positions requiring these subjects in the schools of the province, the candidate in chemistry and natural sciences would have twenty-seven chances of promotion to one for Latin and Greek. But there are more teachers wanted for the classics than for the sciences. An examination of the faculty lists of three typical schools shows sixteen teachers of Latin and Greek to seven teachers of chemistry and natural sciences (or either). This reduces the chances of the candidate in science very materially, and yet the ratio is about twelve to one in his favour. But the law of supply and demand will regulate all these defects in time. This happens to be a period of rapid advancement in science, and good teachers are few.

Combination of Subjects.

There is still another factor that influences appointments and tends to delay promotion. When vacancies occur from death or retirement, the probabilities are that superior places are to be filled, and that many changes will be made before there is need of calling in a new man. Untried men are never appointed to any particular position, but rather to *a* position which is pretty certain to be near the foot of the faculty list. Young men often have to stand aside and let experienced teachers from other schools step into the places that seemed to be theirs. In fact, the transfer of teachers from school to school is much more frequent than would seem possible under the system. Some positions are eagerly sought, because of special advantages attached thereto. The *Friedrichs-Werdersches Gymnasium* of Berlin and *Schulpforta,* for example, have special foundations for teachers, widows and orphans, and valuable stipends for the education of teachers' sons. But despite all such attractions, a vacancy will be sifted out somewhere to which a young candidate may be appointed.

Transfers of Teachers.

It is not to be understood that the candidate spends the time intervening between the trial year and his permanent appointment in idleness. Some are employed as assistant teachers at a salary of 1,500 marks ($375) per year. Others seek employment as private tutors, journalists, book-keepers or what-not. Practically, however, most candidates are unable to do anything but teach; they have had no training for anything else, and competition is too severe in Germany to let choice positions go a-begging. Often a candidate prefers to serve a number of years as assistant in a good school, awaiting appointment in that place, than to accept a permanent position in an undesirable locality. In Hesse-Nassau, in 1894, of one hundred and seventeen certificated candidates awaiting appointment, thirty were assistants and ten were employed in other capacities in the public schools. Sixty-five were over thirty years of age. They had spent, on the average, fourteen years in preparation—nine in the *Gymnasium*, three in the university and two in professional study—and were destined to wait full six years after being declared fit for their life work. *[margin: Employment During the Waiting Period.]*

After taking the oath of allegiance and having been installed in a definite position, the teacher is a government officer. His tenure of office is secure, and upon retirement after ten years of service he is entitled to a pension. His salary and pension are determined, primarily, by the position which he occupies and length of service. While a teacher must always confine his instruction to the subjects in which he is certificated, an efficient teacher is certain of advancement in rank. Leaving assistants (*Hilfslehrer*) and special teachers out of account, there are three ranks: regular teachers (*Oberlehrer*), professors and directors. The title of professor, however, is purely honorary, and carries with it no substantial benefits. It is one of the practical results of the Conference of 1890, intended to better the social standing of higher-school teachers. By royal order, it is decreed that one-third of the regular staff of the higher school may be appointed by the ministry to a *[margin: Honours.]*

rank equivalent to that of university professor and have the title. The honour is intended to be an award of merit; but in practice it is the upper—and older—third of the faculty who receive it, regardless of merit.

Special privileges are granted to teachers in accordance with their rank. All state officials of Prussia are carefully classified, and the gradation is punctiliously observed on all state occasions. The ordinary higher-school teachers belong to the fifth class; directors and professors of twelve years' service belong to the fourth class; and occasionally the crown honours a very old man who is distinguished as a teacher and director with the privileges of the third class and the title of *Geheimer-Regierungs-Rat*. Provincial school inspectors and ministerial councillors, being administrative officers, are ranked by themselves in higher classes.

<small>Privileges.</small>

Great care is exercised in the selection of directors of higher schools, not only for the professional responsibilities involved, but also because through them the government expects to watch over the political development of future leaders in the state. From the time of the Reformation down to 1810, it was the custom for the city magistrates to nominate principals of schools under their patronage, subject to the confirmation of the local pastor and the superintendent of the ecclesiastical district. Humboldt made the election of directors of *Gymnasien* dependent upon the approval of the crown. In 1817 the provincial consistories were given the right to appoint, or approve the appointment, of all higher-school teachers, except that the assent of the ministry was necessary in case of head-teachers and directors. A few years later the ministry assumed the entire appointive powers, and in 1836 the appointment of directors was again direct from the crown. And there it remains to-day. By custom, however, the choice of director is almost entirely left to the judgment of the provincial inspector—himself *persona grata* to the king and ministry who retain him in office. The inspector, as he

<small>Selection of Directors.</small>

moves about the schools of his province, marks those teachers who seem to have the quality of leadership. When a vacancy occurs in a state school, he knows at once the man for the place. Whenever possible, the selection is made from the faculty of the school; but petty jealousies often make this impracticable. In case of city schools, the local board usually seeks the advice of the provincial inspector. But no city is bound to take the man who may be the choice of the inspector; on the other hand, the inspector, with the consent of the crown, can veto any appointment the city board may make. Thus a dead lock may occur if a city government is strongly liberal or progressive, and aims at getting a school director of the right political stripe. The government would unhesitatingly refuse to confirm the appointment of any man known to be of a socialistic turn of mind. In such an event the local board must proceed to another election, and so on till a compromise candidate is found. The state is bound to win in the end; it is extremely imprudent to oppose one's superiors in Prussia.

The successful candidate for the vacant principalship is generally the one who has made no move to secure it. Electioneering on a candidate's part would surely defeat him; such action is branded as unprofessional in Germany, and unworthy of a teacher and a gentleman. Nothing prevents a person making an application for a position, even in a state school; but a good deal depends on how it is done. Public advertising or the exertions of "teachers' agencies" would be of little use. The approved method is to keep in close touch with the provincial inspector. There is nothing discreditable in a young man's telling the inspector that he prefers promotion in line of principalship, rather than as master. If such a man is willing to take the leadership of a small provincial school, his chances of advancement are good. Promotion to a better post may come, if one's record is good; but it will come slowly. The typical director of a higher school is a man above fifty years of age; the directors of the state schools in Berlin in 1894 were of the average age of sixty years.

Individual Efforts.

The installation of a director of a higher school is an interesting ceremony. A representative of the government, generally a provincial school inspector, makes an address and inducts the director into office.

Installation of Director.

Besides this, there is generally a place on the program for music, speeches by local dignitaries and an inaugural address by the newly installed officer. No oath is required, as the director is already in the civil service; he is merely transferred to a new field. And, in general, no examination of any kind is required, although provision is made for a *Colloquium pro rectoratu*, which is specially designed to test the director's familiarity with the laws and ordinances governing his office. These are so many and so intricate that, as a provisional inspector once said to me, "the average teacher can hardly be expected to know them." Hence the omission of this test.

It would far exceed the limits of this essay were I to attempt to give in detail the duties of higher-school directors, as defined by the ministerial orders, circular rescripts and provincial regulations which have been issued for the guidance of these officials.

Duties of Directors.

Suffice to say, that there is no code of school laws in Prussia, and that precedent determines everything. The briefest possible summary of the official orders given to the directors from 1867 to 1873 covers over one hundred finely printed pages in Wiese-Kübler's *Laws and Orders*. Besides being required to teach at least twelve hours a week, the director is charged with the entire responsibility of his school. He oversees the work of all his teachers, and is obliged personally to observe their work and to keep a written record of his observations. He must settle all disputes within his faculty, and report cases of negligence to the provincial school-board; he must be the leader in the professional life of his school; he must be in constant communication with the parents of his pupils, and see to it that the regular notices and reports are issued at the proper time; he must make exhaustive annual and semi-annual reports to his superiors, and be ready at any time to supply all statistics and special information that the government may require; and once in three years he must file a comprehensive report of his administration, which informs the government of the condition of his school, its needs and the quality of the work and character of each instructor. In short, there is nothing that a school principal can be conceived as doing which is not directly enjoined or prohibited in the numerous precedents established by official orders. And I wish to say that, so far as my observation goes, the conscientious director of a higher school in Germany is the hardest worked man I have ever seen in the profession. Principals of schools and colleges in England and America may occasionally be charged with greater responsibility; but I have never found elsewhere so much detail work and so much teaching coupled with the necessity of professional growth and intellectual productivity, nor have I ever seen elsewhere so much energy wasted for lack of clerical assistance. It is painful to see a great school-master doing unaided what a third-rate stenographer could better do. But the day of typewriters has not yet dawned on the fatherland; the old way is quite satisfactory, if the new happens to cost money.

An extract from a private letter from one of the foremost directors in all Germany tells its own story: "I am at present quite overwhelmed with work, which, to my regret, is chiefly administrative and always uncongenial to me. I am still compelled to turn night into day, in order to perform the most necessary duties. Then, all my spare time is taken up with class visitation, criticism of teachers' work and devising means of assisting them to better results. It takes so much time; but I must do it, as I can find no other way of interesting them in new methods. Besides, my notion of a pedagogue compels me to regard this work as my highest duty; it is in the interests of the moral education of my pupils, which is certainly not less important than their intellectual development. The next step is to secure the friendly co-operation of the parents, for the sake of complete harmony between home and school. All

A Typical Instance.

this is desirable, and I am compelled to do it. Note, too, that I must also keep regular office hours for parents and pupils; hold conferences; that I give thirteen hours of instruction a week, for which papers must be prepared and corrected; that I have two trial teachers entrusted to me, whose training I must supervise with special care; that I must, unaided, make up the numerous government reports and conduct all my correspondence. Note all this, and you will readily see that more than one man's strength is demanded or much must be neglected. But even this is not the end: I had almost forgotten the regular directors' meeting (of the city); consultation with the local board; special conferences (just now it is the question of school gardens); the numerous educational meetings which one must attend occasionally, for the sake of appearances; social obligations, which one can never entirely shake off; and, finally, family—but there is nothing left for them, poor things!" One wonders that there is anything left of the man. But the picture is true to life, as I can testify from personal observation of the school. I need scarcely add that for six years this man has been vainly trying to revise a little book of his which the public demands in a new edition.

Necessity has invented a way of piecing out a director's strength and extending his authority. It is the discovery of the class-master, or *Ordinarius*, and his possibilities. The *Ordinarius* is a regular teacher who is chosen by the director, with the consent of the provincial school-board, to act as the director's representative in a particular class. There are, therefore, as many class-masters as there are classes in the school. Each class-master is selected from the teachers who give instruction in the class —generally the one who teaches the largest number of hours. The class-master is expected to be teacher, guide and friend of his class. All other teachers report to him, and the class record is his special care. Pupils must first seek his advice before going to the director; he becomes personally acquainted with the parents of his boys; he studies the condition of their home life and their conduct out of school; he has charge of the trial teachers who may be assigned to the class, and sees to it that no harm comes from their teaching; and in all faculty conferences he acts as spokesman for his class. *His Duties.* From the reports of other teachers he knows just what each boy is doing, and is prepared to talk intelligently with teacher or boy, as the case may be. Thus, he is responsible for the industry, progress and morals of his charges. But he is not allowed to hear pupils' complaints against other teachers, nor can he interfere with the execution of any order that a colleague may give. A question involving the judgment or goodwill of another teacher must go to the director.

It will be evident that the class-master can be of great service to the director. When the office is faithfully filled, as I believe it generally is, not only is the director saved much anxious care, but the work of the school is wonderfully improved. And, best of all, the system provides for that close and intimate contact between pupil and teacher which is so essential in a secondary school; at no time in a boy's course is it so necessary to have the close, personal and intensely interested guidance of some one upon whose experience and advice he may rely. To be sure, not all class-masters are successful, or even conscientious, in the performance of their duties; but enough of them are to remove all basis for that charge which is so often, and so falsely, made against German school-masters—namely, that they have no personal interest in their pupils.

Regular teachers are required to give at least twenty-two hours of instruction per week, but professors may fall under this minimum two hours without losing a proportionate amount of their salary. Assistants must teach twenty-four hours, and special teachers twenty-six hours per week. *Duties of Regular Teachers.* Every instructor is liable to be called upon at any time for extra service, in case of need, without remuneration. The teacher is required to obey the orders of the director in all official matters. He must faithfully carry out the official program, keeping in mind the general administration and educational purposes of the school. He must see that the physical powers of the pupils are not overtaxed, and that all instruction is made pedagogical and clear. He must hold all recitations punctually; make all corrections of pupils' work regularly and exactly; record all cases of punishment, with explanations, and report such cases to the class-masters and director. He can communicate with higher state officials only through the director. He cannot marry without the consent of the provincial school-board. He may not take up outside duties, nor give instruction to pupils in the regular course, without the consent of the director. He must notify the director in case he wishes to make a journey during vacation; or, if he wishes to resign his position, he must notify the provincial school-board at least three months in advance. Especially are teachers required to hold themselves aloof from all political controversies, and from publishing or writing essays or themes on political subjects.

The director is expected to supervise and criticise the work of his staff. If a teacher remains indifferent, he may be reproved by his colleagues in faculty meeting, or the director may report the case direct to the provincial school-board, which is authorized, after special investigation, to take final action. The offender may be fined, suspended from office for a time or dismissed from the service altogether. Naturally, extreme measures are taken very seldom, and only for the grossest misconduct or impropriety. The usual means of whipping a negligent teacher into line are the director's criticisms and the fear of losing caste with his colleagues. It is a hard blow for a teacher to be proved inefficient by his successor in the next higher class. Such a condition is sufficient reason for faculty censure, which is about as hard to bear as the extreme penalty. Indeed, it is generally felt that the teacher who conducts himself in a manner to merit the disapprobation of his fellows would accept dismissal quite as gracefully as censure

School Supervision.

from the faculty. It happens very seldom, therefore, that a teacher is publicly reprimanded—probably all too seldom. The *esprit de corps* of German teachers is very marked; but action—or rather inaction—is more influenced by the university custom of letting each man do as he will, than by the military ideal of upholding the honour of the profession. The fact is—and there is no denying it—a large percentage of the staff of each school is a dead weight which the rest must carry. Whatever be the theoretical means of detecting poor work, and of prodding the inefficient teacher, in practice all depends upon the personality of the director. If he is a progressive man, and knows how to inspire his teachers with high ideals, all goes well; but if he is himself weak, or too diplomatic to stir up bad odours, the rotten parts will be discreetly covered. This is undoubtedly the usual state of affairs, due in a large measure to the fact that in each school some teachers are long past their prime. These men may have been good teachers twenty years ago; but the times have changed. New tasks have been imposed upon the school, and there is not enough vitality in reserve to meet the emergencies. In many cases it is not a lack of goodwill, but absolute inability to see things in their modern perspective.

The advantages of the Prussian system are obvious. Its chief defect is the difficulty of getting rid of incompetent teachers. The teacher's tenure of office is based upon such grounds, and governed by such laws, as make expulsion from the service exceedingly difficult. Not only is it difficult to prove charges of inefficiency, but it injures a school to make the trial. The next best plan—the one that is regularly enforced in the army—is to force the incompetent teacher to retire and make way for a better. This step, however, necessitates the payment of the pension to which every retiring higher-school teacher is entitled. It costs money, and consequently the step is reluctantly taken. *Defects of the Prussian System.*

The teaching profession in Germany cannot expect to rival the military, but the two are drawing nearer together. The effort is being made to establish a professional code of honour, as in the army, in which the younger teachers are trained by the older ones. The policy of having a generous sprinkling of reserve officers in the teachers' ranks is decidedly helping to establish a norm. The ideal teacher of to-day is not that of twenty or thirty years ago. He is not the absent-minded, black-coated, seedy individual that once typified the scholar, but a wide-awake man of the world. Of course, the gradual separation of the schools from clerical influence is largely responsible for this change; yet it is the military spirit that has set the ideal for the modern teacher. The man who stands before his class erect and stiff as a statue, buttoned to the chin and in faultless attire—this is the man who inspires German pupils with the highest respect, even though his speech in the classroom is as short, sharp and imperious as that of the parade field. In referring to my observations on this point, one of the most progressive inspectors of Prussia freely expressed himself as convinced that the military type of teacher was the coming one. He maintained, too, that the increased attention to gymnastics and field-sports was tending to strengthen the military spirit among the pupils. "For us there is no other way," he said; "we are and must remain a nation of soldiers. When we cease to be that we are nothing." It remains to be seen whether the military spirit will sufficiently penetrate the profession as to make it impossible for a master to shirk his duty; whether the best interests of all will be sacrificed to the indolence, indifference or inability of a few.

The Military Ideal.

The salaries of teachers in the higher schools of Prussia vary, as has been said, according to rank and length of service. Directors of full nine-year schools in Berlin receive from $1,500 to $1,800 a year, and $375 for house rent if an apartment is not provided in the school building. The initial salary of directors of complete schools in cities of over 50,000 inhabitants is $1,275; after fifteen years of service the maximum, $1,800, is reached. The initial salary in smaller cities is $1,200. Directors of six years'

Salaries.

schools begin in Berlin and other large cities with $1,275, and work up to $1,500; in the smaller cities, the limits are $1,125 and $1,500. Regular teachers in state schools receive an initial salary of $675, which is increased $75 triennially until the maximum, $1,275, is reached, after twenty-four years of service. One-half of all the teachers in the complete schools and one-fourth of those in the incomplete schools may receive an additional allowance of $225 per year for distinguished services. The salaries of technical teachers, assistants and others of like grade range from $375 to $900. To these amounts should be added the annual allowances for house rent: directors, $150 to $250; regular teachers, $90 to $225; and others, $40 to $135—according to the size of the city in which the teacher must reside. City schools and those under private patronage may be permitted to pay larger salaries than the state allows, but in no case can they pay less.[1]

Directors.

Regular Teachers.

Special Teachers.

The salaries of directors and teachers of higher schools are very low in comparison with the salaries paid to men of equal worth in American or British schools. It will be seen that $2,000 is beyond the reach of the best men in the state schools, even after twenty years of service. A few city schools, and some on special foundations, do approximate that amount. And these men, be it understood, are holding positions equivalent to the presidency of a high-grade American college or the headmastership of an English public school. The discrepancy is often explained on the theory that it costs correspondingly less to live in Germany. That living expenses are less in Germany than in America is true, but it is not because foods are cheaper there than here. The fact is, as everyone knows who has tried it, that it costs more to live in Germany than in America, *if you live in the same way*. Provisions of all kinds are more expensive; clothing and domestic service

Income vs. Expenses.

---

[1] The complete salary schedules of Prussia, Saxony, Bavaria and Würtemberg are given in Appendix.

alone are cheaper. The German family has learned the lesson of economy; the same economy, if practised in America, would yield still better results. The sole advantage which the German teacher has, as I see it, is in his tenure of office and pension. This may make good the difference or not, just as one looks at it.

It is no wonder that with such meagre income German teachers rarely travel beyond the fatherland. Leave of absence may be granted, but the teacher must bear the expense of a substitute. Prussia, however, expends yearly 5,000 marks in assisting teachers, especially of modern languages, to study abroad. The city of Berlin provides an annual fund of 6,000 marks for the same purpose, and a few other cities do almost as much. Special foundations exist, too, for the purpose of assisting classical teachers to a period of travel in Italy and Greece. These grants range, according to the circumstances, from 500 marks upwards. In case of illness, no deduction is made; the director will divide up the work among the other members of his staff. If, however, there are no signs of ultimate recovery, the teacher is ordered before an examining board for retirement.

Travelling Stipends.

Teachers of all grades in the civil service retiring after ten years of service—or earlier, if because of disabilities incurred in the discharge of their duties—receive a pension of $\frac{1}{6}\frac{5}{0}$ of their last year's salary. For each year of service beyond ten years, $\frac{1}{60}$ of the last year's salary is added, until, after thirty years, the maximum of $\frac{4}{6}\frac{5}{0}$ is reached. A teacher who has an income, from all official sources, of $1,600 will receive, therefore, a pension of $1,200 for the rest of his life. More than that, after his death his widow is entitled to one-third of his pension; and each child under eighteen years of age, to one-fifth as much as the mother.[1]

Pensions.

On the whole, it must be conceded that the German teacher is tolerably well provided for. His income is small; but in

---

[1] See Appendix for a summary of pension laws.

comparison with members of other learned professions, he is not far in the rear. He can live as his neighbours do, enjoy cultivated society, rear a large family, send his sons to the university, fit his daughters to be as cheerful, industrious and frugal as their mother, and be assured of a competency in his old age.

GENERAL REFERENCES :— Wiese, *Das höhere Schulwesen in Preussen;* Wiese-Kübler, *Verordnungen und Gesetze ; Instruction für die Directoren an den höheren Unterrichtsanstalten der Provinz Brandenburg* (and same for *Lehrer* and *Ordinarien*), Berlin, 1868; *Bestimmungen über das Mädchenschulwesen, 31 Mai, 1894,* Berlin, 1895; Wychgram, *Handbuch des höheren Mädchenschulwesens,* Leipsic, 1897; Encyclopedias of Schmid and Rein; *Stätistisches Jahrbuch der höheren Schulen ;* Kunze, *Kalendar für das höhere Schulwesen Preussens,* Breslau, 1894; *Centralblatt für die gesammte Unterrichts-Verwaltung in Preussen* (official organ of the Prussian Education Department).

CHAPTER XX

TENDENCIES OF SCHOOL REFORM

THE German school system in its present form is the outcome of a long process of development, in which there has been continual adaptation of means to ends. The system of the future will be the result of an evolution in what is now at hand. The factors in this problem are so numerous, and their interrelations so complex, that it is almost presumptuous in a foreigner to suggest a possible solution. Nevertheless, there are certain tendencies so manifestly important that they deserve special mention. This chapter, therefore, is the projection of the historical introduction to this study into the present and future.

A Complex Problem.

The pressing problems in German educational affairs are unmistakably those relating to the function of the higher schools—questions of the end and means of secondary education, of state control and individual freedom. Of course, there are many less important questions; and it is characteristic of the German way of doing things to slight nothing because of its apparent insignificance. There are questions of methods of teaching, of internal organization and conduct of school work, of hygiene, of salaries and pensions, of the social rank and standing of teachers, of the professional training of teachers—all these and many more are constantly in the minds of German educators, as the flood of current literature clearly demonstrates. At intervals, these questions come into prominence, but with few exceptions the course of development is well

The Main Questions.

understood, or waits on the solution of more fundamental problems.

The struggle between humanism and realism in higher education goes back centuries. It had passed through several stages even before Sturm and Comenius entered the lists; since their day there has been no cessation of hostilities. The latest stage of development was entered on in Germany about forty years ago, when *Real*-schools began to be fostered by the state. Then, for the first time, the "gymnasial monopoly" was forced to reckon with a real adversary. It is the same old struggle, but in modern dress. In this case both humanism and realism have been touched with the prevailing civic ideals of education. The problem is to reconcile the conflicting claims of humanism, realism and nationalism. *Humanism vs. Realism.*

I have already attempted to show that the higher schools are expected to enter readily into the service of the state. The emperor, in an order dated May 1, 1889, said: "I have for a long time been occupied with the thought of making use of the schools in their separate grades for combating the spread of socialistic and communistic ideas. The prime object of the schools will ever be to lay the foundations for a sound comprehension of both civic and social relations, by cherishing reverence for God and love for the fatherland. But I cannot fail to recognise that in a time when the errors and misrepresentations of social democracy are spread abroad with increased zeal, the school is called upon to make increased efforts to advance the recognition of the true, the real and the possible in the world. The school must endeavour to create in the young the conviction that the teachings of social democracy contradict not only the Divine commands and Christian morals, but are, moreover, impracticable and, in their consequences, destructive alike to the individual and to the community. The school must bring the new and the newest history of the times more than hitherto into the circle of the subjects of instruction, and show that the power of the state alone can protect for the in- *Civic Ideals.*

dividual his family, his freedom and his rights. And it must bring the youth to know how Prussia's kings have exerted themselves to elevate the condition of the labourers, in a continuous development from the legal reforms of Frederick the Great, and from the abolition of serfdom to the present day. Moreover, the school must show by statistics how considerably and constantly in this century the wages and condition of the labouring classes have improved under this monarchical protection." [1]

This led to definite proposals by the ministry of state for carrying out the emperor's wishes. In August of the same year another imperial order directed the calling of the Conference which met in Berlin in December, 1890. This order supported the position formerly taken in the following terms: "The duty falls upon the higher-school system, in a more effective pursuit of its former objects, not only to equip those social classes that are called to exercise a critical influence upon the entire life of our people with the knowledge necessary to produce such results, but also to give them, by means of an education based upon Christianity and the national German spirit, a permanent tendency of the will and of the character. Therefore, above all, those subjects of instruction which are calculated to determine immediately the sensibility and will are to be employed to the greatest extent possible. Along with these duties, common to all the higher schools, the goals fixed for individual classes of schools are to be kept firmly in view. If, however, in this, not merely a more highly cultured personality, but also an intellectually composed and a morally confirmed personality, is everywhere striven for as the result of the instruction, then all the scientific work of the higher schools will serve the ends of true education. This is universally recognised; but different views prevail as to the way that should be taken to reach this goal, and these views are in part contradictory. Therefore, it has been recommended

Schools Must Serve the State.

---

[1] *Report of the Commissioner of Education*, Washington, 1889-1890, p. 344.

to ascertain, through the joint deliberations of men of different positions in life, which of the numerous proposals for improving our school system are justified, and how the same are to be equalized; especially, however, how they are to be made available for school forms that have come down to us through history."[1]

Again, in his address before the assembled Conference, he returned to the same theme. "This order in council," he said, "would, perhaps, have been unnecessary, if the schools had stood at the stand-point which they ought to occupy. If I shall become somewhat sharp in my subsequent remarks, I will state here, in advance, that these remarks refer to no one in particular, but to the system, to the whole situation of affairs. If the schools had accomplished what must be demanded of them—I speak to you as one who is not unfamiliar with them, for I have attended the *Gymnasium* and know how things go there—they, of their own accord, would have undertaken the fight against social democracy from the very beginning. The teaching faculties of our schools ought to have taken a firm hold of the situation, and ought to have instructed the growing youth in such a way that the young people who are of my own age, about thirty, would now furnish me the material wherewith I might accomplish the overthrow of this movement. But such has not been the case. . . . But just here lies the *punctum saliens*. Why are so many of our young people led astray by crude theories? Why is it that so many so-called reformers of the universe (*Weltverbesserer*) make their appearance among us, with their confused and incoherent notions? What is the reason why so much fault is continually found with our government, and we are perpetually referred to foreign nations for example? Because our young people are ignorant as to the historical evolution of the conditions of our time, and as to the fact that they are the outgrowth of the

_{The Opinion of the Emperor.}

---

[1] See *Verhandlungen über Fragen des höheren Unterrichts*, Berlin, 1891; also *Report of Commissioner of Education*, Washington, 1889–1890, p. 346.

age of the French Revolution. . . . The question, then, before us is, how can we best reach the desired results with regard to classical and scientific training (*Real-bildung*), and as to the requirements for the one year's service in the army? The easiest way, in my opinion, to get at these results is by changing, with one decisive and radical step, our former views, and by saying: Classical *Gymnasien* for classical education, and another kind of schools for scientific training (*Real-bildung*), but no *Realgymnasien*. The *Realgymnasien* are only half-way measures, which give but a partial education, and produce, therefore, only incomplete preparation for life."[1]

The emperor's words were a direct challenge to all parties. The humanists were charged with being philologists merely, not educators in the truest sense of the term.

The One Thing Needed. "The foundation of our *Gymnasium* must be German. It is our duty to educate young men to become young Germans, and not young Greeks and Romans." The *Realgymnasium* was declared to be a hybrid institution, which gives "but a partial education and . . . incomplete preparation for life." And, lastly, the entire system, *Realschulen* included, was condemned as wanting a national basis.

While the charge that the higher schools were responsible for the growth of social democracy was indignantly repudiated by the conference, the results of their **Triumph of Nationalism.** deliberations appear in the school curricula of 1892, in which the subjects of religion, German and history are made the centres of instruction. To that extent nationalism, as represented by the emperor, might claim a victory.

The cause of ultra-realism was decidedly advanced, in that the *Realschulen* were given a definite place in the school system, and endowed with some privileges hitherto **Growth of Real-Schools.** confined to the classical course of training. In consequence, these schools have had a remarkable growth in the last five years. In 1890 there were in

---

[1] *Educational Review*, I., pp. 201 ff.

Prussia only nine *Oberrealschulen* and twenty *Realschulen;* these numbers had increased in 1896 to twenty-four and seventy-three respectively. In the meantime the attendance had increased from 4,177 and 6,940 to 10,288 and 19,675.[1]

The signal advantages accorded to the *Realschulen* have put the advocates of a humanistic education on the defensive. The emperor's advice to convert all *Realgymnasien* into *Oberrealschulen,* and the action of the ministry in discrediting classical instruction in classical schools, precipitated a heated discussion concerning the true significance of humanistic training.

Advocates of the *Realgymnasium* have always insisted that that institution was designed to afford a liberal education on the basis of modern culture. They contend that no secondary school can give both the ancient point of view and the modern also ; that the attempt to do both is the only "half-training" which is known in German schools. *The Problem of the Realgymnasium.* Better cut the knot at once, then, and acknowledge that Greek is not absolutely essential to a well-rounded humanistic training. You can have a humanistic education founded on the Greek and Roman culture, with a modicum of the modern added ; or you can have a humanistic training based on Latin, French and English, with such understanding of Greek culture as can be gained through art and philosophy and literature, without a knowledge of the Greek language. They point out that in the ministerial order of 1859, which established the *Realgymnasien,* it was expressly stated that these institutions were not intended to be schools merely for the furtherance of realistic education. "They are not technical schools (*Fachschulen*), but, like the *Gymnasien,* have to do with the general means of education and fundamental knowledge. Between *Gymnasien* and *Realschulen,* therefore, there is no essential opposition, but a relation of mutual support. *Original Purpose.* They share the task of providing the basis for the higher education necessary for the learned

---

[1] *Statistisches Jahrbuch der Höheren Schulen.*

professions. This division has become necessary through the development of the sciences and social conditions." This principle was again recognised in 1882, when the *Real*-schools with Latin (*Realschulen I. Ordnung*) were given the gymnasial title.

But time effects many changes—among them changes in the *personnel* of the ministry of education. Hence in 1890 the proposition to abolish these modern humanistic institutions altogether. But the attempt was a failure; these schools exist, and are probably stronger to-day, because of the persecution, than they were in 1890.

The humanistic party is divided against itself. Both factions accord the *Oberrealschulen* a legitimate place in the school system. The realists, therefore, are for the nonce quite satisfied. The out-and-out classicists claim that enough is conceded; the *Realschulen* are pre-eminently the schools for those who want only modern culture. The more liberal faction asserts that there can be no understanding of modern culture without the historical setting that comes from a study of the life and language of Rome. Greek, too, is desirable; but it should be an optional subject.

Current Opinions.

This is the attitude of Professor Paulsen; and it accounts for the fact that, in gymnasial circles, he is one of the most cordially hated men in Germany. He is at the same time, I may also add, one of the most popular men in other circles. He is a hard fighter, and cannot be terrified into silence. His creed is as follows: " A school without Latin cannot be the culture-school (*Gelehrtenschule*) of the present. It may be that the *Oberrealschule* is the school of the future; it may be that, in one hundred, or two hundred, or five hundred years, a school not only without Greek but also without Latin will suffice in preparation for the learned studies of that period. In fact, I have no doubt that the significance of the ancient languages will continue to decrease, just as in the past three hundred years. But this must be said : The school of the future is

Professor Paulsen.

not the school of the present. The knowledge of the Latin language is to-day indispensable for most higher studies. . . . If Latin is no longer the universal literary language, it is still the language without which a deep historical education is impossible. He who undertakes Latin has the possibility of stepping out of the narrow circle of the present. He has access to a world that lies entirely beyond the interests and passions of the day, a world that has become entirely historical. Thus he can observe the present as from outside; in old Rome he moves in a world which had its own centre, and knew nothing of the world that stirs about Berlin and Paris, London and Moscow, and which fights about popedom and Lutherdom, revolution and reaction, and whatever other names are given to the antitheses of the present time. So he gains an objective point of view for these things, to use Spinoza's expression *sub quadam æternitatis specie*. Just as Rome is the Eternal City, so is Latin also the language of eternity. Indeed, a language of an astonishing range: Cæsar wrote in it his reminiscences and Augustine his confessions; Catullus sang in it his songs and the mediæval church its awe-inspiring hymns; Lucretius composed in it his poem 'On the Nature of Things' and Spinoza his ethics; and twice did Rome write in it laws for the world."[1]

Professor Ziegler, of the University of Strasburg, is of the same opinion. In a public address in 1894 he spoke thus plainly to the representatives of the *Gymnasien*: "We do not at all deny the educational value of Greek. We do not for a moment dispute the splendour and lustre of the Greek spiritual life, its ideal worth and its great educational value. But when we lead our youth to Lessing and Schiller and Goethe, and, instead of Sophocles, to Shakespeare, we also mean thereby to open to them the highest spheres of the spiritual life of man; and when we let them look deeper than you do into the secrets of nature, an ideal element of a different kind reveals itself, which consists in the recognition of the subjection of man to Nat-

Professor Ziegler.

---

[1] *Über die gegenwärtige Lage des höheren Schulwesens*, Berlin, 1893.

ure's Law, and which can be made by us a great educational power. But we want to meet you on the same ground in the study of the mother-tongue and of history, as well as instruction in Latin for the sake of linguistic culture and for the recognition of the historical connections of our whole civilization and spiritual life. And when you seek to strengthen your Latin instruction because it no longer adequately serves its purpose, we stand with you shoulder to shoulder; for we are *Gymnasien* as well as you, *i.e.*, preparatory schools for the university."[1]

The leaders of the conservative wing are Professor Uhlig, of Heidelberg, and Dr. Jaeger, of Cologne. They uncompromisingly opposed all suggestions for reform in the Berlin Conference, and on principle never fail to urge the advantages of a complete classical training. It is not how many things a pupil knows, but what he knows, that counts; and not so much what he learns as how he learns it. Everything cannot be taught in the schools; a selection must be made, and it is well to choose what is of lasting worth. "In every word of Latin a bit of *Culturgeschichte* is hidden away, and that prevents the instruction from sinking into triviality; it makes it scientific even for nine-year-old boys. . . . The *Gymnasium* must be preserved in its integrity. The essence of the *Gymnasium* does not consist in that the pupil reads any particular Greek or Latin author in his fourteenth, or even in his sixteenth year, and also not altogether in that he is introduced to antiquity; but it consists in this alone, that by a gradual accustoming to exact knowledge, however it is grasped, the pupil is educated to knowledge in its highest sense."[2]

Opposition Leaders.

Their Arguments.

The same idea came to expression over and over again in the conference. The *Realgymnasium* was charged with being

---

[1] *Notwendigkeit und Berechtigung des Realgymnasiums*, Stuttgart, 1894.

[2] Jaeger in *Verhandlungen über Fragen des höheren Unterrichts*, Berlin, 1891.

a school with no "centre;" with a curriculum made up of a little of everything that seemed to cater to popular needs. "Above all," said one speaker, "it matters not so much what is taught as how it is taught. 'Man lives not, nor shall live, by the bread alone that the school crumbles for him.' He lives also from that which other forces reach out to him—the force of the family, that of the church and that of the entire life of the people. These forces must also share in the school; must take hold and co-operate with it. Not knowledge, but culture is the chief thing."[1]

It is evident that the opponents of the *Realgymnasium* put the emphasis on the *Real*, while its advocates are anxious to lay stress on the latter part of the compound. In other words, what is troubling the German educational world is the "Greek question." British and American school-masters know well what that is; but it is doubtful if any of us can imagine what it might have been if every gate to our leading public and professional occupations had been barred by six years of prescribed Greek. That is precisely the rub in Germany to-day. Six years of Greek and nine years of Latin are required of every applicant for the coveted posts in professional and civil service. The prevailing opinion is that these positions should be occupied only by men who have enjoyed a humanistic training. But what is humanistic training? and how should it be rewarded?

The Greek Question.

A calm view of the situation seems to me to present a twofold opposition to the "gymnasial monopoly." One force is represented by those who would make Greek optional; these support the *Realgymnasium*. The other element will hold tenaciously to Greek, but make the gymnasial course more popular, and thus overcome the opposition to the classical training; these are the advocates of the *Reform-Schulen*, as found, for example, in Frankfort-am-Main. It is a curious fact, too, that in all

The Gymnasial Monopoly.

---

[1] Dr. Uhlhorn. See Professor Thurber's excellent review of the proceedings of the Berlin Conference in the *Report of the Commissioner of Education*, Washington, 1889-1890.

the discussions very little is heard of the value of Greek. The struggle turns on the position of Latin. Indeed, it comes near being a contest between scholasticism and humanism. The conservatives will hear nothing of optional Greek. They will not concede to the *Realgymnasium* the gymnasial Latin course; they will not grant additional privileges to the schools which offer Latin, but no Greek. They lose no chance to take unfair advantage of their opponents; even the Berlin Conference, it is charged, was a "packed" convention, and destined for its initiation to oppose any proposition looking to equal rights for all humanistic schools.[1] In the eyes of the liberals, the representatives of the *Gymnasien* are dogs in the manger.

---

[1] "Dr. Hornemann, Dr. Albrecht and Dr. Holzmüller were all well-known opponents of the *Real*-institutions." All the most prominent representatives of the *Realgymnasien*, as, for example, Steinbart, Schwalbe, Schmeding, Krumme in Brunswick, and Dillman in Stuttgart and Prof. Preyer in Berlin, were not summoned. All members of the congressional committee on education who had spoken in favour of the equalization of the *Realgymnasien*, like Seyffardt, Schmelzer and Arendt, were also missing. On the other hand, the deputies Graf and Kropatschek, who had always opposed the wishes of the *Real*-school, were included. There was one mathematician—Holzmüller, he a declared opponent of the *Realgymnasien*; no naturalist, unless we count the physicians as such; no teacher in a technical high school; no artist; no architect; no engineer; no forester; no merchant; one manufacturer, and one mine-owner. The association of *Real*-schoolmen had good reason to complain; its most violent opponents were summoned, and its chief advocates were not. Much might be expected, however, in the way of such reforms as did not involve a serious change in school organization. Schenkendorf, Eitner and others might be expected to advocate warmly the cause of physical culture. Frick and Schiller would take ground for a pedagogical preparation of teachers. There was ground to hope that some measure would be taken against over-pressure and the causes of near-sightedness. There was lamentation that no one appeared to plead the cause of drawing and art in the *Gymnasium*. Some practical improvements in existing institutions might be expected from such a commission, but no radical changes. The friends of the new German school, however, expected little; and they would have been less disappointed than they were but for the energetic interference of the Emperor."—Professor Thurber, in *Report of Commissioner of Education*, 1889-1890, p. 349.

The truest friends of classical culture, in my opinion, are the liberals. Germany is no longer a part of the Holy Roman Empire. Since 1870 the German nation has stood on a modern basis. Her civilization is, indeed, rooted in classical culture, and she feels her kinship with the past more certainly than can England or America. It must needs be, therefore, that her education, under wise management, will long continue to be of the classical type. But the conservatives fail to recognise that social conditions are not what they were; that modern life is differentiated to a far greater degree than the life of the past, and that this differentiation demands variety in the training of youth. Moreover, they fail to appreciate the significance of the constantly increasing encroachments of the government. The mere fact that the government has been partial to the classical schools for seventy-five years does not necessarily guarantee the same attitude during the next seventy-five. The general will is long-suffering in Germany; but once let popular opinion become hostile to the *Gymnasien*, the cause of humanistic education will be set back a century, if not utterly ruined. And when classical education breaks down in Germany, classical culture will vanish from the earth —unless, perchance, a better than Germany arises.

German Education Must be Classical.

I have already spoken at length of one liberal movement, the *Realgymnasium;* the other—and the one which seems to me to promise better immediate results—is the *Reform*-school movement. It has already been referred to several times in this book as the Frankfort plan.

The Reform-School.

The idea of national unity which pervaded all classes of German society at the time of the revolution in 1848, and which later found expression in the new German Empire, has as its correlate in the educational world the idea of an *Einheitsschule*. This "Union School" was intended to absorb all the existing common and higher schools, and, by welding them together, to make one school suitable for all purposes, continuous from the lowest grades to the university. This ideal was heralded as the panacea for all educational ills by zealous pedagogues, who established unions, founded journals and made many speeches in its support. The movement was popular—altogether too popular to suit German bureaucracy. The emperor agreed with Bismarck in thinking that the "educated proletariat" were already too numerous; fewer university graduates, rather than more, was the chief desideratum. The *Einheitsschule* was snuffed out, therefore, by the Berlin Conference. It was too democratic for Prussia.[1]

The *Reform-Schule* is not the descendant of the *Einheitsschule*, although it bears some relationship to it. In 1865 Director Ostendorf, of Lippstadt, began the agitation for the earlier introduction of French, as a step toward Latin. The attempt was first made at Altona, in 1871, but complete arrangements were delayed until 1878. In that year Dr. Schlee was allowed to make the course in the first three years of the *Realschule* and *Realgymnasium* identical. During the first three years French was the only language taught at both schools; in the fourth year Latin was introduced in the *Realgymnasium*, and English in the *Realschule*. In 1892 the plan was adopted in the city schools of Frankfort-am-Main, and was extended to include a half of the *Gymnasium*, two *Realgymnasien*, the *Oberrealschule* and all the *Realschulen* of the city. The comprehensiveness of the trial in Frankfort has given it first place in public opinion; hence the popular term, "Frankfort system," has replaced the older and more strictly historical term, "Altona system."

Origin and Development.

The principle underlying the *Reform-Schule* is that of comparatively short and intensive courses. In Frankfort, six years of Latin and four of Greek replace the usual nine and six years' courses in these subjects. Hence the decision on which a boy's future rests is postponed from three to five years later than in the regular royal schools. This gives time for teachers to

Educational Principles.

---

[1] The important literature on the *Einheitsschule* is given in the *Educational Review*, I., 380.

test his ability, and a basis on which they can intelligently advise his parents. It retains for the strict classical course all those who are by nature fitted for it; it gives the *Real*-schools the material which can best profit from realistic instruction. The tendency is to relieve the higher schools of all kinds from the dead weight which each must carry when pupils are forced to decide upon their course before their powers have been tested.

Undoubtedly, school politics has much to do with the introduction of the reformed organization. The middle class in society looks upon the long classical training as an evil—a necessary evil, perhaps, but still something that should be swallowed as quickly as possible. A diminution of three years in the Greek and Latin courses, therefore, is likely to meet with popular favour. But a pedagogical principle is also involved which commends itself to many school-masters, the expediency of prefacing the study of a dead language with a good working knowledge of a living tongue. The three years exclusively devoted to French works wonders, as I have related elsewhere; and if present indications mean anything, the Frankfort experiment will demonstrate that as great proficiency in Latin can be attained in six years, if preceded by French, as in nine years without it. On this point I quote from a report, made in 1896 by the mayor of Kiel to the city magistrates, recommending the adoption of the Frankfort plan, which he had personally investigated both in Frankfort and Altona. His recommendation is significant of the attitude of many thoughtful men outside of the teaching profession; his opinion of the quality of work done accords with the estimate that has been given by all unprejudiced observers. He says:

Shorter and More Intensive Courses.

"In Altona, where at present we find the only opportunity of seeing a *Reform-Schule* carried through to the highest class, I was especially interested in the instruction in Latin. I followed it through classes from the *Untertertia* to the *Prima* of the *Realgymnasium*. In the *Untertertia*, where Latin is begun, the pupils showed an unmistakable interest in the new language; the grammatical questions of the teachers were answered with great readiness, and short sentences were translated with ease from German into Latin. In the *Obertertia* a connected passage unfamiliar to the class was translated into Latin with remarkable confidence. Latin authors are taken up only in the *Secunda*. Cæsar's *Gallic War* is read in *Untersecunda* exclusively, and in the *Obersecunda* simultaneously with Sallust and Ovid. I heard the pupils of the *Untersecunda* translate a chapter from Cæsar at sight, and it seemed to present to them no difficulties whatever; the Latin text was read aloud by the teacher only. In the *Obersecunda* a similar extempore translation of a particularly difficult chapter from the same author was given with equal success. In *Prima* Livy and Tacitus, of the historians, are read; of poets, Vergil and Horace. The director himself conducts this instruction. He had his pupils read for us two chapters from Livy, XXII. (chapter 39 after preparation, and chapter 56 extempore), and proved his skill in the highly developed ability of the pupils at once to fully understand the meaning of the Latin construction and to translate it into good German. The recitation of an ode of Horace (II., 10, in praise of the *aurea medocritas*) finally showed that the pupils fully enjoyed the exquisite music of these lines. The aim of Latin instruction has been attained by the *Primaner* of the Altona *Gymnasium* at least as successfully, if not more so, than in any *Realgymnasium* of the old sort. . . . In Frankfort-am-Main Latin has been so far introduced only in the *Untertertia*. The instruction had begun three-fourths of a year before; still, that short period was sufficient to show how easily the pupils who have had a three years' preparatory course in French can overtake the pupils trained in the old way. The city *Gymnasium* at Frankfort has the advantage of a first-class corps of teachers and a highly gifted director, whose fame to a great extent consists in his allowing the teachers to use their own methods. Naturally, the *Gymnasium* attracts superior material. Still, I would attribute a great part of the successful work I have seen there to reformed methods. I witnessed the Latin instruction in both parallel classes of *Untertertia,* one of which was taught by the director himself. The readiness with which the pupils answered the rapid questions of the teachers was really astonishing. Even when the director put his questions in Latin, the answers in short Latin sentences were promptly given—a readiness which I can only explain by the pupils' confidence obtained in the use of the related language, the French."

The following extracts from a circular letter addressed to the patrons of the higher schools in Hanover, advising them of the introduction of the *Reform*-school curricula in that city, shows the arguments which appeal to parents: "The *Reform-Schule* obviates the necessity of parents' choosing for their nine-year-old son what career he shall follow. This important decision is postponed until his natural inclinations and abilities can be more readily ascertained. Very often, too, a change in the circumstances of the parents makes it desirable that there should be more freedom in the choice of education for their children. . . . French is the foreign language first taught, and it is from the very beginning treated as a living tongue. . . . Such a beginning accords with the pedagogical requirement that the subject-matter of instruction should correspond to the mental development of the pupil, and that the easier should precede the more difficult. When Latin is begun in *Untertertia,* the pupil is mentally ready for it. . . . Since by the new program of instruction the Latin essay is abolished, the scope of Greek prose composition limited and the interpretation of the literature is made the chief object in classical instruction, it follows that . . . there can be no great difference between the gymnasial pupils and those from the new schools as shown in the final examination. For in the development of mental power the new school will not have less means, nor will it be behind the other schools in directing the mind toward the ideal. . . . Through the prominence given to the study of French, and

<small>Views of Parents.</small>

because of the increase in the number of hours given to German, the *Reform-Schule* becomes an institution resting on a modern basis, and meets the needs of the times for an education more independent of the ancient languages. 'The spirit of the school must be nourished by the life surrounding us, with whose changing tides the principles of education vary; but for the success of all instruction faith in the utility and necessity of the knowledge acquired is of the greatest significance.' The new school believes in connecting the present with the historic past."[1]

It is easy to detect in this announcement the mingling of politics, expediency and pedagogy. But what the people really want they will some time get, in Germany as elsewhere. It matters not that the old party predict the failure of the new school on *a priori* grounds; the trial is being made with the consent of the government. In one form or another, it is being tried in Altona, Frankfort, Güstrow, Magdeburg, Essen, Iserlohn, Hildesheim, Harburg, Osnabrück, Lippstadt, Bremen, Breslau, Hanover, Schöneburg, Charlottenburg, in the French *Gymnasium* of Berlin and in the *Realgymnasium* of Carlsruhe. If the experiment is a failure, it will be because the task is an impossible one. The first real test will come in 1901, when the first graduates from the Frankfort schools will have a chance to demonstrate their knowledge of Greek and Latin side by side with those who complete the regular course.

Spread of the Reform-School.

It is dangerous to venture a prediction as to the final outcome of the present struggle; but to a person with a democratic turn of mind, one of two possible solutions seems inevitable: either Greek will be made optional, or the gymnasial monopoly will be broken down. If additional privileges are given to the *Real*-schools, Greek may be preserved in its integrity for many years to come; if six years of Greek must continue to bar the way to

The Outlook.

---

[1] *Jahresbericht des städtischen Leibniz-Realgymnasium zu Hannover*, 1895.

professional life, then Greek will eventually become what it was before 1810—a dead weight in the curriculum. An American or an Englishman, with his national predilection for freedom, finds it almost inconceivable that the Frankfort plan should fail; it is essentially that which we ourselves are rapidly coming to believe in. The first three years, in which the course is common to all, are our "grammar-school" grades; the upper six classes differentiate along the "classical," the "Latin-scientific" and the "scientific" lines. But the German mind is not democratic; it is monarchical, and accepts class distinctions. The old gymnasial course is the aristocratic course, and the privileged classes are determined to keep it so. The *Gymnasium*—or, rather, its supporters—is largely at fault for the growth of social democracy; but not, as the emperor thought, because it is doing so much, but because of what it is not doing. It will not grant that freedom of choice, variety in education and equal opportunity for all, which modern life demands. I have more faith in modern ideals—even in Germany—than I have in German bureaucracy. The bane of the German schools is the system of privileges. When that is abolished, humanism and classical education of the right sort will flourish as never before.

GENERAL REFERENCES:—*Verhandlungen über Fragen des höheren Unterrichts*, Berlin, 1891; Paulsen, *Geschichte des gelehrten Unterrichts* (new edition, last chapter)—*Das Realgymnasium und die humanistische Bildung*, Berlin, 1889; *Über die gegenwärtige Lage des höheren Schulwesens in Preussen*, Berlin, 1893; Ziegler, *Die Fragen der Schulreform*, Stuttgart; *Notwendigkeit und Berechtigung des Realgymnasiums*, Stuttgart, 1894; Bahnsch, *Der Streit um den griechischen Sprachunterricht*, Dantzic, 1893; Ohlert, *Die deutsche höhere Schule*, Hanover, 1896; Wernicke, *Kultur und Schule*, Osterwieck-Harz, 1896; Munch, *Neue pädagogische Beiträge*, Berlin, 1893; Frick, *Die Einheit der Schule—Möglichkeit der höheren Einheitsschulen* in *Päd. und didak. Abhandlungen*, Halle, 1893; Rein, *Am Ende der Schulreform?* Langensalza, 1893 (gives bibliography down to 1893); *Das humanistiche Gymnasium; Zeitschrift für das Gymnasialwesen; Central-Organ für die Interessen des Realschulwesens.*

CHAPTER XXI

MERITS AND DEFECTS OF GERMAN SECONDARY EDUCATION

THE two dominant forces in the later development of the German school system have proceeded from the State and the University. The one has made the system; the other, the school. Whatever merits or defects are discernible, therefore, in German secondary education, aside from those due to local influences, which might arise anywhere and under almost any circumstances, can be traced to one or both of these sources. In their tendencies these forces are radically different; it is an opposition of the centripetal and the centrifugal. The state is authoritative, autocratic, conservative; the university is free, liberal and democratic. The university embodies the highest ideals of the spiritual life and culture of the German people; the state represents their genius for self-control, organization and government. It is at once the strength and the weakness of the school system·that it is the resultant of several forces.

Two Dominant Forces.

1. The State.

2. The University.

In ascribing to the state so large a share of honor in the development of secondary education, I do not mean to discredit the influence of the Church. Until the present century the church was practically in supreme control. But since the Napoleonic Wars, the state has superseded the church in the management of school affairs. The spiritual leadership of the church is perhaps as strongly marked now as ever, but it is maintained

The Church also a Power.

indirectly through the good offices of the state and university. The university provides for the theological training of intending teachers; the state prescribes the course of religious instruction in the schools.

It is not too much to say that without the fostering care of the state the present efficiency of secondary education could hardly have been attained. The state compels parents to send their children to school, *Service of the State.* provides ample means for their instruction, cares for their physical well-being, directs their course of training and sets standards for promotion and graduation; it has perfected an organization which permits a high degree of central control, and yet allows considerable freedom in the local direction of school affairs; it insists on high scholarship, thorough professional training and pedagogical skill from all its teachers; it recognises a teaching profession, and agrees to support it even unto death. All this has been achieved by the German state in less than a century. It is an achievement of which any people might well be proud.

The compulsory school laws of Germany are most salutary in their effects. They are severe, but they work no hardships. It has come to be so much a matter of course for children to enter school at six and *Compulsory School Laws.* attend every day regularly until they are fourteen, that to the average child it seems as inevitable as his birthdays. This assures to every child who is physically and mentally able to receive it full eight years of schooling. Luther proclaimed it the right and duty of the state to compel parents to send their children regularly to school; Weimar enacted the first compulsory education law in 1619; Gotha followed in 1642; Brunswick in 1647; Würtemberg in 1649; and finally, in the reign of Frederick the Great, Prussia introduced the plan which has since become universal in Germany. The responsibility is placed where it belongs—on the parent. Complete census lists are kept by the local police; and twice a year, before the opening of each term, the school authorities are given the names of all children who should enter school. Those who are not enrolled in the higher schools, and who have not received permission to undertake private study, are required to show cause for not attending the common schools. Delinquents who do not satisfactorily excuse their shortcomings are reported to the police or truant officers, whose duty it is to make investigations and institute the necessary legal proceedings. In the higher schools the problem is much simpler than it is in the common schools, simple as it is anywhere. The necessity of earning the privileges connected with promotion in the higher schools effectually keeps all laggards in line; the assistance of the law is rarely necessary.

The care of the state is most beneficent in the regulations concerning hygienic conditions of school work. No school building can be constructed, whether by royal or municipal authority or by private or corporate bodies, which does not conform to officially accepted standards of sanitary science. In the selection of school sites; in the arrangements for heating, lighting, ventilation and plumbing of school-houses; in the precautions taken for the prevention of contagious and infectious diseases, the government has taken modern science into its service. If the construction, equipment and management of German schools are not the best in the world, it is not the fault of the system. The health of the children in school is everywhere looked upon as a matter of grave importance, which is greatly complicated by the natural inclinations of the German boy to lead a sedentary life. The German boy seems to have an aversion for outdoor games; it is partly the fault of the pressure he works under in the schools, partly because he is a German. Whatever else may be done or left undone, the state insists on its children having sound bodies, as the fundamental condition of developing sound minds. The emperor told the Berlin Conference that he was " looking for soldiers; . . . for a robust generation who can also serve the fatherland as intellectual leaders and public officials. . . . I consider it very urgent that the question of hygiene be taken up in the training schools for teachers, and that with it be joined the requirement that every teacher who is healthy must be able to go through the gymnastic exercises, and must do it every day."

A uniform course of study for all schools of a particular grade, and a common standard for promotion and graduation, can be made most serviceable in a national scheme of education. There is, however, one important proviso: The regulations must be wisely made and still more wisely administered. The German states have not always acted thus wisely, but no one can deny that much good has resulted from uniformity. Under the old *régime* there were some grand schools, some great school-masters, some excellent scholars; but the average level was deplorably low. For every really good school a score of wretchedly poor ones could be cited; and with each student who entered the university well prepared, fifty others were admitted who had no business there. The present plan insures a high standard for all: it protects the university from being deluged with immature students; it guards the pupil against incompetent leadership and partisan interference. *Uniform Curricula.*

The organization of the higher-school system, especially in Prussia, is worthy of general imitation. It provides for a central bureau, local school-boards and provincial *Schulcollegien* intermediate between the two. The provincial inspectors of schools supervise and unify the educational interests of their respective districts; the central authority is extended immediately over the provincial boards, and through them indirectly over all schools in the kingdom. The provincial inspectors, organized as they are in semi-independent bureaus, have practically entire control of all ordinary school affairs within their respective territories; and thus they can do much toward granting local option. On the other hand, matters in dispute can always be appealed to the ministry, or even to the crown in the last resort. Each school is given considerable freedom in working out its own policy, and each teacher has *Organization of the School System.*

a chance to stamp his own individuality on all his work.
Courses of study and the regulations for school management
are seldom minutely prescribed; they are transmitted in outline, with a statement of the minimum standards, leaving to
individual initiative entire freedom in practical application.
The many defeats suffered by the government in attempting
to codify the school laws are popular recognitions of local
rights. It is greatly to the credit of the Prussian schoolmasters that, while granting to the state general directive and
supervisory powers, they have tenaciously adhered to their
individual and professional rights in the exercise of these
duties. No ministry has, thus far, violated these rights with
impunity. I have stated elsewhere my reasons for thinking
that much credit is due to the provincial school-boards for
this good fortune. The partial isolation of the boards, their
personal contact with the schools on the one hand, and their
dependence on the ministry on the other hand, tend to make
them peace-makers. In theory, if not always in practice,
their mission is blessed.

The greatest service that the German states have done for
the cause of education is unquestionably the creation of a
teaching profession. That first step taken by
Humboldt in 1810, which provided for the examination and certification of teachers, was the
inauguration of a policy to which Prussia has converted the
civilized world. And as Prussia was the first to take her
teachers into the service of the state, so she has maintained
her leadership in making the profession worthy of public
honour and preferment. No other country has done so much
to dignify teaching, and to attract to it the best talent; none
has so persistently and intelligently pursued the policy of
making the teacher's position worthy of the man; nowhere
else can such teachers be found. Prussia has not only created
a teaching profession, but she has trained up a body of men
to occupy it who are without rivals the world over. This is
not mere flattery. It is a calm conviction growing out of
a long personal acquaintance with the men of whom I speak,

and a somewhat intimate knowledge of conditions in other European countries. The Prussian teacher has his faults, and I have taken occasion elsewhere to expose them; but when these are set off against his virtues, it seems almost trivial to criticise. The Prussian teacher, generically speaking, is a man of noble character, high ideals, generous impulses, broad and accurate scholarship and technical skill; he is a gentleman, patriot and educator.

The making of teachers is the joint work of state and university. The state has made the teaching profession attractive by protecting it at all points, and supporting it most generously; the university has trained the teacher, given him his ideals and sent him forth thoroughly equipped for his life's work. *Teachers' Equipment.* The character of his equipment may well be shown by a comparison. Public opinion in America is coming, somewhat tardily it must be confessed, to demand a college training of its high-school teachers. In Prussia the teacher in a higher school has a training equivalent to the American college course, plus two years of post-graduate study, plus other two years of professional training and trial teaching. Those who believe in the all-sufficiency of erudition, as well as those who believe in the necessity of professional training, must grant the superiority of the German teacher in point of preparation. And even those very respectable people who profess to believe that teachers, like poets, are born, not made, must confess that Germany has, at least, a fair chance for distinction if the laws of heredity operate elsewhere than in their own families.

It should be remembered that Germany is in Europe, and that Europe stands armed for war. "The first and paramount duty of our European States is to guard against aggression from without; and this duty, *German Militarism.* which is forced upon them by the enmity and rivalry of their neighbours, frequently overshadows the higher aims of civilization and culture."[1] This is a condition

---

[1] Professor Ziegler, of the University of Strasburg, in *Forum*, XXV., 4, p. 457.

which has to be reckoned with in estimating the merits and defects of the German school system. War demands men; they should be both intelligent and loyal. The schools are institutions supported by the state in the interests of the state. What more likely than that the government should seek to convert the schools into training camps for the army?

It should also be remembered that the government is monarchical; the crown is established by divine right—so, at least, runs a recent dictum from the throne. *German Absolutism.* What more likely than that patriotism should be officially interpreted as loyalty to the crown and established institutions?

The chief defects in the German school system may be traced to these sources. For upward of a century the management of the schools has steadily been becoming more bureaucratic. *Sources of Chief Defects.* The demands of militarism have begotten the privilege of one-year volunteer army service; the *Abschlussprüfung* is the latest encroachment on the domain of public secondary education for military purposes. Indeed, the whole system of privileges, which I have characterized as the bane of German secondary schools, is an evidence of bureaucratic control. Year by year new regulations are made which tighten the grip of the central authority, and leave correspondingly less freedom for local option. The trend is toward officialism and formalism. It weighs on the teachers in their class-rooms, in so far as they are required to observe ends which are foreign to true pedagogical ideals; it distracts the pupil's attention from his study for its own sake, and centres it on rewards to be attained out of school; it lowers the standards of scholarship, by forcing schools to carry too heavy a load of superannuated teachers and unambitious scholars. In a word, the tendency is to place altogether too little reliance on individual liberty and personal ambition.

The German university is the nursery of German idealism and individual liberty. From the days of Luther until the present time it has been the mother of revolutions. The

Reformation centred about Wittenberg, and Halle was founded two centuries ago on the principle of *Lernfreiheit*. Freedom of research, freedom in teaching, is the cornerstone of university education in German. And yet the universities are state institutions and stand under royal patronage. It is a curious and instructive fact that such a democratic institution as the German university, pledged as it is to absolute freedom and independence in all its work, can exist in a German state. They are essentially in opposition to each other at every point. Time and again this opposition has resulted in open hostilities, and many learned professors have found it prudent to accept voluntary exile. Twice within five years the attempt has been made to enact imperial laws restraining the freedom of speech in university circles. In the session of 1894–1895 the government introduced a bill in the *Reichstag* which provided a penalty of imprisonment for not longer than two years or a fine of not more than six hundred marks, in case of derogatory expressions publicly directed against religion, monarchy, marriage, family or property.[1] The aim of the government was to combat the rising social democracy, and in order to do that the law had to be all-embracing. Freiherr von Stumm, one of the stanchest supporters of the government, expressly stated that the intention was to put down by "the iron hand" all opposition to authority wherever found. "Though I have said some hard things against the employer of labour, yet I am willing to acknowledge a shadow of excuse for him, *viz.*, the coquetting of certain learned circles with social democracy—or, what is the same thing, with revolution, as was the case shortly before the French Revolution. Gentlemen, right here in Berlin has been developed a complete university socialism. Every professor, especially in political economy, who does not fall in with socialistic views

---

[1] " . . . *welcher in einer der öffentlichen Frieden gefahrdenden Weise die Religion, die Monarchie, die Ehe, die Familie, oder das Eigenthum durch beschimpfende Aeusserungen öffentlich angreift.*"

is boycotted, as was the case in France; he is persecuted, pronounced unscientific and is never advanced. Under such influences our future officials are being trained! Things have come to such a pass that the attempt is being made to bring the social democratic students into closer association with the others. . . . A certain part of the Evangelical Church is directly aiding the democrats. The civil service is becoming tainted. It is high time that something be done. This bill is the first step toward a cure. Its great advantage is that it reaches not only the law-breakers, but those who directly or indirectly incite to crime. There can be no exceptions; there can be no law of exceptions."

Another speaker, a representative of the powerful Catholic "Centre," which is stronger since the election of 1898 than ever, disclosed the attitude of the clerical party toward the freedom of the university. "This protection of the German professor is, in my opinion, exceedingly imprudent and wrong. Imprudent—for how can we prevent the people from saying and doing precisely what these professors are saying in their lecture-rooms, repeating in popular forms and writing in their books? It is sheer nonsense to permit in the upper strata what is forbidden in the lower. And more—it is wrong. The great danger comes not from below, but from above."[1]

The astonishment produced by this debate among progressive university men can well be imagined. It had an inquisitional sound that harmonized ill with nineteenth century ideals. So great indignation was aroused, and so fierce opposition, that the government abandoned the bill. The principle, however, that was involved has not been abandoned. Very recently another attempt has been made to stifle free speech in the universities of Prussia; and it has partially succeeded, in that men of known progressive views have been put aside for those who will yield to authority. But no one really believes that the

Freedom in Teaching.

---

[1] See my paper on *The University Crisis in Germany*, *Educational Review*, April, 1895.

universities will give up their independence. When the university falls, the throne will go with it. The one expresses the traditional love for personal liberty; the other embodies the national sense of law, order and authority. These two irreconcilable facts are characteristic of the German mind.

In one important respect the universities, contradicting themselves, join hands with the bureaucracy in perpetuating class distinctions. Theoretically, it is the pride of the German university that its doors are open to all, high or low, rich or poor, democrat or royalist; practically, however, the universities are to blame for the present chaotic condition of secondary education. The "gymnasial monopoly" has been fostered in season and out of season by the great majority of university men. Even the medical faculties, supposedly composed of scientific men, and imbued with the modern spirit, have repeatedly rejected all overtures from the *Realgymnasien*. It is impossible to give a satisfactory excuse for such action on the part of an institution which professedly stands for equality and freedom, and which prides itself on recognising no distinctions but those of worth. *Lernfreiheit* is the necessary corollary of freedom in teaching. A university bureaucracy that attempts to deprive students of the benefits of higher study for which they are fully prepared (as is granted by all who are best qualified to judge in the matter of admitting graduates of the *Realgymnasium* to the study of medicine) deserves itself to be subjected to some higher power.

University Defects.

Fosters Gymnasial Monopoly.

The truth is, that at bottom this question, like a good many others that interrogate educationists, is one of expediency. It involves class distinctions. The *Gymnasium* is the aristocratic school, and he who would be counted among the elect must tread its narrow path. The physician who has completed the gymnasial course is socially correct, and that covers a multitude of sins.

The boasted freedom of the universities is again contradicted in their attitude toward the education of women. No one expects the state to be liberal, but liberality is looked for in the highest educational centres of the country. But with what results? Determined, almost fanatical opposition to the extension of university privileges to women. I do not refer now to the general policy in girls' education, for in the main I am in hearty accord with it. Ninety per cent., or more, of German women are better off with the German training than they would be with the results of such a system as is in vogue in England and America. But for those women who desire to secure a broader education than is afforded by the girls' schools, and who can easily enough take up university work and profit from it, there can be no valid reason for keeping them out. It makes one lose faith in the ideals of university enlightenment. But that would be judging a German institution from an American stand-point. It is difficult for us to realize the strength of tradition in the German universities. Indeed, if it were not for this very potent force, the radical tendencies in university life would long ago have been their destruction. But whatever the reason, it remains a fact that, while women have gained access to university study, the doors are being opened very slowly and with unusual circumspection. In effect, the universities have joined with the bureaucracy in upholding the gymnasial monopoly, not only against the advocates of a modern humanistic training, but against the advocates of classical training as well, if it happens to have been taken by a woman.

Opposes Admission of Women.

The precedent has been established of admitting graduates of girls' *Gymnasien* to university study. Prussia and Baden grant them the privilege of taking the regular *Maturitätsprüfung*. In 1896 six girls from one school took the final examination set for the boys of a Berlin *Gymnasium*, and received high rank. Four or five other schools are graduating classes of six or eight. As yet the movement is in its infancy; the time will come when another *Schulfrage*, infinitely more troublesome

The Woman Question.

than any of its predecessors, will confront German educationists and demand a hearing.

The general policy of Germany in respect to woman's education is, in my opinion, eminently satisfactory. The masses of women receive a far better training than the American plan would give them under similar conditions. Life is hard, but it is not the fault of the schools. A university, or even a high school, training for every woman would not lessen the ills of militarism; no amount of higher education would nullify the aggression of foreign powers. "Let us not forget," says an ardent advocate of the higher education of women, "that the most pressing necessity is not found in universities for women, nor in the participation of women in the scientific labour of the times, nor in the opening of higher professions for women, but in the care and extensive education of the millions of girls—indeed, for the education of the mothers of the coming generation. The graceful structures of a higher education and the capstone of the edifice will remain insecure until they can rest upon the broad and secure foundation of a general education of the people. A state which neglects this and promotes higher education exclusively, works for show and neglects the general weal of the people, while it may satisfy the desires and claims of a noisy minority. Let us not forget that more important than the results of intellectual education, which are easily recognised and estimated, are the ethical effects of education which are taken into life and manifest themselves as determination of the will—a quality which is not easily estimated, because not visible to the eye."[1]

General Policy in Woman's Education.

The government seconds this view by publishing the address in the official organ of the education department. The poverty of the state is urged as the sole excuse for not granting financial aid to girls' schools. "As yet the lecture-rooms

---

[1] Dr. Waetzoldt, provincial inspector of schools, in *Centralblatt* for 1895, p. 741. The entire address is translated in the *Report of the Commissioner of Education*, 1894–1895.

of our universities are open only to very few women; as yet the professions which do not agree with the constitutions of women, and for which the state demands an academic preparation, are still closed to them, while in other civilized states the women have succeeded in securing admission. Is this fact explained simply by an unjust valuation of woman's work, by the undervaluation of woman's capacity, by the imperiousness of man and his anxiety lest woman's competition will interfere with his success? Let me say, first, that the state with us is not only a police institution to protect life and property, but its object is the promotion and equalization of all interests and culture. It is obliged to ask, with every newly arising claim, whether and how far it meets recognised needs. It is a sound and safe policy of the public-school authorities not to interfere with things that are only beginning and developing, but to give time and space for healthy growth; not to feed and nurse young forms artificially, but to wait patiently and see whether they have a vigorous life and find good soil among the people. To remodel anything ancient that has long stood the test, in order to introduce something new that has not yet proved its value, is always doubtful. Now, with us, as it is well understood, the condition for academic or university study is the graduation diploma, which is granted alone by classical high schools, called *Gymnasien*, for young ladies. Shall the state establish them? Prussia is not wealthy enough for that, and should we really lead our girls upon an educational path which is exclusively designed and planned for boys intending to devote themselves to the higher professions and offices of the state? Shall we for the girls fix a course of study with the authority of the state, a course which many and many of us think badly needs reform? When, as in Berlin, Leipsic and Carlsruhe, private *Gymnasien* for girls were established in order to give them an education such as the boys' schools offer, the state authorities certainly did not interfere or prohibit them. The first Prussian female graduate has passed her examination well. That which is

Financial Considerations.

wanting in the realm of higher education of women here in Germany is not so much favours from the state as from great philanthropists, such as Rockefeller and Holloway, and wealthy corporations, such as the Brewers' Guild in London, who gave large donations for the higher education of women. Such means flow very scantily in Germany, as the interest for our aspirations is not very extended as yet among the people. More pressing needs claim the strength and means of the state."[1]

Such excuses, however, have little influence on the minds of the women of Germany who demand equal rights for their sex. They insist that not only should the universities be opened to women who are prepared to enter, but also that they should be admitted to the professions of teaching and medicine. Forty-five per cent. of the women of the upper classes have no chance to marry, for the simple reason that the men who are their equals hesitate to incur the expense. They will not be dependent; they must have equal rights with men. They ask no favours from the state, except the opportunity to demonstrate their ability to undertake university study and professional employment. *Equal Rights for Women.*

Such arguments are convincing, and are bound in time to win their way. At present, however, the government is engaged in checking the growth of *Gymnasien* for girls. In April, 1898, a petition from Breslau for permission to establish such a school was curtly refused by the Prussian ministry. When the government was interpellated in the Diet by the member from Breslau, the minister of public instruction gave, as his chief reason for denying the petition, the answer that the proper function of women was to be intelligent helpmates to men, that equal rights involved the sharing of burdens as well as privileges, and that until women were ready to enter the army and serve in the Reserve and *Landwehr* the govern- *Official Interference.*

---

[1] *Centralblatt*, 1895, p. 469–470.

ment could not consistently advocate unrestricted competition of the sexes. Later in the summer, if press accounts are reliable, the national association of physicians and surgeons, in a meeting at Wiesbaden, resolved that with their permission no woman should study medicine. The reasons alleged for this action were that woman is by nature unfit for scientific work; her mental powers are acquisitive rather than inventive; memory and imagination, rather than observation and reason, are the faculties on which she naturally relies. In short, they are in accord with the emperor's dictum that woman's province is *Küche, Kinder und Kirche*—cooking, children and church.

It will be seen that the "woman question" will soon supersede the "Greek question." There would be no serious consequences from the discussion of either were it not that class and sex prejudices are involved.

Results of Class Distinctions.

As it is, neither problem can be satisfactorily solved until society is reorganized on a basis of equality of opportunity and freedom of choice for all. The gravest defect in the German school system is the organization which fosters distinctions of class and sex. The common schools are for the common people; the *Real*-schools are for the middle classes; the classical schools are for the aristocracy; and in secondary education the sexes are kept apart. The lines of cleavage are distinctly marked, and in practice generally observed. Were conditions otherwise, there would be no quibbling over an *Einheitsschule*. If class prejudice did not exist, one high school could easily perform all the functions of secondary education by the simple arrangement of elective subjects. But class distinctions do obtain in German society, and are not likely soon to be obliterated. Hence differentiation in school organization is inevitable. It may be theoretically deplorable, but it is a practical necessity in German society.

No such axiom as that the school exists for the pupil is recognised in German educational philosophy. The German school exists primarily for the state. The pupil is a citizen in training. That he should be an obedient, loyal, submissive subject is a self-evident truth. Respect for authority is the one essential prerequisite to German citizenship. In the selection of a school and the course of study, in seeking admission to the university and the vocations of civil life, the individual has little freedom of choice. *Individualism vs. Nationalism.* The rigorous discipline of the schools, which brooks no opposition and tolerates no parental interference; the methods of instruction, which leave nothing to chance and individual initiative; the system of privileges, which dominates teachers and pupils alike—all tend to the development of character which feels no restriction of personal liberty in the constant surveillance of the police and the rule of a military despotism. The social institutions, the school system and the methods of instruction in Germany are calculated to beget dependence on authority, rather than independence and freedom of action. Individualism in education yields to paternalism in government. German society is founded on the principle that the greatest good of each is included in the greatest good of all, rather than on the principle that the greatest good of all is subserved by the highest individual development of each.

It is to the credit of the German school system that it is thoroughly German; that it promotes German culture and German civilization; that it strives to realize German ideals in the social, industrial and political life of the German people. *German Schools for German People.* The foreigner may not admire German ideals, he may even despise German culture and German civilization; but if he is an observant school-master, he cannot fail to admire the practical workings of the German schools. The sole test that can reasonably be applied is adaptation of means to ends; and, judged by this standard, it must be acknowledged that the German schools are master-pieces of intelligent design. To criticise them for not serving other ends is like criticising a delicately adjusted watch for not recording changes in temperature. So long as schools remain social institutions designed to realize in the young the ideals of the social whole, so long must they be regarded entirely apart from national and racial prejudices. It follows that, just in proportion as German schools are German are they un-American, and incapable of satisfying American needs. It is not to be expected, therefore, that the German system or German methods can be directly applicable to American schools. Only in so far as German education is concerned with the development of man as man, apart from his relations to any particular society or special end, can it be immediately serviceable. To be sure, much can be learned from a comparative study of national school systems; but whatever information is gained from foreign sources must be transformed and readjusted to home conditions. What is eminently fitting in one place may be ill adapted to another environment. Each nation must work out its own educational salvation in fear and trembling. It is a work that should be free from servile imitation, but ever ready to profit from the experience of others. The experience of Germany can teach us much, if we will but learn to consider it aright. Indeed, the future of American civilization and the rich blessings of republican institutions will be assured if we can interest the best talent of the country in education, and evolve a school system which shall be as nicely adjusted to our national requirements as the German system is to German needs.

The Point of View.

APPENDICES

A. THE PRIVILEGED HIGHER SCHOOLS OF GERMANY IN 1897.
B. ATTENDANCE IN HIGHER SCHOOLS OF PRUSSIA.
C. SYSTEM OF PRIVILEGES.
D. SALARY SCHEDULES.
E. PENSIONS OF TEACHERS IN HIGHER SCHOOLS OF GERMANY.
F. EXTRACTS FROM THE PENSION LAWS OF PRUSSIA.
G. LEADING EDUCATIONAL JOURNALS OF GERMANY.

APPENDIX A

THE PRIVILEGED HIGHER SCHOOLS OF GERMANY IN 1897

Statistisches Jahrbuch der Höheren Schulen, 1897–1898.

	Gymnasien.	*Progymnas.*	*Realgymn.*	*Realprogymn.*	*Oberrealschul.*	*Realschul.*	*Höhere Bürgerschulen.*	*Schullehrer-Seminarien.*	Other Schools. Public.	Other Schools. Private.
1. Prussia	277	53	85	67	26	60		114	16	19
2. Bavaria	40	26	5			46		12	6	6
3. Saxony	17		10			23		18	5	6
4. Würtemberg	16	4	3	4	6	9		6		2
5. Baden	14	2	2	5	3	14		4		2
6. Hesse	9	2	3			16	1	3	1	2
7. Mecklenburg-Schwerin	7		6	3		2	1	1		
8. Mecklenburg-Strelitz	3			1		1				
9. Saxe-Weimar	3		2			2		2		2
10. Oldenburg	5			1	1	1			1	
11. Brunswick	6		1	1	1	1		1		1
12. Saxe-Meiningen	2		2			2		1		1
13. Saxe-Altenburg	2		1					1		1
14. Saxe-Coburg-Gotha	2	1	1	2		1		2		
15. Anhalt	4		2	1		1		1		1
16. Schwarzburg-Sondershausen	2					2		1	1	
17. Schwarzburg-Rudolstadt	1			2						1
18. Waldeck	1			1						1
19. Reuss, a. L.	1			1				1		
20. Reuss, j. L.	2		1					1		1
21. Schaumburg-Lippe	1			1						
22. Lippe-Detmold	2			1				1		
23. Lübeck	1		1			1		1		1
24. Bremen	2		2	1		2		1		1
25. Hamburg	2		1	1		6		1		6
26. Alsace-Lorraine	17	4			3	8		6	1	
Total in 1897	439	92	128	93	40	198	2	181	32	56
Total in 1896	436	92	129	98	35	183	2	170	33	56
Changes	+3	±0	−1	−5	+5	+15	±0	+11	−1	±0

$$1145 + 28 = 1173$$
Total number $= 1173 + 88 = 1261.$

$$89 − 1 = 88$$

APPENDIX B

ATTENDANCE IN HIGHER SCHOOLS OF PRUSSIA

Report of the Commissioner of Education, Washington, 1896–1897.

YEAR.	Gymnasien.		Progymnasien.		Realgymnasien.		Realprogymnasien.		Oberrealschulen.		Realschulen.		TOTAL.	
	Schools.	Students.	Schools.	Students.	Schools.	Students.	Schools.	Students.	Schools.	Students.	Schools.	Students.	Schools.	Students.
1830–31	110	(?)	23	(?)	0	0	0	0	0	0	0	0	133	0
1837–38	113	(?)	34	(?)	0	0	0	0	0	0	0	0	147	0
1846–47	116	(?)	28	(?)	0	0	0	0	0	0	0	0	144	0
1853–54	121	33,036	28	2,796	0	0	0	0	0	0	0	0	149	0
1859–60	135	37,746	31	2,614	30	12,317	11	1,581	0	0	27	7,706	234	54,508
1863–64	145	43,809	26	2,602	64	22,692	(?)	(?)	0	0	(?)	(?)	288	(?)
1867–68	(?)	(?)	(?)	(?)	(?)	(?)	65	10,130	0	0	14	4,125	(?)	(?)
1868–69	198	57,171	29	3,294	(?)	(?)	(?)	(?)	0	0	(?)	(?)	(?)	(?)
1873–74	218	63,207	29	3,617	80	31,080	(?)	(?)	0	0	17	6,896	(?)	(?)
1875–76	(?)	(?)		(?)	(?)	(?)	92	17,086	0	0	(?)	(?)	(?)	(?)
1877–79	245	71,324	32	4,141	(?)	30,822	101	16,369	0	1,833	19	7,249	498	134,637
1880–81	250	73,922	35	4,372	85	30,457	103	16,511	8	4,296	19	7,083	505	136,780
1881–82	251	74,085	35	4,296	86	30,406	88	10,498	12	4,402	37	11,891	513	138,441
1882–83	253	76,356	36	4,556	90	30,406	88	10,520	12	4,419	35	11,908	514	138,804
1883–84	258	77,043	36	4,648	90	30,366	88	10,479	12	5,817	37	12,228	522	139,741
1884–85	257	77,979	37	4,337	89	29,901	86	10,450	14	5,380	30	13,466	525	140,615
1885–86	259	77,718	39	4,958	89	28,623	87	10,696	13	5,671	39	14,034	530	142,879
1886–87	263	78,498	40	5,251	89	28,925	87	10,695	12	5,305	44	15,892	535	145,062
1887–88	264	78,683	39	4,681	88	29,442	80	11,060	11	5,449	48	17,475	537	145,839
1888–89	266	77,629	38	4,545	87	29,815	87	10,026	11	5,301	50	18,696	540	145,875
1889–90	267	76,537	41	4,442	86	30,345	84	10,464	10	4,865	56	21,366	551	147,197
1890–91	270	75,599	45	5,444	86	29,706	85	10,217	9	4,737	55	23,081	554	146,970
1891–92	271	74,907	44	4,906	89	29,252	85	10,085	12	6,419	55	23,037	555	147,639
1892–93	272	74,951	44	4,614	88	28,962	84	9,677	20	9,686	64	22,116	568	148,563
1893–94	274	75,266	44	4,286	87	28,402	73	8,667					568	
1894–95	274	75,233	44	4,634	86	28,420	74	7,930	24	12,111	67	22,330	569	150,548

426

APPENDIX C

SYSTEM OF PRIVILEGES

The following table shows the rights and privileges attached to the completion of the various grades of the higher schools of Germany (arranged from Rein's Encyclopædia, the *Centralblatt* and *Statistisches Jahrbuch der höheren Schulen*).

A. CIVIL SERVICE.

	Gymnasium.	Realgymnasium.	Oberrealschule.
1. Study of Theology and Admission to State Examination...	IA.	....	....
2. Study of Law and Political Science and Admission to State Examination..................................	IA.[1]	....	....
3. Study of Medicine and Admission to State Examination...	IA.	....	....
4(a). Study of Ancient Philology and History; Teachers' Certificate..	IA.	....	....
4(b). Study of Modern Languages; Teachers' Certificate... ...	IA.	IA.	... ...
4(c). Study of Mathematics and Natural Sciences; Teachers' Certificate..	IA.	IA.	IA.
5. Study of Architecture and Mechanical Engineering; State Examination..................................	IA.[2]	IA.	IA.
6. Study of Forestry; State Examination................	IA.[3]	IA.[3]	IA.[3]
7. Study of Mining Engineering; State Examination.......	IA.	IA.	IA.
8. Admission to Schools of Agriculture.................	IIB.	IIB.	IIB.
9. Admission to Academies of Art......................	IIB.	IIB.	IIB.
10. Admission to Higher Postal and Telegraph Service.......	IA.	IA.	IA.
11. Admission to Customs Service.......................	IB.	IB.	IB.
12. State Examination for Surveying.....................	IIA.	IIA.	IIA.
13. Telegraph Inspectorship at State Railways.............	IIA.	IIA.	IIA.
14. Study of Dentistry and Admission to State Examination...	IIA.	IIA.	....
15. Study of Veterinary Medicine; State Examination.	IIA.	IIA.	....
16. Study of Pharmacy; State Examination for Druggists....	IIB.	IIB.	....
17. Admission to Imperial Bank Service.................	IIB.	IIB.	IIB.
18. Subaltern Service, in Dept. of Justice, in Provincial Service and State Railway Service......................	IIB.	IIB.	IIB.
19. Admission to Horticultural Institute at Potsdam..........	IIB.	IIB.	IIB.[4]

[1] Würtemberg and Bavaria admit graduates of *Realgymnasien* to the study of Finance and the State Service.
[2] Graduates of *Gymnasien* in Würtemberg must show a knowledge of English.
[3] "Good" in mathematics is required of all candidates.
[4] And Latin enough to enter IIIA.

B. MILITARY SERVICE.

	Gymnasium.	Realgymnasium.	Oberrealschule.
20. Exemption from Ensign's Examination	IA.	IA.	....
21. Exemption from Midshipman's Examination	IA.¹	IA.¹	....
22. Admission to Ensign's Examination	IIA.	IIA.	....
23. Admission to Midshipman's Examination	IIA.	IIA.	....
24. Study of Farriery; Admission to State Examination	IIA.	IIA.	....
25. Paymastership in Army and Subaltern Supervisory Service	IIA.	IIA.	....
26. Admission to Marine Superintendency	IB.²	IB.²	....
27. Superintending Secretaryship at Imperial Wharves	IB.³	IB.³	....
28. Study of Ship-Building and Engineering; State Exam.	IA.	IA.	IA.
29. Exemption from One Year of Service in Army	IIB.	IIB.	IIB.
30. Paymastership in Navy	IIIA.	IIIA.	....

[1] "Good" in English is required of all candidates.
[2] Candidates for Paymasterships need only pass IIA.
[3] English is required.

APPENDIX D

SALARY SCHEDULES — ARRANGED AND CONDENSED FROM OFFICIAL SOURCES

I. SALARIES OF TEACHERS IN THE HIGHER SCHOOLS OF PRUSSIA.

A. Schools Supported by the State and Schools under State Control.

According to the scale of salaries (based on length of service) instituted by the law of May 4, 1892, and modified April 1, 1897, the teachers are divided into six classes:

1. Principals of complete (nine years' course) schools.
    a. In Berlin:
Initial salary, 6,000 marks; after 3 years, 6,400; after 6 years, 6,800; after 9 years, 7,200.
    b. In cities of more than 50,000 inhabitants:
Initial salary, 5,100 marks; after 3 years, 5,600; after 6 years, 6,000; after 9 years, 6,400; after 12 years, 6,800; after 15 years, 7,200.
    c. In all other places:
Initial salary, 4,800 marks; after 3 years, 5,300; after 6 years, 5,700; after 9 years, 6,100; after 12 years, 6,500; after 15 years, 6,900.
2. Principals of incomplete (six years' course) schools.
    a. In Berlin and cities of more than 50,000 inhabitants:
Initial salary, 5,100 marks; after 3 years, 5,400; after 6 years, 5,700; after 9 years, 6,000.

b. In all other places :

Initial salary, 4,500 marks; after 3 years, 4,800; after 6 years, 5,100; after 9 years, 5,400; after 12 years, 5,700; after 15 years, 6,000.

If no dwelling is provided, principals under Classes 1 and 2 also receive an allowance for house rent from 600 to 1,500 marks, according to the size of the city.

3. Permanently appointed regular teachers (*definitiv angestellte wissenschaftliche Lehrer*) :

Initial salary, 2,700 marks; after 3 years, 3,000 ; after 6 years, 3,300 ; after 9 years, 3,600 ; after 12 years, 3,900 ; after 15 years, 4,200; after 18 years, 4,500 ; after 21 years, 4,800 ; after 24 years, 5,100.

One-half of the total number of those teachers employed in the complete schools, as well as one-fourth of those employed in the incomplete schools, receive the additional sum (*Zulage*) of 900 marks a year. This allowance is granted, whenever a vacancy occurs, for excellence in scholarship and skill in teaching.

4. Permanently appointed drawing teachers (*definitiv angestellte Zeichenlehrer*), also teachers of technical and elementary subjects and teachers in preparatory schools (*Vorschulen*) of Berlin :

Initial salary, 1,800 marks ; after 3 years, 2,000 ; after 6 years, 2,200; after 9 years, 2,400 ; after 12 years, 2,600 ; after 15 years, 2,800 ; after 18 years, 3,000 ; after 21 years, 3,200 ; after 24 years, 3,400 ; after 27 years, 3,600.

5. Teachers of technical and elementary subjects and teachers in preparatory schools outside of Berlin :

Initial salary, 1,500 marks; after 3 years, 1,700; after 6 years, 1,900 ; after 9 years, 2,100 ; after 12 years, 2,250 ; after 15 years, 2,400 ; after 18 years, 2,550 ; after 21 years, 2,700 ; after 24 years, 2,850 ; after 27 years, 3,000.

6. Regular assistant teachers (*wissenschaftliche Hilfslehrer*) :

Initial salary, 1,700 marks ; after 2 years, 1,900 ; after 3 years, 2,100.

Besides their salaries, teachers of Classes 3 and 4 receive an allowance for house rent, according to the size of the city in which the school is located, varying from Berlin to cities of the fifth-class, as follows:

	(Berlin)	I.	II.	III.	IV.	V.
Class 3	900	660	540	480	420	360
Class 4	540	432	360	300	216	160

The time of service is counted:

(1) For principals, from the time of appointment as principal of a higher school;

(2) For regular teachers, from the time of permanent appointment, from which time they are also entitled to a pension;

(3) For drawing teachers; and

(4) For teachers of technical and elementary subjects and teachers in preparatory schools, from the day of permanent appointment in public service (service in excess of four years before permanent appointment may also be counted);

(5) For regular assistant teachers, from the day of appointment to a position of not less than 1,500 marks a year.

Time spent in higher-school service abroad, also time spent either at home or abroad as instructor at a university, as supervisor of schools, or in church service, may be taken into account by the Minister of Public Instruction either in whole or in part. Similarly, a principal may have so much of his previous service as regular teacher counted in his time of service as is necessary to make his salary equal the salary he would have received if he had continued to serve as regular teacher (*wissenschaftlicher Lehrer*).

B. *Higher Schools which Receive Subsidies from the State.*

The regulations concerning salaries, their increase and house-rent allowances, enumerated under A, apply also to these schools, with the following limitations:

(1) The acceptance of the above-mentioned time of foreign service, church service, university service and school supervision depends on a mutual agreement between the teacher and the financial supporters of the school.

(2) The Minister of Public Instruction can, on application by the financial supporters of a school, exempt principals and fully occupied (*vollbeschaeftigte*) drawing teachers from the system of increase of salaries by length of service, whenever the new law would interfere with the steady promotion of the teachers toward the highest salary.

(3) The financial supporters of a school can exempt "regular" teachers from the operation of the new law, under special regulations by the Minister for the particular school or for a number of schools. In that case the average salary of regular teachers in state schools ($2100 + 4500 = 6600$; $6600 \div 2 = 3300$) is taken as many times as there are positions, and the sum is divided among the teachers in amounts from 2,100 to 4,500 marks, according to the ratios provided by the normal schedule for state schools. (This calculation is made on the old schedule—before April, 1897.)

(4) The income of fully employed teachers of technical and elementary subjects, and of teachers in "preparatory" schools not coming under *A, 4,* is to be fixed within the limits given under *A, 5;* so that their income shall not fall lower than that of the common school teachers (*Volksschullehrer*) in the given locality. Besides, these teachers are to receive an additional allowance of not less than 150 marks a year.

C. Higher Schools not under State Control and Receiving no Support from the State (Nicht-staatliche höhere Schulen).

According to the law of July 2, 1892, the regulations of the *Normal Etat* of May 4, 1892, also apply to these schools, with the following limitations:

The municipality may resolve that promotions of regular teachers in salary in the municipal schools shall be made according to special regulations provided for one particular city or for a number of cities. In that case the method of procedure is the same as that mentioned under *B, 3.* For principals and fully employed drawing teachers the same exceptions can be made by the Minister of Public Instruction.

The average salaries on which calculations are made are accordingly:
1. For principals of complete (nine years' course) schools:
   a. In Berlin, 6,000 marks (unalterable, by the law of 1892);
   b. In cities of more than 50,000 inhabitants, 5,550 marks;
   c. In all other places, 5,250 marks.
2. Principals of incomplete (six years' course) schools:
   a. In Berlin and cities of more than 50,000 inhabitants, 5,250 marks;
   b. In all other places, 4,950 marks.
3. Permanently employed regular teachers, 3,300 marks; in addition to which the extra allowance of 900 marks for a certain number of teachers must be considered (see *A, 3*). If the number of regular teachers in a nine-year school is not divisible by two, or the number in a six-year school is not divisible by four, the remaining positions are not entitled to the allowance of 900 marks. But those incomplete schools where less than four regular teachers are employed must provide one such allowance (*Zulage*), if it employs a teacher who by length of service and efficiency would be entitled to it in a state school.
4. Fully employed drawing teachers, 2,400 marks. Permanently employed but not fully engaged drawing teachers, also other teachers of technical subjects and teachers coming from seminaries, come under *B, 4*. Regular assistant teachers come unexceptionally under *A, 6*.

II. SALARIES OF TEACHERS IN THE HIGHER SCHOOLS OF BAVARIA.

The teachers are divided into four classes:
1. Rectors;
2. Professors;
3. Higher-school teachers (*Gymnasiallehrer*);
4. Assistants.

The following table gives the salaries of the first three classes:

	Initial Salary.	Increases every 5 years.	After 20 years.
Class 1	4,920	360	6,000 marks.
Class 2	3,720	360	5,220 "
Class 3	2,280	180	3,540 "

Rectors are generally provided with a dwelling—if not, there is a special grant of 540 marks annually for house rent. Professors get 420 marks, *Gymnasiallehrer* 180 marks, for house rent. Assistant teachers are not entitled to a pension, and receive 1,323–1,800 marks a year.

For the first three classes, after a period of 20 years the quinquennial increase is only 180 marks.

III. SALARIES OF TEACHERS IN THE HIGHER SCHOOLS OF SAXONY.

1. In the twelve royal *Gymnasien* and three royal *Realgymnasien* the teachers receive:
   a. 15 rectors, 6,600–7,200 (average, 6,900) marks and free rent, or 900–1,200 marks for house rent;
   b. 261 regular teachers (*wissenschaftliche Lehrer*), 2,400–6,000 (average, 4,000) marks;
   c. 32 special teachers, 1,500–2,100 (average, 1,800) marks;
   d. 3 teachers of agriculture and commercial science, 2,700–5,000 (average, 4,000) marks;
   e. 21 technical teachers, 1,500–4,000 (average, 2,850) marks.

2. In the four municipal *Gymnasien* and *Realgymnasien* in Dresden the salaries are as follows:
   a. Rectors, 6,600 marks and free rent; also two quinquennial increases of 300 marks each, *i.e.*, to 7,200 marks;
   b. Conrectors (associate principals), 5,500 marks, an increase of 300 marks after 5 years and 200 marks after 10 years, *i.e.*, to 6,000 marks;

c. Head-teachers (*Oberlehrer*), 76 regular positions, divided into eight classes:

    I. 10 positions at 4,500 marks.
    II. 10 positions at 4,200 marks.
    III. 9 positions at 3,900 marks.
    IV. 9 positions at 3,600 marks.
    V. 9 positions at 3,300 marks.
    VI. 9 positions at 3,000 marks.
    VII. 10 positions at 2,700 marks.
    VIII. 10 positions at 2,400 marks.

Moreover, Class IX. contains 5 special positions at 2,100 and 5 at 1,800 marks.

In addition to these salaries, each teacher receives an increase of 300 marks after 5 years, 300 after 10 years and 400 after 15 years of service (counting from the time of his appointment as assistant).

The average salary of the teachers embraced by Classes I. to VII. is 4,100 marks.

3. The salaries in the three *Gymnasien* at Leipsic are somewhat higher:

    a. 3 rectors, 6,900 marks; after 5 years, 7,200; after 10 years, 7,500, and free rent or 1,050 marks;
    b. 3 conrectors, 5,700 marks;
    c. 70 head-teachers (*Oberlehrer*): 6 positions at 5,100, 4,800, 4,500, 4,200, 4,000, 3,800, 3,600, 3,300, 3,000, 2,700 marks, respectively; 5 at 2,400, and 5 at 2,200.

Assistants get 1,700 marks; after 2 years, 1,900; after 4 years, 2,100.

In addition to this, the conrectors, head-teachers and assistants receive increases of 200, 400 and 600 marks after 6, 12 and 18 years of service respectively.

Besides this schedule of salaries, there is a subsidy list (*Notstafel*), guaranteeing certain salaries to teachers who do not reach them in the regular manner. According to that list, teachers of *Gymnasien* must receive after 5 years, 2,400 marks; after 10 years, 3,000; after 15 years, 3,600; after 20 years, 4,200, and after 25 years, 4,800.

The regular teachers of gymnastics in all higher schools and the regular teachers of drawing in the *Realgymnasium* receive from January 1, 1893:

  1st to 5th year.....................2,000 marks.
  6th to 10th " ....2,400 "
  11th to 15th " ....2,800 "
  16th to 20th " ....3,100 "
  21st to 25th " ....3,400 "

They are engaged 28 hours a week.

Teachers of these subjects who also hold a regular municipal office receive 90 marks a year per week-hour.

IV. SALARIES OF TEACHERS IN HIGHER SCHOOLS OF WÜRTEMBERG.

1. The minimum salaries are as follows:
   a. Rectors of *Gymnasien*, *Realgymnasien* and ten-year *Realschulen*, also ephors of elementary theological seminaries, 4,400 marks and free rent;
   b. Rectors of *Lyceen*, *Reallyceen* and eight-year *Realschulen*, 4,200 marks;
   c. Head-teachers of the higher classes in complete schools, 3,600 marks;
   d. Head-teachers of the lower classes in complete schools, 2,100 marks;
   e. Teachers of elementary Latin and *Real*-schools, 2,100 marks;
   f. Assistant-teachers, 1,850 marks.

Teachers under (b) to (f) receive a rent subsidy (*Wohnungsgeldzuschuss*) according to the following schedule (since 1889): In Stuttgart, 9% of the salary; in communities of the second class (more than 6,000 inhabitants), 7%; in all other communities, 6%. But this subsidy is computed not on the present salaries, but on those paid before 1889, when they were raised 5%. Before 1889 no rent subsidies were given.

2. The salaries are raised every 5 years as follows :
   a. Preceptors (*Praeceptoren*), *Real*-school teachers and assistants :

After 5 years, 100 marks; after 10 years, 300 ; after 15 years, 400; after 20 years, 500 ; after 25 years, 600 ; after 30 years, 700.

   b. Teachers of lower and middle classes of *Gymnasien, Realgymnasien, Lyceen, Reallyceen* and *Realschulen :*

After 10 years, 100 marks; after 15 years, 200 ; after 20 years, 300 ; after 25 years, 400 ; after 30 years, 500.

   c. (1) Principals of elementary seminaries, schools under 2 (b) and the *Bürgerschule* at Stuttgart :

After 15 years, 200 marks ; after 20 years, 300; after 25 years, 400 ; after 30 years, 500.

   (2) Head-teachers (*Oberlehrer*) in elementary seminaries and higher classes of schools under 2 (c) :

After 15 years, 200 marks; after 20 years, 300 ; after 25 years, 400 ; after 30 years, 500.

These increases in salary are counted for pension. The time of service is counted from the first permanent appointment. Promotion to higher salaries depends on vacancies.

APPENDIX E

PENSIONS OF TEACHERS IN THE HIGHER SCHOOLS OF GERMANY

Statistisches Jahrbuch der Höheren Schulen, 1897–1898.

	Minimum Amount.		Amounts in Terms of the Last Salary After			Maximum Amount.		Amount of yearly dues.
	Begins after	Amounts to % of last salary.	10 yrs.	25 yrs.	40 yrs.	Reached after	Amounts to	
	Yrs.	%	%	%	%	Yrs.	%	
1. Prussia and Alsace-Lorraine..	10	25	25	50	75	40	75	None.
2. Bavaria........................	4	70	70	80	90	......	100[1]	"
3. Saxony........................	10	30	30	51	80	40	80	"
4. Würtemberg....................	10	40	......	......	[2]	......	......	......
5. Baden.........	10	30	30	52.5	75	40	75	None.
6. Hesse...............	5	40	50	72.5	90	50	100	"
7. Mecklenburg-Schwerin.......	20	50	......	55	75	50	90	"
8. Saxe-Weimar...........	0[3]	40	40	62.5	80	36	80	"
9. Oldenburg.....................	0	50	50	65	80	50	90	"
10. Brunswick....................	3[4]	33⅓	40.8	63⅓	85.8	50	100	"
11. Saxe-Meiningen............	0	45	45	60	75	40	75	"
12. Saxe-Altenburg..	0	25	30	50	80	40	80	3%
13. Saxe-Coburg-Gotha..........	0	40	55	77.5	100	40	100	1%
14. Anhalt..	0	33⅓	40.8	63⅓	85.8	49	100	None.
15. Schwarzburg-Rudolstadt.....	0	40	40	62.5	80	36	80[5]	"
16. Schwarzburg-Sondershausen.	0	40	40	62.5	80	37	80	"
17. Waldeck....	0	33⅓	33⅓	50	66⅔	26	66⅔	"
18. Reuss, a. L.....................	0	40	40	62.5	80	37	80	"
19. Reuss, j. L.....................	3	40	40	62.5	80	37	80	"
20. Schaumburg-Lippe	10	30	30	45	70	45	80	"
21. Lippe-Detmold...............	0	40	40	62.5	80	37	80	"
22. Lübeck..........................	10	33⅓	33⅓	58⅓	75	35	75	"
23. Bremen........	0	40	40	70	80	30	80	"
24. Hamburg......................	0	40	40	62.5	85	50	100	"

In Mecklenburg-Strelitz the amount of pension depends on the will of the Sovereign.

[1] Reached at seventy years of age.

[2] The teacher pays 2% toward the pension fund. The pension rises with every year of service—(a) 1⅔% for salaries not higher than 2,400 marks; (b) 1½% for those higher than 2,400 marks. The maximum is reached at forty years of service, and cannot exceed 6,000 marks.

[3] That is, immediately after permanent appointment.

[4] The pension begins to rise 1½% only after five years.

[5] After fifty years of service the pension reaches 100%.

APPENDIX F

EXTRACTS FROM THE GENERAL PENSION LAWS OF PRUSSIA OF 1872, 1882, 1884 AND 1890

1. Every official drawing salary from the state treasury is entitled to a pension, if after ten years' service he becomes incapable, in consequence of bodily injury or physical or mental weakness, of performing his duties. But if his disability is the result of an injury or disease contracted in the performance of his official duties, he is entitled to a pension even before the expiration of the ten-year period. Those who have reached the age of sixty-five years need not show disability in order to receive a pension.

2. The pension laws do not apply to teachers in universities; but they do apply to teachers and officers in all higher schools, normal schools, institutions for the deaf and blind, art schools and *Bürgerschulen*.

3. If an official becomes unable to perform his duties before the lapse of the ten-year period, and yet does not come under (1), he may be granted a pension with the approval of the crown.

4. A pension amounts to $\frac{16}{60}$ of the last total income if an official is retired after ten years' service, $\frac{18}{60}$ after eleven years' service and so on, increasing $\frac{1}{60}$ up to forty years' service. This gives a maximum of $\frac{45}{60}$ of the last salary.

5. Regular allowances and supplies, as house rent, fuel, etc., if entered on the budget as part of the official's remuneration, are counted for pension.

Thus, an official with a salary of 4,800 marks and 492

marks for house rent will receive on retirement, after fifteen years' service, $\frac{1}{60}$ of 5,292 marks, or 1,764 marks, annually.

6. An official who accepts voluntarily a position at a lower salary than is attached to the office to which he is justly entitled receives on retirement a pension estimated on the basis of the higher salary.

7. Time of service includes time spent (a) under leave of absence, (b) in the service of the North German Confederation, (c) in the service of the German Empire, (d) in technical studies required for admission to the civil service, (e) in the trial year of a teacher, (f) in the military service, and (g) as prisoner of war.

8. Pensions are paid monthly, in advance.

9. No pension can be transferred or seized for debt.

10. A pensioner loses the right to state aid (a) when he ceases to be a German subject, and (b) when he receives a salary for service to the state or empire which, added to his pension, exceeds the amount of his original salary. In the latter case, he may draw such part of his salary as will make his income equal to his original salary.

The pension laws are strictly applicable to teachers in schools supported entirely by the state. Patrons of schools which are in part supported by the state must provide a pension schedule at least as good as the state schedule; they may do better, with the approval of the government. No provision is legally made for teachers in private schools and schools not under state control. Such teachers must rely on insurance companies and organizations for mutual assistance of members.

Pensions for Widows and Orphans of Prussian Higher School Teachers.

Extracts from Laws of 1882 and 1897.

1. Widows and legitimate children of public officials are entitled to pensions, if the official himself was entitled to one.

2. A widow's pension is four-tenths of the pension which

her husband would have received if he had been regularly retired on the day of his death. A widow's pension, however, cannot be less than 216, or more than 2,000, marks.

3. The pensions of orphans whose mother is living are each one-fifth of the widow's pension; in case of the death of both parents, each child receives one-third of the pension to which the widow would be entitled. But in no case can the total pension paid to the family of a deceased official amount to more than he himself would have received upon retirement.

4. A widow is not entitled to a pension if married to the deceased within three months of his death, and it is proved that she married him for sake of the pension.

5. Neither the widow nor her children are entitled to a pension if the marriage occurred after the official's retirement.

6. Pensions of widows and orphans are paid monthly, in advance.

7. Such pensions cannot be transferred or seized for debt.

8. The pension of a widow or an orphan lapses upon the death or marriage of the person receiving it. An orphan's pension lapses when the person reaches the age of eighteen years.

APPENDIX G

LEADING EDUCATIONAL JOURNALS OF GERMANY

EDITORS. TITLES.

SALVISBERG : *Academische Revue*, Munich.
HORNEMANN : *Blätter für Höheres Schulwesen*, Leipsic.
MELBER : *Blätter für das Bäyerische Gymnasialschulwesen*, Munich.
KURZ : *Blätter für das Bäyerische Realschulwesen*, Munich.
(OFFICIAL) : *Centralblatt für die Gesammte Unterrichts-Verwaltung in Preussen*, Berlin.
STRACK, FREYTAG and BÖTTGER : *Centralorgan für die Interessen des Realschulwesens*, Berlin.
UHLIG : *Das Humanistische Gymnasium*, Heidelberg.
MANN : *Deutsche Blätter für Erziehenden Unterricht*, Langensalza.
SCHILLMAN : *Deutsche Schulgesetz-Sammlung*, Berlin.
VIETOR : *Die Neueren Sprachen*, Marburg.
HETTNER : *Geographische Zeitschrift*, Leipsic.
BENDER and RAMSLER : *Korrespondenzblatt für die Gelehrten- und Realschulen Würtembergs*, Stuttgart.
FRIES and MEIER : *Lehrproben und Lehrgänge*, Halle.
DAHN : *Pädagogisches Archiv*, Osterwieck-Harz.
REIN : *Pädagogische Studien*, Dresden.
WYCHGRAM : *Zeitschrift für Ausländisches Unterrichtswesen*, Leipsic.
LYON : *Zeitschrift für den Deutschen Unterricht*, Leipsic.
HOFFMAN : *Zeitschrift für Mathematischen und Naturwissenschaftlichen Unterricht*, Leipsic.
KÖRTING and KOSCHWITZ : *Zeitschrift für Neufranzösische Sprache und Litteratur*, Leipsic.
BUCHNER : *Zeitschrift für Weibliche Bildung in Schule und Haus*, Leipsic.
MÜLLER : *Zeitschrift für das Gymnasialwesen*, Berlin.
HOLZMÜLLER : *Zeitschrift für die Lateinlose höhere Schulen*, Leipsic.
HARTEL : *Zeitschrift für die Österreichischen Gymnasien*, Vienna.

APPENDIX G

EDITORS.   TITLES.

POSKE : *Zeitschrift für den Physikalischen und Chemischen Unterricht*, Berlin.
FLÜGEL and REIN : *Zeitschrift für Philosophie und Pädagogik*, Langensalza.
CZUBER : *Zeitschrift für das Realschulwesen*, Vienna.
SEIBERT : *Zeitschrift für Schulgeographie*, Vienna.
KOTELMANN : *Zeitschrift für Schulgesundheitspflege*, Hamburg.

YEAR-BOOKS.

RETHWISCH : *Jahresberichte über das Höhere Schulwesen*.
VOGT : *Jahrbücher des Vereins für Wissenschaftliche Pädagogik*.
FLECKEISEN and MASIUS : *Neue Jahrbücher für Philologie und Pädagogik*, Leipsic.
RICHTER : *Pädagogischer Jahresbericht*, Leipsic.

INDEX

ADMINISTRATION, school, development of central control, 86-92; no imperial system of, 108, 191; basis of Prussian school laws, 109; Prussian administrative system, 111; department of education, 112; provincial school-boards, 113; examination commission, 114; local school-boards, 116; merits of Prussian system, 119; in other states, 119; restrictions on private venture, 135; difficulties of, due to established precedents, 141-143; founding of new schools, 143 ff.; rules, regulations and customs, 156-174; examinations and privileges, 175-193; in relation to student life, 194 ff.; in relation to school officers, 370-387; tendencies of school reform, 388-405; merits and defects of German secondary education, 406-422

Agricola, 20

Alcuin, 5, 9, 10

Allgemeine Landrecht, Prussia, 88, 109

Altenstein, 101, 102

Altona Reform School, 251, 400-402

Appointment, of minister of education, 111; of provincial school inspectors, 113; of state examiners, 114; of local school-boards, 116; of teachers, 370 ff. See Teachers

Architect, duties of supervising, 146

Arndt, 79, 91

Attendance, compulsory school, 151, 407; table of, in higher schools of Prussia, 1830-1895, 426

Auditorium of school building, 150; used on public occasions, 195; for religious exercises, 157, 164

BADEN, 98, 125, 128, 248, 425, 438

Basedow, 65

Bavaria, 98, 124, 126, 127, 128, 249, 425, 438

Benedictines, services to church and school, 3

Berlin, Conference of 1890, 105, 390-398; schools and school expenses, 154; University of, founded, 93

Bible, and the Reformation, 28 ff.; in German schools, 213

Boarding-schools, 196-212; clientele of, 135

Boards, provincial school, organization and duties of, 113; importance of, 119; control of profes-

445

sional training of teachers, 363 ff.; of appointment and promotion of teachers, 370 ff.; local school, 116; organization of, 116; powers of, 117
Boniface Romanizes and Christianizes Germany, 3
Botany, 330, 333 ff. See Sciences
Buildings, school, 145 ff. See Schools
Bureaucracy, triumph of, 90; German absolutism, 412
Burschenschaften, 91

CALENDAR, Academic, 156
Charles the Great, first general charter of education, 5; educational progress under, 8; the palace school, 9
Chemistry, 330, 343 ff., 346. See Sciences
Church, influence of, on education, 1, 16, 88, 406; attitude of, toward city schools, 12, 15; toward common schools, 15; and the Reformation, 23 ff.; development of a territorial, in Germany, 36; and state, 89; attendance, 164; and religious instruction, 224
Cities, function of, in creating a middle class, 11; rapid growth of, in modern Germany, 142
City schools, rise of, 13; administration of, 117; foundation of, 144; for girls, 129-132; selection of teachers for, 371
Civic ideals of education, development of, 76 ff.; as evidenced in examination system, 175 ff.; in system of privileges, 189; attitude of the government, 389; service of the state, 406-412; the German point of view, 420

Civil service, in Prussia, 90; conditions of admission to, 192, 427; teachers members of, 352-354; oath of office, 372
Class distinctions, evils of, 420
Class-master, 380; duties of, 381
Class rooms, specifications for and dimensions of, 145, 146; lighting of, 147; heating of, 148; ventilation of, 148; seating of, 149; equipment of, 149. See School Buildings
Classes, in Gymnasium, 122; in Progymnasium, 124; in Realschules, 127; in girls' Gymnasien, 132
Clergy, low condition of, in the time of Charles the Great, 9; attitude toward secular schools, 12; need of trained, in Reformation, 28; Luther's appeal for schools for, 31, 34; Landesschulen for, in Saxony, 38; in Würtemberg, 41; Jesuits, 47; and religious instruction, 224
Co-education, 129, 132. See Women
Columban, 1
Comenius, 58, 59, 291, 389
Compulsory school laws, 151, 407; suggested by Luther, 30 ff. See Schools
Conference, Berlin, of December, 1890, 105, 390-398
Constitution of Prussia, 88, 109. See Allgemeine Landrecht
Courses of study, in religion, 213 ff.; in German, 227 ff.; in Greek and Latin, 245 ff.; in modern languages, 266 ff.; in history and geography, 291 ff.; in mathematics, 312 ff.; in the natural sciences, 329 ff. See Curriculum

INDEX

Culture studies, employed by early humanists, 17-19, 24, 35; at variance with aims of the reformers, 27 ff.; Sturm's position, 42-44; influence of French ideals, 51, 54; of pietism and rationalism, 60; return to the Greeks, 71 ff.; modern problems, 95

Curriculum, of the Prussian Gymnasium, 123; comparative table, 124; of Prussian Realgymnasium, 125; comparative table, 126; of Prussian Oberrealschule, 128; of Prussian Höhere Mädchenschule, 131

——— Lehrplan of 1816, 97; place of Greek and Latin in, 247; of French, 267; of history, 293; of mathematics, 312; of sciences, 330

——— Lehrplan of 1837, 247; place of Greek and Latin in, 247; of French, 267; of mathematics, 312

——— Lehrplan of 1859, 104; problem of the Realgymnasium, 393-399

——— Lehrplan of 1882, 248; place of Greek and Latin in, 248; of French, 268, 270; of mathematics, 312

——— Lehrplan of 1892, 248, 249; place of Greek and Latin in, 248; of French, 268; of other modern languages, 289; of history, 294; of mathematics, 312; of sciences, 330

Customs, rules, regulations and, 156-174

DEFECTIVE CHILDREN, administration of schools for, 113

Deventer, 20

Director, selection of, 376; installation of, 378; duties of, 378-380, 382; salaries of, in Prussia, 429; in Bavaria, 433; in Saxony, 434; in Würtemberg, 436

Disciplinary studies, 74. See Culture Studies

Discipline, 161-171, 211

Drinking customs, 165

EDUCATION, history of, in Germany, 1-107

——— Elementary, in Middle Ages, 15; after the Reformation, 28 ff.; in Würtemberg, 40; revival of, under Humboldt, 92; administration of, 113

——— Secondary, in Middle Ages, 2 ff.; church schools, 8; humanistic schools, 25; protestant schools, 37-44; schools for nobles, 51 ff.; Real-schools, 64; recent reforms in, 86 ff.; present tendencies in, 388-405; merits and defects of, 406-422; administration of, in Prussia, 108-120; higher schools of Prussia, 121-137; foundation and maintenance of higher schools, 138-155; rules, regulations and customs of, 156-174; examinations and privileges, 175-193; student life in higher schools, 194-212; methods of instruction in, 213-351; professional training of teachers for, 352-369; appointment, promotion and emoluments of teachers, 370-387

——— Higher, in Middle Ages, 13; spread of humanism, 24; founding of protestant universities, 36; decadence of, 50-55; founding of Halle, 61; work of Humboldt,

93; university influence on secondary education, 114, 355–361, 406, 413–419
Einheitsschule, 399 ff.
Eisleben, 37
Elective studies, 65, 123, 266 ff., 420
English, instruction in, 266 ff.; controversies about, 272; gymnasial course of study in, 273, 274; Real-school course of study in, 275–277; typical lessons, 278–282; direct method, 283–288; training of teachers of, 288, 289
Enlightenment, coincident with Frederick the Great, 62; motives of, 63; influence of, on education, 63–75
Erasmus, 20, 21, 24
Ernesti, 73
Examinations, students' final, 88, 90, 96; subjects of final, in Gymnasium, 182; in other higher schools, 185; in six-year schools, 186; in the mid-course, 187; examining board, 181; privileges attached to, 189–193, 427, 428; in mathematics, 325; in sciences, 384
——— teachers', 97; organization of commission, 114, 115, 356–358; development of, 352–355; purpose of, 356; subjects of, 357; conduct of, 359–361; grade and rank of certificates for, 357, 361, 362; in professional training, 363, 364, 368; of directors, 378; results, 407, 410

FEUDALISM, influence of, on education, 10
Fichte, 80, 84
Francke, 63–65, 329
Franckesche Stiftungen, 134, 368

Frankfort plan, of shorter courses, 136, 252, 399, 402; Lehrplan, Gymnasium and Realgymnasium, 136
Frederick the Great, reforms of, 62, 87; on the study of French, 267; on the study of history, 291–293; on the training of teachers, 352–354
French, instruction in, 266 ff.; historical development of, 266–268; controversies about, 272; gymnasial course of study in, 273, 274; Real-school course of study in, 275–277; methods of teaching, 278; typical lessons, 282; direct method, 283–288; training of teachers for, 288, 289
Frick, 297, 298, 309, 368
Fries, 368
Fürstenschulen, 38, 39, 196–198

GEDIKE, 73, 74, 88, 124, 245, 246
Geography, 297; relation to history, 298; Jena course of study, 298 ff.; methods of teaching, 299, 300 ff.; correlation with other studies, 308; criticisms, 309–311
German, instruction in, 227–244; aim of, 227; historical development of, 229; Prussian course of study in, 230, 235, 239; grammar, 231, 236; literature, 228, 233, 238, 241; composition, 234, 236, 240; ideals and results of, 243
Gesner, 72, 97
Giessen, University seminar, 367
Girls, schools for, in Prussia, 129; in Berlin, 155; in Hamburg, 133; curriculum of, 131; Gymnasien for, 132; problems of education of, 416–420. See Women

Goethe, 71, 84, 101
Greek, in the Middle Ages, 9; the revival of letters, 18, 20, 23, 25; Luther's attitude toward, 32 ff.; in protestant schools, 37-44; and the new humanism, 70-75; later development, 95 ff., 245-249; in the curriculum, 98, 99, 101, 104, 123, 124, 136, 137, 245 ff.; instruction in, 245 ff.; methods of teaching, 258; text-books, 264; criticisms, 264
Grimma, 38, 98, 140, 144
Gymnasium, so-called since the middle of the sixteenth century, 39; official designation, 96; object of, 74, 122; original aim of, 138; some old foundations, 138-140; Lehrplan of Prussian, 123; comparative curricula of, in Prussia, Bavaria, etc., 124; function and position of, 124; teachers in, officers of the state, 110; numbers of, and attendance at, 125, 140; educational problem of, 397 ff. See Altona, Frankfort, Civic Ideals, Conference, Curriculum, Greek, Latin, Realgymnasium

HALLE, the first modern university, 61; university seminar, 368
Hardenburg, 77, 78
Head-masters. See Directors
Hegel, 84, 100, 101
Hegius, 20, 23
Herbart, 99, 292, 302
Herder, 71, 84, 94, 95
Hesse, 128, 248, 425, 438
Higher Schools, definition of, 121; aim of, 175 ff.; statistics of, in Germany, 425. See Gymnasium, Realgymnasium, Realschulen
History, instruction in, 291 ff.; Comenius on, 291; historical developments of, 291; Frederick the Great on the study of, 291, 293; subject-matter used in instruction, 294 ff.; Prussian course of study in, 295; Jena course of study in, 299 ff.; methods of teaching, 300 ff.; correlation with other subjects, 308; criticisms, 309-311
Holidays, 157. See Calendar
Home study, 158, 160, 315
Honours attached to the teaching profession in Germany, 375
Humanism, in Germany in the fifteenth century, 20; rapid spread of, 24, 25, 26; influence of, 44; and Lutheranism, 34, 44; Sturm's position, 42, 43; repression of, by counter-Reformation, 47; by French ideals, 51 ff.; by Thirty Years' War, 52; by pietism, 59 ff.; revival of, 69-75; incorporated in school curricula, 95 ff.; tendencies of school reform, 388-405
Humboldt, 89, 92-94, 101; on the training of teachers, 354
Hygiene, school, 145-149, 159, 160, 408

IDEALISM, German, 83, 413
Imperial school commission, 191
Instruction. See Courses of Study, Curriculum

JAEGER, 264, 396
Jena, University, founding of, 36; Gymnasium, 302, 341; seminar, 367
Jesuits, 47 ff.; success of, 48, 49; influence on German school system, 49; evidences of the work of, 139

Journals, list of leading educational periodicals of Germany, 442, 443
Journeys, school, in Stoy school, 209-211; excursions, 300, 335, 341

KANT, 83, 84
Kiepert, 297
Kirchner, 224
Klinghardt, 272
Klopstock, 71
Kühn, 272

LABORATORIES in school buildings, 150; for science teaching, 339, 348
Landesschulen, 38, 39, 196, 198
Lange, 132
Latin, in various curricula, 2, 8, 13, 15, 18, 25, 38, 40, 66, 74, 96, 98, 99, 101, 103, 104, 123, 124, 125, 126, 136, 137, 142; first begins to give way to the vernacular, 15; in the Renaissance period, 19, 23, 25; in the protestant schools, 32, 33-44; reaction against formalism in teaching, 66 ff.; recent development of, 99 ff., 246 ff.; instruction in, 245 ff.; Prussian course of study in Gymnasium, 254 ff.; methods of teaching, 258 ff.; textbooks, 264; criticisms, 264; in the Realgymnasium, 249; Prussian course of study in, 254 ff.; educational problems, 393-405
Lehrfreiheit, beginning of, in Germany, 61; recent attempts at restriction of, 413-415
Leibnitz, 56
Leipsic, University, 14, 25, 36, 61, 133; seminar, 367
Lessing, 71

Libraries, defects and merits of school, 150; defects of cataloguing, 150, 151; system throughout Germany prevailingly bad, 151; redeeming features, 151; pupils may not use public, 166
Luther, 25 ff.; insight into educational needs in Reformation times in Germany, 28; on school curricula, 33; on school libraries, 33; and Melanchthon, 34, 37; on instruction in religion, 213

MÄDCHENSCHULE, Höhere. See Girls' Schools, Women
Manual training in Stoy school, 206
Marking system, 177, 178
Mathematics, instruction in, 312-328; arithmetic, 314 ff.; algebra, 314, 322 ff.; geometry, 319, 321, 324; course of study in Realgymnasium, 314, 320, 323; Austrian methods, 317, 318; final examinations in, 325; criticisms, 326-328
Meierotto, 73
Meissen, 38, 98, 140, 144, 197
Melanchthon, and Erasmus, 23; and Luther, 34, 37; pedagogical ideas of, 35; as an organizer, 36, 37
Middle Ages, German education during, 1-16; ideals of, 17
Militarism, effects on education, 78, 121, 161, 162, 200, 212, 383, 411
Mittelschulen, 130. See Schools
Mosellanus, 23
Muff, 262, 264
Museums, school, for teaching sciences, 336
Music, in mediæval church schools, 4, 8, 13; in protestant schools, 37, 38, 40; in teaching patriotism, 79, 93; in school curricula. See Curriculum

INDEX 451

NATURAL HISTORY, 330, 333-341.
See Sciences
Nature study, 341-343. See Sciences
Nuremberg, 25

OBERREALSCHULE, 104, 105; graduates of, 127; Lehrplan, 128; numbers, 128. See Realschule
Oberschulcollegium, 87-89. See Administration
Ordinarius, 380. See Class-master

PAULSEN, 23, 37, 74, 394
Pensions, of teachers, 386; comparative table for all German states, 438; extracts from the general pension laws of Prussia, 439, 440; for widows and orphans of higher school teachers, 440
Periodicals, current educational, of Germany, 442, 443
Pestalozzi, 92, 297
Pforta. See Schulpforta
Philanthropinists, 66
Philosophy, scholastic, 11; of the seventeenth century, 55 ff. ; rationalistic, 59 ff.; German idealism, 83, 84; the romantic school, 85
Physical training in Stoy school, 207; Turnhalle, 147
Physics, 343-346. See Sciences
Pietism, 60, 64
Play-grounds, 146. See School Buildings
Principal. See Director
Privileges, system of, 189-193; military service, 190 ; university study, 192; state examinations, 192; tabulated statement of, 427, 428; relation to school reforms, 397, 404, 415

Professions, preparation of students for, 174. See Privileges
Program, school. See Calendar, Courses of Study, Curriculum
Progymnasium, 124. See Gymnasium
Promotion, of pupils, conditions of, 177, 189; of teachers, 370-383
Protestant schools, rise and character of, 22, 23, 26-45; and the counter-Reformation, 46, 47, 50, 52-54; reaction against, 66
Prüfungscommission, Wissenschaftliche, 114, 115, 352-358. See Examinations, Teachers'
Prussia, development of, 76; constitution of, 109; and War of Liberation, 77; civil and military reforms, 78-82; central control in school administration, 86-92; school system of, 108-120; higher schools of, 121-137; old schools of, 138-142; school-year in, 156; system of examinations and privileges of, 175-193, 427, 428; professional training of teachers in, 352-369; appointment, promotion, and emoluments of teachers in, 370-387; tendencies of school reform in, 388-405; merits and defects of secondary education in, 406-422; attendance in higher schools of, 426; salary schedules in, 429-433; extracts from pension laws of, 439-441
Publications, student, 166
Punishments in schools, 167. See Discipline

QUADRIVIUM, 4 ff.
Quiehl, 272, 278
Quintilian, 24

Rationalism, 59, 62 ff.
Ratke, 68
Ratzel, 297
Realgymnasium, rise of, 64, 104, 105; aim of, 125; Lehrplan of Prussian, 125; comparative curricula of, in Prussia, Bavaria, etc., 126; position of, 126; similar to American high school, 126, 127; number of, in the states of Germany, 127; attendance, 127; examinations in, 185; Latin in, 249; Prussian Latin course in, 254-257; modern languages in, 274 ff.; mathematics in, 312 ff.; natural sciences in, 345 ff.; the problem of, 393-399, 415; privileges of, 427, 428
Realschule, rise of, 64, 65, 104; aim of, 127; Lehrplan of, in Prussia, 128; in Würtemberg, 128; numbers in German states, 128; examinations in, 186; modern languages in, 274 ff.; mathematics in, 312 ff.; natural sciences in, 345 ff.; recent growth of, 392; outlook for, 250, 389, 392, 394, 415; privileges of, 427, 428; attitude of teachers toward, 326, 340
Reformation, influence of, on education in Germany, 22, 26-45, 138; counter, 47. See Luther
Reformschule, 251 ff.; Frankfort plan, 399, 402-404; Altona, 400-402; recent growth of, 404
Rein, 367
Reinhardt, 262
Religion, Luther's position, 27-32, 34, 37, 38, 213; supervision of, in schools, 115, 164; preferences of students, 173; instruction in, 213-226; teachers of, 214; Prussian course of study in, 216-218; confirmation, 220; subject matter of instruction in, 220; text-books, 221; defects of the system of instruction, 223 ff.
Renaissance, ideals of, 17, 20; influence of, 19-22, 24-26, 138
Reuchlin, 20, 21, 23
Richter, 262, 298, 367
Ritter, 297
Ritterakademie, 52, 54, 56
Romantic school of philosophy, 85
Rossleben, 197
Rules, regulations and customs for guidance of students, 156-174

Salaries, teachers', 154, 384, 385; official schedules of, in Prussia, 429; in Bavaria, 433; Saxony, 434; Würtemberg, 436
Saxony, school system of, in 1538, 37; in 1580, 41; old schools of, 144, 197, 198; teachers' salaries in, 434; pensions in, 438
Schiller (Fr.), 71, 84
Schiller (Prof. H.), 306, 367
Schlee, 400
Scholarships, 36, 41, 152, 153
Scholasticism, influence of, on education, 11; tendency toward, in seventeenth century, 50
Schools, boarding, 133, 134, 135, 140, 196 ff.; cathedral, 8; church, 133; city, designed for the middle classes, 12; foundations of, 144; status of, 117, 143; cloistral, 41, 98; common, 15; commercial, 133; Einheitsschule, 399 ff.; Fürstenschule, 38, 39; girls', 129; present status of, 130, 131; Gymnasium, see Gymnasium; higher, definition of, 121; classification of, 122; aim of, 175 ff.; attendance upon, in Prussia from

1830-1895, 426; list of privileged, 425; Höhere Mädchenschule, 129-131; Jesuit, see Jesuits; Landesschule, 38, 39; Mittelschule, 130; normal, 113; Oberrealschule, see Oberrealschule; protestant, first, 37; private, status of, 111, 116, 118; Progymnasium, 124; Realgymnasium, see Realgymnasium; Realschule, see Realschule; Reformschule, see Reformschule; secondary, see Education; state, status of, 117; ideals of, 389; Stoy school, 199 ff.; union (Einheitsschule), 399 ff.; Volksschule, 129; destroyed by the Thirty Years' War, 54; history of secondary, 1-107; supervision of, 382; ecclesiastical supervision of, 215; first step in secularization of, 88; administrative system of, 111; maintenance of, 153; expense of maintenance in Prussia, 153; inter-relations, 135; punishments, 167; regulations of a typical school, 168 ff.; some old, 138, 139, 140; confessional character of, 214; reform of, 388 ff.; conference of December, 1890, 105, 390

School system, of Saxony, 37, 38, 41; complete, first organized in Würtemberg, 40; centralization of, 86-96; not imperial in Germany, 108; and the state, 99, 105, 106, 109, 110, 406-412; a product of German ideals, 107, 406-412; the Prussian, 108-120; merits of the Prussian, 119; in the smaller German states, 119; sources of chief defects of, 412; expense of maintenance in Prussia, 153; in Berlin, 154, 155

School buildings, construction and equipment of, 145, 146; location of, 146; lighting of, 147; ventilation of, 148; heating of, 148; seating of, 149; general equipment of, 149; equipment of, for teaching sciences, 331; auditorium of, 150; hygienic precautions, 408

School laws, not codified in Prussia, 108; basis of, 109; rule of precedent binding, 111 ff.; compulsory, 407

School year, 156

Schulpforta, 38, 95, 98, 140, 144, 197, 198

Schulze, 99, 247

Sciences, development of, and influence on educational ideals, 56, 57, 63-66, 102-105; instruction in, 329 ff.; historical development of, 329, 330; chief aim, 330; equipment for teaching, 331; Prussian course of study—natural history, 333; physics and chemistry, 343 ff.; school museums, 336; methods of teaching, 337-339; laboratory work, 339, 348; nature study, 341-343; final examinations, 348, 349; recent tendencies, 351

Secondary education schools. See Education

Seminars, pedagogical, early foundations, 97; state, 365; gymnasial, 365; university, 367

Sessions, daily, 157. See Calendar

Sievers, 297

Social rank, of students, 172; of teachers, 326, 340, 375; results, 420

State, control of school system, 86-96, 108-120, 409; influence on education, 406, 407-412; and

454   INDEX

compulsory school laws, 407;
and hygienic precautions, 408;
and uniform curricula, 409; and
teaching profession, 410
Stein, 77, 78, 89, 90, 93, 354
Stoy school, 199; regulations of,
200; student life in, 202-212
Students, rules, regulations and
customs, 156-174; non-resident,
163; social rank of, 172; conditions of promotion of, 177; examination of, 178-189; life in
higher schools, 194 ff.; public exercises, 195; privileges attached
to completion of various grades of
higher schools, 189-193, 427, 428
Studies. See Courses, Curriculum
Study, home, 158, 160, 315
Sturm, 42, 43, 141, 389
Suicides among school children in
Germany, 147
Superintendent. See Director
Supervision. See Administration
Süvern, 96

TEACHERS, training of professional,
97, 352-369; university study for,
355; state examinations, 356;
examination commission, 358;
conduct of examinations, 360;
subjects for examinations, 357;
certification of, 95, 114, 115, 357,
361, 362; university degrees, 358;
trial teaching, 97, 98, 364, 368;
seminar year, 364; present requirements, 364; Prussian seminars, 365; university courses, 367,
368; religious training, 215; of
religion, duties of, 215; general
duties of teachers, 381, 382;
women as, 130, see Women; tenure of office, defects, 383; officers
of state, 161, 162; professional
strength of, 411; appointment of,
114, 118, 370 ff.; in royal schools,
371; in city schools, 371; oath
of office, 372; waiting period,
373; salaries, 384; salary schedules in Prussia, 429; Bavaria,
433; Saxony, 434; Würtemberg,
436; travelling stipends, 386;
honours, 375; pensions, 118, 386;
comparative table of pensions for
the German states, 438; for widows and orphans, 440; pension
laws of Prussia, 439-441
Teaching, freedom of, 61, 413-415;
methods of. See Religion, Greek,
Latin, etc.
Tenure of office of teachers, 383,
386, 407, 410
Text-books, for protestant schools,
35; control of, 113, 114; nature
of, in religion, 221; in German,
231, 233; in Greek and Latin,
264; in French and English, 274,
288; in history, 307; in mathematics, 321, 322; in sciences, 346
Thiersch, 98
Thirty Years' War, evil consequences of, 52, 53, 54
Thomasius, 61, 68
Thurber, 398
Travelling stipends for teachers,
386
Trial year of teaching, 97, 98, 364,
368
Trivium, 4 ff.
Trustees, powers of school, 117
Tuition, in royal secondary schools,
151, 152; in city schools, 152
Turnhalle, 147

UHLIG, 396
Universities, founding of Paris, 13;
founding of, in Germany, 14;

INDEX

protestant, 36; decadence of, in the seventeenth century, 55; founding of Berlin, 93; influence on secondary education, 406, 413–416; idealism of, 413; struggle between the state and, 413; Lehrfreiheit in, 414; defects of, 415 ff.; foster gymnasial monopoly, 415; oppose admission of women, 416; Giessen seminar, 367; Halle, 61, 368; Jena, seminar, 367; Leipsic, seminar, 367

VACATIONS, 156
Victor, 271, 272, 273
Volksschulen, 15, 33, 40, 54, 64, 92, 129

WAETZOLDT, 272, 417
Walter, 272, 280, 282, 283, 284
War of Liberation—Humboldt, Arndt, Fichte, 77; effects of, 81 ff.
Weimar, 95, 314, 323
Wernekke, 314
William II., views on educational matters, 105, 143, 389, 392

Wimpheling, 20, 23
Windscheid, 132
Wittenberg, 25
Wittich, 313
Wolf, 74, 93, 94, 95, 96, 97, 99, 101, 245, 292
Wolff, 61, 68
Women, teachers' association of, 129; as teachers, 130; higher education of, 416–420; admission to universities, 416; admission to professions, 419; attitude of Prussian state toward education of, 419. See Girls' Schools
Württemberg, school system of, first complete, 40; school curricula, 98, 124–128, 249; schools of, 425; teachers' salaries in, 436, 437; teachers' pensions in, 438

YEAR-BOOKS, educational, in Germany, 443

ZEDLITZ, 73, 87, 88, 293
Zeller, 92
Ziegler, 395, 411
Zoölogy, 330, 333 ff. See Sciences

COLLEGE HISTORIES OF ART.

Edited by JOHN C. VAN DYKE, L.H.D., Professor of the History of Art in Rutgers College.

*** The object of the series is to furnish clear, concise histories of the different Arts for use as text-books in Schools and Colleges. In order that the text-book need shall be well met each volume of the series is written by a College Professor teaching in the Department of which he writes, and presumably well qualified for his task: The Text is critical as well as historical. The books are brief in accordance with the amount of time usually given to the study of Arts in Schools and Colleges; each consists of about 250 pages, very freely illustrated.

A History of Painting.

By the Editor of the Series. With Frontispiece and 109 Illustrations in the Text. Crown 8vo. 307 pages. $1.50.

Nation, New York:—"Professor Van Dyke has performed his task with great thoroughness and good success.... He seems to us singularly happy in his characterization of various artists, and amazingly just in proportion. We have hardly found an instance in which the relative importance accorded a given artist seemed to us manifestly wrong, and hardly one in which the special characteristics of a style were not adequately presented."

A History of Architecture.

By Prof. A. D. F. HAMLIN, Adjunct Professor of Architecture, School of Mines, Columbia College. With Frontispiece and 229 Illustrations in the Text. Crown 8vo. 470 pages. $2.00.

Providence Journal:—"The work is ... not only extremely valuable for reference, but it may also be commended to those who wish to obtain an adequate knowledge of the fundamental laws of architecture."

Boston Advertiser:—"... probably presents more comprehensively, and, at the same time, concisely, the various periods and styles of architecture, with a characterization of the most important works of each period and style, than any other published work.... The volume fills a gap in architectural literature which has long existed."

A History of Sculpture.

By Profs. ALLAN MARQUAND and A. L. FROTHINGHAM, Jr., of Princeton College. With Frontispiece and 112 Illustrations in the Text, chiefly in half tone. Crown 8vo. 313 pages. $1.50.

Critic, New York:—"A model of condensation ... should meet with an enthusiastic reception among students and amateurs of art, not so much, however, because it is the only book of its kind, as for its intrinsic merit and attractive form."

Henry W. Kent, Curator of the Seater Museum, Watkins, N. Y.:—"Like the other works in this series of yours, it is simply invaluable, filling a long-felt want. The bibliographies and lists will be keenly appreciated by all who work with a class of students."

NEW BOOKS FOR TEACHERS.

Teaching and School Organization.

A Manual of Practice, with Especial Reference to Secondary Instruction. Edited by P. A. Barnett. Crown 8vo. 438 pages. $2.00.

The object of this Manual is to collect and co-ordinate for the use of students and teachers, the experience of persons of authority in special branches of educational practice, and to cover as nearly as possible the whole field of the work of Secondary Schools of both higher and lower grades.

The subjects treated in the 22 chapters are as follows: The Criterion in Education—Organization and Curricula in Boys' Schools—Kindergarten—Reading—Drawing and Writing—Arithmetic and Mathematics—English Grammar and Composition—English Literature—Modern History—Ancient History—Geography—Classics—Science—Modern Languages—Vocal Music—Discipline—Ineffectiveness of Teaching—Specialization—School Libraries—School Hygiene—Apparatus and Furniture—Organization and Curricula in Girls' Schools.

A New Manual of Method.

By A. H. GARLICK, B.A., Head-master of the Woolwich P. T. Centre. Crown 8vo. 398 pages. $1.20 *net*. *New Edition*.

"It is the best manual of its scope and size in English."—*Nation*, New York.

"The notes given on all these topics are those of a master, and of a master from whom any teacher in these grades of instruction might be glad to receive suggestions."—*The Independent*, New York.

"It is excellent. No teacher can do without it."—Prof. CARLA WENCKEBACH, Wellesley College, Wellesley, Mass.

Kindergarten Guide.

By LOÏS BATES. With numerous Illustrations, chiefly in half-tone, and 16 colored plates. 388 pages. Crown 8vo. $1.50 *net*.

In addition to a full description of the kindergarten gifts and occupations, the book shows how ordinary subjects may be taught on kindergarten principles.

"A long needed hand-book for the kindergarten teacher. . . . The whole course of instruction is elaborately explained with full illustrations, so that the teacher possesses, in this 12mo volume, a complete compendium for her work."—*Churchman*, New York.

"Never before has there been so full, varied, and detailed a treatment of the subject from the standpoint of teacher, parent, and child. No family in which there are little children should be without this sum of all kindergarten virtues."—*Journal of Education*, Boston, Mass.

Longmans, Green, & Co's Publications.

Books for Teachers.—*Continued*

The Art of Teaching.

By DAVID SALMON, author of Longmans' School Grammar. Crown 8vo, 289 pages, $1.25.

"We have not seen the thing nearly so well done before. It is an actual and serviceable reduction of the principles to possible present day practice in every existing kind and type of school. It should have a place in every educationalist's collection."—*London School Board Chronicle.*

Work and Play in Girls' Schools.

By Three Head Mistresses. I.—Intellectual Education, including Humanities, Mathematics, Science, and Æsthetics, by DOROTHEA BEALE. II.—The Moral Side of Education, by LUCY II. M. SOULSBY. III.—Cultivation of the Body, by JANE FRANCES DOVE. Crown 8vo, 443 pages, $2.25.

"Yesterday I received from you the new book, 'Work and Play in Girls' Schools.' I find it full of the most interesting matter and a very profitable book to be read by all teachers, not only in England, but in America, North and South. The book suggests not only useful devices in the teaching of special branches, but abounds in profound discussion on the very nature of school education itself. I think you ought to bring this book to the attention of our teachers by advertisements and circulars."— Hon. W. T. HARRIS, United States Commissioner of Education.

Psychology in the Schoolroom.

By T. F. G. DEXTER, B.A., B.Sc., and A. H. GARLICK, B.A., author of "A New Manual of Method." 421 pages. Crown 8vo. $1.50.

Many students have little difficulty in mastering the general principles of the science of Psychology, but experience considerable difficulty in applying those principles to the Art of Teaching; and it is because special attention has been paid to the *application* of the subject that it is hoped that this book will be of some service, not only to the student and young teacher, but also to teachers generally.

It has been thought advisable to exclude polemical discussions, since they are believed to be out of place in this elementary book, which is an attempt to apply the laws of Mental and Moral Science to school work—to take the elements of Psychology into the Schoolroom.
—*Extract from the Preface.*

Boyhood: a Plea for Continuity in Education.

By ENNIS RICHMOND. Crown 8vo. 154 pages. $1.00.

"We are quite sure that this book will prove very helpful, especially to mothers, upon whom, after all, mainly rests the responsibility of guidance in the early days of childhood."—*Derby Mercury.*

Books for Teachers—*Continued.*

Games Without Music for Children.

By LOIS BATES, Author of "Kindergarten Guide," etc. 12mo, cloth. 112 pages. $0.60 *net*.

Contents: I. Games for the Schoolroom—II. Games for the Playground—III. Guessing Rhymes.

The object of these games is to introduce variety when it is needed in the ordinary school routine, and to form a means of recreation to the children when unfavorable weather makes the usual playtime impossible.

Briefs for Debate on Current, Political, Economic, and Social Topics.

Edited by W. DuBOIS BROOKINGS, A.B., and RALPH CURTIS RINGWALT, A.B. With an Introduction on "The Art of Debate" by ALBERT BUSHNELL HART, Ph.D. Crown 8vo. With Full Index. 260 pages. $1.25

In use as a text-book in Harvard University, Columbia University, University of Pennsylvania, University of Michigan, and other leading institutions.

"I cannot resist telling you that 'Briefs for Debate' has proved itself to be one of the most useful books in the library. We use it constantly in connection with the High School work."—C. K. BOLTON, Librarian, Public Library, Brookline, Mass.

The Will to Believe, and Other Essays in Popular Philosophy.

By WILLIAM JAMES, LL.D., Professor of Psychology in Harvard University. Large crown 8vo. Pp. xvii-332. Cloth, gilt top. $2.00

Pre-Christian Education.

By S. S. LAURIE, A.M., LL.D., of the University of Edinburg. 444 pages. $3.50

This book is an attempt to survey the education of ancient nations in relation to those factors in civilization which govern the thought and life of communities—the political and the ethical. The nations specially considered are the Egyptians, Chinese, Jews, Babylonians and Assyrians, Persians and Hindus. The education of Greece, and Rome receives fuller consideration than that of other nations.

Recently adopted as a text-book for Radcliffe College, Columbia University, and Teachers' College, New York, and in use in other leading Institutions.

Messrs. Longmans, Green, & Co. will be happy to send their Catalogue, describing more than 1,000 text-books and works of reference, to any teacher on request.